BLOOD OF THE ICENI

AQUILA CREATED BY GORDON RENNIE & LEIGH GALLAGHER

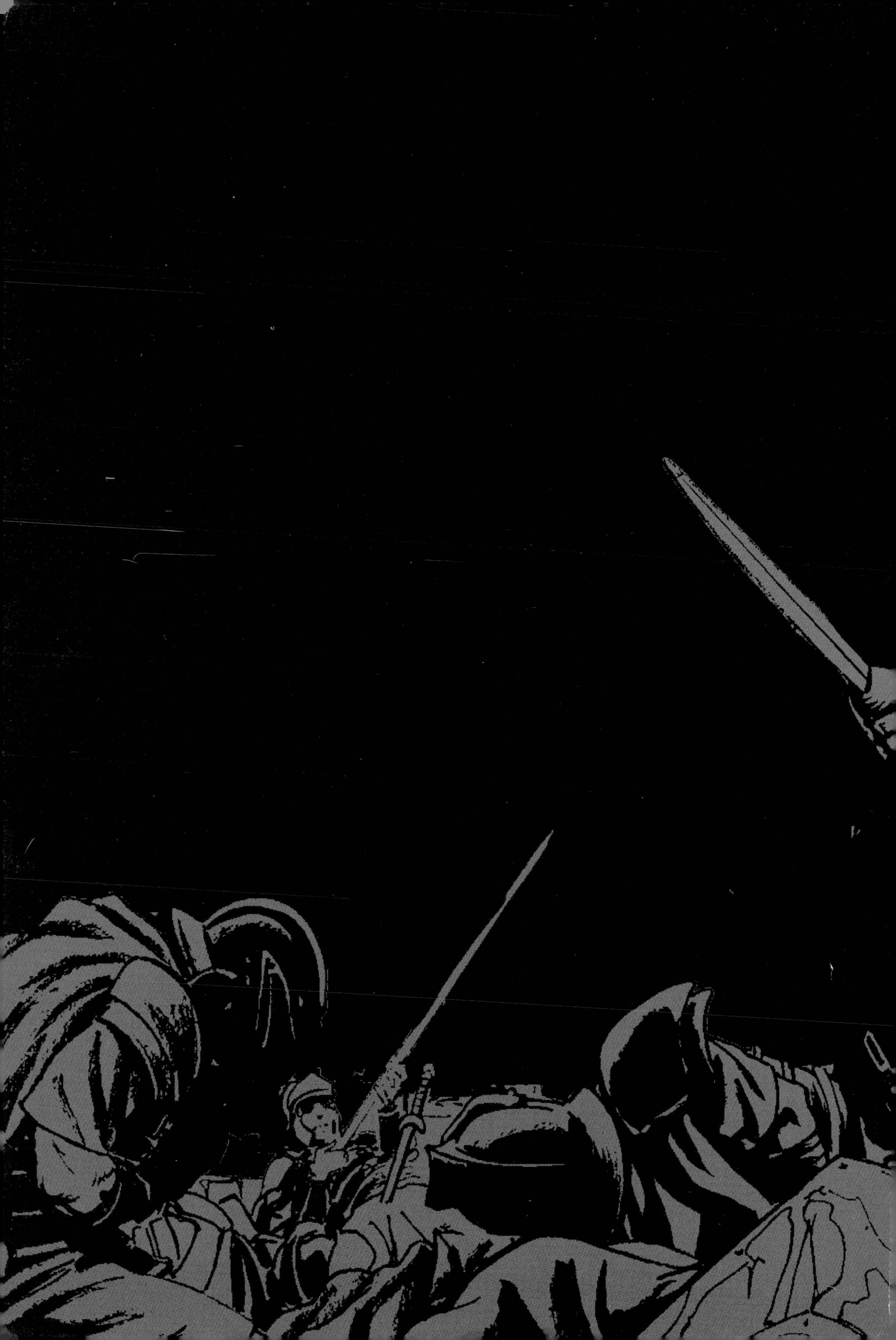

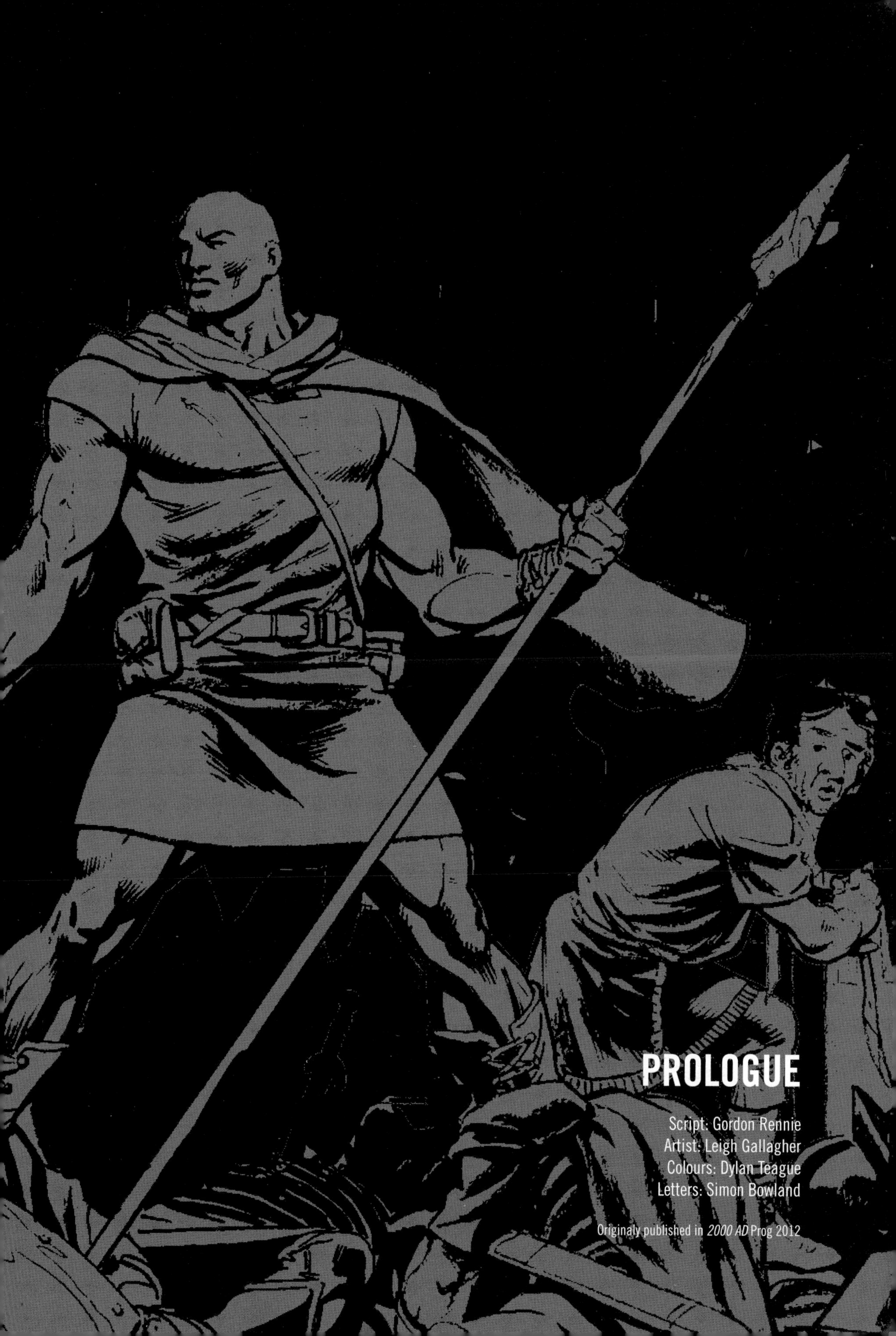

PROLOGUE

Script: Gordon Rennie
Artist: Leigh Gallagher
Colours: Dylan Teague
Letters: Simon Bowland

Originaly published in *2000 AD* Prog 2012

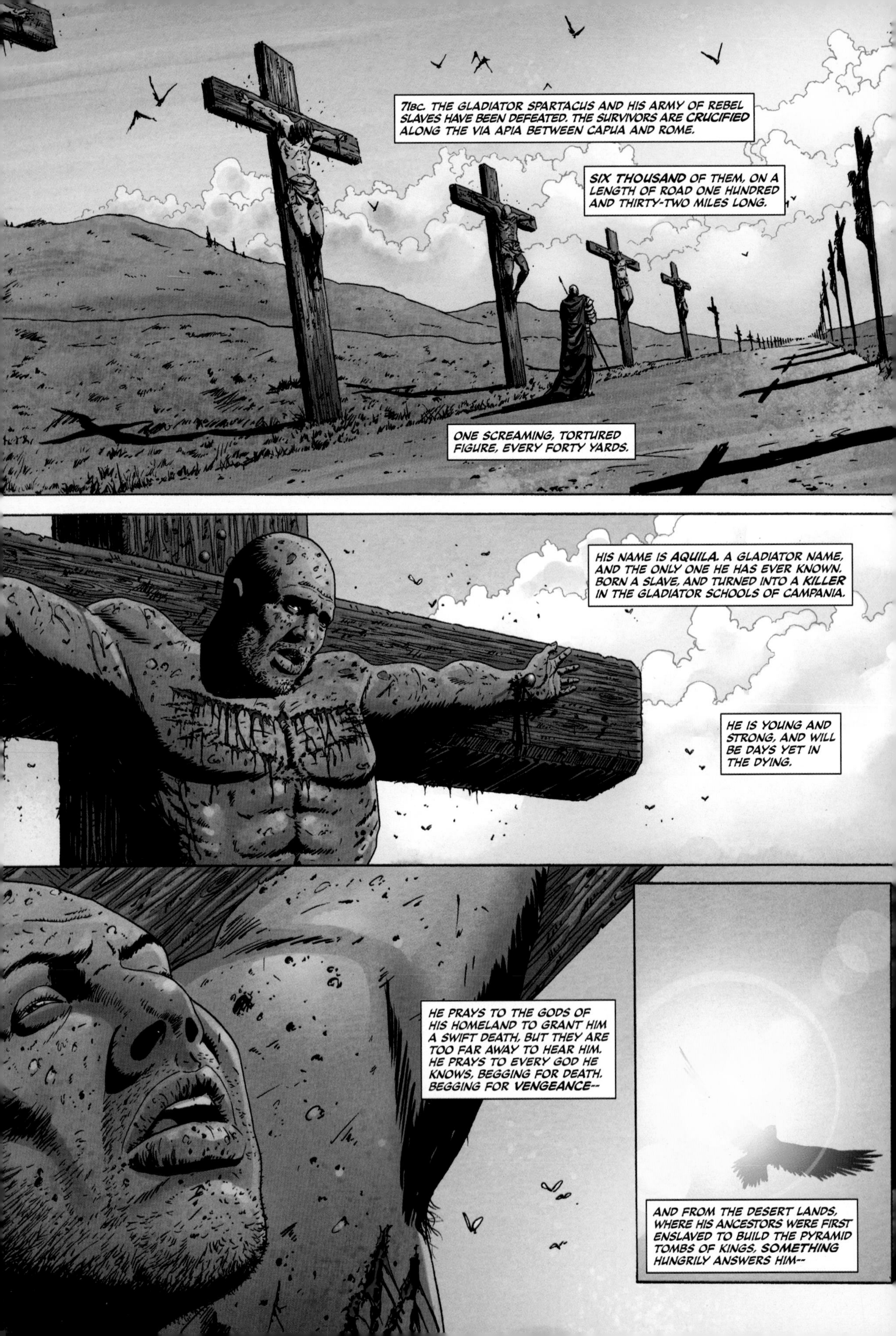
71BC. THE GLADIATOR SPARTACUS AND HIS ARMY OF REBEL SLAVES HAVE BEEN DEFEATED. THE SURVIVORS ARE CRUCIFIED ALONG THE VIA APIA BETWEEN CAPUA AND ROME.
SIX THOUSAND OF THEM, ON A LENGTH OF ROAD ONE HUNDRED AND THIRTY-TWO MILES LONG.
ONE SCREAMING, TORTURED FIGURE, EVERY FORTY YARDS.
HIS NAME IS AQUILA. A GLADIATOR NAME, AND THE ONLY ONE HE HAS EVER KNOWN. BORN A SLAVE, AND TURNED INTO A KILLER IN THE GLADIATOR SCHOOLS OF CAMPANIA.
HE IS YOUNG AND STRONG, AND WILL BE DAYS YET IN THE DYING.
HE PRAYS TO THE GODS OF HIS HOMELAND TO GRANT HIM A SWIFT DEATH, BUT THEY ARE TOO FAR AWAY TO HEAR HIM. HE PRAYS TO EVERY GOD HE KNOWS, BEGGING FOR DEATH. BEGGING FOR VENGEANCE--
AND FROM THE DESERT LANDS, WHERE HIS ANCESTORS WERE FIRST ENSLAVED TO BUILD THE PYRAMID TOMBS OF KINGS, SOMETHING HUNGRILY ANSWERS HIM--

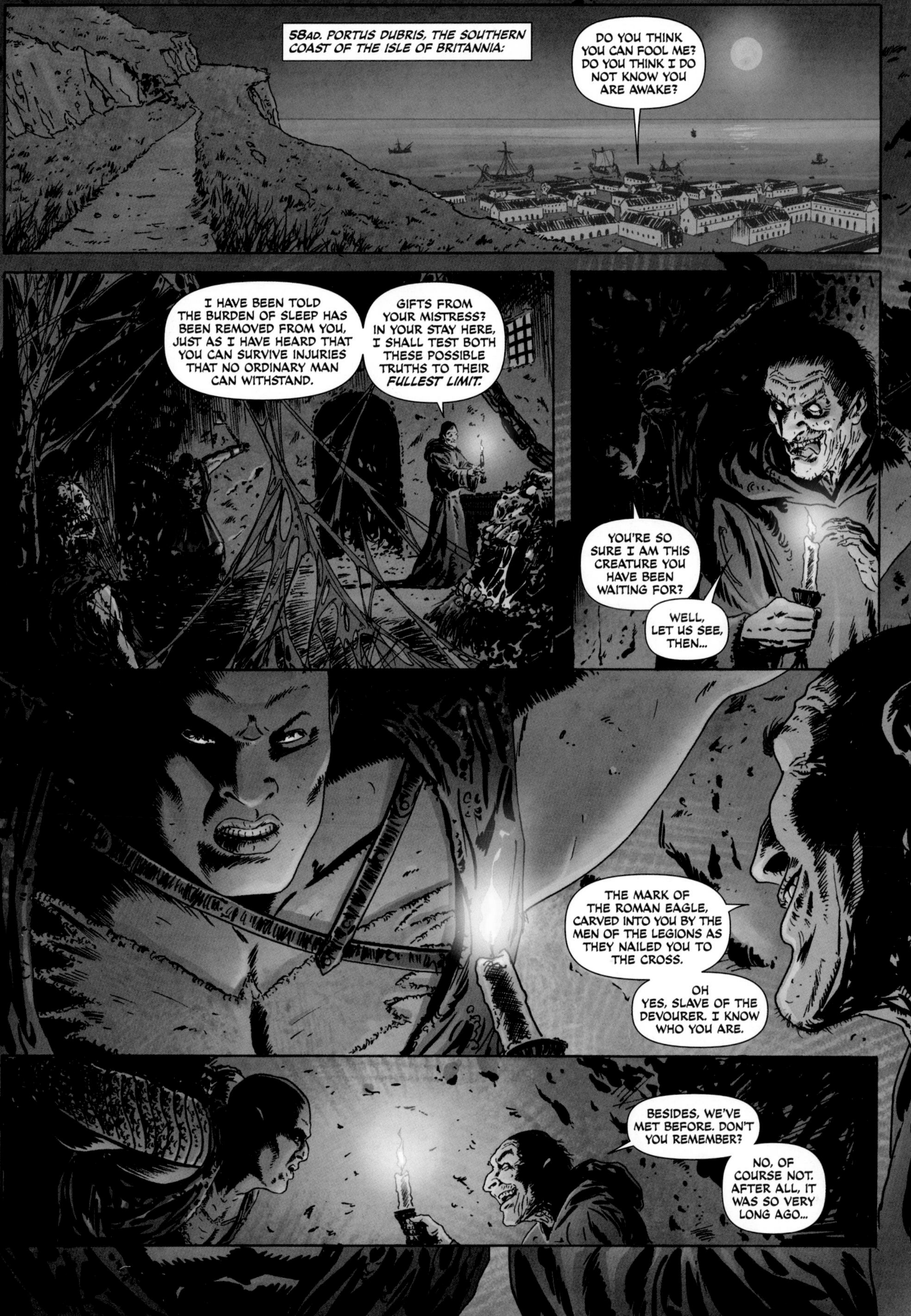
58AD. PORTUS DUBRIS, THE SOUTHERN COAST OF THE ISLE OF BRITANNIA:
DO YOU THINK YOU CAN FOOL ME? DO YOU THINK I DO NOT KNOW YOU ARE AWAKE?
I HAVE BEEN TOLD THE BURDEN OF SLEEP HAS BEEN REMOVED FROM YOU, JUST AS I HAVE HEARD THAT YOU CAN SURVIVE INJURIES THAT NO ORDINARY MAN CAN WITHSTAND.
GIFTS FROM YOUR MISTRESS? IN YOUR STAY HERE, I SHALL TEST BOTH THESE POSSIBLE TRUTHS TO THEIR FULLEST LIMIT.
YOU'RE SO SURE I AM THIS CREATURE YOU HAVE BEEN WAITING FOR?
WELL, LET US SEE, THEN...
THE MARK OF THE ROMAN EAGLE, CARVED INTO YOU BY THE MEN OF THE LEGIONS AS THEY NAILED YOU TO THE CROSS.
OH YES, SLAVE OF THE DEVOURER. I KNOW WHO YOU ARE.
BESIDES, WE'VE MET BEFORE. DON'T YOU REMEMBER?
NO, OF COURSE NOT. AFTER ALL, IT WAS SO VERY LONG AGO...

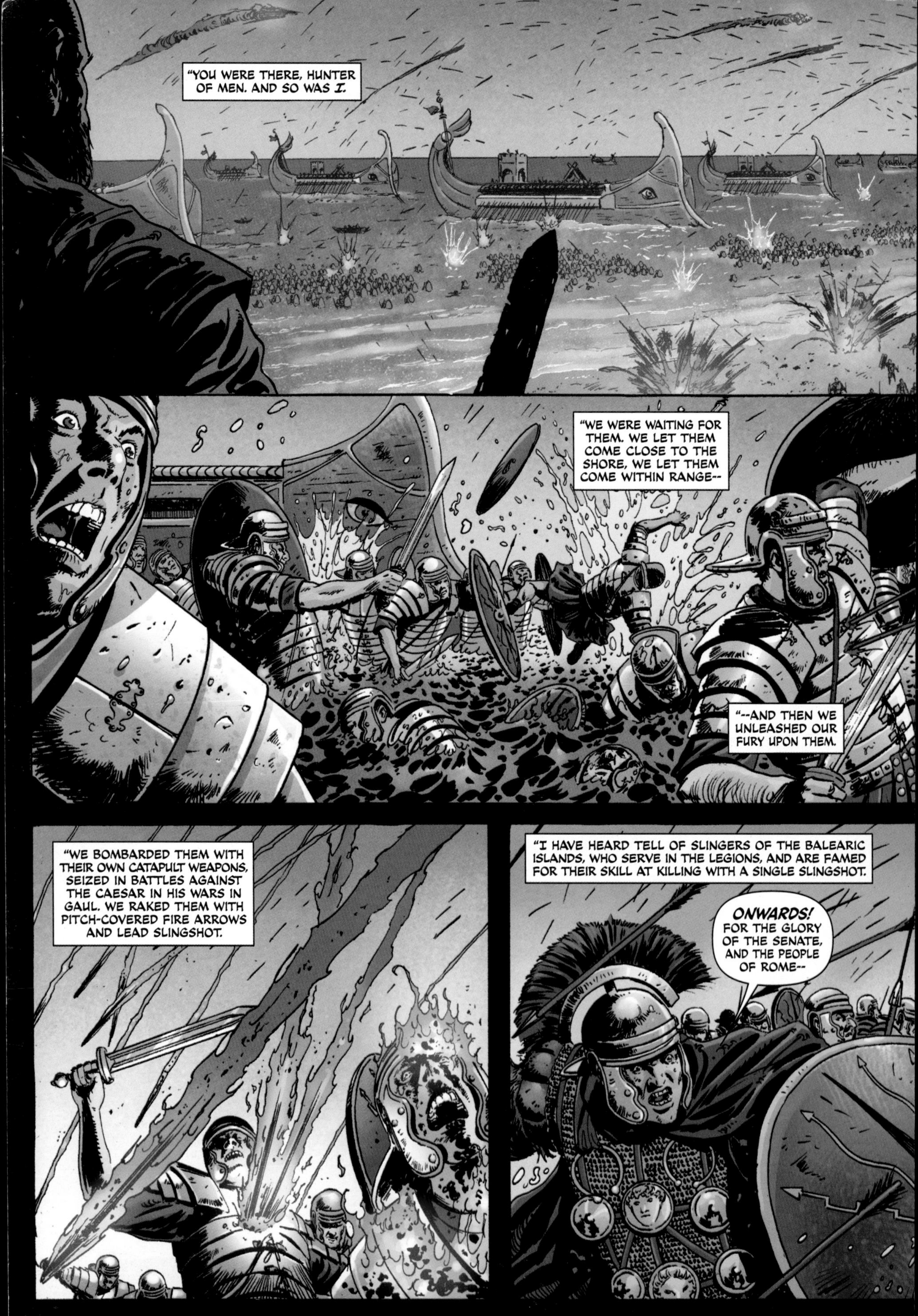
"YOU WERE THERE, HUNTER OF MEN. AND SO WAS *I*.
"WE WERE WAITING FOR THEM. WE LET THEM COME CLOSE TO THE SHORE, WE LET THEM COME WITHIN RANGE--
"--AND THEN WE UNLEASHED OUR FURY UPON THEM.
"WE BOMBARDED THEM WITH THEIR OWN CATAPULT WEAPONS, SEIZED IN BATTLES AGAINST THE CAESAR IN HIS WARS IN GAUL. WE RAKED THEM WITH PITCH-COVERED FIRE ARROWS AND LEAD SLINGSHOT.
"I HAVE HEARD TELL OF SLINGERS OF THE BALEARIC ISLANDS, WHO SERVE IN THE LEGIONS, AND ARE FAMED FOR THEIR SKILL AT KILLING WITH A SINGLE SLINGSHOT.
ONWARDS! FOR THE GLORY OF THE SENATE, AND THE PEOPLE OF ROME--

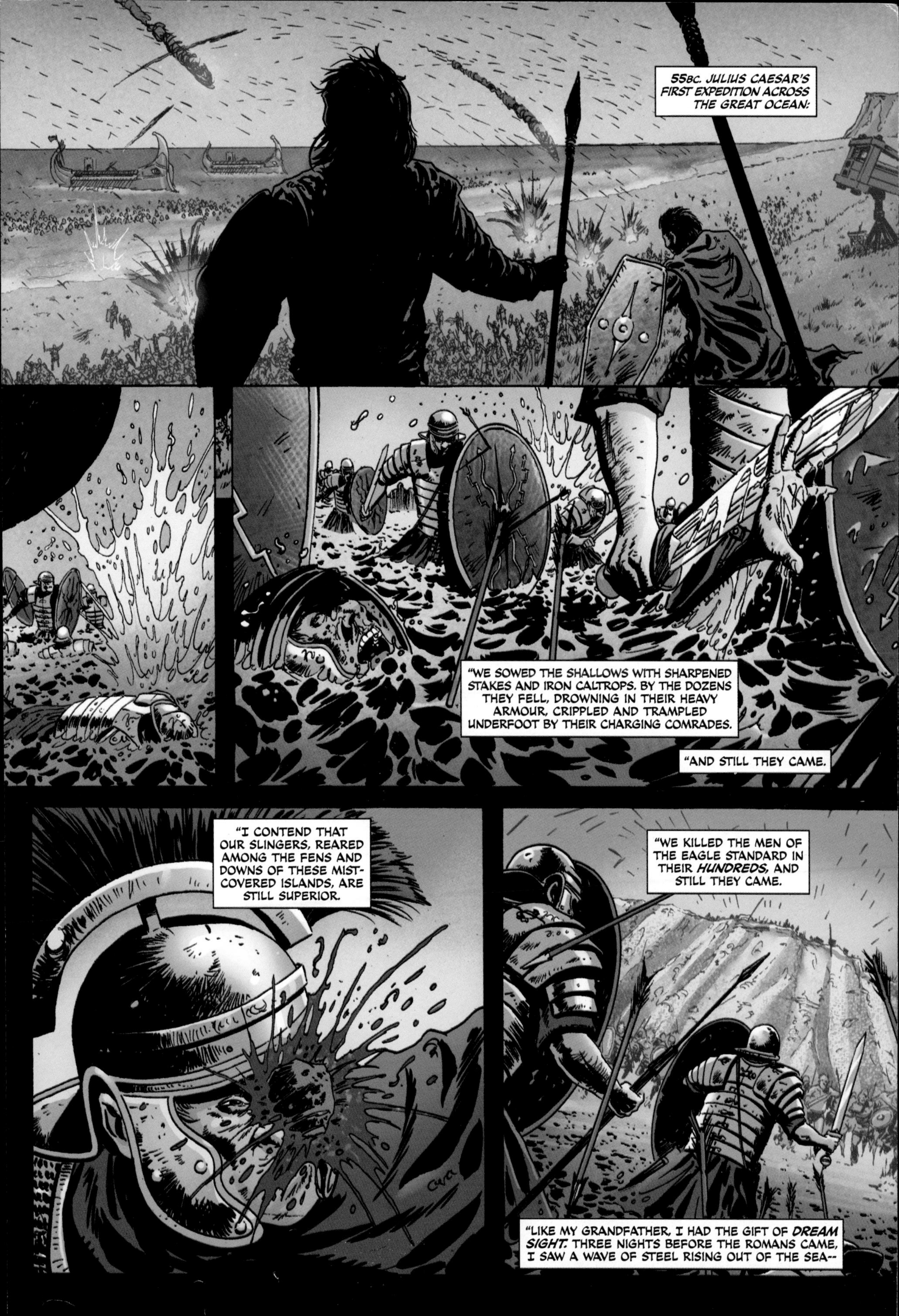
55BC. JULIUS CAESAR'S FIRST EXPEDITION ACROSS THE GREAT OCEAN:
"WE SOWED THE SHALLOWS WITH SHARPENED STAKES AND IRON CALTROPS. BY THE DOZENS THEY FELL, DROWNING IN THEIR HEAVY ARMOUR, CRIPPLED AND TRAMPLED UNDERFOOT BY THEIR CHARGING COMRADES.
"AND STILL THEY CAME.
"I CONTEND THAT OUR SLINGERS, REARED AMONG THE FENS AND DOWNS OF THESE MIST-COVERED ISLANDS, ARE STILL SUPERIOR.
"WE KILLED THE MEN OF THE EAGLE STANDARD IN THEIR *HUNDREDS,* AND STILL THEY CAME.
"LIKE MY GRANDFATHER, I HAD THE GIFT OF *DREAM SIGHT.* THREE NIGHTS BEFORE THE ROMANS CAME, I SAW A WAVE OF STEEL RISING OUT OF THE SEA--

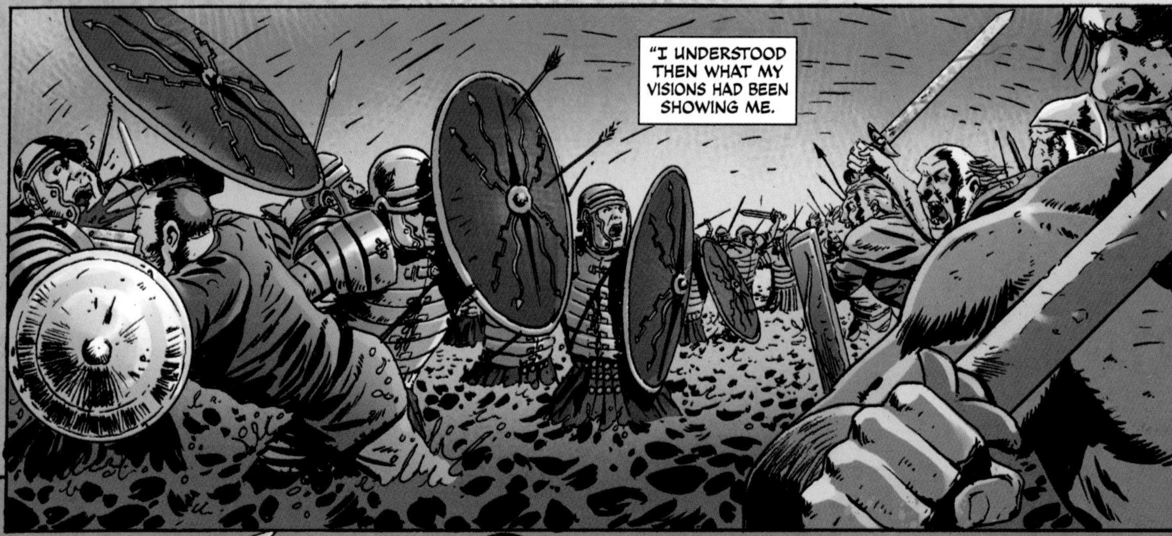
"I UNDERSTOOD THEN WHAT MY VISIONS HAD BEEN SHOWING ME.

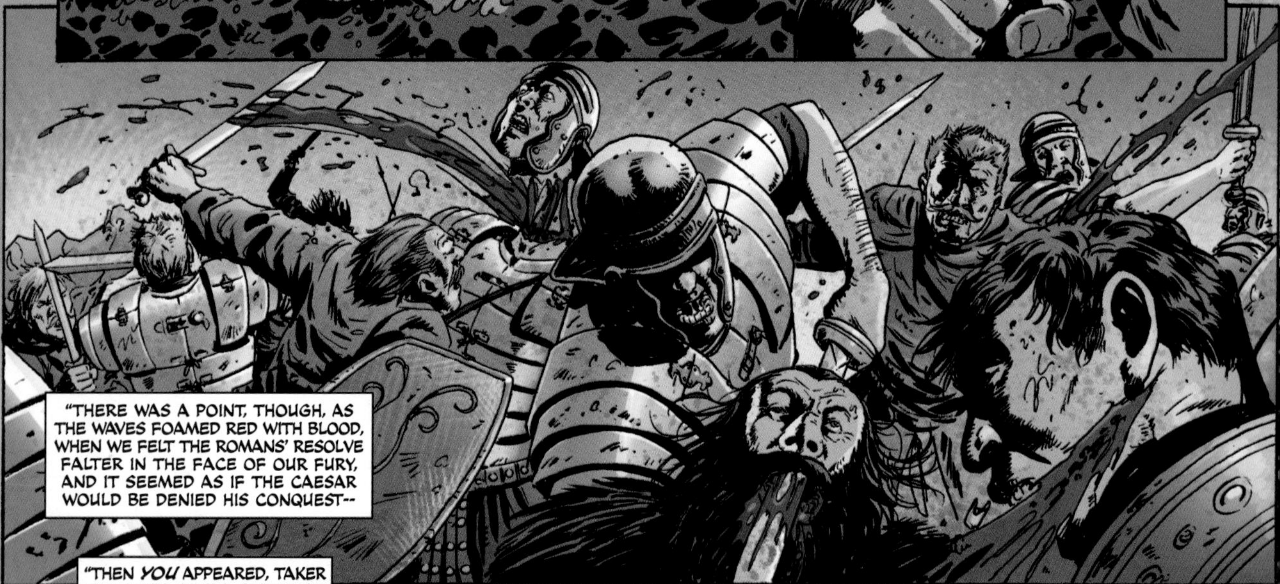
"THERE WAS A POINT, THOUGH, AS THE WAVES FOAMED RED WITH BLOOD, WHEN WE FELT THE ROMANS' RESOLVE FALTER IN THE FACE OF OUR FURY, AND IT SEEMED AS IF THE CAESAR WOULD BE DENIED HIS CONQUEST--

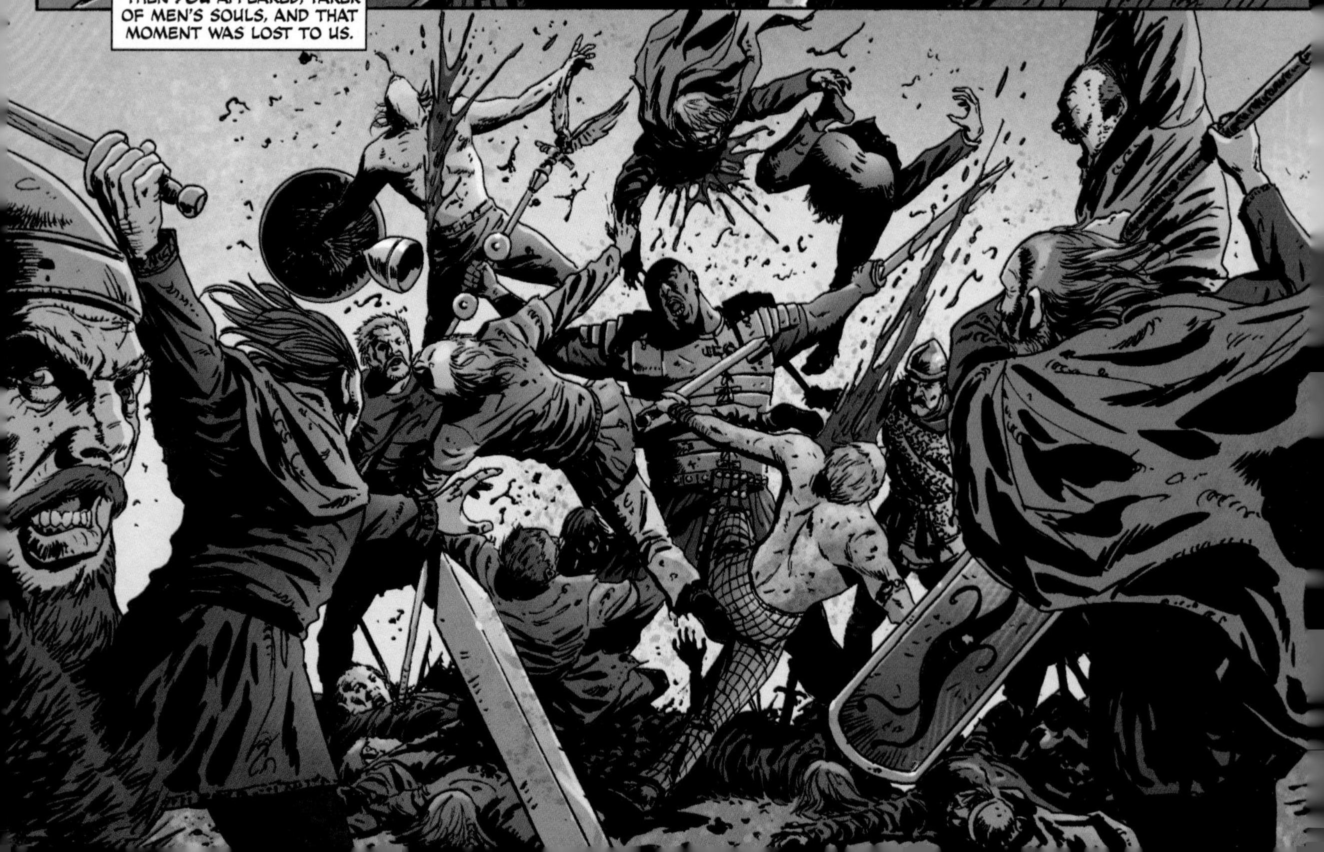
"THEN *YOU* APPEARED, TAKER OF MEN'S SOULS, AND THAT MOMENT WAS LOST TO US.

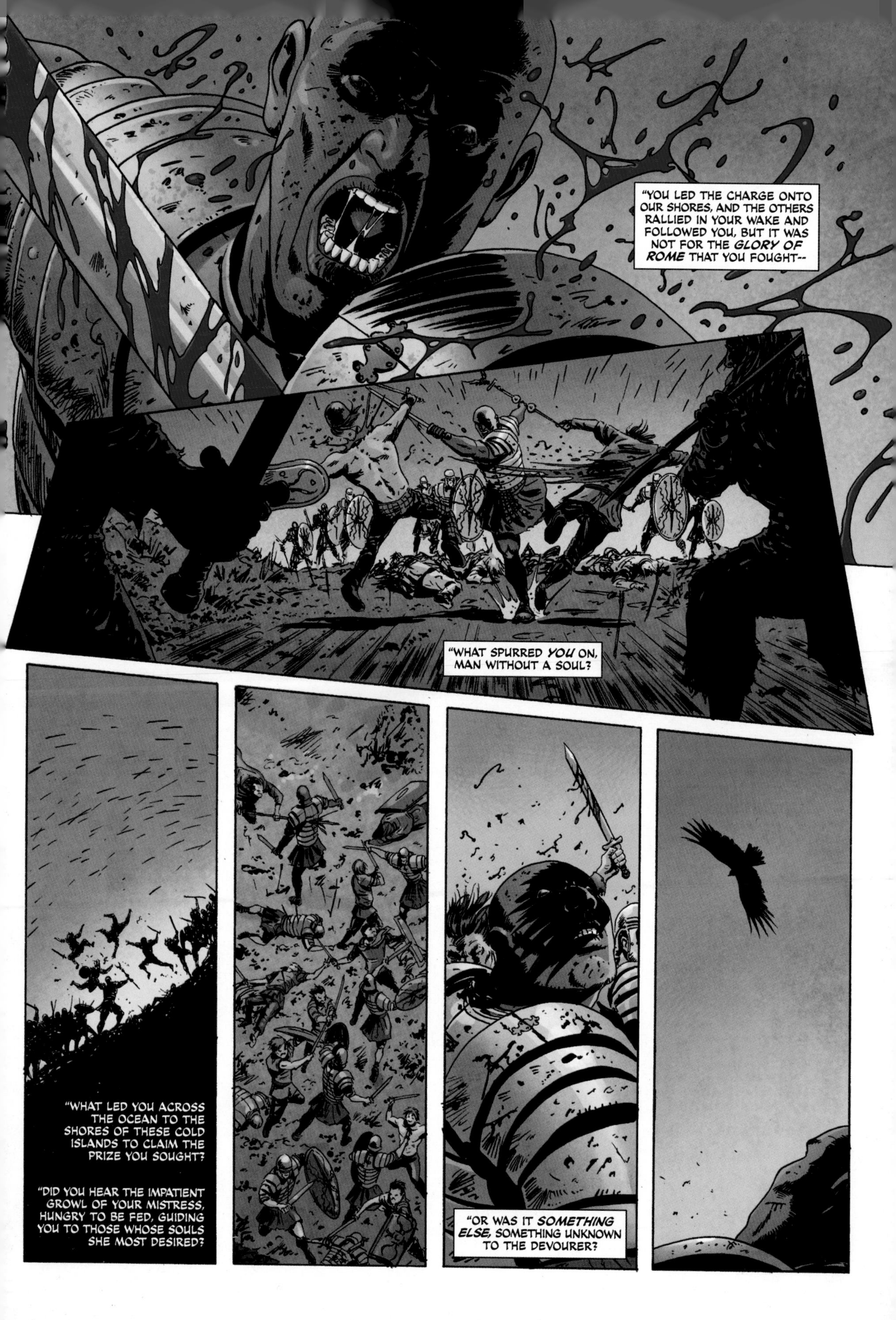
"YOU LED THE CHARGE ONTO OUR SHORES, AND THE OTHERS RALLIED IN YOUR WAKE AND FOLLOWED YOU, BUT IT WAS NOT FOR THE GLORY OF ROME THAT YOU FOUGHT--
"WHAT SPURRED YOU ON, MAN WITHOUT A SOUL?
"WHAT LED YOU ACROSS THE OCEAN TO THE SHORES OF THESE COLD ISLANDS TO CLAIM THE PRIZE YOU SOUGHT?
"DID YOU HEAR THE IMPATIENT GROWL OF YOUR MISTRESS, HUNGRY TO BE FED, GUIDING YOU TO THOSE WHOSE SOULS SHE MOST DESIRED?
"OR WAS IT SOMETHING ELSE, SOMETHING UNKNOWN TO THE DEVOURER?

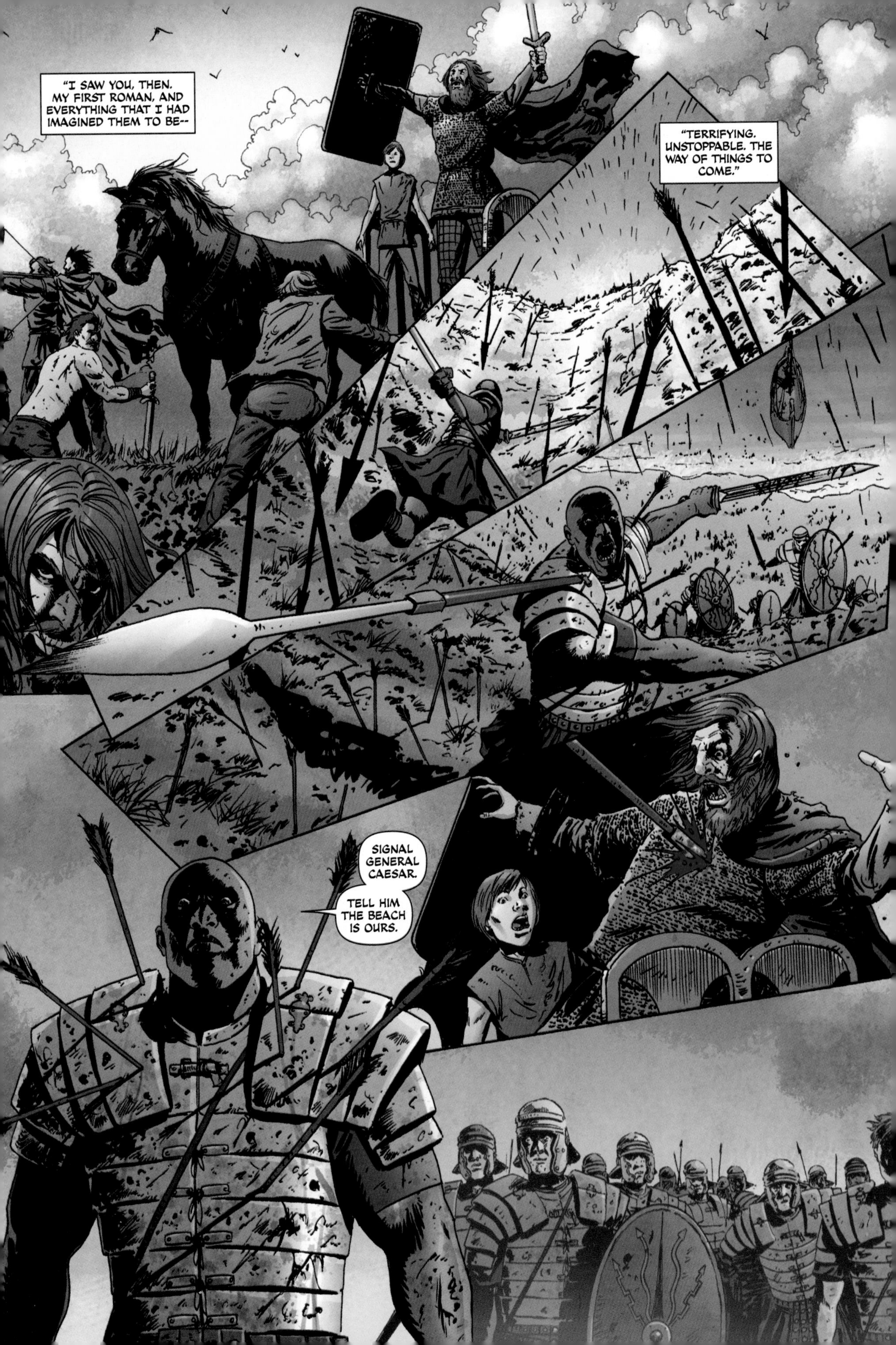
"I SAW YOU, THEN. MY FIRST ROMAN, AND EVERYTHING THAT I HAD IMAGINED THEM TO BE--
"TERRIFYING. UNSTOPPABLE. THE WAY OF THINGS TO COME."
SIGNAL GENERAL CAESAR.
TELL HIM THE BEACH IS OURS.

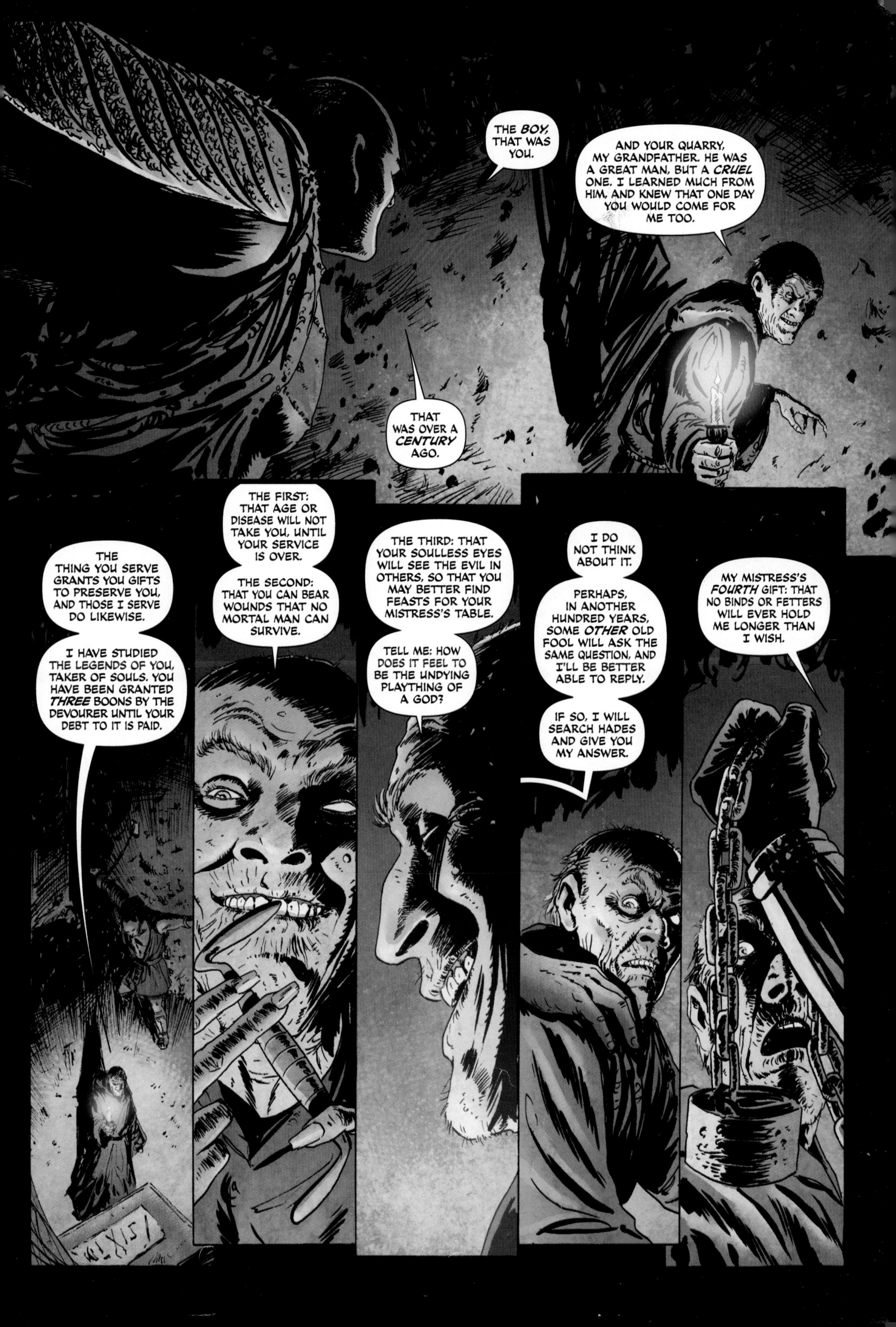
THE BOY, THAT WAS YOU.
AND YOUR QUARRY, MY GRANDFATHER. HE WAS A GREAT MAN, BUT A CRUEL ONE. I LEARNED MUCH FROM HIM, AND KNEW THAT ONE DAY YOU WOULD COME FOR ME TOO.
THAT WAS OVER A CENTURY AGO.
THE THING YOU SERVE GRANTS YOU GIFTS TO PRESERVE YOU, AND THOSE I SERVE DO LIKEWISE.
I HAVE STUDIED THE LEGENDS OF YOU, TAKER OF SOULS. YOU HAVE BEEN GRANTED THREE BOONS BY THE DEVOURER UNTIL YOUR DEBT TO IT IS PAID.
THE FIRST: THAT AGE OR DISEASE WILL NOT TAKE YOU, UNTIL YOUR SERVICE IS OVER.
THE SECOND: THAT YOU CAN BEAR WOUNDS THAT NO MORTAL MAN CAN SURVIVE.
THE THIRD: THAT YOUR SOULLESS EYES WILL SEE THE EVIL IN OTHERS, SO THAT YOU MAY BETTER FIND FEASTS FOR YOUR MISTRESS'S TABLE.
TELL ME: HOW DOES IT FEEL TO BE THE UNDYING PLAYTHING OF A GOD?
I DO NOT THINK ABOUT IT.
PERHAPS, IN ANOTHER HUNDRED YEARS, SOME OTHER OLD FOOL WILL ASK THE SAME QUESTION, AND I'LL BE BETTER ABLE TO REPLY.
IF SO, I WILL SEARCH HADES AND GIVE YOU MY ANSWER.
MY MISTRESS'S FOURTH GIFT: THAT NO BINDS OR FETTERS WILL EVER HOLD ME LONGER THAN I WISH.

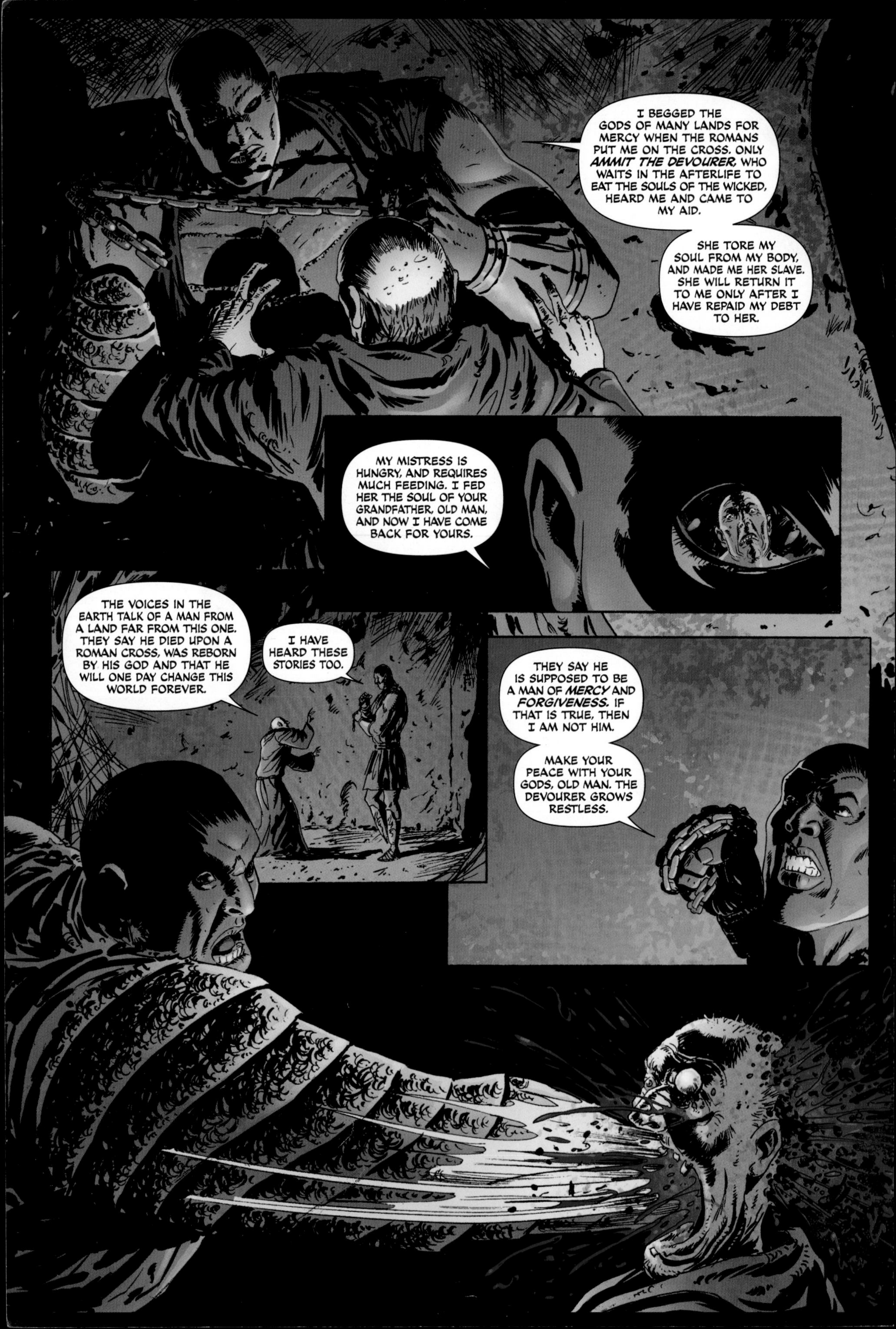
I BEGGED THE GODS OF MANY LANDS FOR MERCY WHEN THE ROMANS PUT ME ON THE CROSS. ONLY *AMMIT THE DEVOURER,* WHO WAITS IN THE AFTERLIFE TO EAT THE SOULS OF THE WICKED, HEARD ME AND CAME TO MY AID.
SHE TORE MY SOUL FROM MY BODY, AND MADE ME HER SLAVE. SHE WILL RETURN IT TO ME ONLY AFTER I HAVE REPAID MY DEBT TO HER.
MY MISTRESS IS HUNGRY, AND REQUIRES MUCH FEEDING. I FED HER THE SOUL OF YOUR GRANDFATHER, OLD MAN, AND NOW I HAVE COME BACK FOR YOURS.
THE VOICES IN THE EARTH TALK OF A MAN FROM A LAND FAR FROM THIS ONE. THEY SAY HE DIED UPON A ROMAN CROSS, WAS REBORN BY HIS GOD AND THAT HE WILL ONE DAY CHANGE THIS WORLD FOREVER.
I HAVE HEARD THESE STORIES TOO.
THEY SAY HE IS SUPPOSED TO BE A MAN OF *MERCY* AND *FORGIVENESS.* IF THAT IS TRUE, THEN I AM NOT HIM.
MAKE YOUR PEACE WITH YOUR GODS, OLD MAN. THE DEVOURER GROWS RESTLESS.

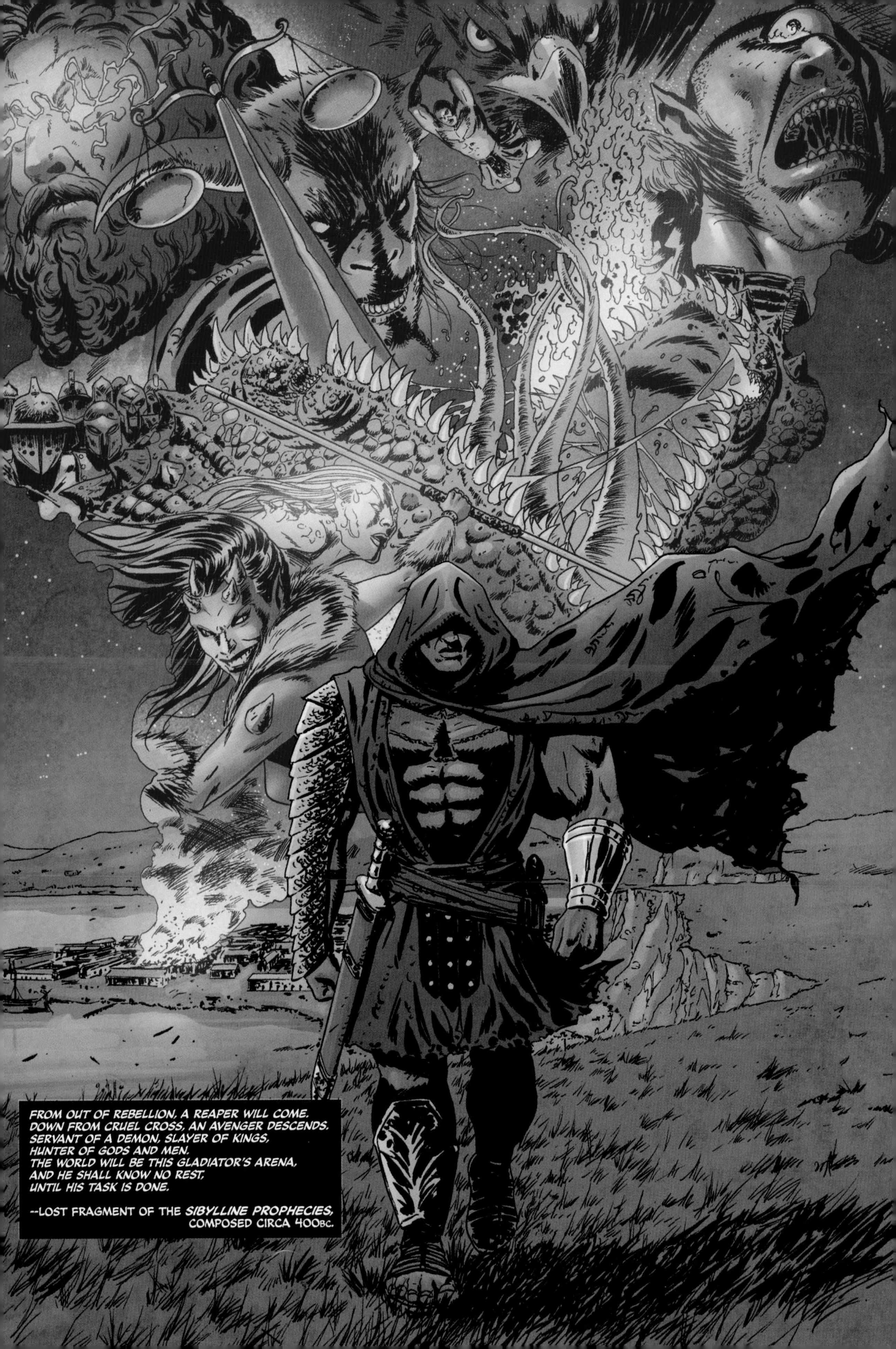
FROM OUT OF REBELLION, A REAPER WILL COME.
DOWN FROM CRUEL CROSS, AN AVENGER DESCENDS.
SERVANT OF A DEMON, SLAYER OF KINGS,
HUNTER OF GODS AND MEN.
THE WORLD WILL BE THIS GLADIATOR'S ARENA,
AND HE SHALL KNOW NO REST,
UNTIL HIS TASK IS DONE.
--LOST FRAGMENT OF THE SIBYLLINE PROPHECIES,
COMPOSED CIRCA 400BC.

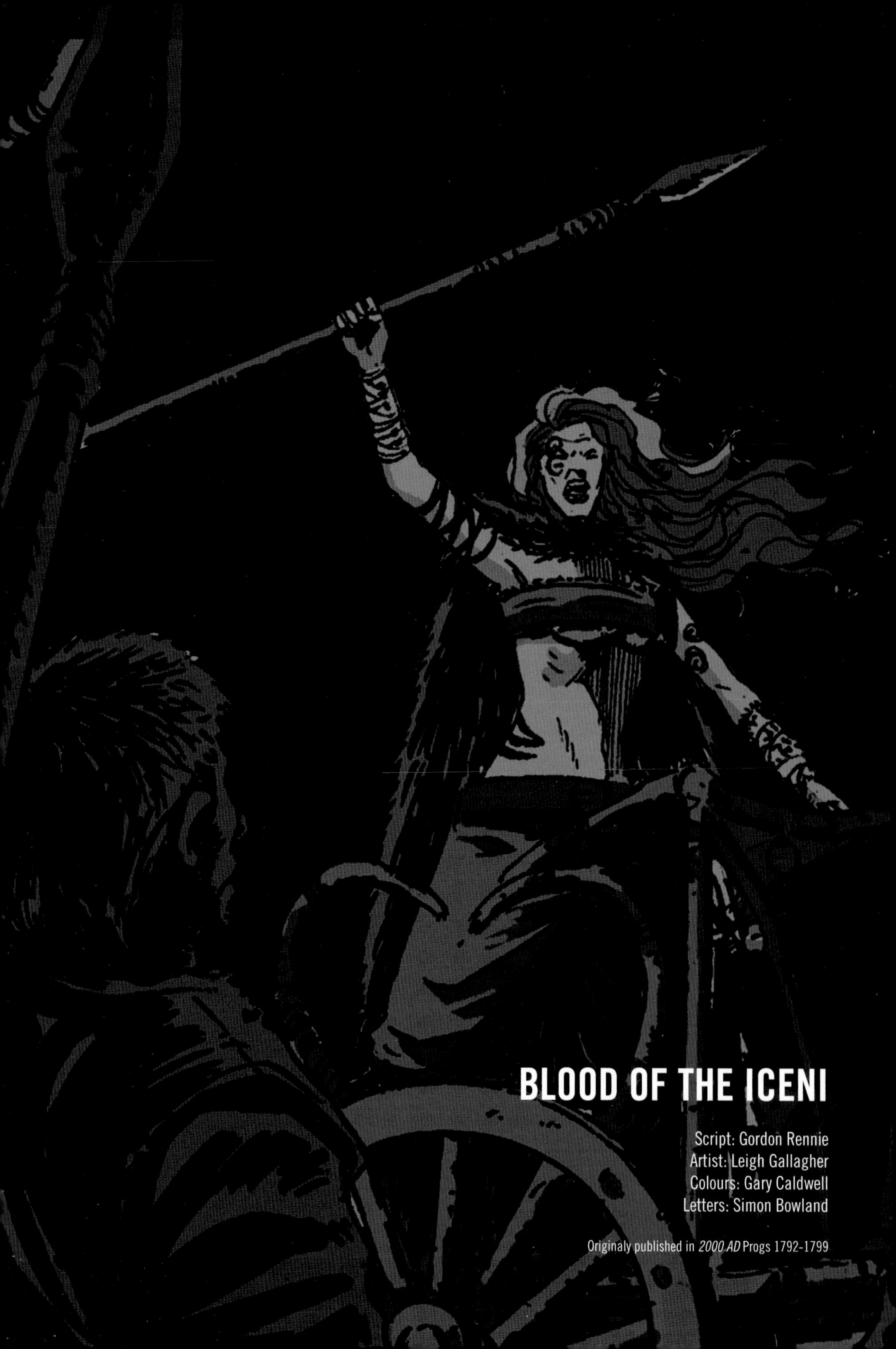

BLOOD OF THE ICENI

Script: Gordon Rennie
Artist: Leigh Gallagher
Colours: Gary Caldwell
Letters: Simon Bowland

Originaly published in *2000 AD* Progs 1792-1799

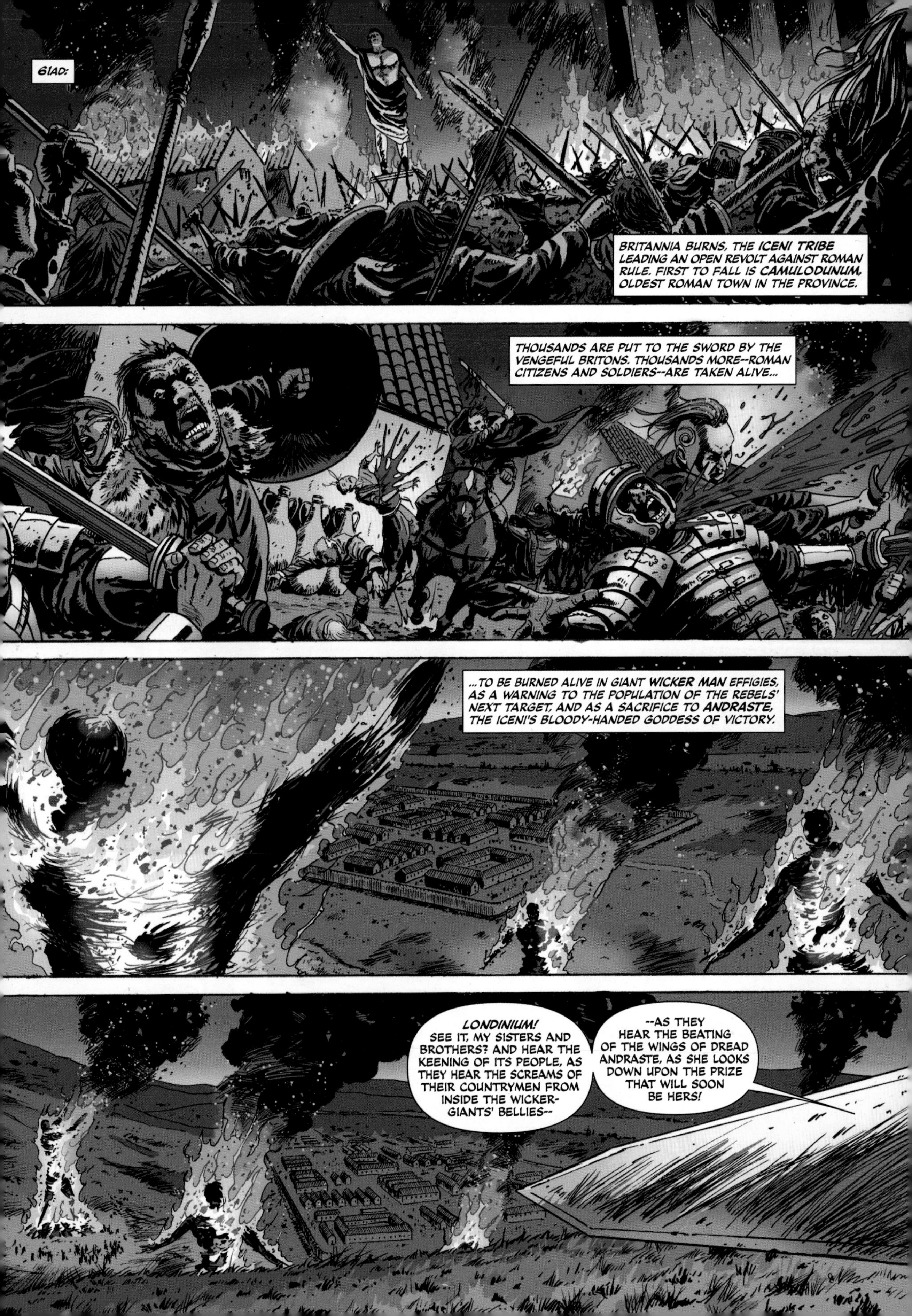
GIAD:
BRITANNIA BURNS, THE ICENI TRIBE LEADING AN OPEN REVOLT AGAINST ROMAN RULE. FIRST TO FALL IS CAMULODUNUM, OLDEST ROMAN TOWN IN THE PROVINCE.
THOUSANDS ARE PUT TO THE SWORD BY THE VENGEFUL BRITONS. THOUSANDS MORE--ROMAN CITIZENS AND SOLDIERS--ARE TAKEN ALIVE...
...TO BE BURNED ALIVE IN GIANT WICKER MAN EFFIGIES, AS A WARNING TO THE POPULATION OF THE REBELS' NEXT TARGET, AND AS A SACRIFICE TO ANDRASTE, THE ICENI'S BLOODY-HANDED GODDESS OF VICTORY.
LONDINIUM! SEE IT, MY SISTERS AND BROTHERS? AND HEAR THE KEENING OF ITS PEOPLE, AS THEY HEAR THE SCREAMS OF THEIR COUNTRYMEN FROM INSIDE THE WICKER-GIANTS' BELLIES--
--AS THEY HEAR THE BEATING OF THE WINGS OF DREAD ANDRASTE, AS SHE LOOKS DOWN UPON THE PRIZE THAT WILL SOON BE HERS!

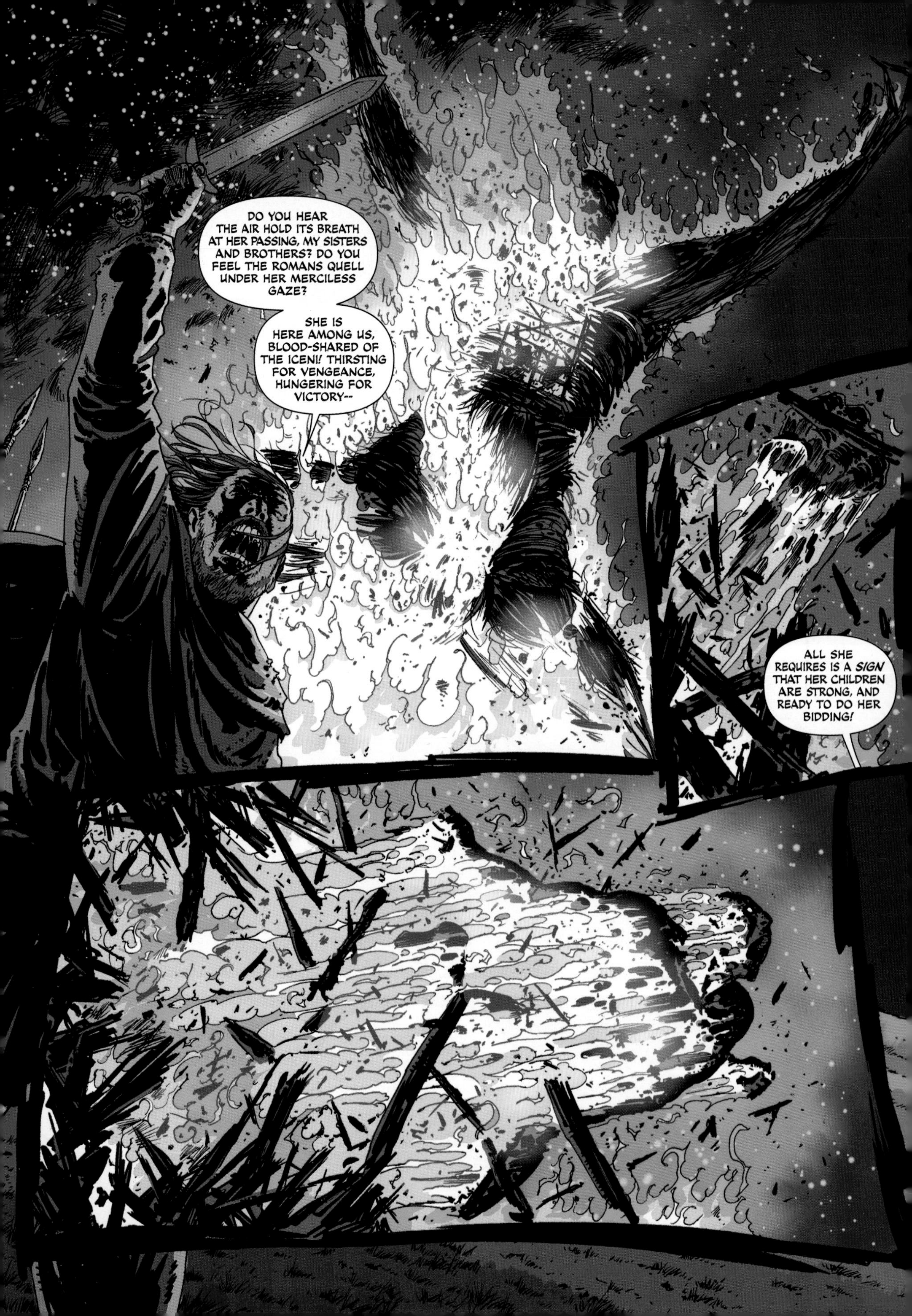
DO YOU HEAR THE AIR HOLD ITS BREATH AT HER PASSING, MY SISTERS AND BROTHERS? DO YOU FEEL THE ROMANS QUELL UNDER HER MERCILESS GAZE?
SHE IS HERE AMONG US, BLOOD-SHARED OF THE ICENI! THIRSTING FOR VENGEANCE, HUNGERING FOR VICTORY--
ALL SHE REQUIRES IS A *SIGN* THAT HER CHILDREN ARE STRONG, AND READY TO DO HER BIDDING!

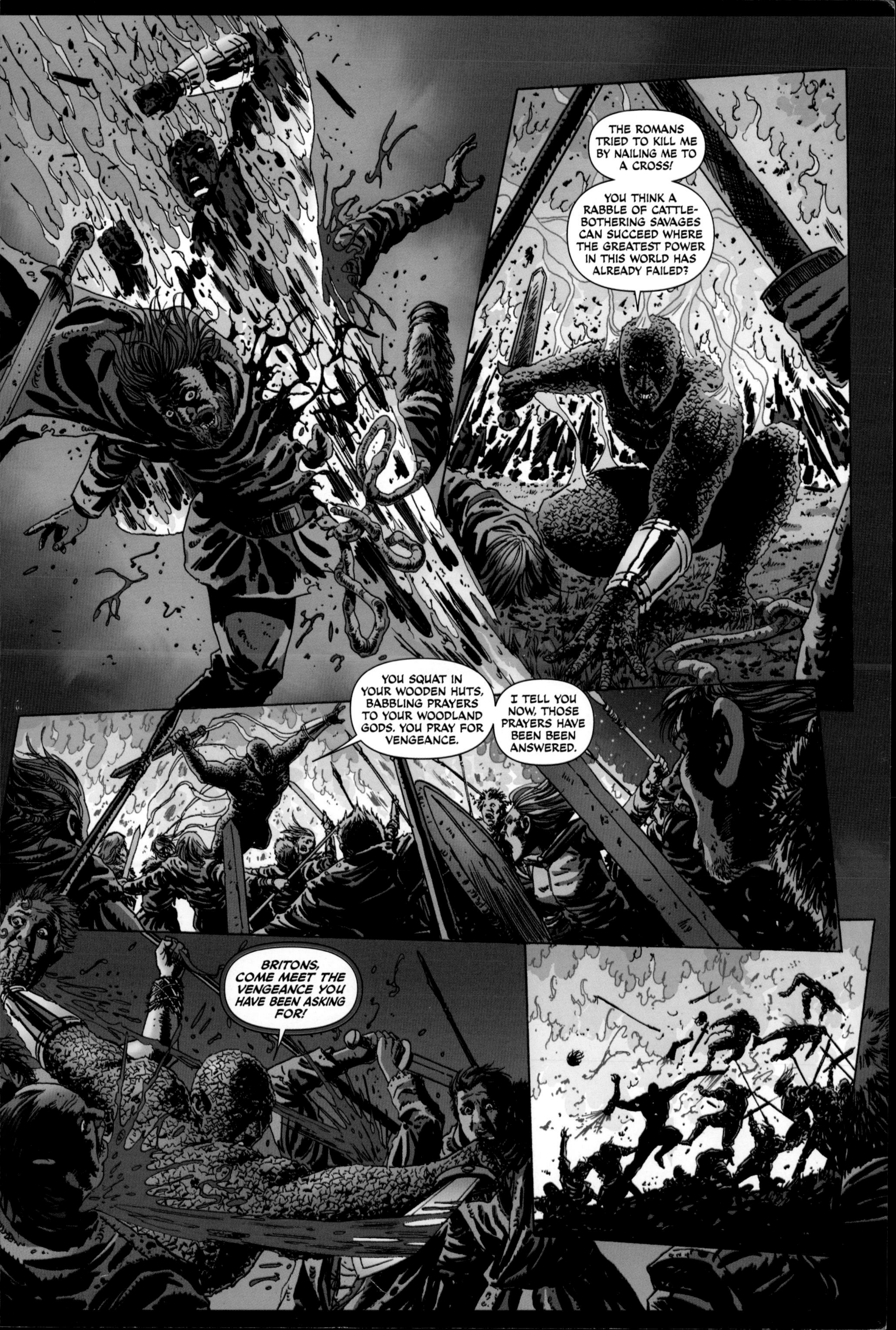
THE ROMANS TRIED TO KILL ME BY NAILING ME TO A CROSS!
YOU THINK A RABBLE OF CATTLE-BOTHERING SAVAGES CAN SUCCEED WHERE THE GREATEST POWER IN THIS WORLD HAS ALREADY FAILED?
YOU SQUAT IN YOUR WOODEN HUTS, BABBLING PRAYERS TO YOUR WOODLAND GODS. YOU PRAY FOR VENGEANCE.
I TELL YOU NOW, THOSE PRAYERS HAVE BEEN BEEN ANSWERED.
BRITONS, COME MEET THE VENGEANCE YOU HAVE BEEN ASKING FOR!

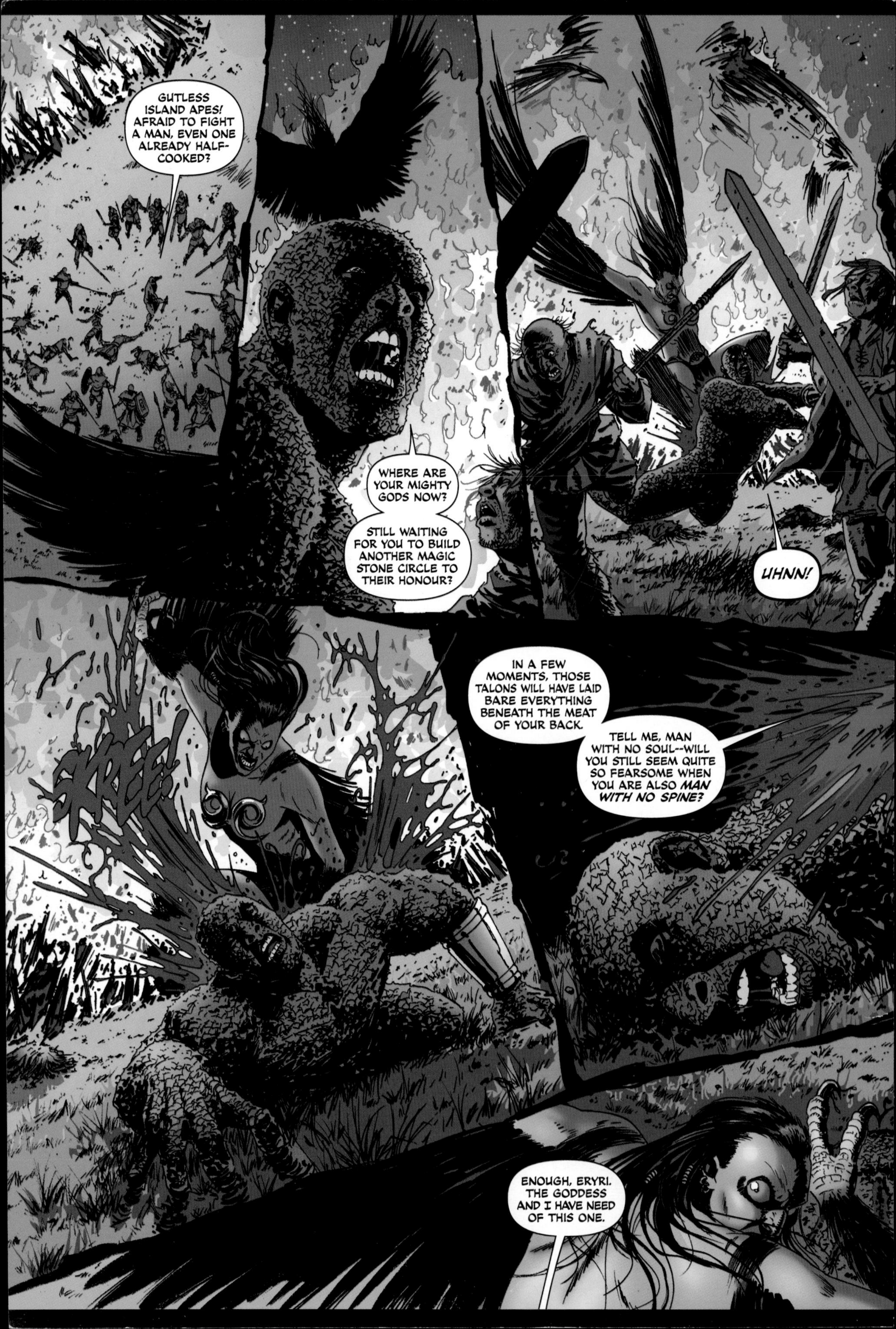
GUTLESS ISLAND APES! AFRAID TO FIGHT A MAN, EVEN ONE ALREADY HALF-COOKED?
WHERE ARE YOUR MIGHTY GODS NOW?
STILL WAITING FOR YOU TO BUILD ANOTHER MAGIC STONE CIRCLE TO THEIR HONOUR?
UHNN!
SKREE!
IN A FEW MOMENTS, THOSE TALONS WILL HAVE LAID BARE EVERYTHING BENEATH THE MEAT OF YOUR BACK.
TELL ME, MAN WITH NO SOUL--WILL YOU STILL SEEM QUITE SO FEARSOME WHEN YOU ARE ALSO *MAN WITH NO SPINE?*
ENOUGH, ERYRI. THE GODDESS AND I HAVE NEED OF THIS ONE.

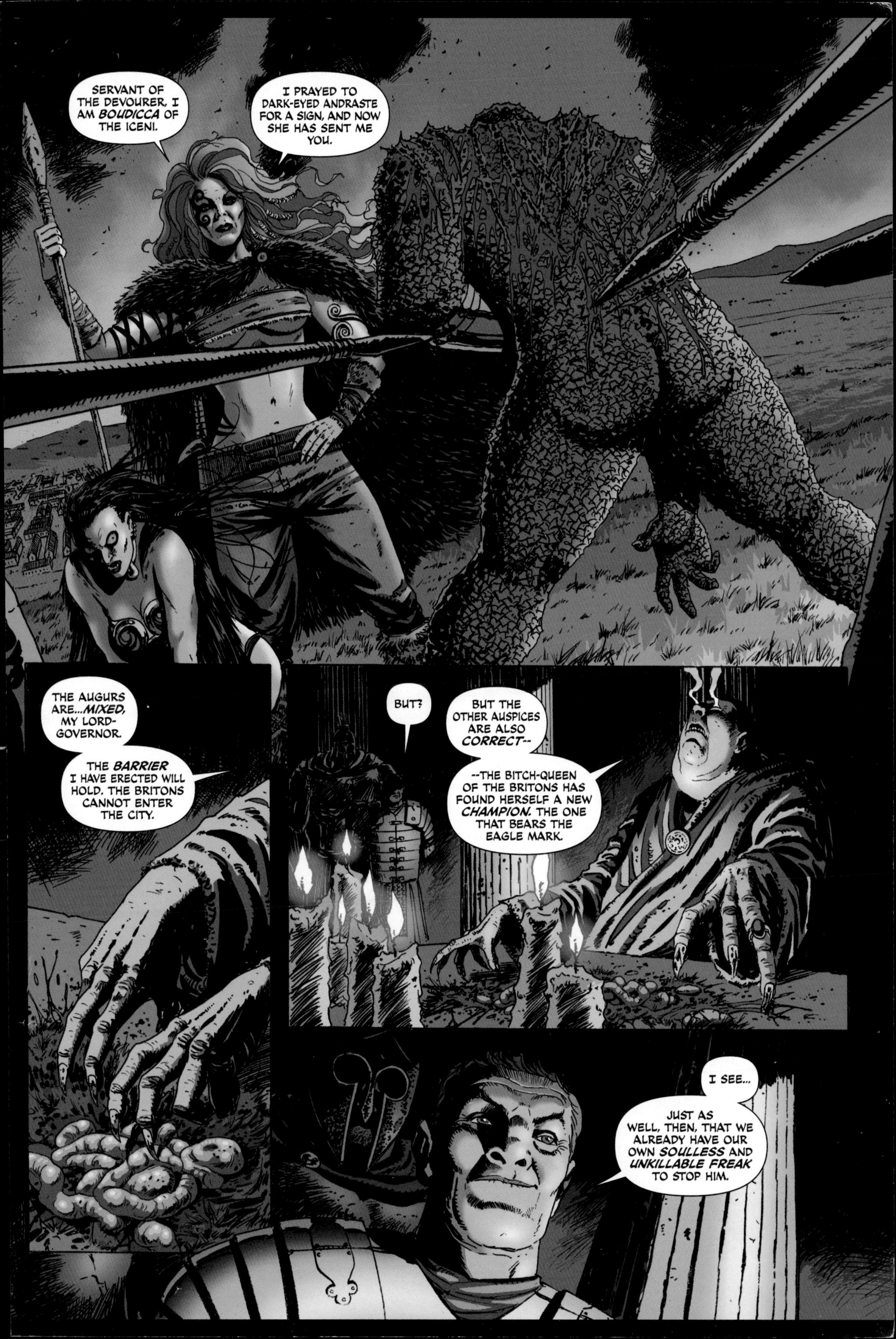
SERVANT OF THE DEVOURER, I AM BOUDICCA OF THE ICENI.
I PRAYED TO DARK-EYED ANDRASTE FOR A SIGN, AND NOW SHE HAS SENT ME YOU.
THE AUGURS ARE...MIXED, MY LORD-GOVERNOR.
THE BARRIER I HAVE ERECTED WILL HOLD. THE BRITONS CANNOT ENTER THE CITY.
BUT?
BUT THE OTHER AUSPICES ARE ALSO CORRECT--
--THE BITCH-QUEEN OF THE BRITONS HAS FOUND HERSELF A NEW CHAMPION. THE ONE THAT BEARS THE EAGLE MARK.
I SEE...
JUST AS WELL, THEN, THAT WE ALREADY HAVE OUR OWN SOULLESS AND UNKILLABLE FREAK TO STOP HIM.

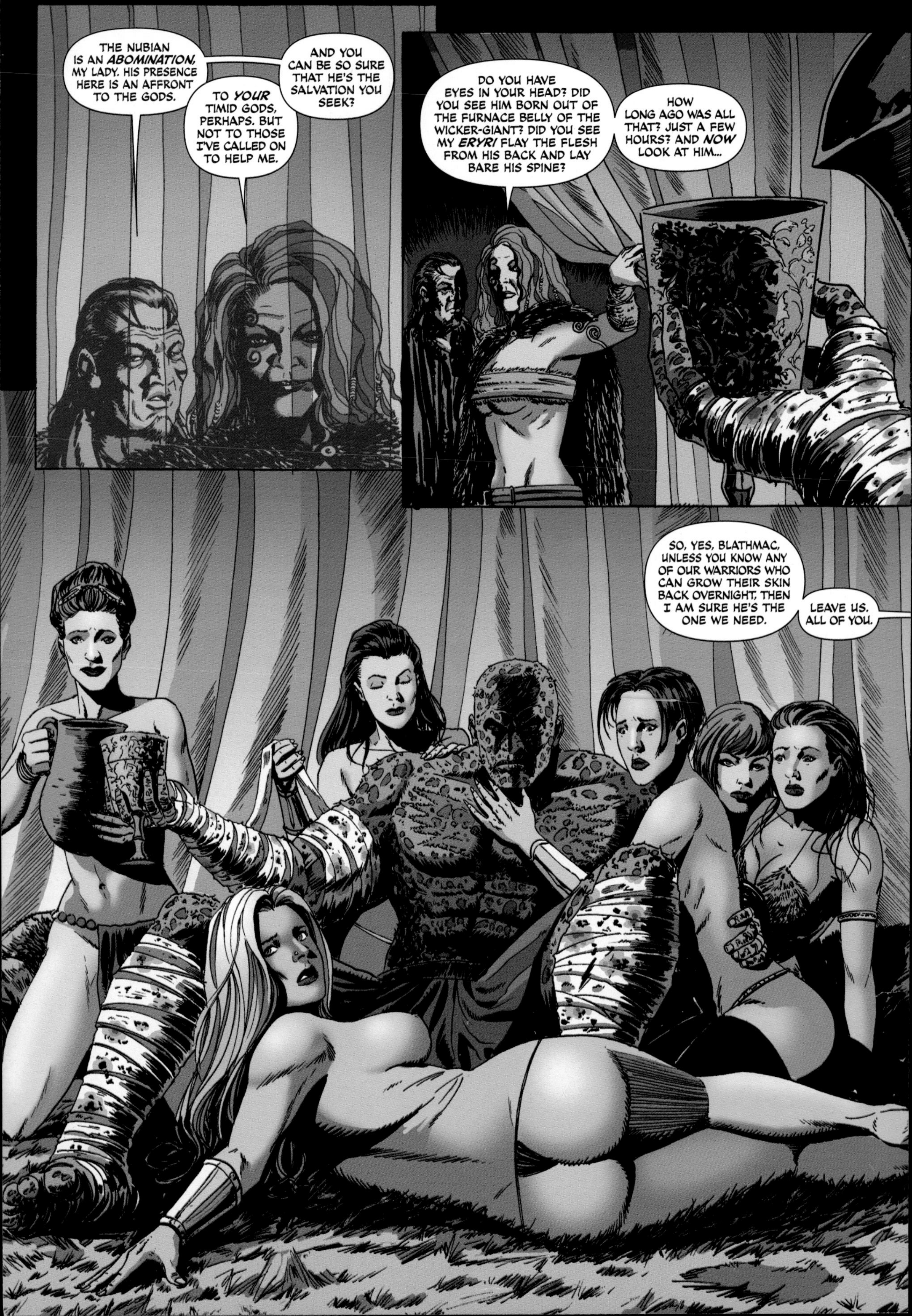
THE NUBIAN IS AN *ABOMINATION,* MY LADY. HIS PRESENCE HERE IS AN AFFRONT TO THE GODS.
AND YOU CAN BE SO SURE THAT HE'S THE SALVATION YOU SEEK?
TO *YOUR* TIMID GODS, PERHAPS. BUT NOT TO THOSE I'VE CALLED ON TO HELP ME.
DO YOU HAVE EYES IN YOUR HEAD? DID YOU SEE HIM BORN OUT OF THE FURNACE BELLY OF THE WICKER-GIANT? DID YOU SEE MY *ERYR!* FLAY THE FLESH FROM HIS BACK AND LAY BARE HIS SPINE?
HOW LONG AGO WAS ALL THAT? JUST A FEW HOURS? AND *NOW* LOOK AT HIM...
SO, YES, BLATHMAC, UNLESS YOU KNOW ANY OF OUR WARRIORS WHO CAN GROW THEIR SKIN BACK OVERNIGHT, THEN I AM SURE HE'S THE ONE WE NEED.
LEAVE US. ALL OF YOU.

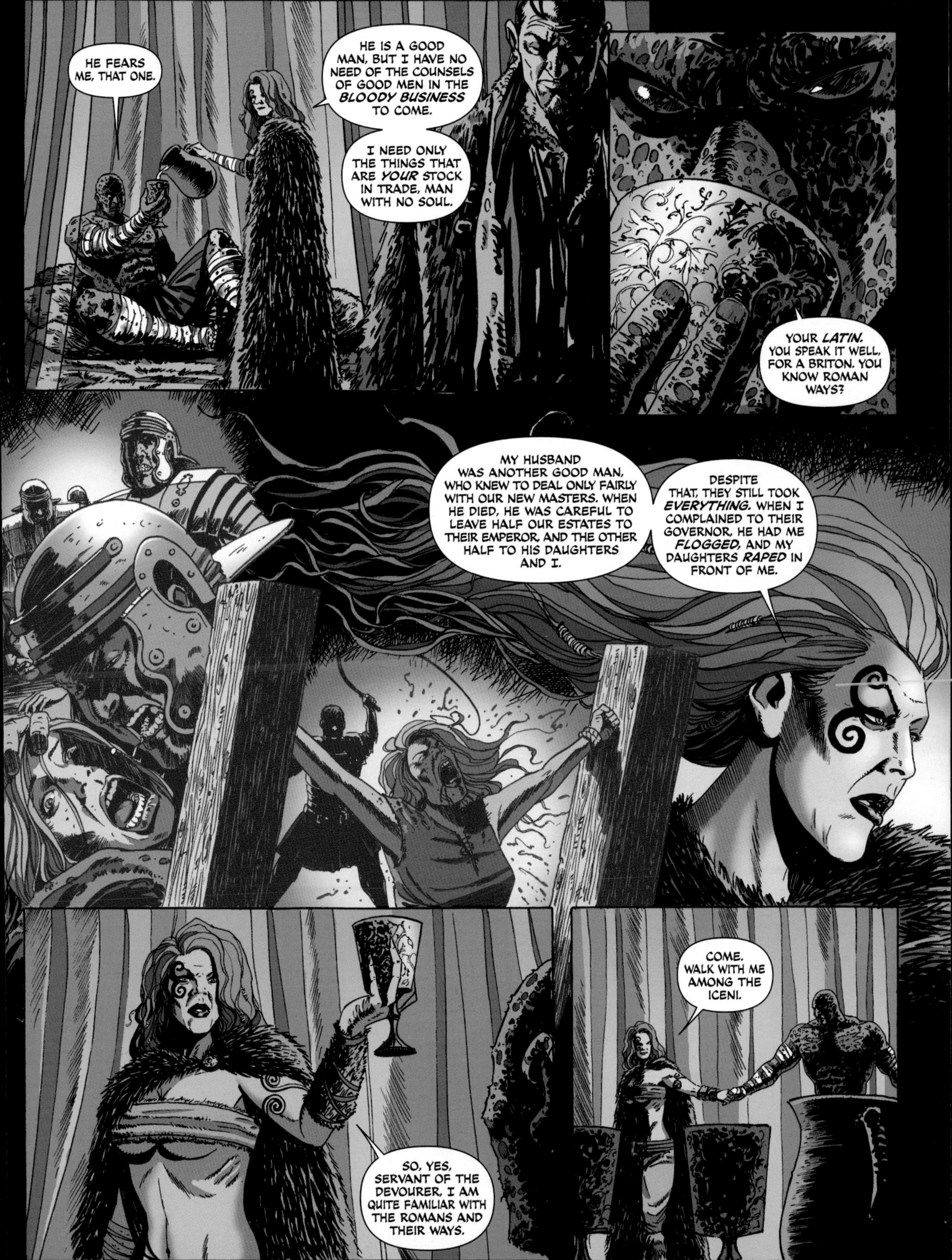
HE FEARS ME, THAT ONE.
HE IS A GOOD MAN, BUT I HAVE NO NEED OF THE COUNSELS OF GOOD MEN IN THE *BLOODY BUSINESS* TO COME.
I NEED ONLY THE THINGS THAT ARE *YOUR* STOCK IN TRADE, MAN WITH NO SOUL.
YOUR *LATIN*. YOU SPEAK IT WELL, FOR A BRITON. YOU KNOW ROMAN WAYS?
MY HUSBAND WAS ANOTHER GOOD MAN, WHO KNEW TO DEAL ONLY FAIRLY WITH OUR NEW MASTERS. WHEN HE DIED, HE WAS CAREFUL TO LEAVE HALF OUR ESTATES TO THEIR EMPEROR, AND THE OTHER HALF TO HIS DAUGHTERS AND I.
DESPITE THAT, THEY STILL TOOK *EVERYTHING.* WHEN I COMPLAINED TO THEIR GOVERNOR, HE HAD ME *FLOGGED,* AND MY DAUGHTERS *RAPED* IN FRONT OF ME.
SO, YES, SERVANT OF THE DEVOURER, I AM QUITE FAMILIAR WITH THE ROMANS AND THEIR WAYS.
COME. WALK WITH ME AMONG THE ICENI.

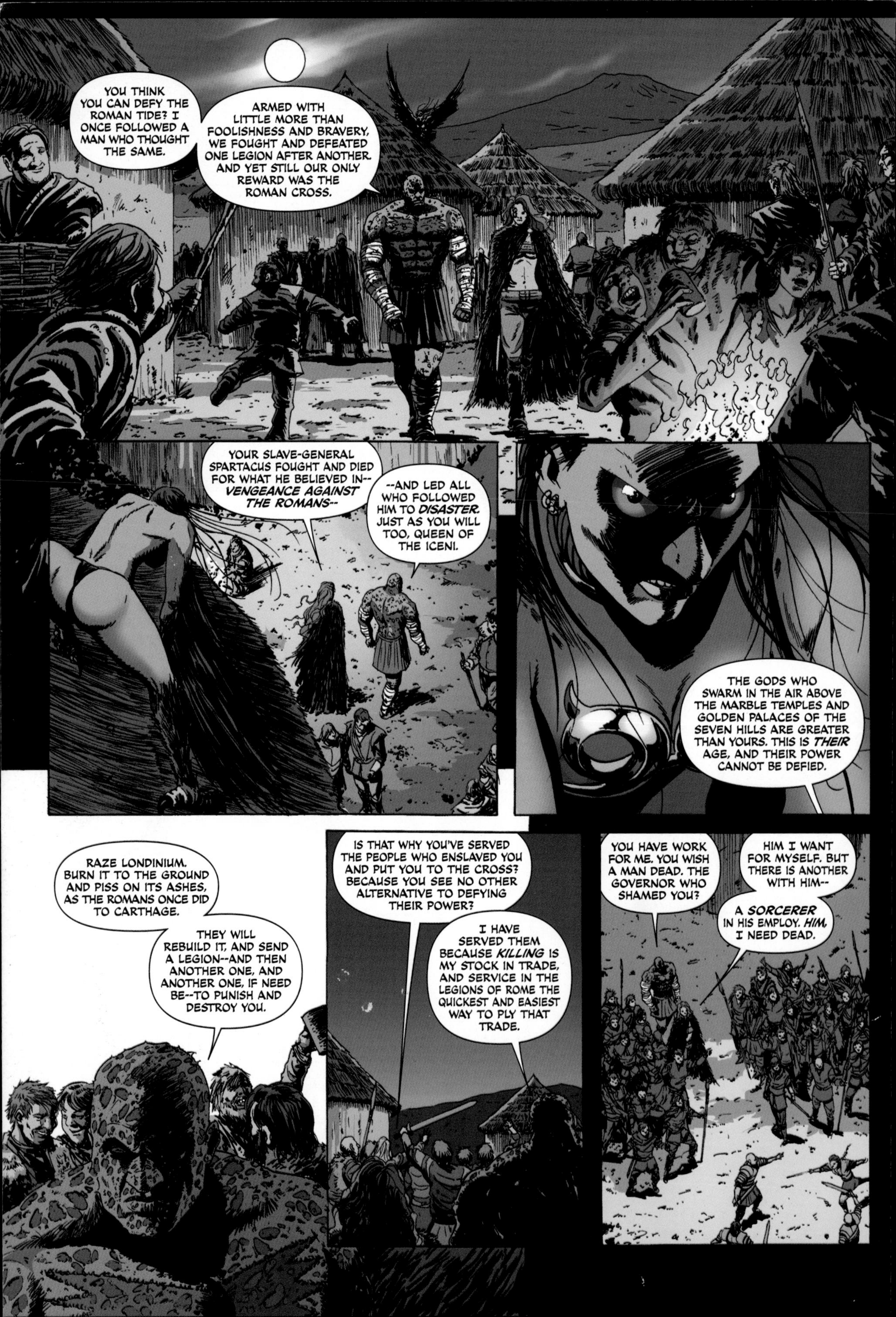
YOU THINK YOU CAN DEFY THE ROMAN TIDE? I ONCE FOLLOWED A MAN WHO THOUGHT THE SAME.
ARMED WITH LITTLE MORE THAN FOOLISHNESS AND BRAVERY, WE FOUGHT AND DEFEATED ONE LEGION AFTER ANOTHER. AND YET STILL OUR ONLY REWARD WAS THE ROMAN CROSS.
YOUR SLAVE-GENERAL SPARTACUS FOUGHT AND DIED FOR WHAT HE BELIEVED IN-- VENGEANCE AGAINST THE ROMANS--
--AND LED ALL WHO FOLLOWED HIM TO DISASTER. JUST AS YOU WILL TOO, QUEEN OF THE ICENI.
THE GODS WHO SWARM IN THE AIR ABOVE THE MARBLE TEMPLES AND GOLDEN PALACES OF THE SEVEN HILLS ARE GREATER THAN YOURS. THIS IS THEIR AGE, AND THEIR POWER CANNOT BE DEFIED.
RAZE LONDINIUM. BURN IT TO THE GROUND AND PISS ON ITS ASHES, AS THE ROMANS ONCE DID TO CARTHAGE.
THEY WILL REBUILD IT, AND SEND A LEGION--AND THEN ANOTHER ONE, AND ANOTHER ONE, IF NEED BE--TO PUNISH AND DESTROY YOU.
IS THAT WHY YOU'VE SERVED THE PEOPLE WHO ENSLAVED YOU AND PUT YOU TO THE CROSS? BECAUSE YOU SEE NO OTHER ALTERNATIVE TO DEFYING THEIR POWER?
I HAVE SERVED THEM BECAUSE KILLING IS MY STOCK IN TRADE, AND SERVICE IN THE LEGIONS OF ROME THE QUICKEST AND EASIEST WAY TO PLY THAT TRADE.
YOU HAVE WORK FOR ME. YOU WISH A MAN DEAD. THE GOVERNOR WHO SHAMED YOU?
HIM I WANT FOR MYSELF. BUT THERE IS ANOTHER WITH HIM--
A SORCERER IN HIS EMPLOY. HIM, I NEED DEAD.

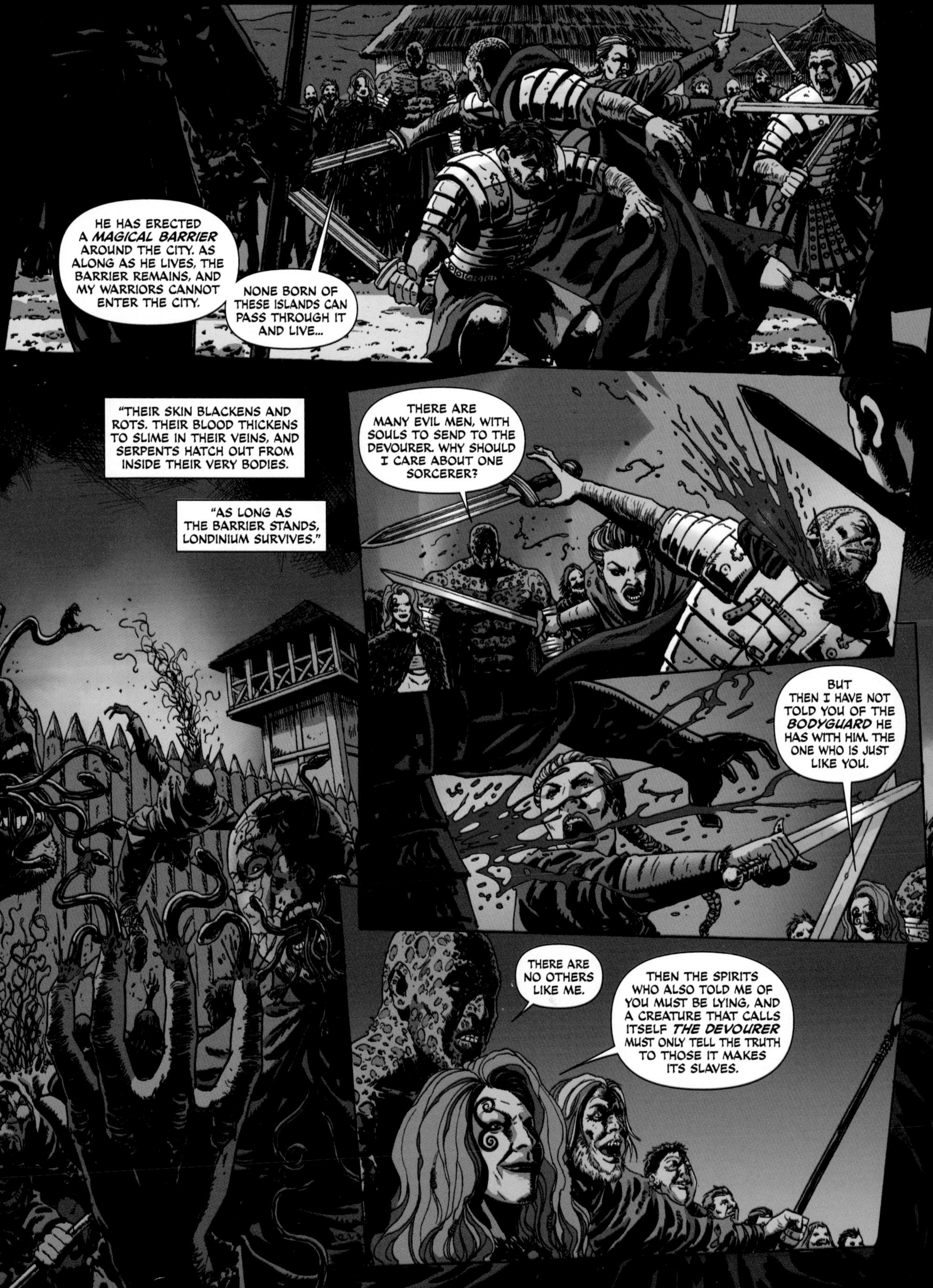
HE HAS ERECTED A MAGICAL BARRIER AROUND THE CITY. AS ALONG AS HE LIVES, THE BARRIER REMAINS, AND MY WARRIORS CANNOT ENTER THE CITY.
NONE BORN OF THESE ISLANDS CAN PASS THROUGH IT AND LIVE...
"THEIR SKIN BLACKENS AND ROTS. THEIR BLOOD THICKENS TO SLIME IN THEIR VEINS, AND SERPENTS HATCH OUT FROM INSIDE THEIR VERY BODIES.
"AS LONG AS THE BARRIER STANDS, LONDINIUM SURVIVES."
THERE ARE MANY EVIL MEN, WITH SOULS TO SEND TO THE DEVOURER. WHY SHOULD I CARE ABOUT ONE SORCERER?
BUT THEN I HAVE NOT TOLD YOU OF THE BODYGUARD HE HAS WITH HIM. THE ONE WHO IS JUST LIKE YOU.
THERE ARE NO OTHERS LIKE ME.
THEN THE SPIRITS WHO ALSO TOLD ME OF YOU MUST BE LYING, AND A CREATURE THAT CALLS ITSELF THE DEVOURER MUST ONLY TELL THE TRUTH TO THOSE IT MAKES ITS SLAVES.

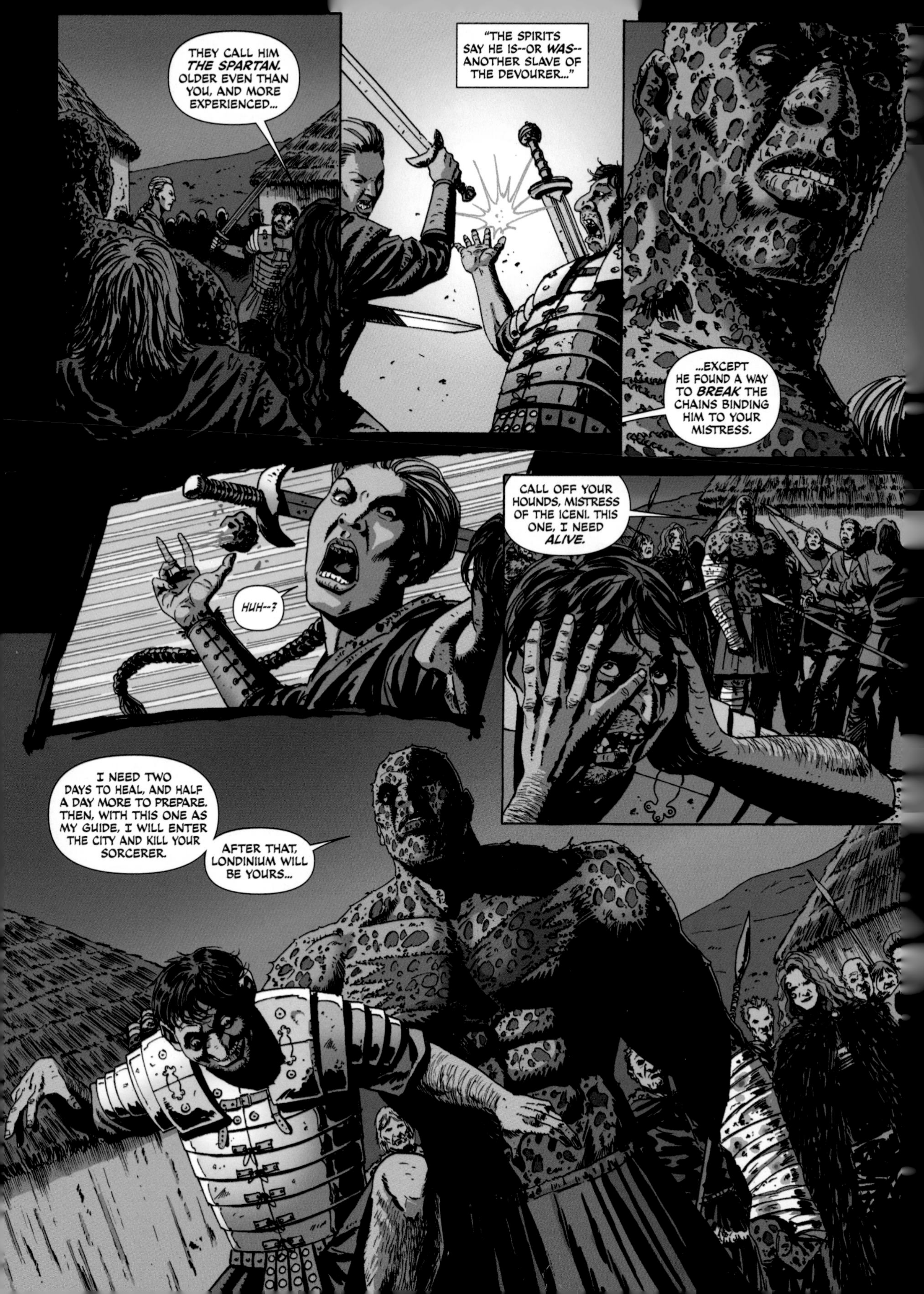
THEY CALL HIM *THE SPARTAN.* OLDER EVEN THAN YOU, AND MORE EXPERIENCED...
"THE SPIRITS SAY HE IS--OR *WAS*--ANOTHER SLAVE OF THE DEVOURER..."
...EXCEPT HE FOUND A WAY TO *BREAK* THE CHAINS BINDING HIM TO YOUR MISTRESS.
HUH--?
CALL OFF YOUR HOUNDS, MISTRESS OF THE ICENI. THIS ONE, I NEED *ALIVE.*
I NEED TWO DAYS TO HEAL, AND HALF A DAY MORE TO PREPARE. THEN, WITH THIS ONE AS MY GUIDE, I WILL ENTER THE CITY AND KILL YOUR SORCERER.
AFTER THAT, LONDINIUM WILL BE YOURS...

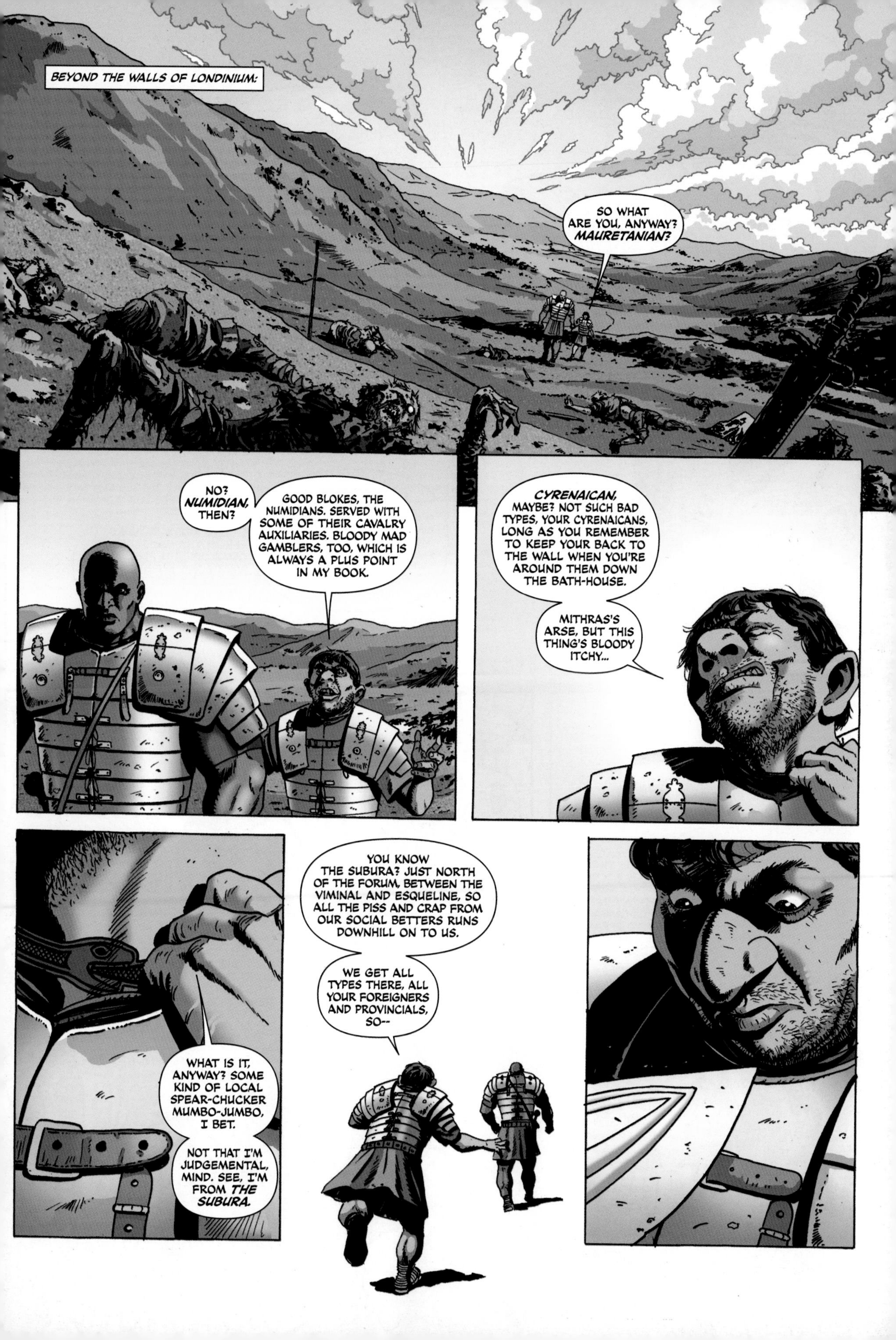

BEYOND THE WALLS OF LONDINIUM:
SO WHAT ARE YOU, ANYWAY? MAURETANIAN?
NO? NUMIDIAN, THEN?
GOOD BLOKES, THE NUMIDIANS. SERVED WITH SOME OF THEIR CAVALRY AUXILIARIES. BLOODY MAD GAMBLERS, TOO, WHICH IS ALWAYS A PLUS POINT IN MY BOOK.
CYRENAICAN, MAYBE? NOT SUCH BAD TYPES, YOUR CYRENAICANS, LONG AS YOU REMEMBER TO KEEP YOUR BACK TO THE WALL WHEN YOU'RE AROUND THEM DOWN THE BATH-HOUSE.
MITHRAS'S ARSE, BUT THIS THING'S BLOODY ITCHY...
WHAT IS IT, ANYWAY? SOME KIND OF LOCAL SPEAR-CHUCKER MUMBO-JUMBO, I BET.
NOT THAT I'M JUDGEMENTAL, MIND. SEE, I'M FROM THE SUBURA.
YOU KNOW THE SUBURA? JUST NORTH OF THE FORUM, BETWEEN THE VIMINAL AND ESQUELINE, SO ALL THE PISS AND CRAP FROM OUR SOCIAL BETTERS RUNS DOWNHILL ON TO US.
WE GET ALL TYPES THERE, ALL YOUR FOREIGNERS AND PROVINCIALS, SO--

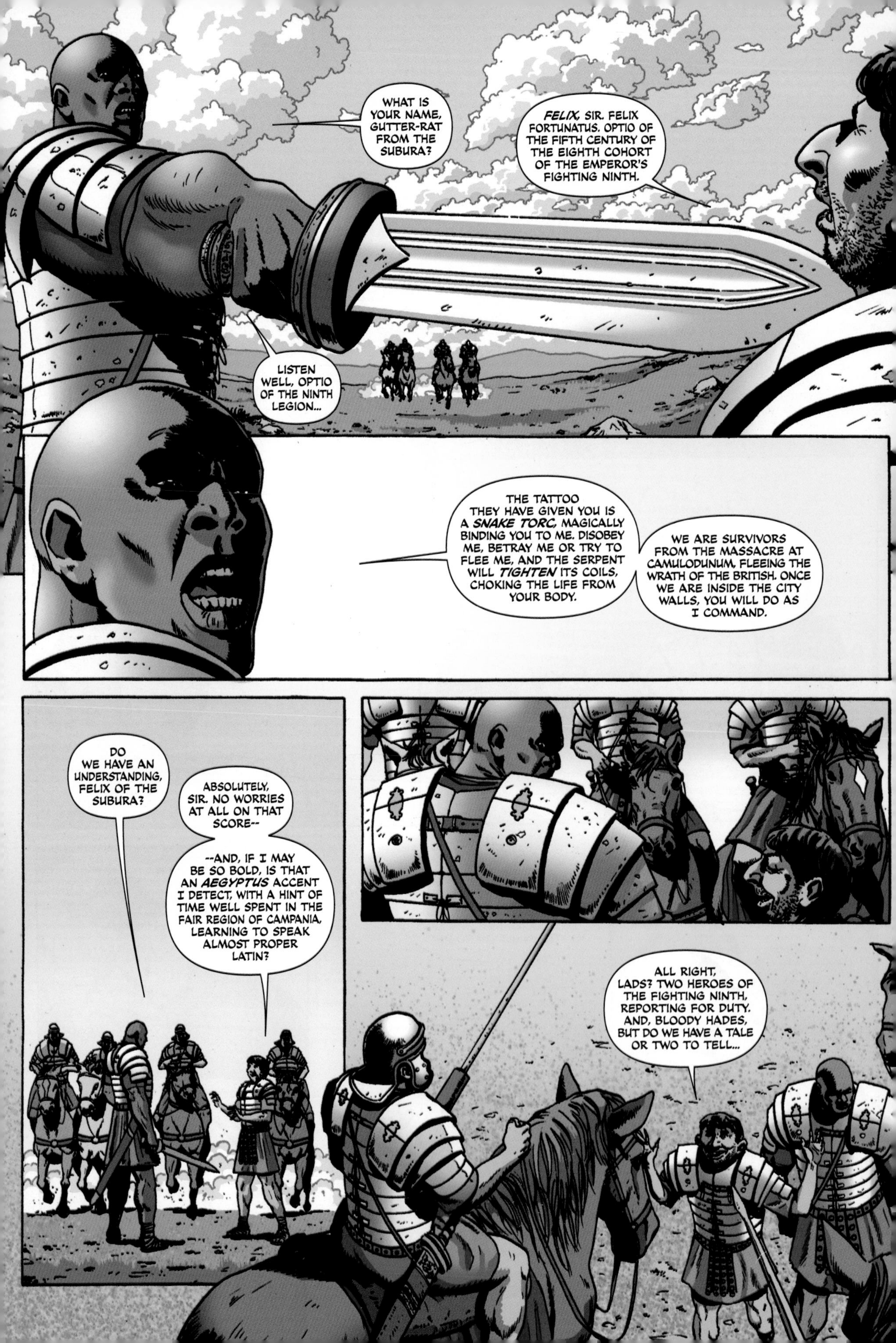
WHAT IS YOUR NAME, GUTTER-RAT FROM THE SUBURA?
FELIX. SIR. FELIX FORTUNATUS. OPTIO OF THE FIFTH CENTURY OF THE EIGHTH COHORT OF THE EMPEROR'S FIGHTING NINTH.
LISTEN WELL, OPTIO OF THE NINTH LEGION...
THE TATTOO THEY HAVE GIVEN YOU IS A SNAKE TORC, MAGICALLY BINDING YOU TO ME. DISOBEY ME, BETRAY ME OR TRY TO FLEE ME, AND THE SERPENT WILL TIGHTEN ITS COILS, CHOKING THE LIFE FROM YOUR BODY.
WE ARE SURVIVORS FROM THE MASSACRE AT CAMULODUNUM, FLEEING THE WRATH OF THE BRITISH. ONCE WE ARE INSIDE THE CITY WALLS, YOU WILL DO AS I COMMAND.
DO WE HAVE AN UNDERSTANDING, FELIX OF THE SUBURA?
ABSOLUTELY, SIR. NO WORRIES AT ALL ON THAT SCORE--
--AND, IF I MAY BE SO BOLD, IS THAT AN AEGYPTUS ACCENT I DETECT, WITH A HINT OF TIME WELL SPENT IN THE FAIR REGION OF CAMPANIA, LEARNING TO SPEAK ALMOST PROPER LATIN?
ALL RIGHT, LADS? TWO HEROES OF THE FIGHTING NINTH, REPORTING FOR DUTY. AND, BLOODY HADES, BUT DO WE HAVE A TALE OR TWO TO TELL...

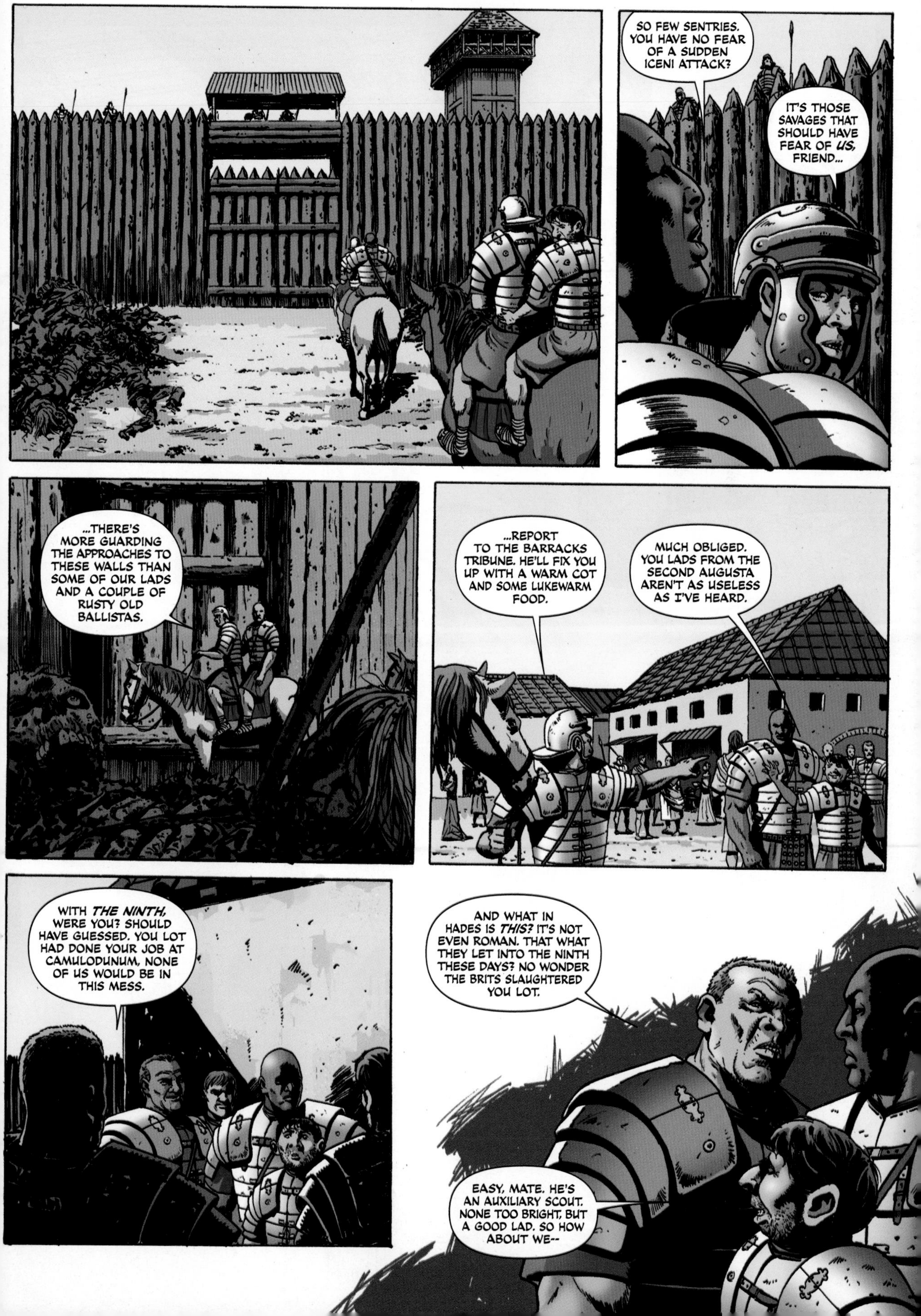
SO FEW SENTRIES. YOU HAVE NO FEAR OF A SUDDEN ICENI ATTACK?
IT'S THOSE SAVAGES THAT SHOULD HAVE FEAR OF *US*, FRIEND...
...THERE'S MORE GUARDING THE APPROACHES TO THESE WALLS THAN SOME OF OUR LADS AND A COUPLE OF RUSTY OLD BALLISTAS.
...REPORT TO THE BARRACKS TRIBUNE. HE'LL FIX YOU UP WITH A WARM COT AND SOME LUKEWARM FOOD.
MUCH OBLIGED. YOU LADS FROM THE SECOND AUGUSTA AREN'T AS USELESS AS I'VE HEARD.
WITH *THE NINTH*, WERE YOU? SHOULD HAVE GUESSED. YOU LOT HAD DONE YOUR JOB AT CAMULODUNUM, NONE OF US WOULD BE IN THIS MESS.
AND WHAT IN HADES IS *THIS?* IT'S NOT EVEN ROMAN. THAT WHAT THEY LET INTO THE NINTH THESE DAYS? NO WONDER THE BRITS SLAUGHTERED YOU LOT.
EASY, MATE. HE'S AN AUXILIARY SCOUT. NONE TOO BRIGHT, BUT A GOOD LAD. SO HOW ABOUT WE--

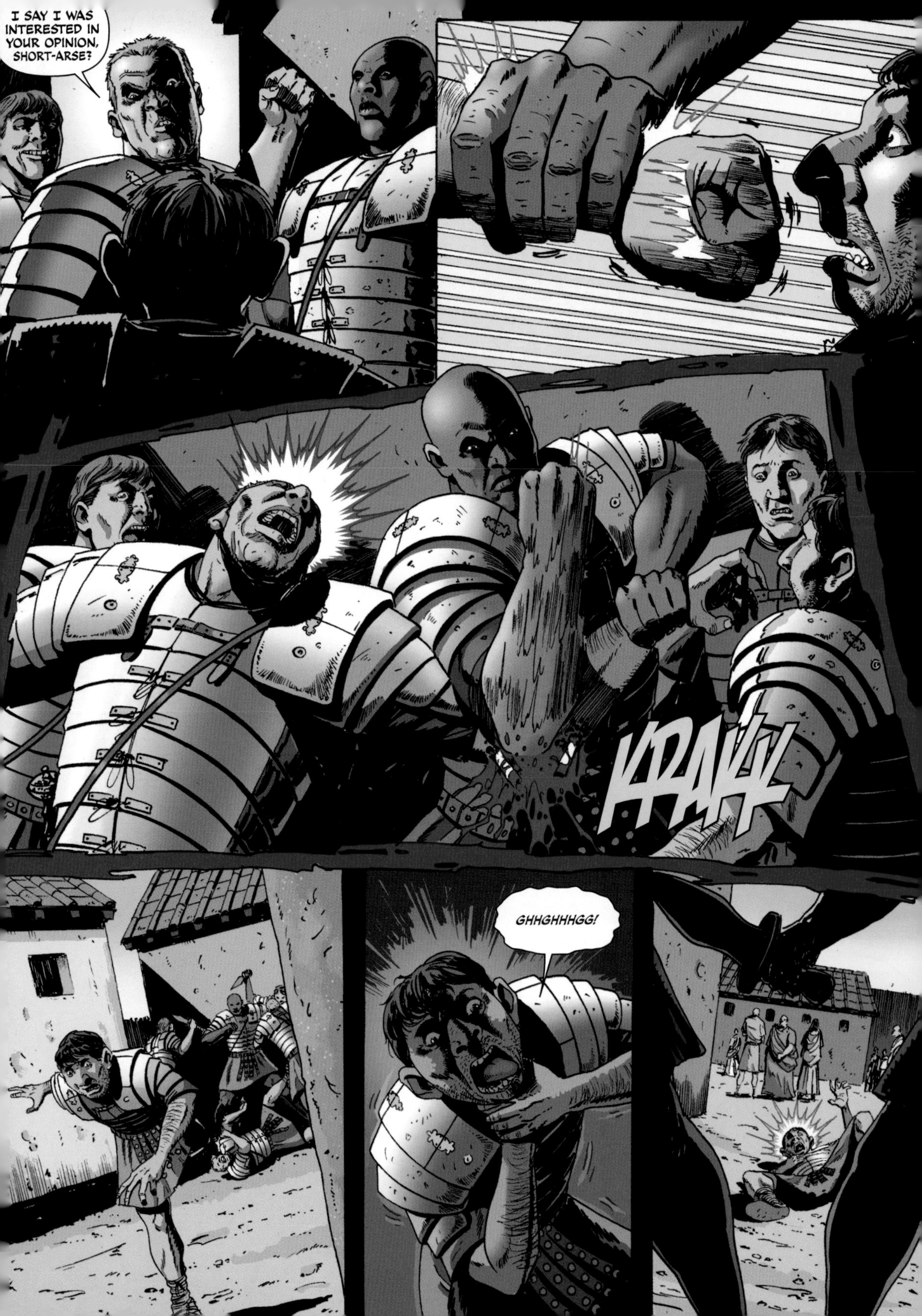
I SAY I WAS INTERESTED IN YOUR OPINION, SHORT-ARSE?
KRAKK
GHHGHHHGG!

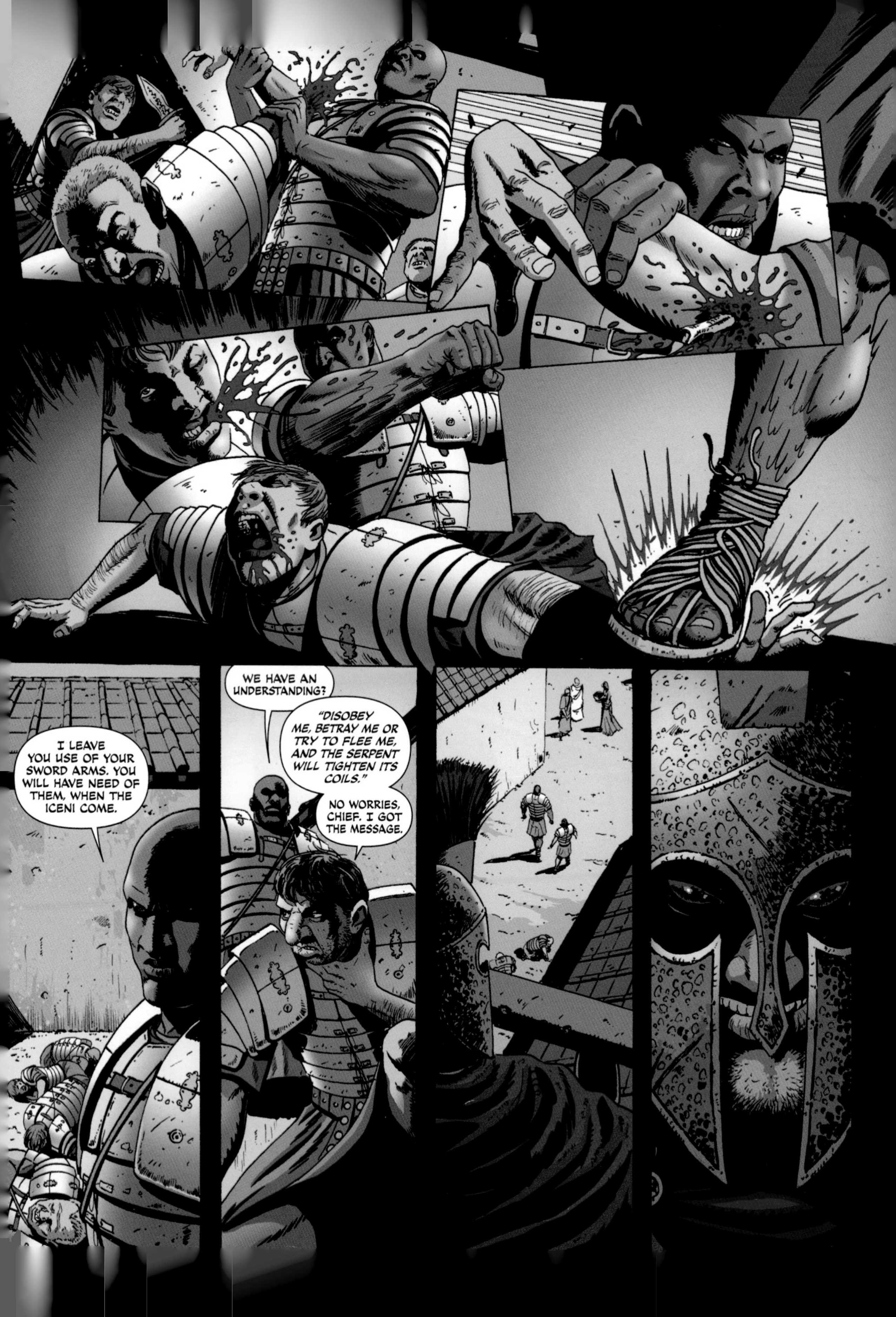
I LEAVE YOU USE OF YOUR SWORD ARMS. YOU WILL HAVE NEED OF THEM, WHEN THE ICENI COME.
WE HAVE AN UNDERSTANDING?
"DISOBEY ME, BETRAY ME OR TRY TO FLEE ME, AND THE SERPENT WILL TIGHTEN ITS COILS."
NO WORRIES, CHIEF. I GOT THE MESSAGE.

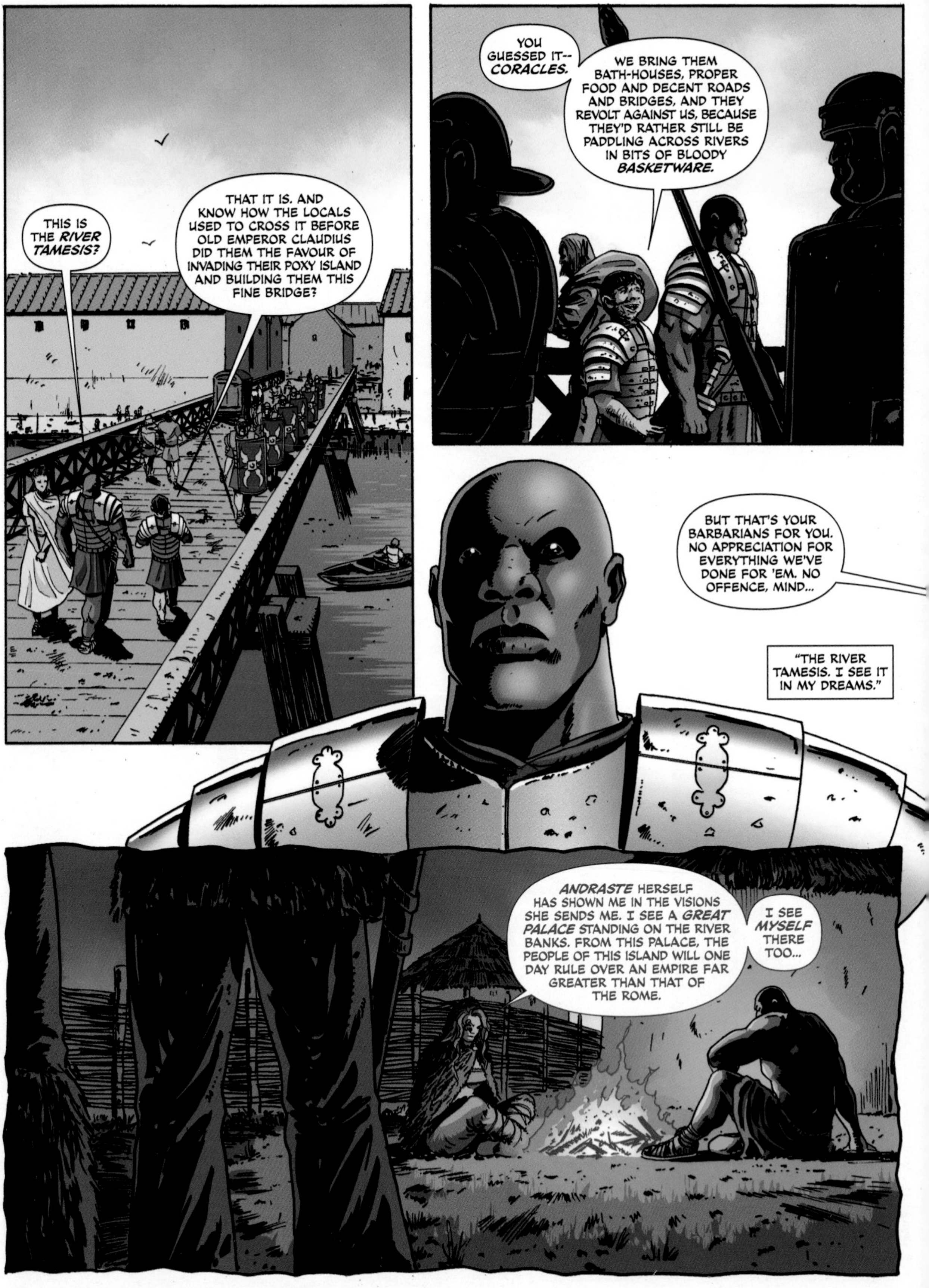
THIS IS THE *RIVER TAMESIS?*
THAT IT IS. AND KNOW HOW THE LOCALS USED TO CROSS IT BEFORE OLD EMPEROR CLAUDIUS DID THEM THE FAVOUR OF INVADING THEIR POXY ISLAND AND BUILDING THEM THIS FINE BRIDGE?
YOU GUESSED IT-- *CORACLES.*
WE BRING THEM BATH-HOUSES, PROPER FOOD AND DECENT ROADS AND BRIDGES, AND THEY REVOLT AGAINST US, BECAUSE THEY'D RATHER STILL BE PADDLING ACROSS RIVERS IN BITS OF BLOODY *BASKETWARE.*
BUT THAT'S YOUR BARBARIANS FOR YOU. NO APPRECIATION FOR EVERYTHING WE'VE DONE FOR 'EM. NO OFFENCE, MIND...
"THE RIVER TAMESIS. I SEE IT IN MY DREAMS."
ANDRASTE HERSELF HAS SHOWN ME IN THE VISIONS SHE SENDS ME. I SEE A *GREAT PALACE* STANDING ON THE RIVER BANKS. FROM THIS PALACE, THE PEOPLE OF THIS ISLAND WILL ONE DAY RULE OVER AN EMPIRE FAR GREATER THAN THAT OF THE ROME.
I SEE *MYSELF* THERE TOO...

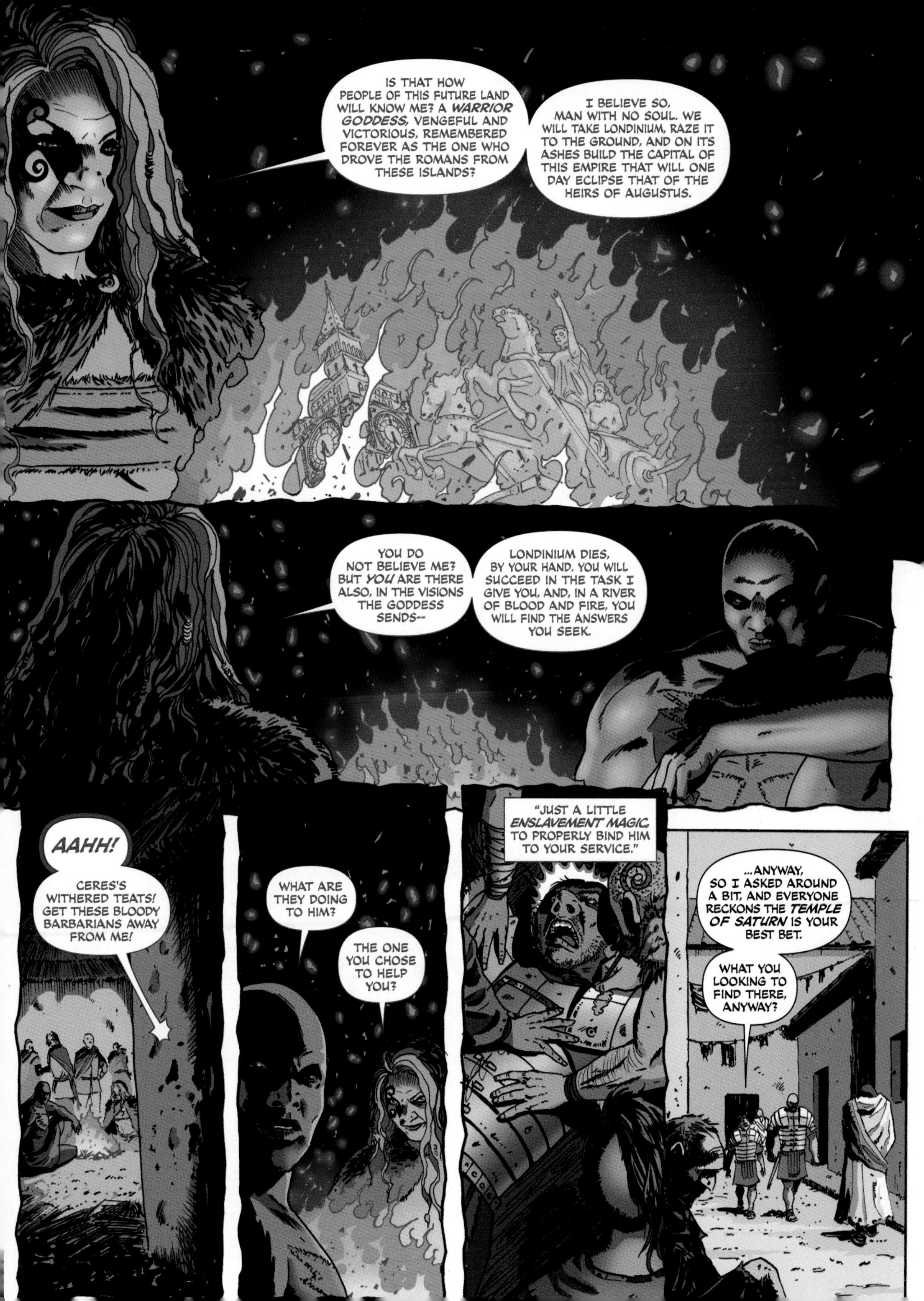
IS THAT HOW PEOPLE OF THIS FUTURE LAND WILL KNOW ME? A *WARRIOR GODDESS,* VENGEFUL AND VICTORIOUS, REMEMBERED FOREVER AS THE ONE WHO DROVE THE ROMANS FROM THESE ISLANDS?
I BELIEVE SO, MAN WITH NO SOUL. WE WILL TAKE LONDINIUM, RAZE IT TO THE GROUND, AND ON ITS ASHES BUILD THE CAPITAL OF THIS EMPIRE THAT WILL ONE DAY ECLIPSE THAT OF THE HEIRS OF AUGUSTUS.
YOU DO NOT BELIEVE ME? BUT *YOU* ARE THERE ALSO, IN THE VISIONS THE GODDESS SENDS--
LONDINIUM DIES, BY YOUR HAND. YOU WILL SUCCEED IN THE TASK I GIVE YOU, AND, IN A RIVER OF BLOOD AND FIRE, YOU WILL FIND THE ANSWERS YOU SEEK.
AAHH!
CERES'S WITHERED TEATS! GET THESE BLOODY BARBARIANS AWAY FROM ME!
WHAT ARE THEY DOING TO HIM?
THE ONE YOU CHOSE TO HELP YOU?
"JUST A LITTLE *ENSLAVEMENT MAGIC,* TO PROPERLY BIND HIM TO YOUR SERVICE."
...ANYWAY, SO I ASKED AROUND A BIT, AND EVERYONE RECKONS THE *TEMPLE OF SATURN* IS YOUR BEST BET.
WHAT YOU LOOKING TO FIND THERE, ANYWAY?

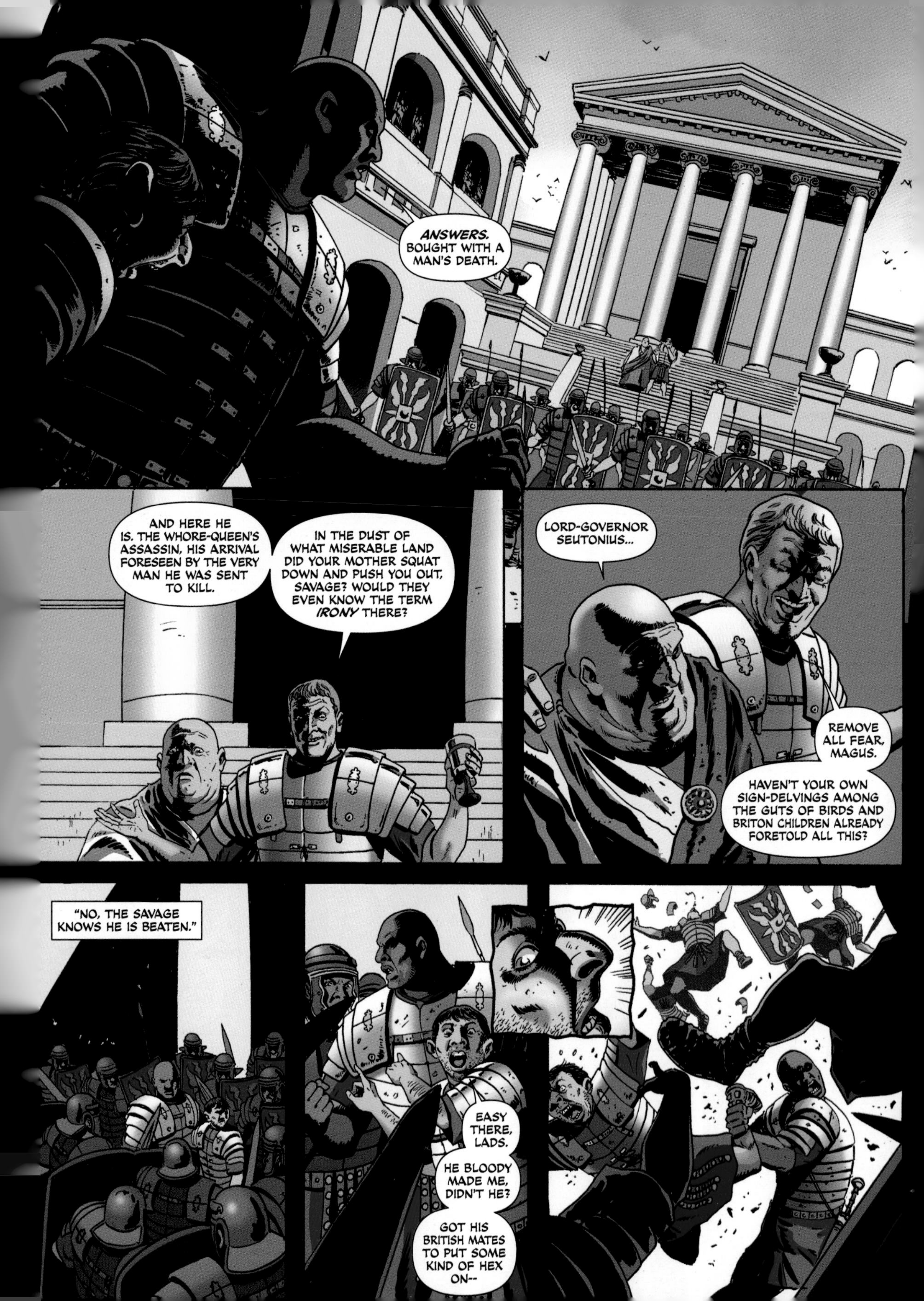

ANSWERS. BOUGHT WITH A MAN'S DEATH.
AND HERE HE IS. THE WHORE-QUEEN'S ASSASSIN, HIS ARRIVAL FORESEEN BY THE VERY MAN HE WAS SENT TO KILL.
IN THE DUST OF WHAT MISERABLE LAND DID YOUR MOTHER SQUAT DOWN AND PUSH YOU OUT, SAVAGE? WOULD THEY EVEN KNOW THE TERM *IRONY* THERE?
LORD-GOVERNOR SEUTONIUS...
REMOVE ALL FEAR, MAGUS.
HAVEN'T YOUR OWN SIGN-DELVINGS AMONG THE GUTS OF BIRDS AND BRITON CHILDREN ALREADY FORETOLD ALL THIS?
"NO, THE SAVAGE KNOWS HE IS BEATEN."
EASY THERE, LADS.
HE BLOODY MADE ME, DIDN'T HE?
GOT HIS BRITISH MATES TO PUT SOME KIND OF HEX ON--

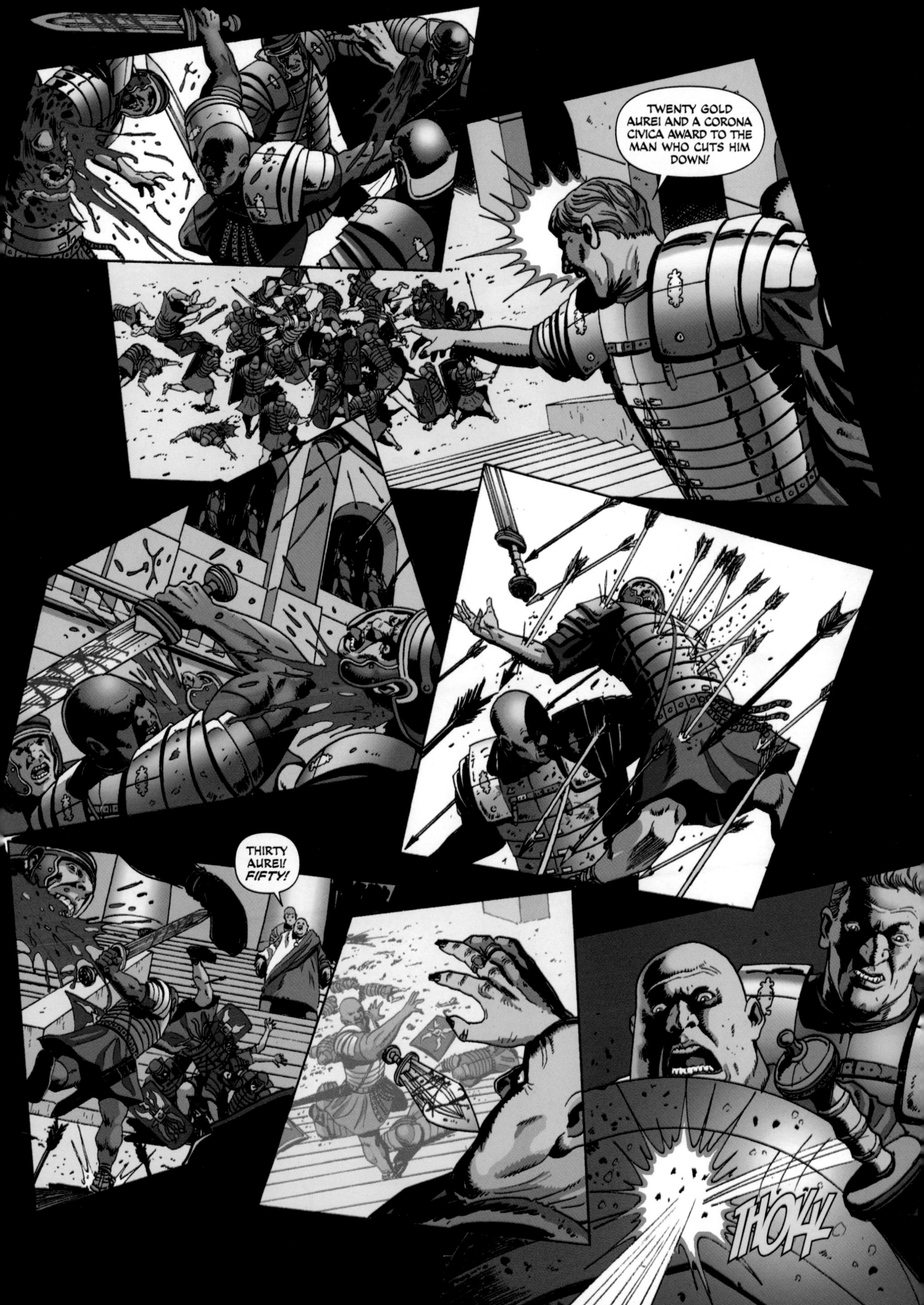
TWENTY GOLD AUREI AND A CORONA CIVICA AWARD TO THE MAN WHO CUTS HIM DOWN!
THIRTY AUREI! FIFTY!
THOK!

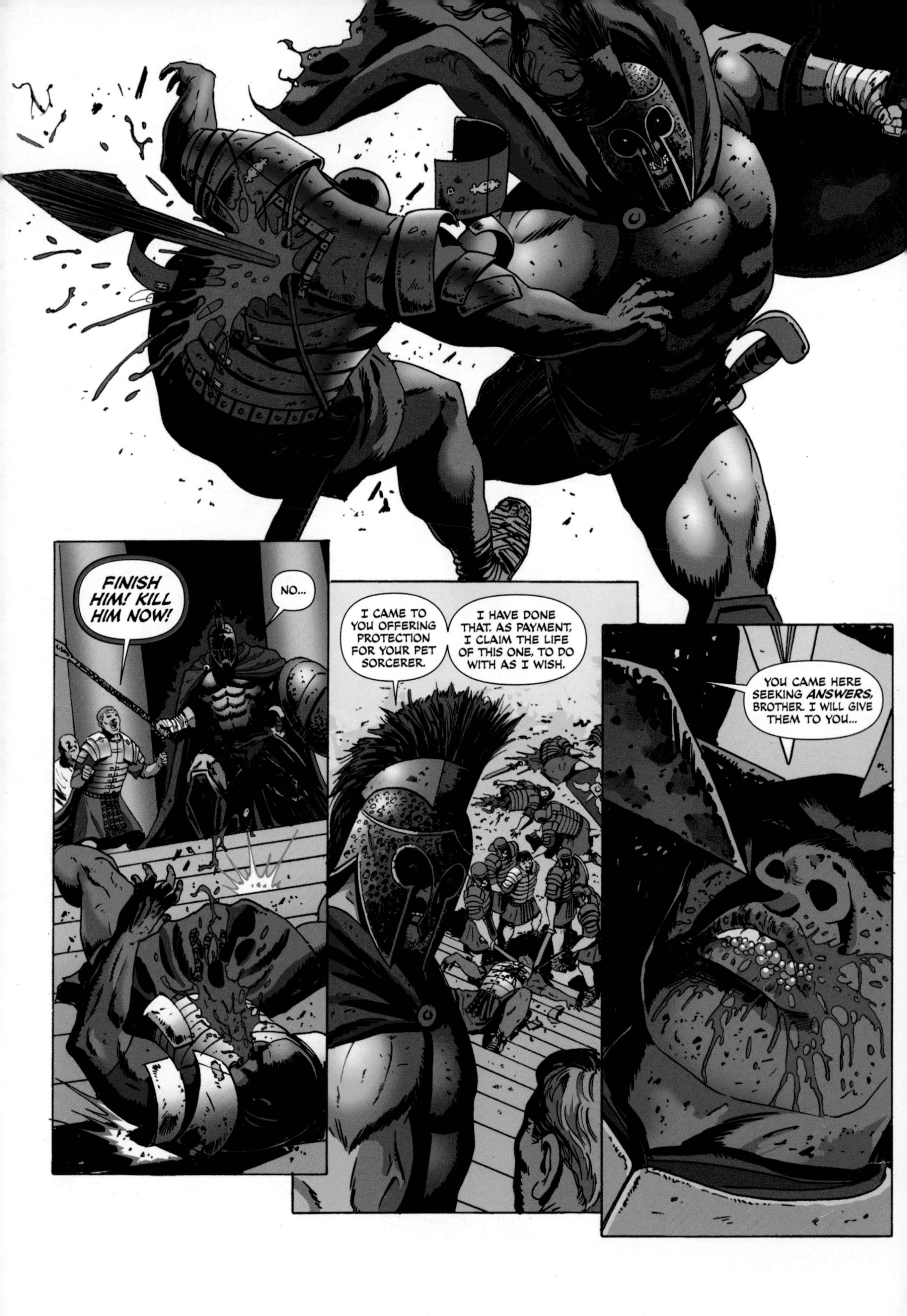
FINISH HIM! KILL HIM NOW!
NO...
I CAME TO YOU OFFERING PROTECTION FOR YOUR PET SORCERER.
I HAVE DONE THAT. AS PAYMENT, I CLAIM THE LIFE OF THIS ONE, TO DO WITH AS I WISH.
YOU CAME HERE SEEKING *ANSWERS*, BROTHER. I WILL GIVE THEM TO YOU...

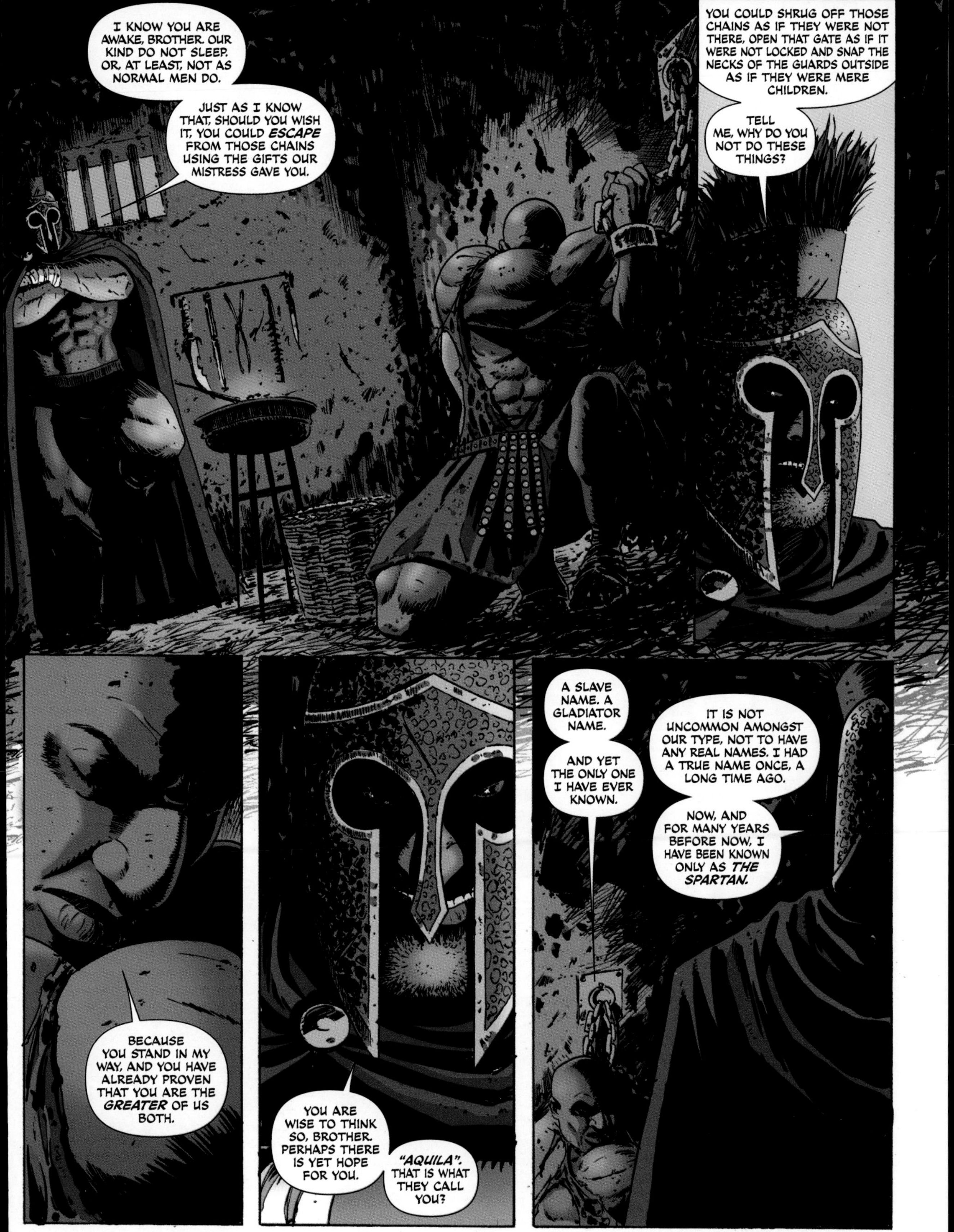
I KNOW YOU ARE AWAKE, BROTHER. OUR KIND DO NOT SLEEP. OR, AT LEAST, NOT AS NORMAL MEN DO.
JUST AS I KNOW THAT, SHOULD YOU WISH IT, YOU COULD ESCAPE FROM THOSE CHAINS USING THE GIFTS OUR MISTRESS GAVE YOU.
YOU COULD SHRUG OFF THOSE CHAINS AS IF THEY WERE NOT THERE, OPEN THAT GATE AS IF IT WERE NOT LOCKED AND SNAP THE NECKS OF THE GUARDS OUTSIDE AS IF THEY WERE MERE CHILDREN.
TELL ME, WHY DO YOU NOT DO THESE THINGS?
BECAUSE YOU STAND IN MY WAY, AND YOU HAVE ALREADY PROVEN THAT YOU ARE THE GREATER OF US BOTH.
YOU ARE WISE TO THINK SO, BROTHER. PERHAPS THERE IS YET HOPE FOR YOU.
"AQUILA". THAT IS WHAT THEY CALL YOU?
A SLAVE NAME. A GLADIATOR NAME.
AND YET THE ONLY ONE I HAVE EVER KNOWN.
IT IS NOT UNCOMMON AMONGST OUR TYPE, NOT TO HAVE ANY REAL NAMES. I HAD A TRUE NAME ONCE, A LONG TIME AGO.
NOW, AND FOR MANY YEARS BEFORE NOW, I HAVE BEEN KNOWN ONLY AS THE SPARTAN.

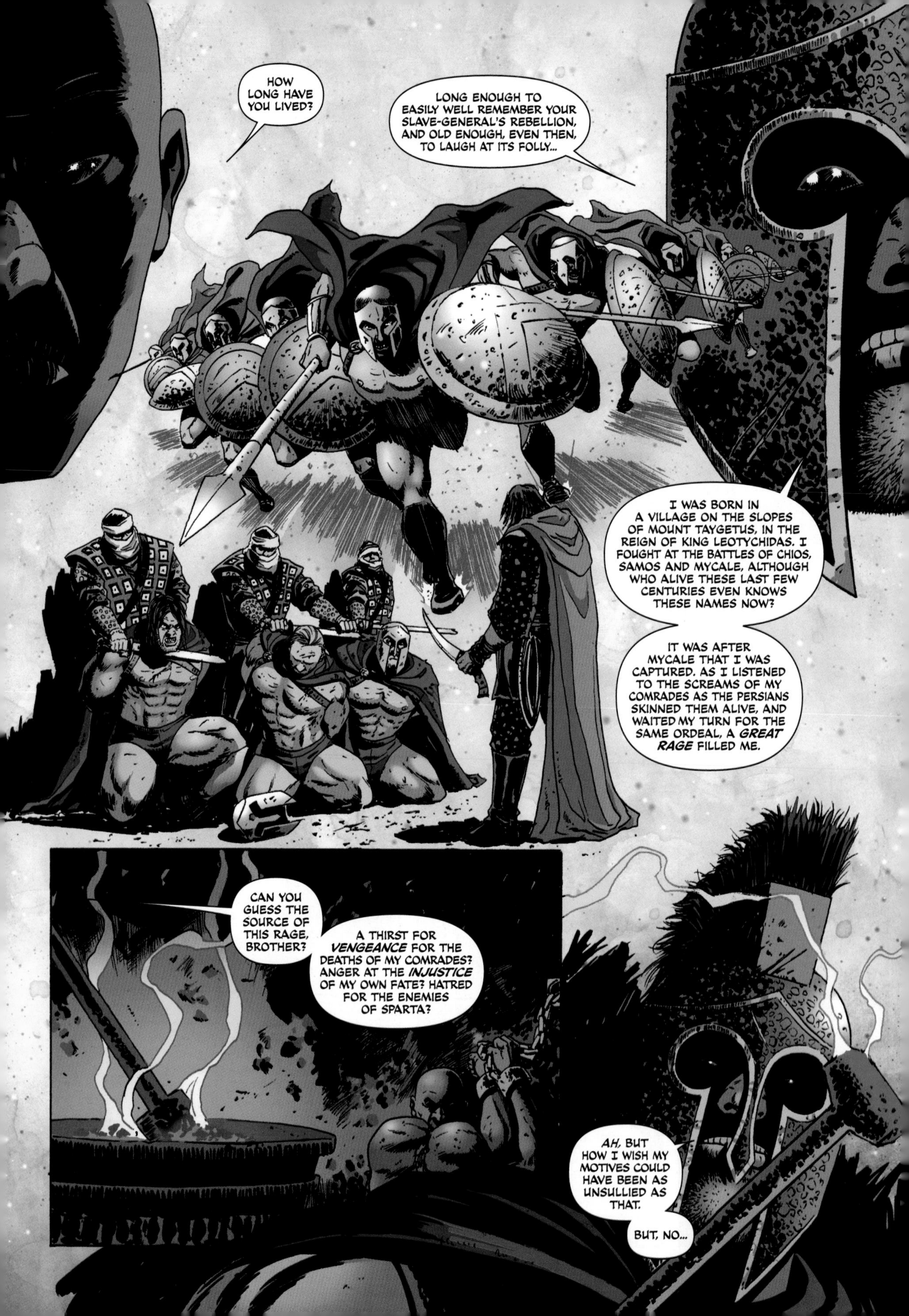
HOW LONG HAVE YOU LIVED?
LONG ENOUGH TO EASILY WELL REMEMBER YOUR SLAVE-GENERAL'S REBELLION, AND OLD ENOUGH, EVEN THEN, TO LAUGH AT ITS FOLLY...
I WAS BORN IN A VILLAGE ON THE SLOPES OF MOUNT TAYGETUS, IN THE REIGN OF KING LEOTYCHIDAS. I FOUGHT AT THE BATTLES OF CHIOS, SAMOS AND MYCALE, ALTHOUGH WHO ALIVE THESE LAST FEW CENTURIES EVEN KNOWS THESE NAMES NOW?
IT WAS AFTER MYCALE THAT I WAS CAPTURED. AS I LISTENED TO THE SCREAMS OF MY COMRADES AS THE PERSIANS SKINNED THEM ALIVE, AND WAITED MY TURN FOR THE SAME ORDEAL, A *GREAT RAGE* FILLED ME.
CAN YOU GUESS THE SOURCE OF THIS RAGE, BROTHER?
A THIRST FOR *VENGEANCE* FOR THE DEATHS OF MY COMRADES? ANGER AT THE *INJUSTICE* OF MY OWN FATE? HATRED FOR THE ENEMIES OF SPARTA?
AH, BUT HOW I WISH MY MOTIVES COULD HAVE BEEN AS UNSULLIED AS THAT.
BUT, NO...

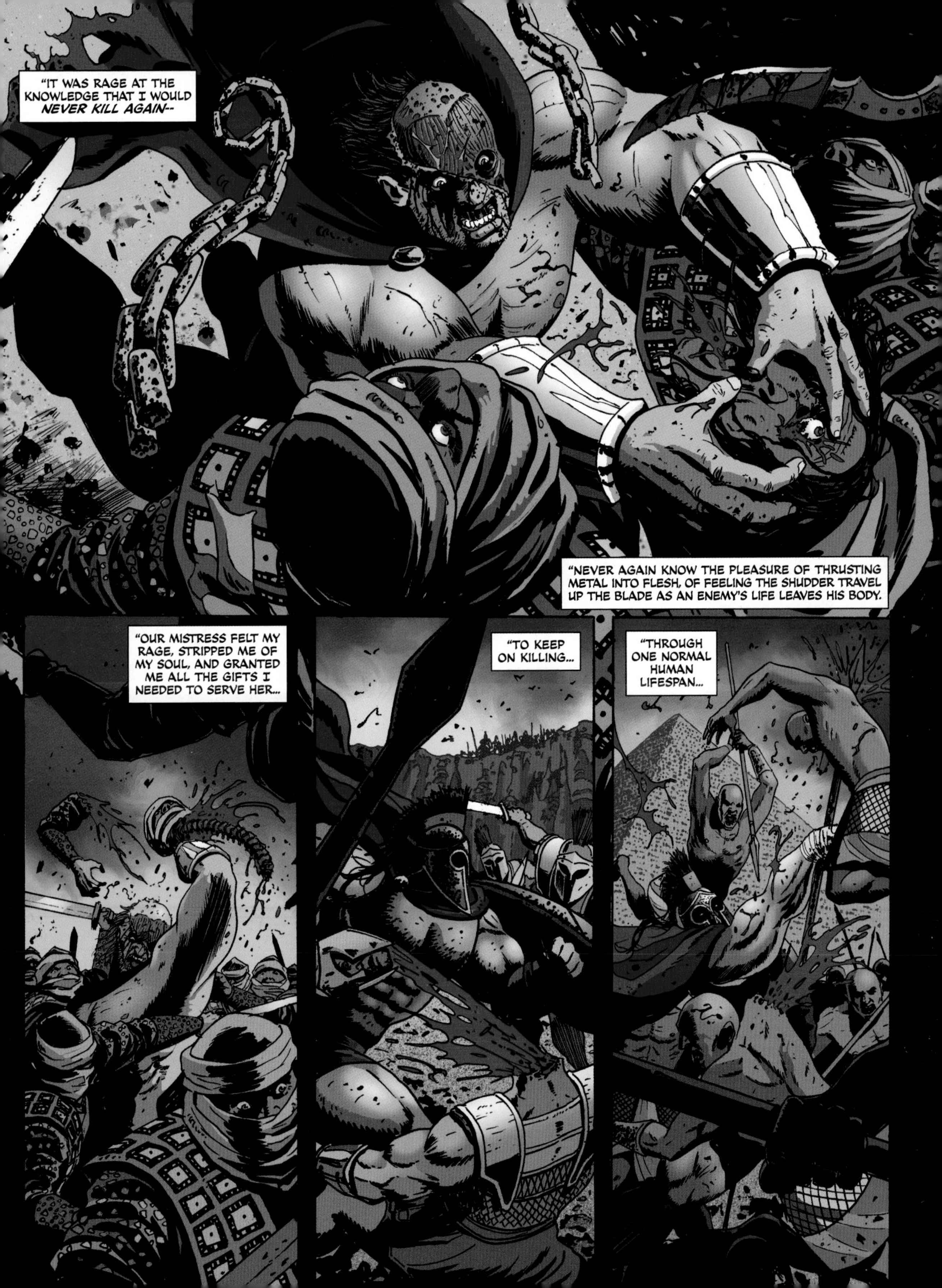
"IT WAS RAGE AT THE KNOWLEDGE THAT I WOULD *NEVER KILL AGAIN*--
"NEVER AGAIN KNOW THE PLEASURE OF THRUSTING METAL INTO FLESH, OF FEELING THE SHUDDER TRAVEL UP THE BLADE AS AN ENEMY'S LIFE LEAVES HIS BODY.
"OUR MISTRESS FELT MY RAGE, STRIPPED ME OF MY SOUL, AND GRANTED ME ALL THE GIFTS I NEEDED TO SERVE HER...
"TO KEEP ON KILLING...
"THROUGH ONE NORMAL HUMAN LIFESPAN...

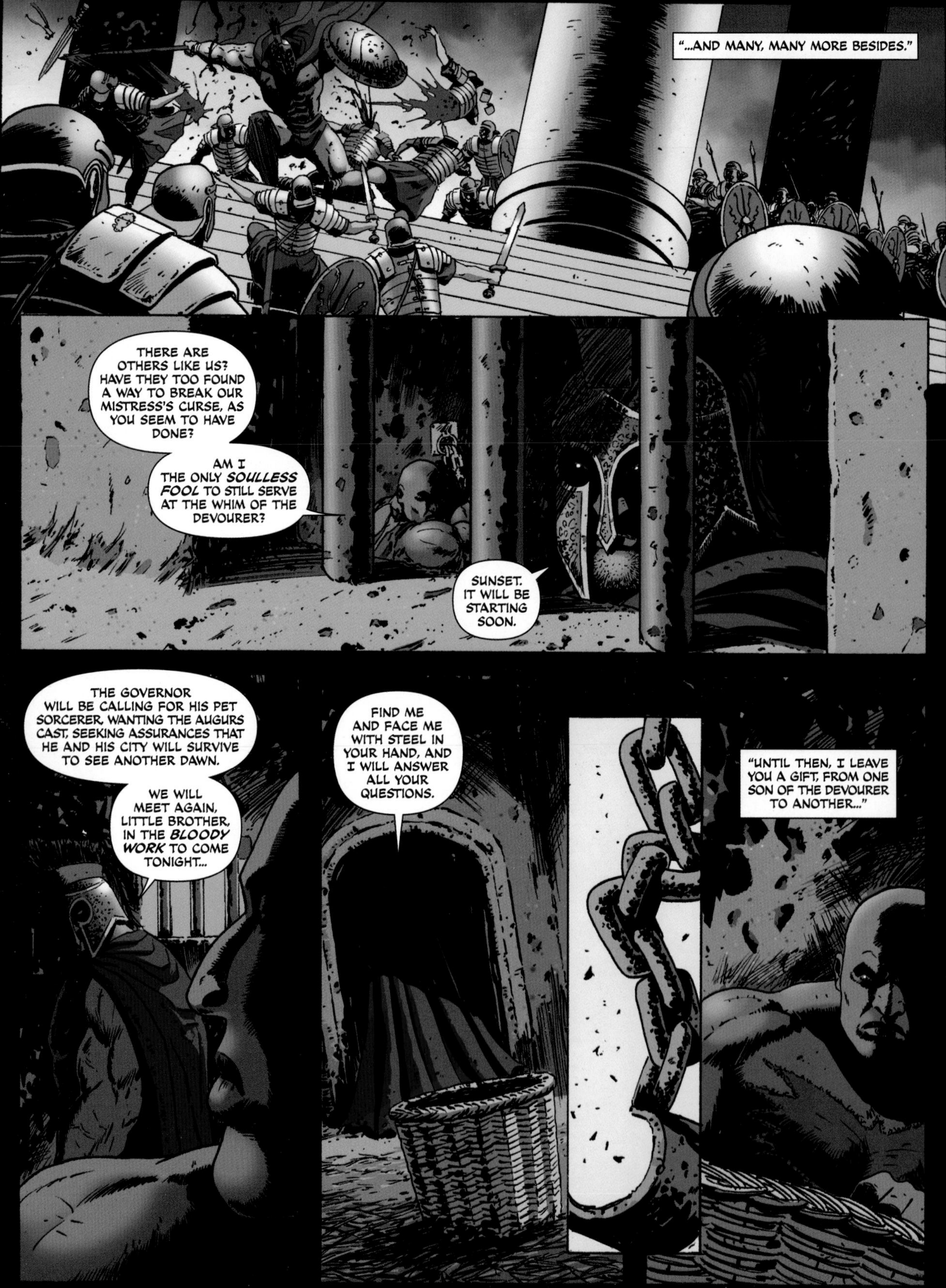
"...AND MANY, MANY MORE BESIDES."
THERE ARE OTHERS LIKE US? HAVE THEY TOO FOUND A WAY TO BREAK OUR MISTRESS'S CURSE, AS YOU SEEM TO HAVE DONE?
AM I THE ONLY SOULLESS FOOL TO STILL SERVE AT THE WHIM OF THE DEVOURER?
SUNSET. IT WILL BE STARTING SOON.
THE GOVERNOR WILL BE CALLING FOR HIS PET SORCERER, WANTING THE AUGURS CAST, SEEKING ASSURANCES THAT HE AND HIS CITY WILL SURVIVE TO SEE ANOTHER DAWN.
WE WILL MEET AGAIN, LITTLE BROTHER, IN THE BLOODY WORK TO COME TONIGHT...
FIND ME AND FACE ME WITH STEEL IN YOUR HAND, AND I WILL ANSWER ALL YOUR QUESTIONS.
"UNTIL THEN, I LEAVE YOU A GIFT, FROM ONE SON OF THE DEVOURER TO ANOTHER..."

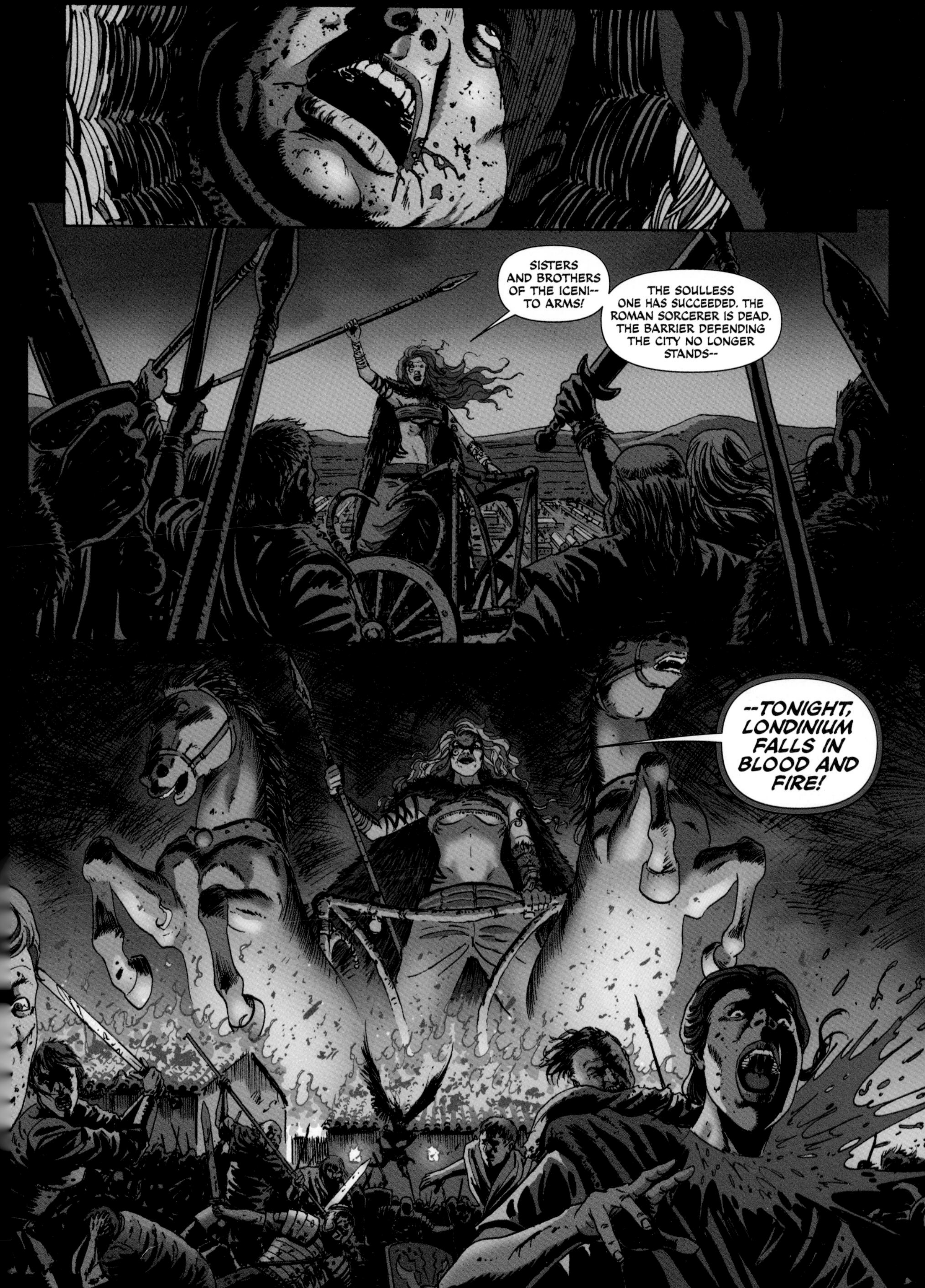
SISTERS AND BROTHERS OF THE ICENI-- TO ARMS!
THE SOULLESS ONE HAS SUCCEEDED. THE ROMAN SORCERER IS DEAD. THE BARRIER DEFENDING THE CITY NO LONGER STANDS--
--TONIGHT, LONDINIUM FALLS IN BLOOD AND FIRE!

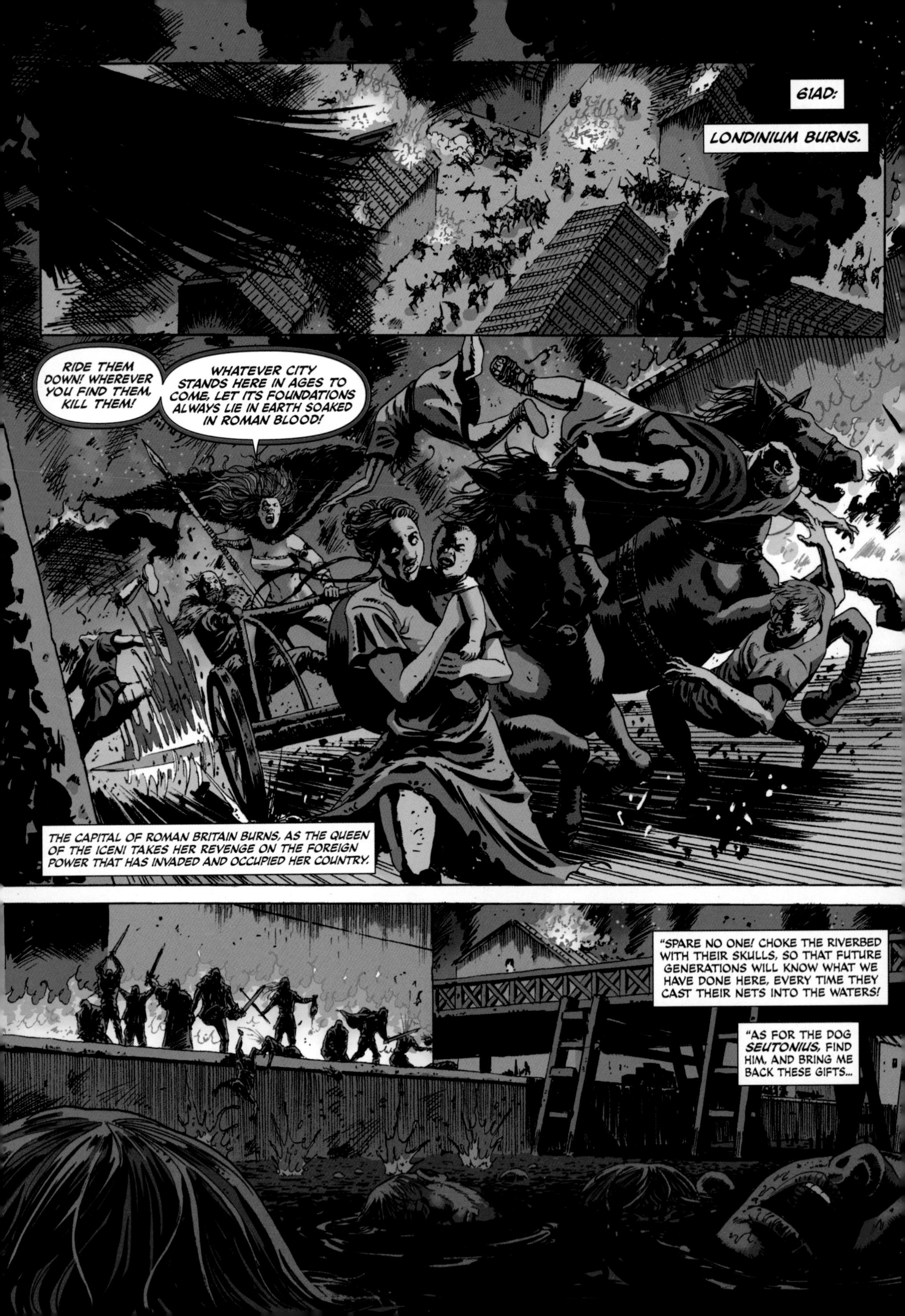
61AD:
LONDINIUM BURNS.
RIDE THEM DOWN! WHEREVER YOU FIND THEM, KILL THEM!
WHATEVER CITY STANDS HERE IN AGES TO COME, LET ITS FOUNDATIONS ALWAYS LIE IN EARTH SOAKED IN ROMAN BLOOD!
THE CAPITAL OF ROMAN BRITAIN BURNS, AS THE QUEEN OF THE ICENI TAKES HER REVENGE ON THE FOREIGN POWER THAT HAS INVADED AND OCCUPIED HER COUNTRY.
"SPARE NO ONE! CHOKE THE RIVERBED WITH THEIR SKULLS, SO THAT FUTURE GENERATIONS WILL KNOW WHAT WE HAVE DONE HERE, EVERY TIME THEY CAST THEIR NETS INTO THE WATERS!
"AS FOR THE DOG SEUTONIUS, FIND HIM, AND BRING ME BACK THESE GIFTS...

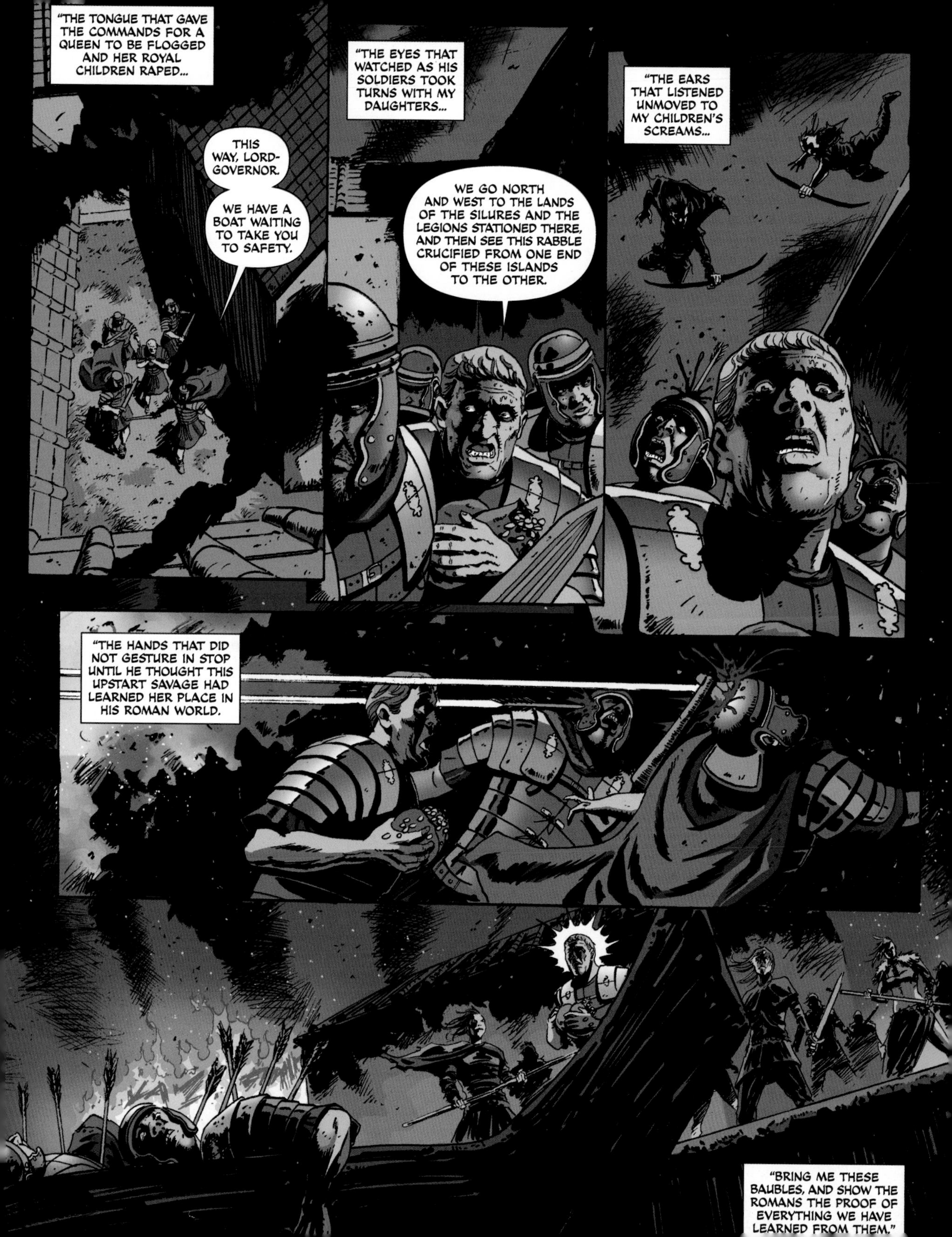
"THE TONGUE THAT GAVE THE COMMANDS FOR A QUEEN TO BE FLOGGED AND HER ROYAL CHILDREN RAPED...
THIS WAY, LORD-GOVERNOR.
WE HAVE A BOAT WAITING TO TAKE YOU TO SAFETY.
"THE EYES THAT WATCHED AS HIS SOLDIERS TOOK TURNS WITH MY DAUGHTERS...
WE GO NORTH AND WEST TO THE LANDS OF THE SILURES AND THE LEGIONS STATIONED THERE, AND THEN SEE THIS RABBLE CRUCIFIED FROM ONE END OF THESE ISLANDS TO THE OTHER.
"THE EARS THAT LISTENED UNMOVED TO MY CHILDREN'S SCREAMS...
"THE HANDS THAT DID NOT GESTURE IN STOP UNTIL HE THOUGHT THIS UPSTART SAVAGE HAD LEARNED HER PLACE IN HIS ROMAN WORLD.
"BRING ME THESE BAUBLES, AND SHOW THE ROMANS THE PROOF OF EVERYTHING WE HAVE LEARNED FROM THEM."

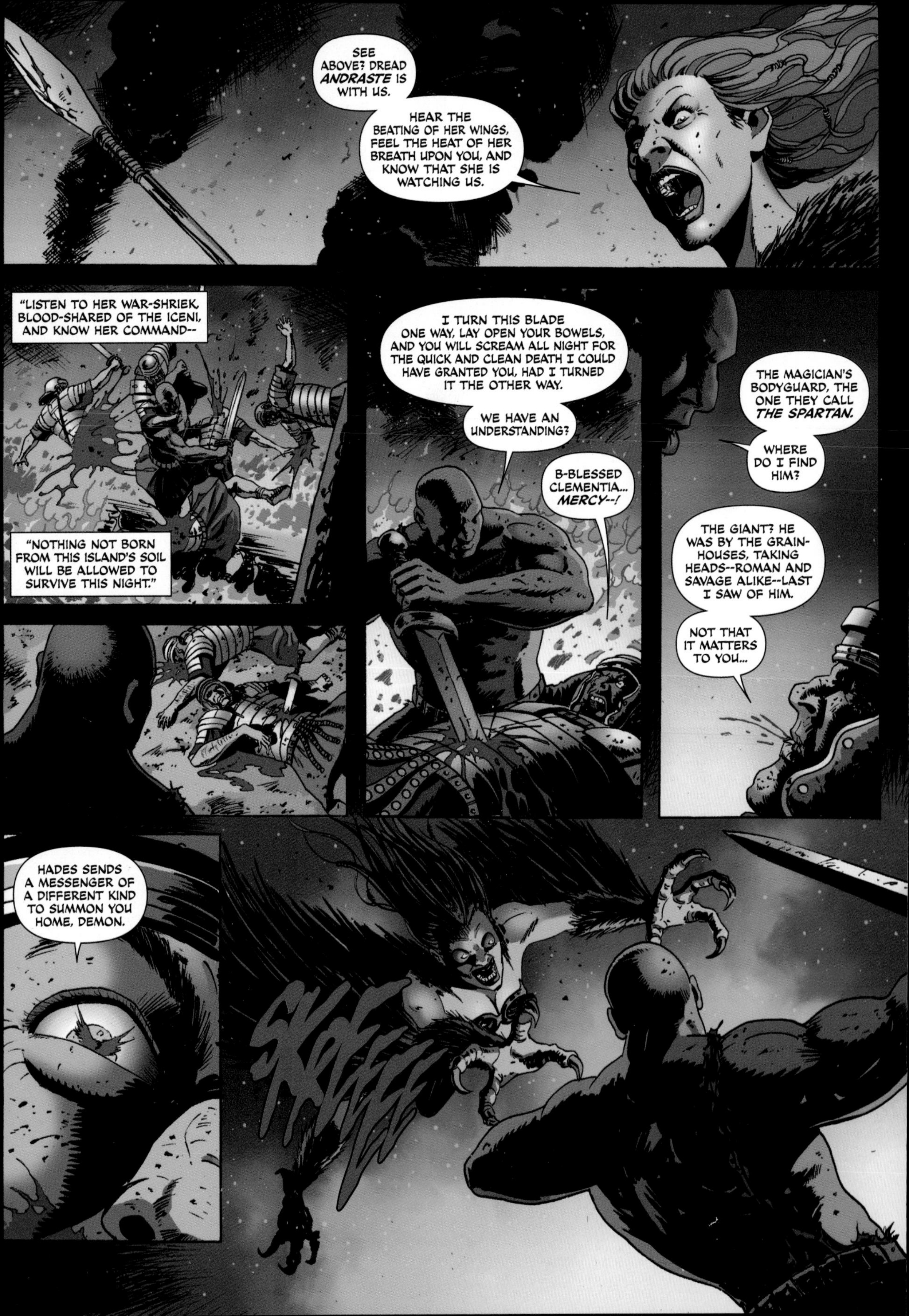
SEE ABOVE? DREAD ANDRASTE IS WITH US.
HEAR THE BEATING OF HER WINGS, FEEL THE HEAT OF HER BREATH UPON YOU, AND KNOW THAT SHE IS WATCHING US.
"LISTEN TO HER WAR-SHRIEK, BLOOD-SHARED OF THE ICENI, AND KNOW HER COMMAND--
"NOTHING NOT BORN FROM THIS ISLAND'S SOIL WILL BE ALLOWED TO SURVIVE THIS NIGHT."
I TURN THIS BLADE ONE WAY, LAY OPEN YOUR BOWELS, AND YOU WILL SCREAM ALL NIGHT FOR THE QUICK AND CLEAN DEATH I COULD HAVE GRANTED YOU, HAD I TURNED IT THE OTHER WAY.
WE HAVE AN UNDERSTANDING?
B-BLESSED CLEMENTIA... MERCY--!
THE MAGICIAN'S BODYGUARD, THE ONE THEY CALL THE SPARTAN.
WHERE DO I FIND HIM?
THE GIANT? HE WAS BY THE GRAIN-HOUSES, TAKING HEADS--ROMAN AND SAVAGE ALIKE--LAST I SAW OF HIM.
NOT THAT IT MATTERS TO YOU...
HADES SENDS A MESSENGER OF A DIFFERENT KIND TO SUMMON YOU HOME, DEMON.
SKREEEE

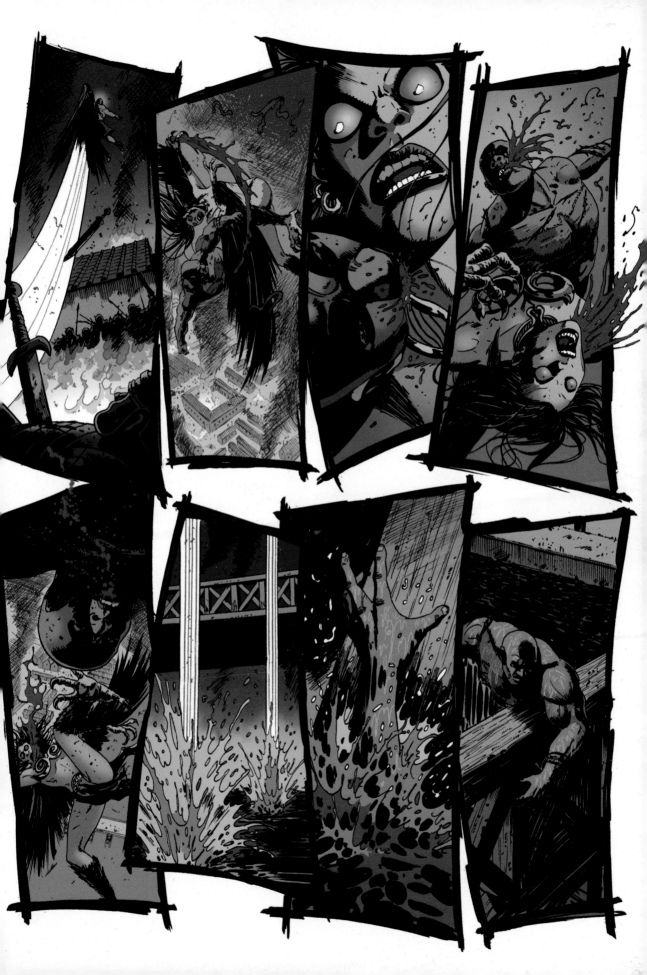

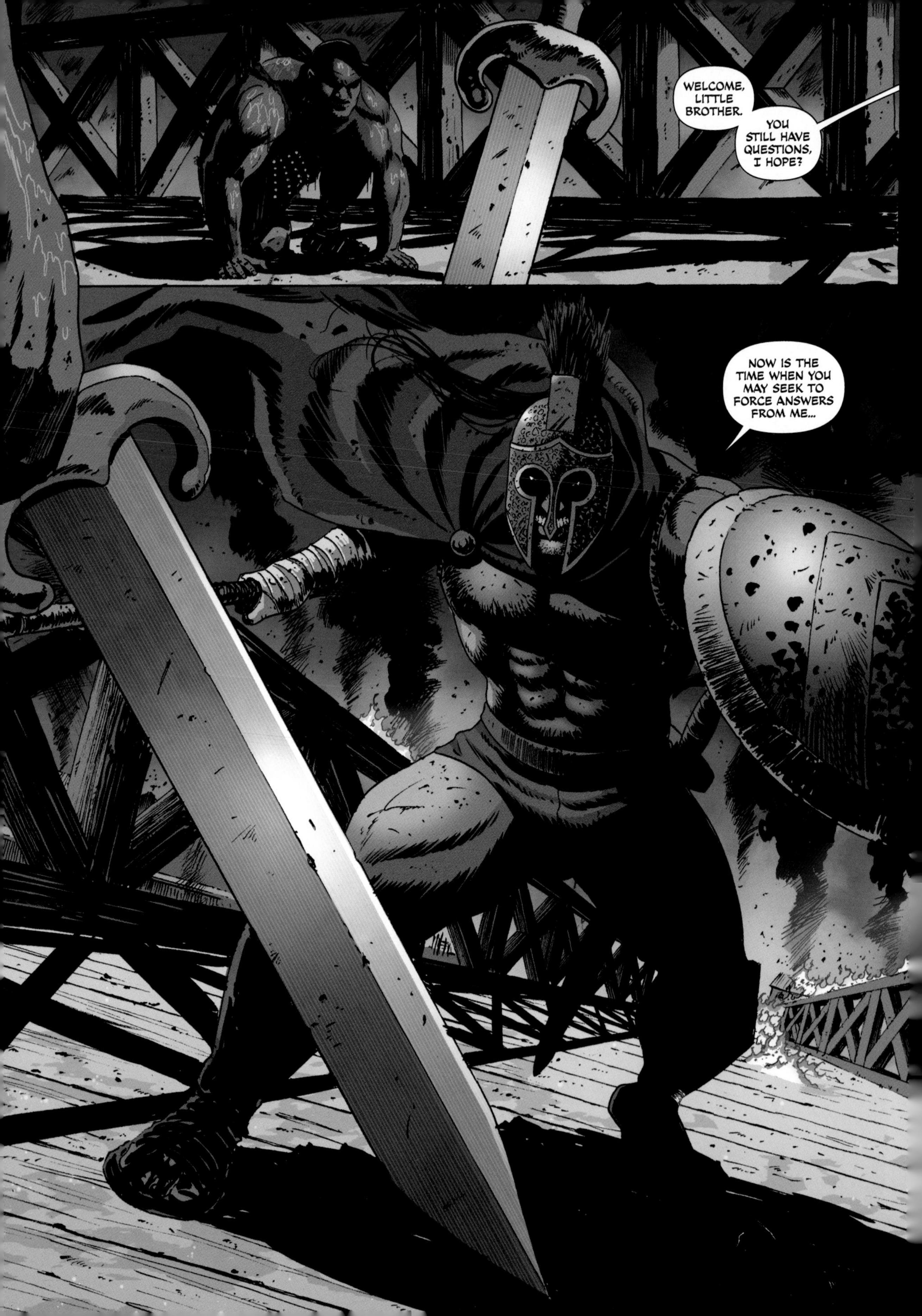
WELCOME, LITTLE BROTHER.
YOU STILL HAVE QUESTIONS, I HOPE?
NOW IS THE TIME WHEN YOU MAY SEEK TO FORCE ANSWERS FROM ME...

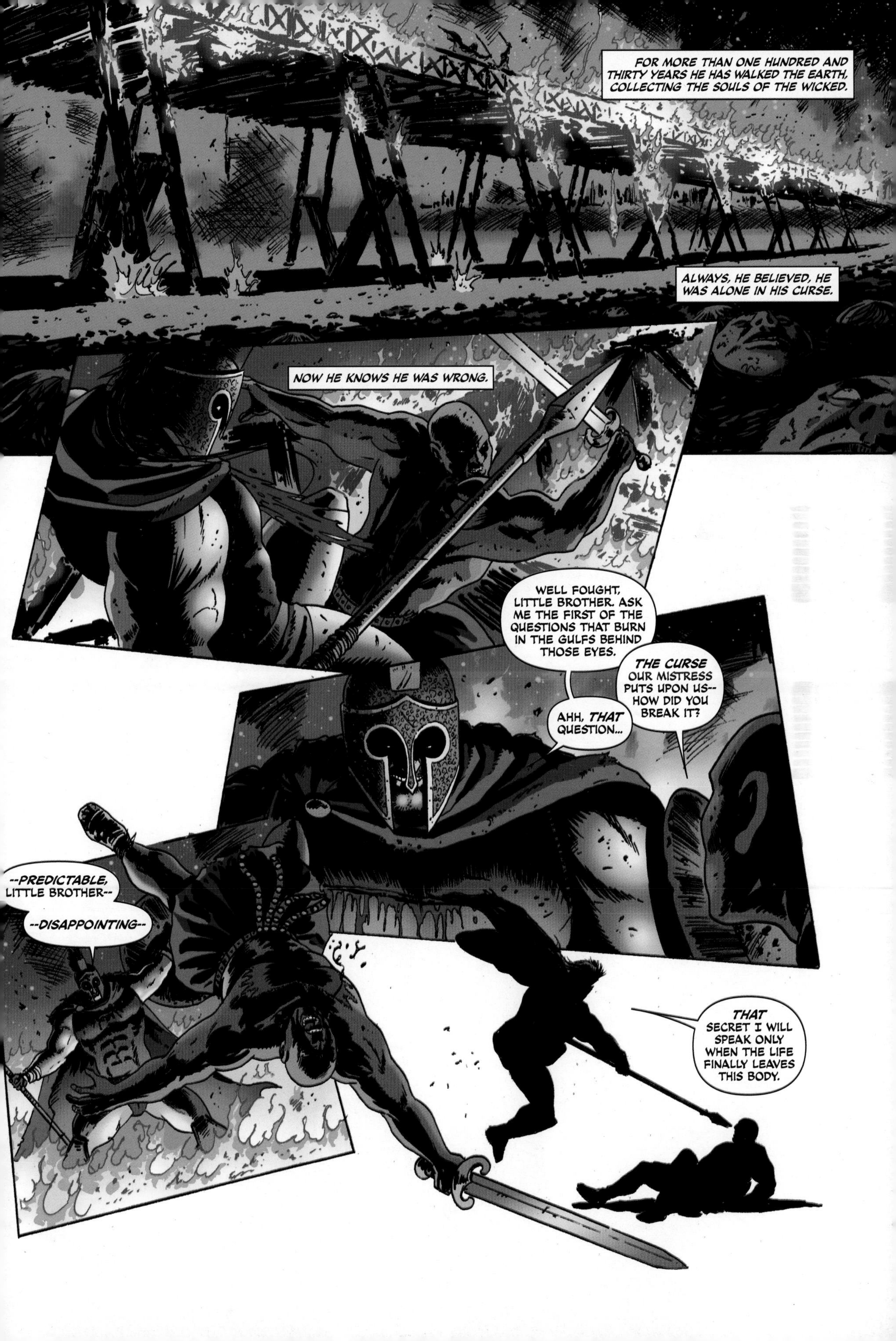
FOR MORE THAN ONE HUNDRED AND THIRTY YEARS HE HAS WALKED THE EARTH, COLLECTING THE SOULS OF THE WICKED.
ALWAYS, HE BELIEVED, HE WAS ALONE IN HIS CURSE.
NOW HE KNOWS HE WAS WRONG.
WELL FOUGHT, LITTLE BROTHER. ASK ME THE FIRST OF THE QUESTIONS THAT BURN IN THE GULFS BEHIND THOSE EYES.
THE CURSE OUR MISTRESS PUTS UPON US-- HOW DID YOU BREAK IT?
AHH, THAT QUESTION...
--PREDICTABLE, LITTLE BROTHER--
--DISAPPOINTING--
THAT SECRET I WILL SPEAK ONLY WHEN THE LIFE FINALLY LEAVES THIS BODY.

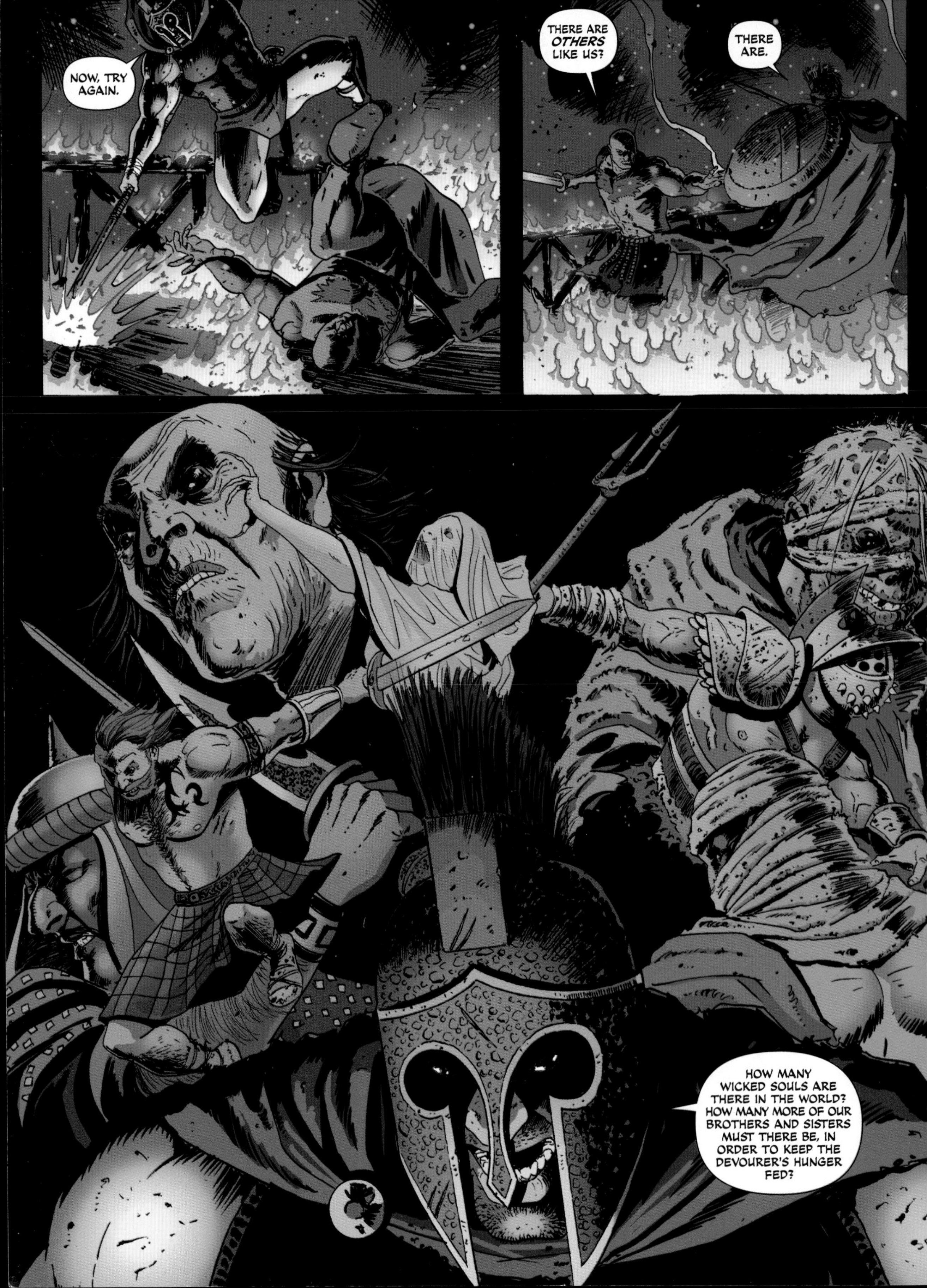
NOW, TRY AGAIN.
THERE ARE OTHERS LIKE US?
THERE ARE.
HOW MANY WICKED SOULS ARE THERE IN THE WORLD? HOW MANY MORE OF OUR BROTHERS AND SISTERS MUST THERE BE, IN ORDER TO KEEP THE DEVOURER'S HUNGER FED?

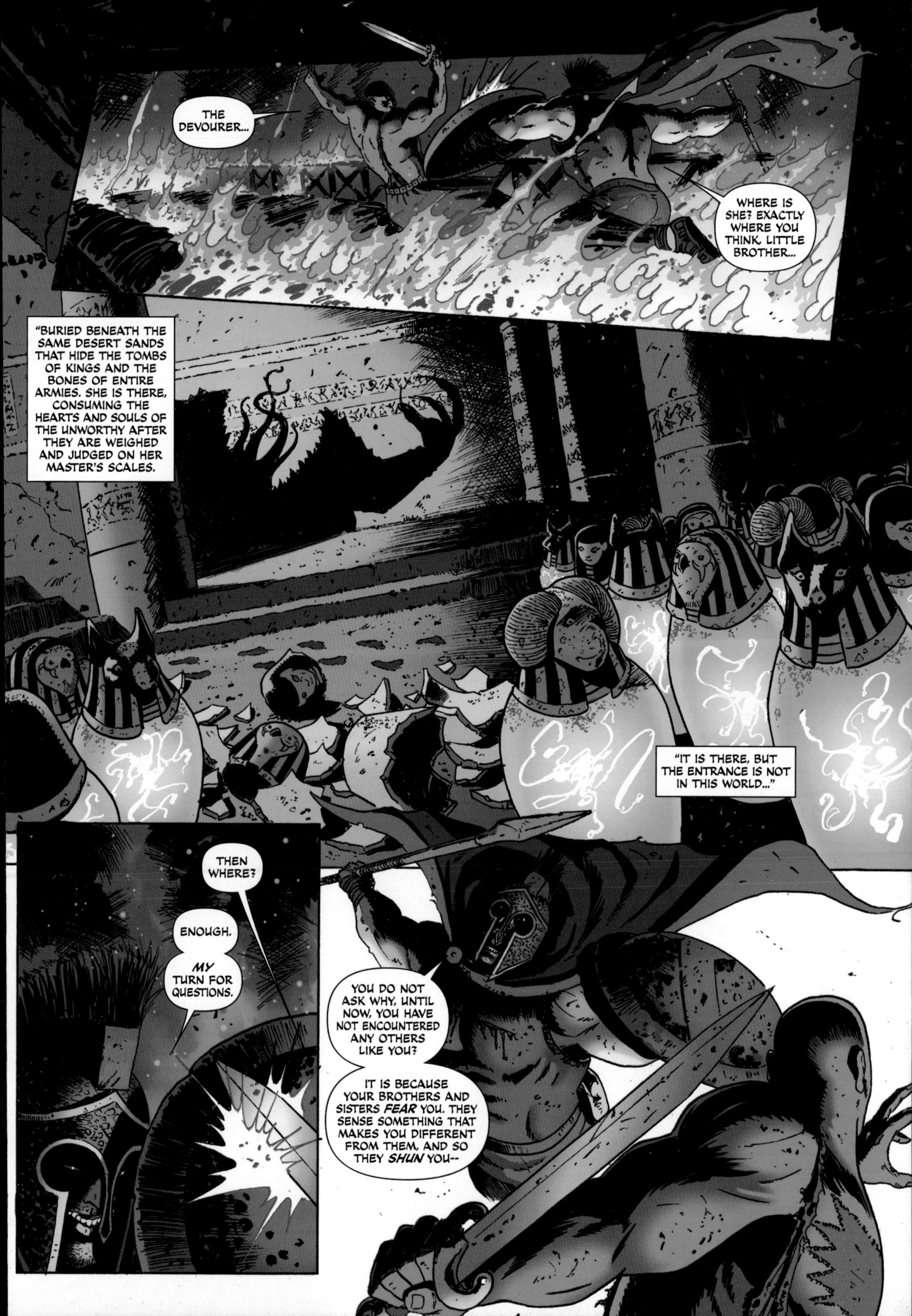
THE DEVOURER...
WHERE IS SHE? EXACTLY WHERE YOU THINK, LITTLE BROTHER...
"BURIED BENEATH THE SAME DESERT SANDS THAT HIDE THE TOMBS OF KINGS AND THE BONES OF ENTIRE ARMIES. SHE IS THERE, CONSUMING THE HEARTS AND SOULS OF THE UNWORTHY AFTER THEY ARE WEIGHED AND JUDGED ON HER MASTER'S SCALES.
"IT IS THERE, BUT THE ENTRANCE IS NOT IN THIS WORLD..."
THEN WHERE?
ENOUGH.
MY TURN FOR QUESTIONS.
YOU DO NOT ASK WHY, UNTIL NOW, YOU HAVE NOT ENCOUNTERED ANY OTHERS LIKE YOU?
IT IS BECAUSE YOUR BROTHERS AND SISTERS *FEAR* YOU. THEY SENSE SOMETHING THAT MAKES YOU DIFFERENT FROM THEM, AND SO THEY *SHUN* YOU--

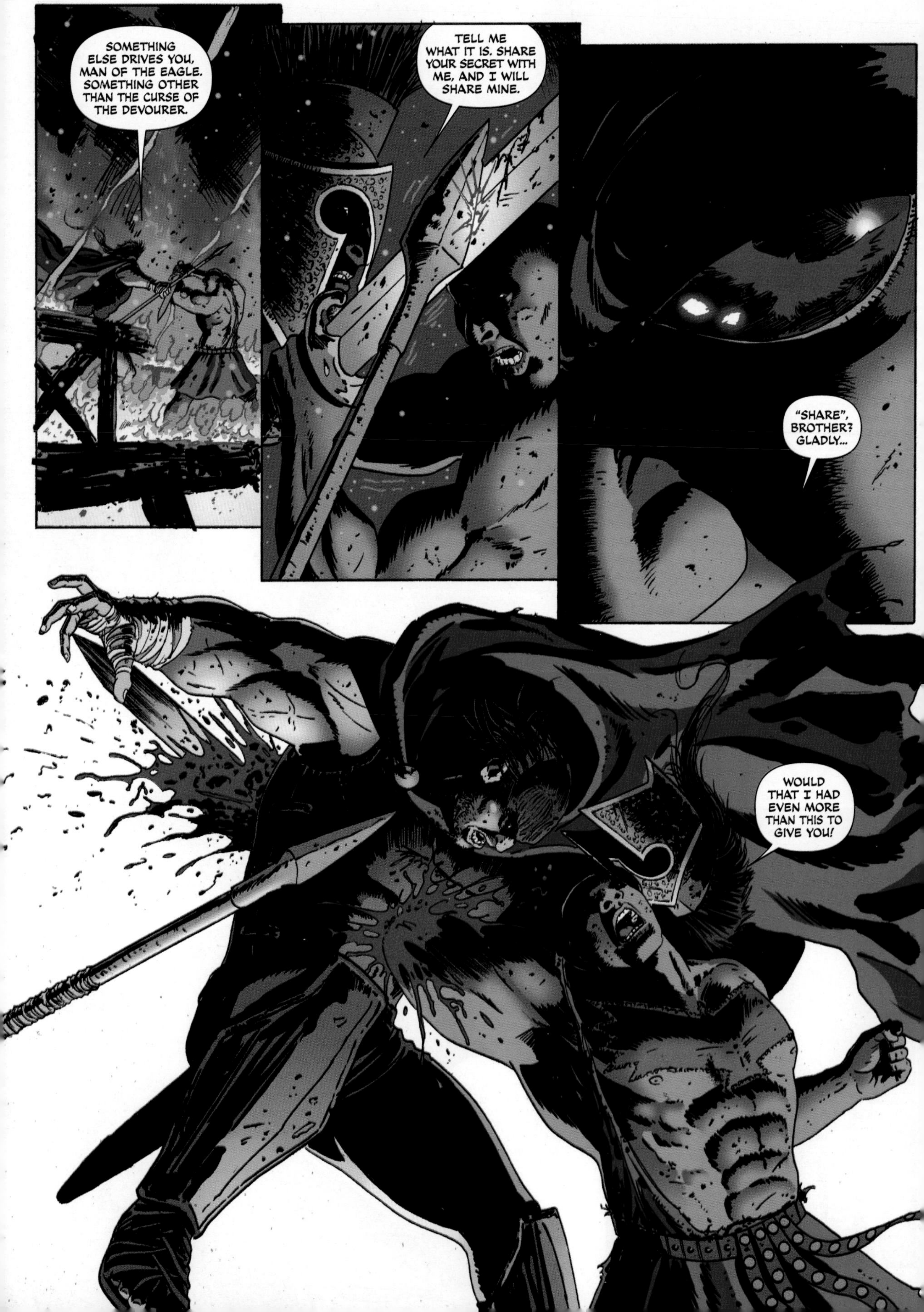
SOMETHING ELSE DRIVES YOU, MAN OF THE EAGLE. SOMETHING OTHER THAN THE CURSE OF THE DEVOURER.
TELL ME WHAT IT IS. SHARE YOUR SECRET WITH ME, AND I WILL SHARE MINE.
"SHARE", BROTHER? GLADLY...
WOULD THAT I HAD EVEN MORE THAN THIS TO GIVE YOU!

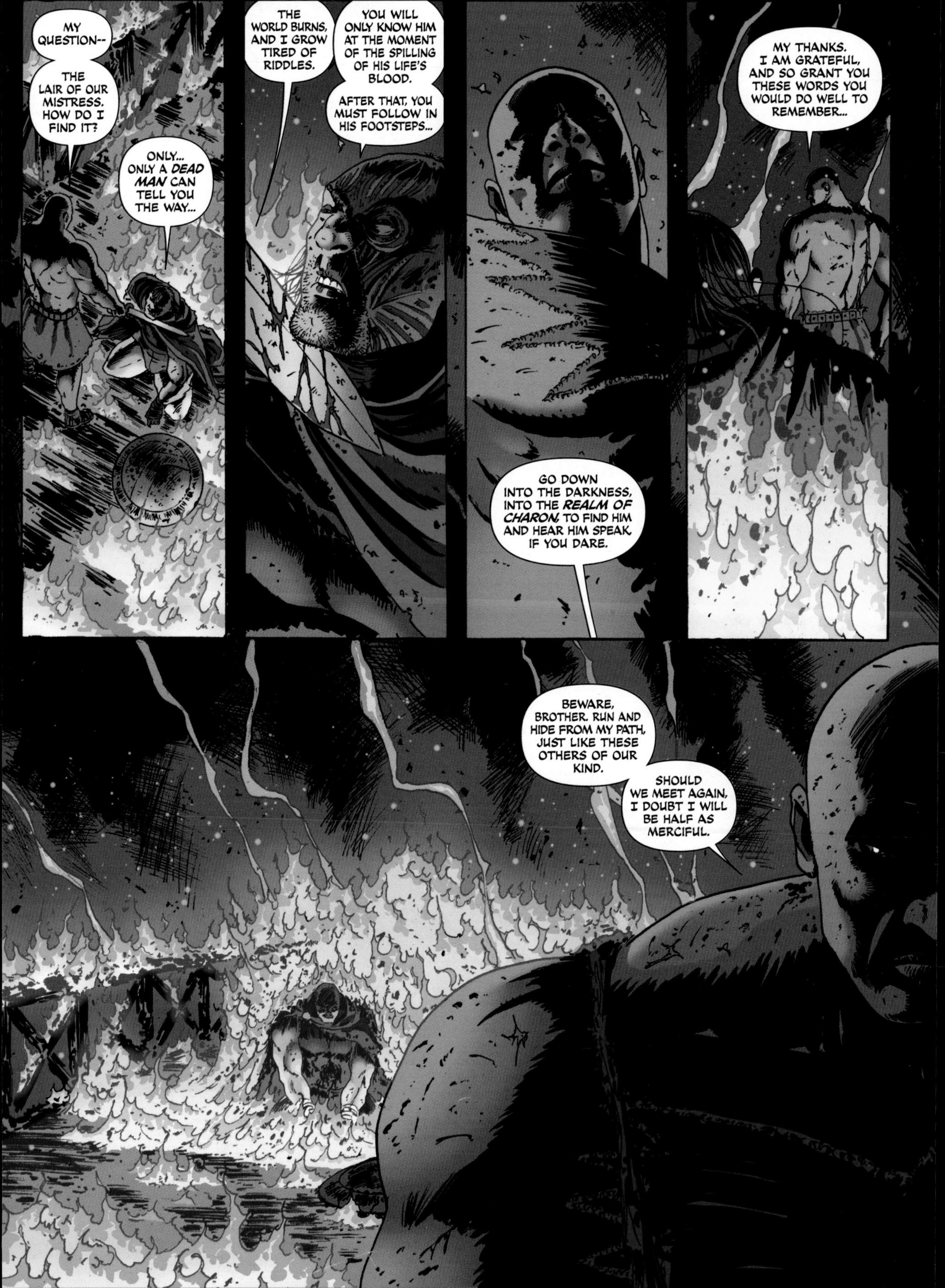
MY QUESTION--
THE LAIR OF OUR MISTRESS. HOW DO I FIND IT?
ONLY... ONLY A DEAD MAN CAN TELL YOU THE WAY...
THE WORLD BURNS, AND I GROW TIRED OF RIDDLES.
YOU WILL ONLY KNOW HIM AT THE MOMENT OF THE SPILLING OF HIS LIFE'S BLOOD.
AFTER THAT, YOU MUST FOLLOW IN HIS FOOTSTEPS...
GO DOWN INTO THE DARKNESS, INTO THE REALM OF CHARON, TO FIND HIM AND HEAR HIM SPEAK IF YOU DARE.
MY THANKS. I AM GRATEFUL, AND SO GRANT YOU THESE WORDS YOU WOULD DO WELL TO REMEMBER...
BEWARE, BROTHER. RUN AND HIDE FROM MY PATH, JUST LIKE THESE OTHERS OF OUR KIND.
SHOULD WE MEET AGAIN, I DOUBT I WILL BE HALF AS MERCIFUL.

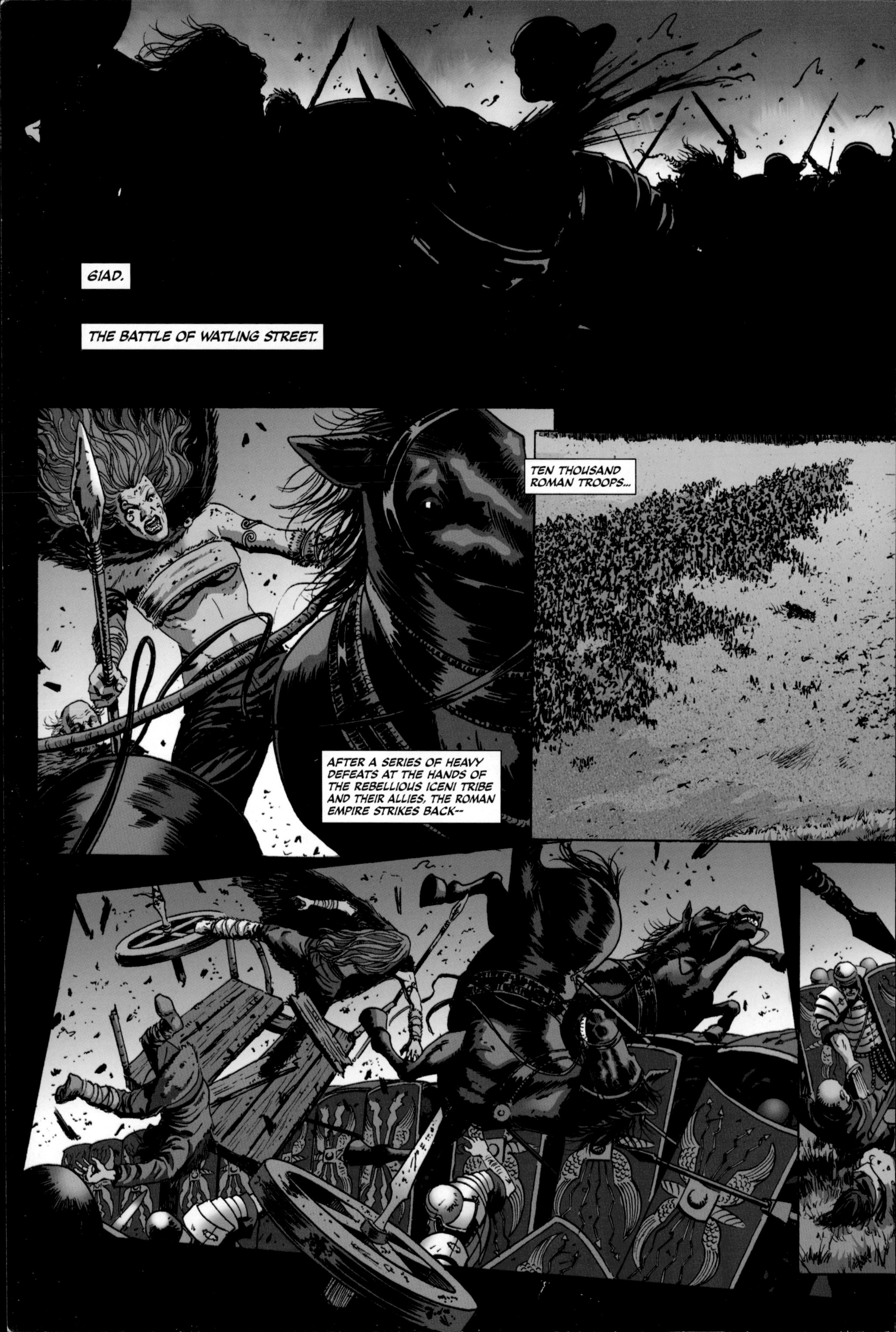
61AD.
THE BATTLE OF WATLING STREET.
AFTER A SERIES OF HEAVY DEFEATS AT THE HANDS OF THE REBELLIOUS ICENI TRIBE AND THEIR ALLIES, THE ROMAN EMPIRE STRIKES BACK--
TEN THOUSAND ROMAN TROOPS...

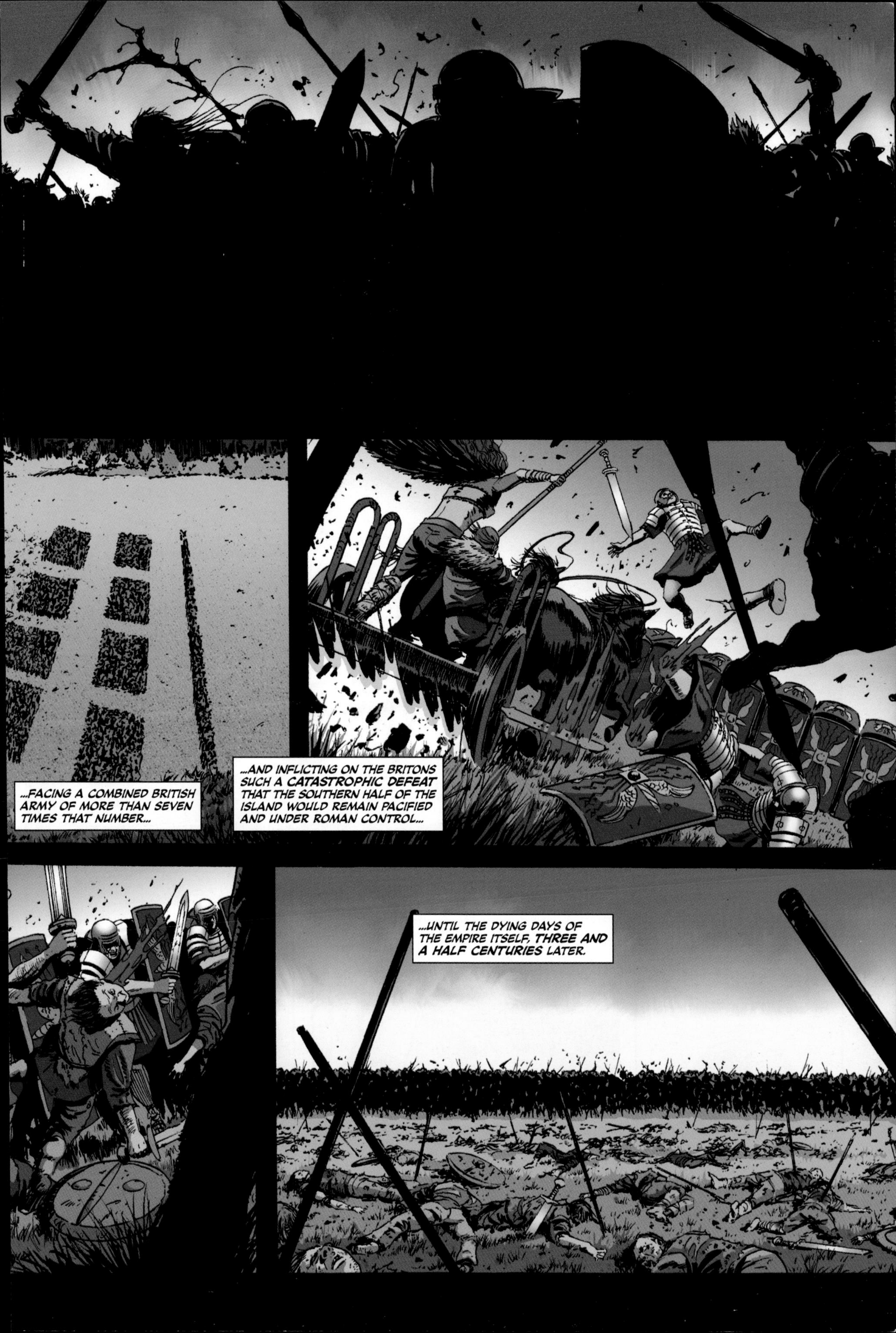
...FACING A COMBINED BRITISH ARMY OF MORE THAN SEVEN TIMES THAT NUMBER...
...AND INFLICTING ON THE BRITONS SUCH A CATASTROPHIC DEFEAT THAT THE SOUTHERN HALF OF THE ISLAND WOULD REMAIN PACIFIED AND UNDER ROMAN CONTROL...
...UNTIL THE DYING DAYS OF THE EMPIRE ITSELF, THREE AND A HALF CENTURIES LATER.

TAKER OF SOULS, I KNEW WE WOULD MEET AGAIN.

YOU ARE HERE FOR ME?

WHEN YOU SACKED CAMULODUNUM, YOU ORDERED THOSE WOMEN THAT HAD LAIN WITH ROMAN SOLDIERS TO BE IMPALED ON WOODEN STAKES...

...BUT NOT BEFORE YOU COMMANDED THAT THOSE WITH CHILD BE CUT OPEN AND THEIR HALF-ROMAN BASTARDS RIPPED FORTH FROM THEM.

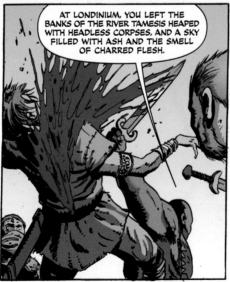

AT LONDINIUM, YOU LEFT THE BANKS OF THE RIVER TAMESIS HEAPED WITH HEADLESS CORPSES, AND A SKY FILLED WITH ASH AND THE SMELL OF CHARRED FLESH.

ON THE MARCH NORTH TO HERE, YOU LEVIED FRESH RECRUITS FROM AMONG THE VILLAGES YOU PASSED THROUGH...

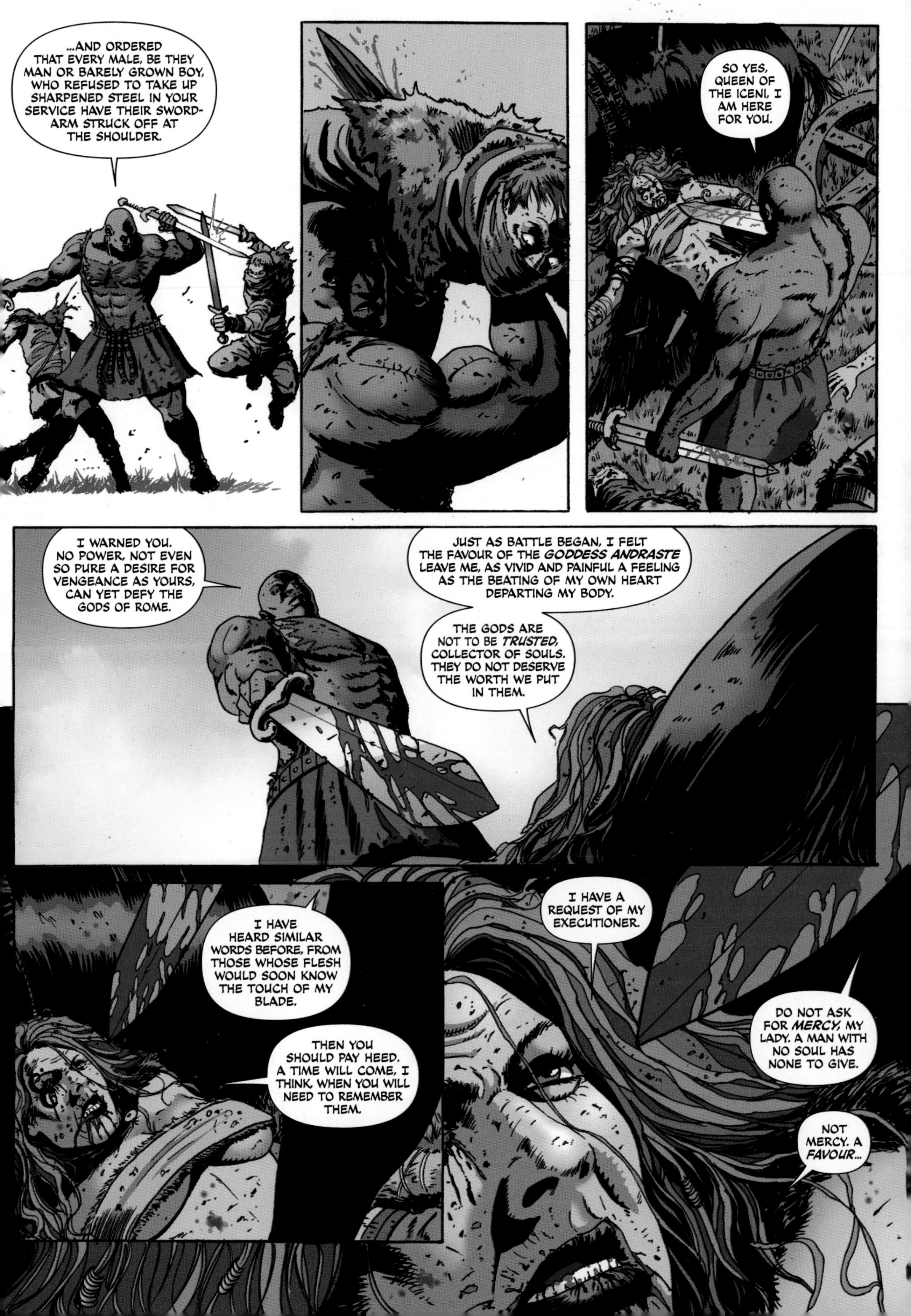
...AND ORDERED THAT EVERY MALE, BE THEY MAN OR BARELY GROWN BOY, WHO REFUSED TO TAKE UP SHARPENED STEEL IN YOUR SERVICE HAVE THEIR SWORD-ARM STRUCK OFF AT THE SHOULDER.
SO YES, QUEEN OF THE ICENI, I AM HERE FOR YOU.
I WARNED YOU. NO POWER, NOT EVEN SO PURE A DESIRE FOR VENGEANCE AS YOURS, CAN YET DEFY THE GODS OF ROME.
JUST AS BATTLE BEGAN, I FELT THE FAVOUR OF THE GODDESS ANDRASTE LEAVE ME, AS VIVID AND PAINFUL A FEELING AS THE BEATING OF MY OWN HEART DEPARTING MY BODY.
THE GODS ARE NOT TO BE TRUSTED, COLLECTOR OF SOULS. THEY DO NOT DESERVE THE WORTH WE PUT IN THEM.
I HAVE HEARD SIMILAR WORDS BEFORE, FROM THOSE WHOSE FLESH WOULD SOON KNOW THE TOUCH OF MY BLADE.
THEN YOU SHOULD PAY HEED. A TIME WILL COME, I THINK, WHEN YOU WILL NEED TO REMEMBER THEM.
I HAVE A REQUEST OF MY EXECUTIONER.
DO NOT ASK FOR MERCY, MY LADY. A MAN WITH NO SOUL HAS NONE TO GIVE.
NOT MERCY. A FAVOUR...

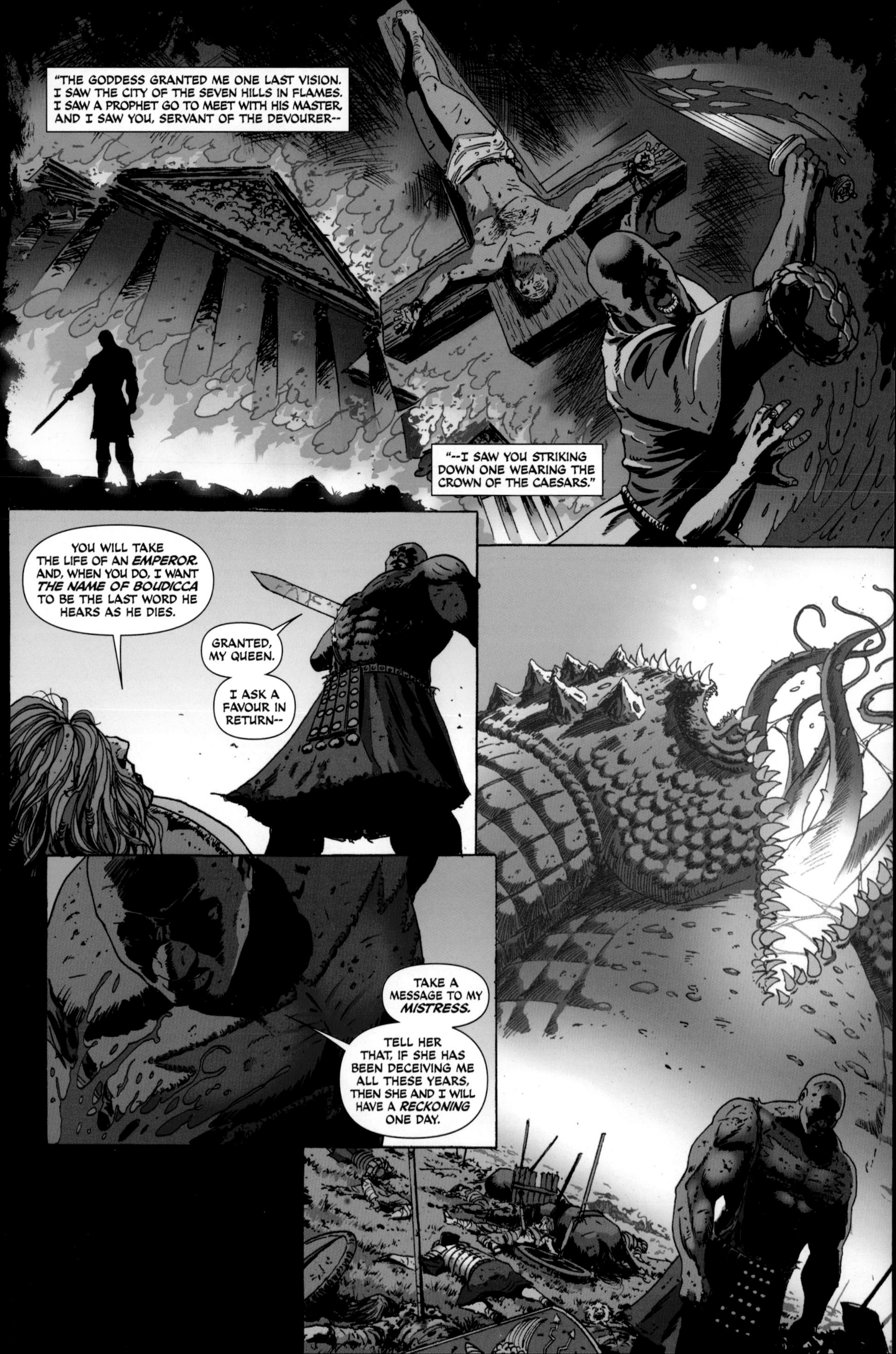
"THE GODDESS GRANTED ME ONE LAST VISION. I SAW THE CITY OF THE SEVEN HILLS IN FLAMES. I SAW A PROPHET GO TO MEET WITH HIS MASTER. AND I SAW YOU, SERVANT OF THE DEVOURER--
"--I SAW YOU STRIKING DOWN ONE WEARING THE CROWN OF THE CAESARS."
YOU WILL TAKE THE LIFE OF AN *EMPEROR*. AND, WHEN YOU DO, I WANT *THE NAME OF BOUDICCA* TO BE THE LAST WORD HE HEARS AS HE DIES.
GRANTED, MY QUEEN.
I ASK A FAVOUR IN RETURN--
TAKE A MESSAGE TO MY *MISTRESS.*
TELL HER THAT, IF SHE HAS BEEN DECEIVING ME ALL THESE YEARS, THEN SHE AND I WILL HAVE A *RECKONING* ONE DAY.

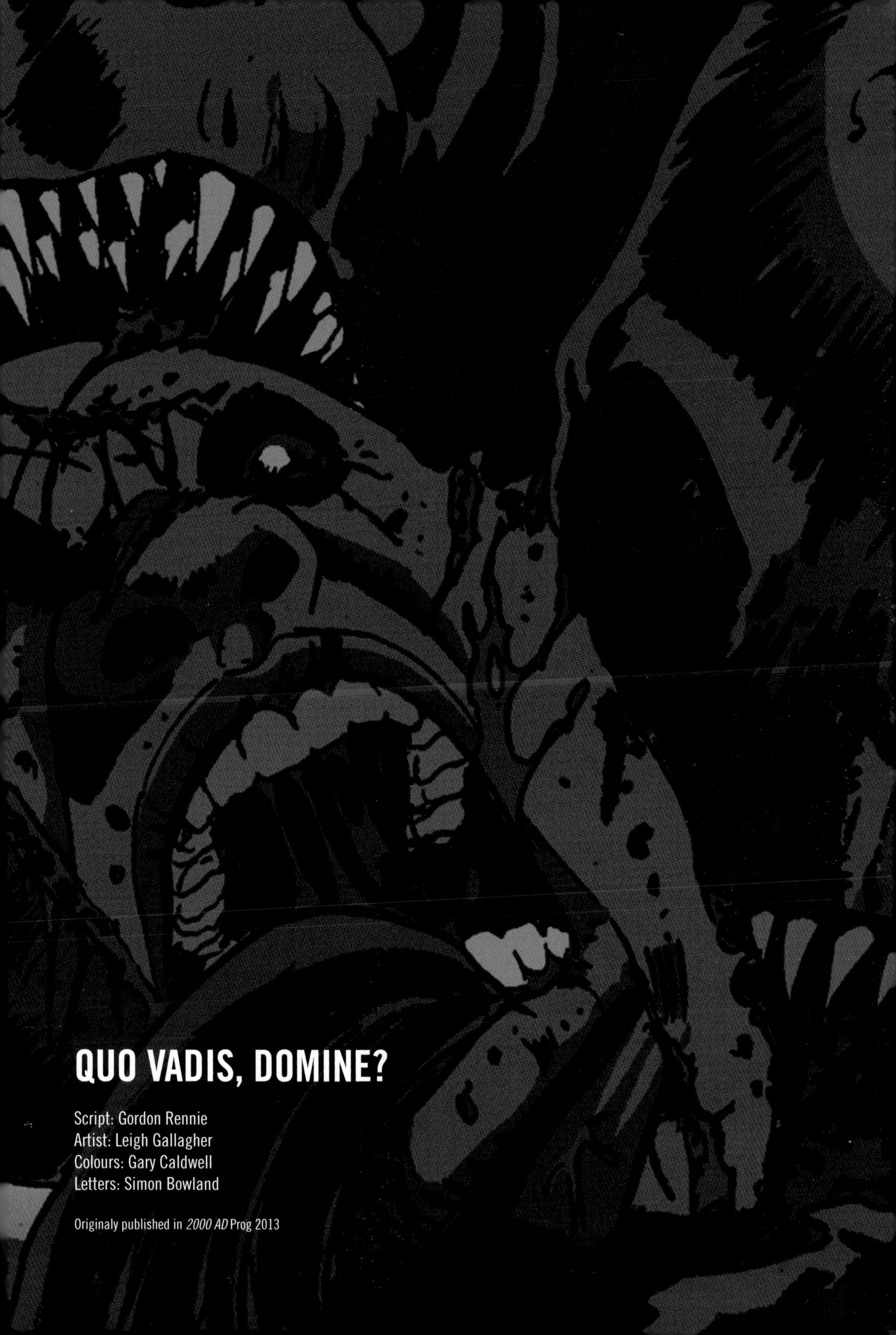

QUO VADIS, DOMINE?

Script: Gordon Rennie
Artist: Leigh Gallagher
Colours: Gary Caldwell
Letters: Simon Bowland

Originaly published in *2000 AD* Prog 2013

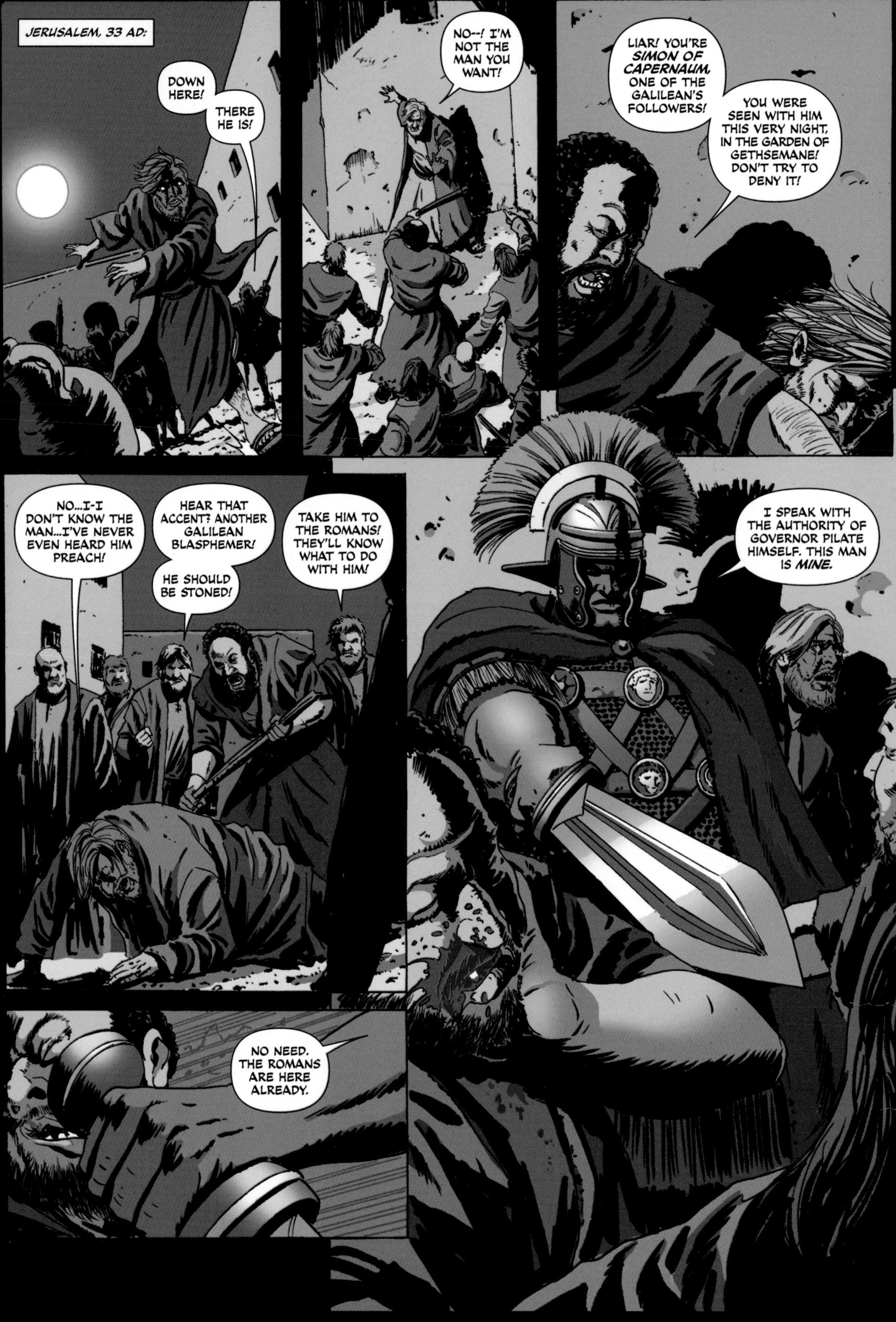
JERUSALEM, 33 AD:
DOWN HERE!
THERE HE IS!
NO--! I'M NOT THE MAN YOU WANT!
LIAR! YOU'RE SIMON OF CAPERNAUM, ONE OF THE GALILEAN'S FOLLOWERS!
YOU WERE SEEN WITH HIM THIS VERY NIGHT, IN THE GARDEN OF GETHSEMANE! DON'T TRY TO DENY IT!
NO...I-I DON'T KNOW THE MAN...I'VE NEVER EVEN HEARD HIM PREACH!
HEAR THAT ACCENT? ANOTHER GALILEAN BLASPHEMER!
HE SHOULD BE STONED!
TAKE HIM TO THE ROMANS! THEY'LL KNOW WHAT TO DO WITH HIM!
NO NEED. THE ROMANS ARE HERE ALREADY.
I SPEAK WITH THE AUTHORITY OF GOVERNOR PILATE HIMSELF. THIS MAN IS MINE.

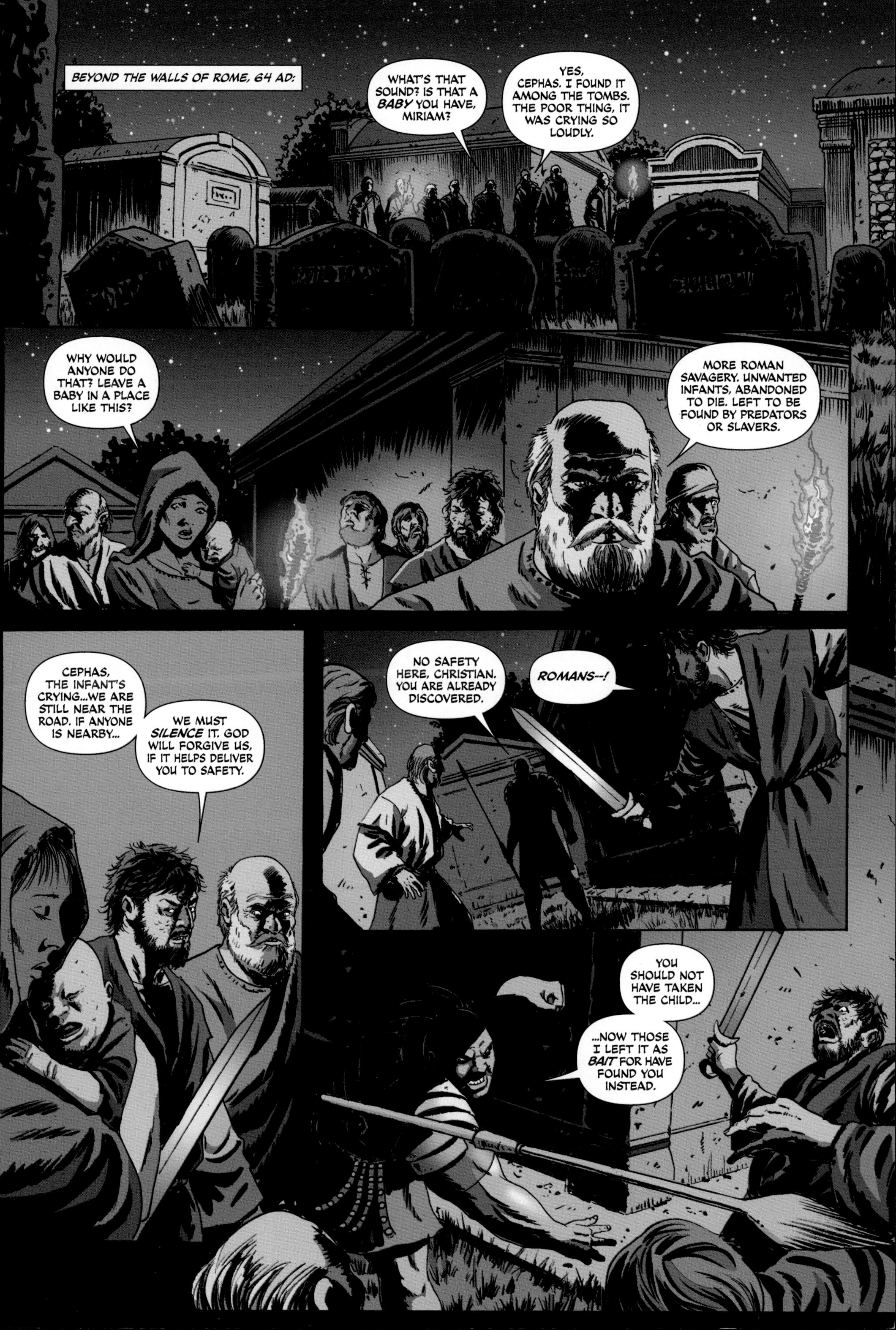
BEYOND THE WALLS OF ROME, 64 AD:
WHAT'S THAT SOUND? IS THAT A BABY YOU HAVE, MIRIAM?
YES, CEPHAS. I FOUND IT AMONG THE TOMBS. THE POOR THING, IT WAS CRYING SO LOUDLY.
WHY WOULD ANYONE DO THAT? LEAVE A BABY IN A PLACE LIKE THIS?
MORE ROMAN SAVAGERY. UNWANTED INFANTS, ABANDONED TO DIE. LEFT TO BE FOUND BY PREDATORS OR SLAVERS.
CEPHAS, THE INFANT'S CRYING...WE ARE STILL NEAR THE ROAD. IF ANYONE IS NEARBY...
WE MUST SILENCE IT. GOD WILL FORGIVE US, IF IT HELPS DELIVER YOU TO SAFETY.
NO SAFETY HERE, CHRISTIAN. YOU ARE ALREADY DISCOVERED.
ROMANS--!
YOU SHOULD NOT HAVE TAKEN THE CHILD...
...NOW THOSE I LEFT IT AS BAIT FOR HAVE FOUND YOU INSTEAD.

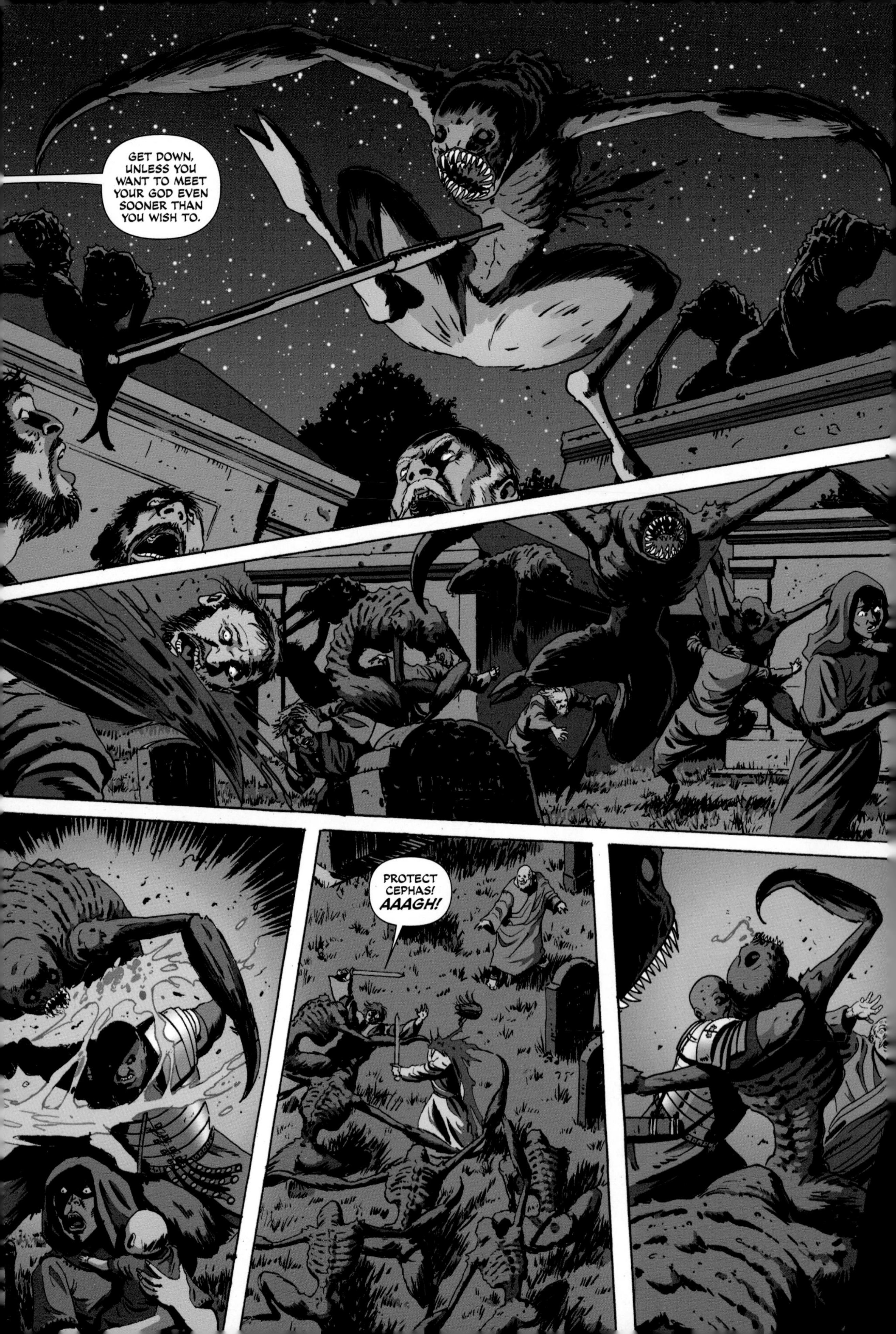
GET DOWN, UNLESS YOU WANT TO MEET YOUR GOD EVEN SOONER THAN YOU WISH TO.
PROTECT CEPHAS! ***AAAGH!***

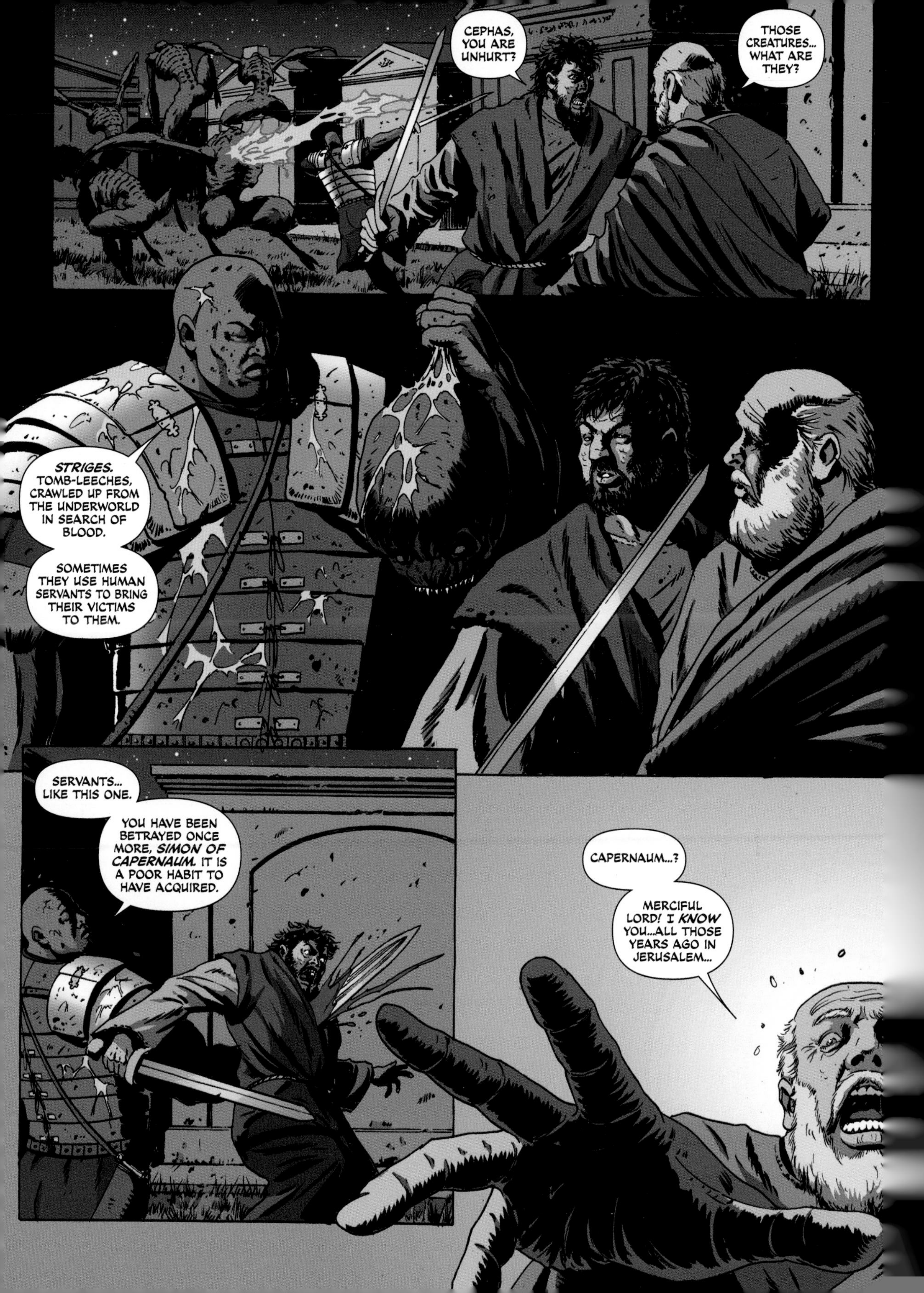
CEPHAS, YOU ARE UNHURT?
THOSE CREATURES... WHAT ARE THEY?
STRIGES. TOMB-LEECHES, CRAWLED UP FROM THE UNDERWORLD IN SEARCH OF BLOOD.
SOMETIMES THEY USE HUMAN SERVANTS TO BRING THEIR VICTIMS TO THEM.
SERVANTS... LIKE THIS ONE.
YOU HAVE BEEN BETRAYED ONCE MORE, SIMON OF CAPERNAUM. IT IS A POOR HABIT TO HAVE ACQUIRED.
CAPERNAUM...?
MERCIFUL LORD! I KNOW YOU...ALL THOSE YEARS AGO IN JERUSALEM...

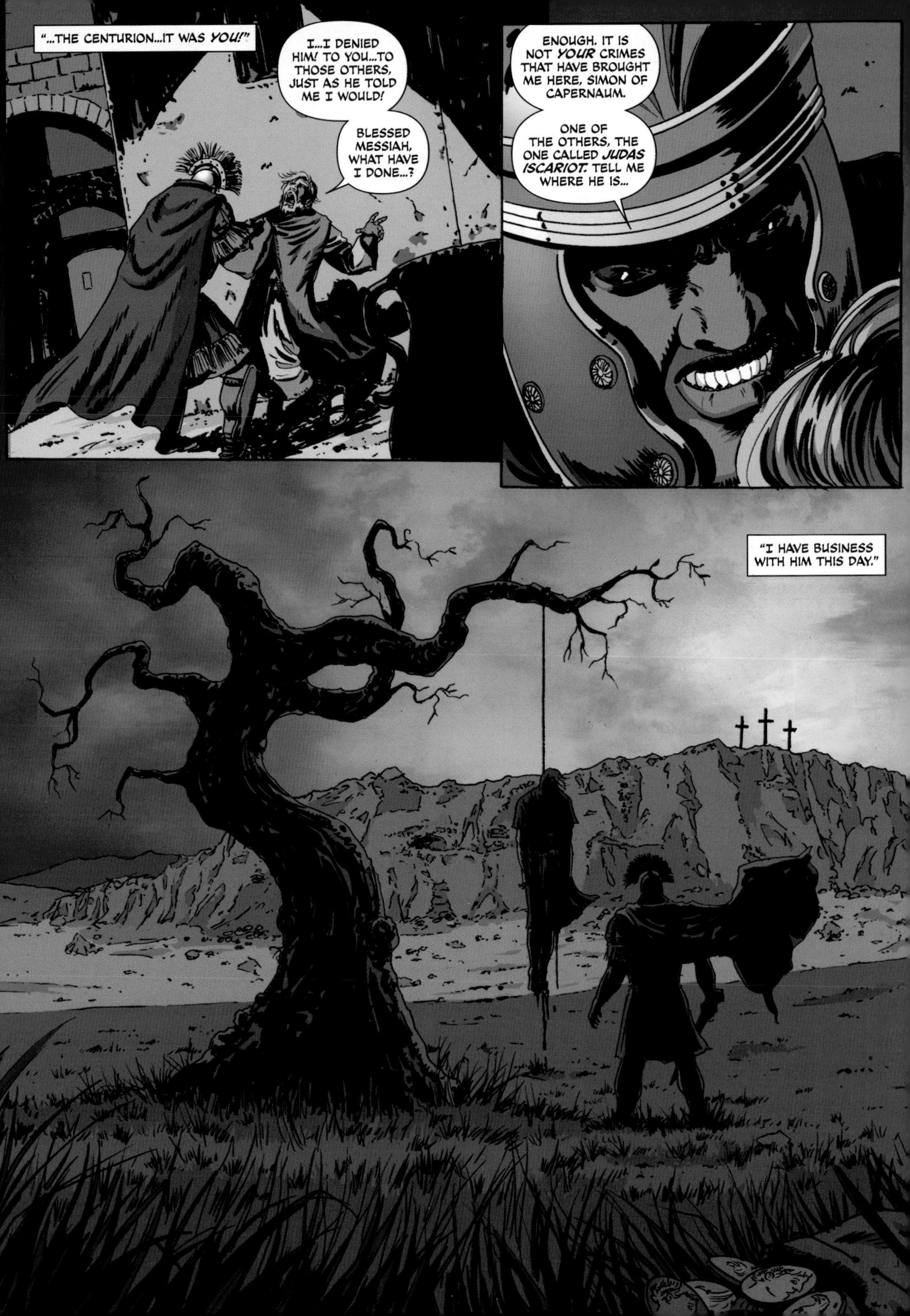
"...THE CENTURION...IT WAS YOU!"
I...I DENIED HIM! TO YOU...TO THOSE OTHERS, JUST AS HE TOLD ME I WOULD!
BLESSED MESSIAH, WHAT HAVE I DONE...?
ENOUGH. IT IS NOT YOUR CRIMES THAT HAVE BROUGHT ME HERE, SIMON OF CAPERNAUM.
ONE OF THE OTHERS, THE ONE CALLED JUDAS ISCARIOT. TELL ME WHERE HE IS...
"I HAVE BUSINESS WITH HIM THIS DAY."

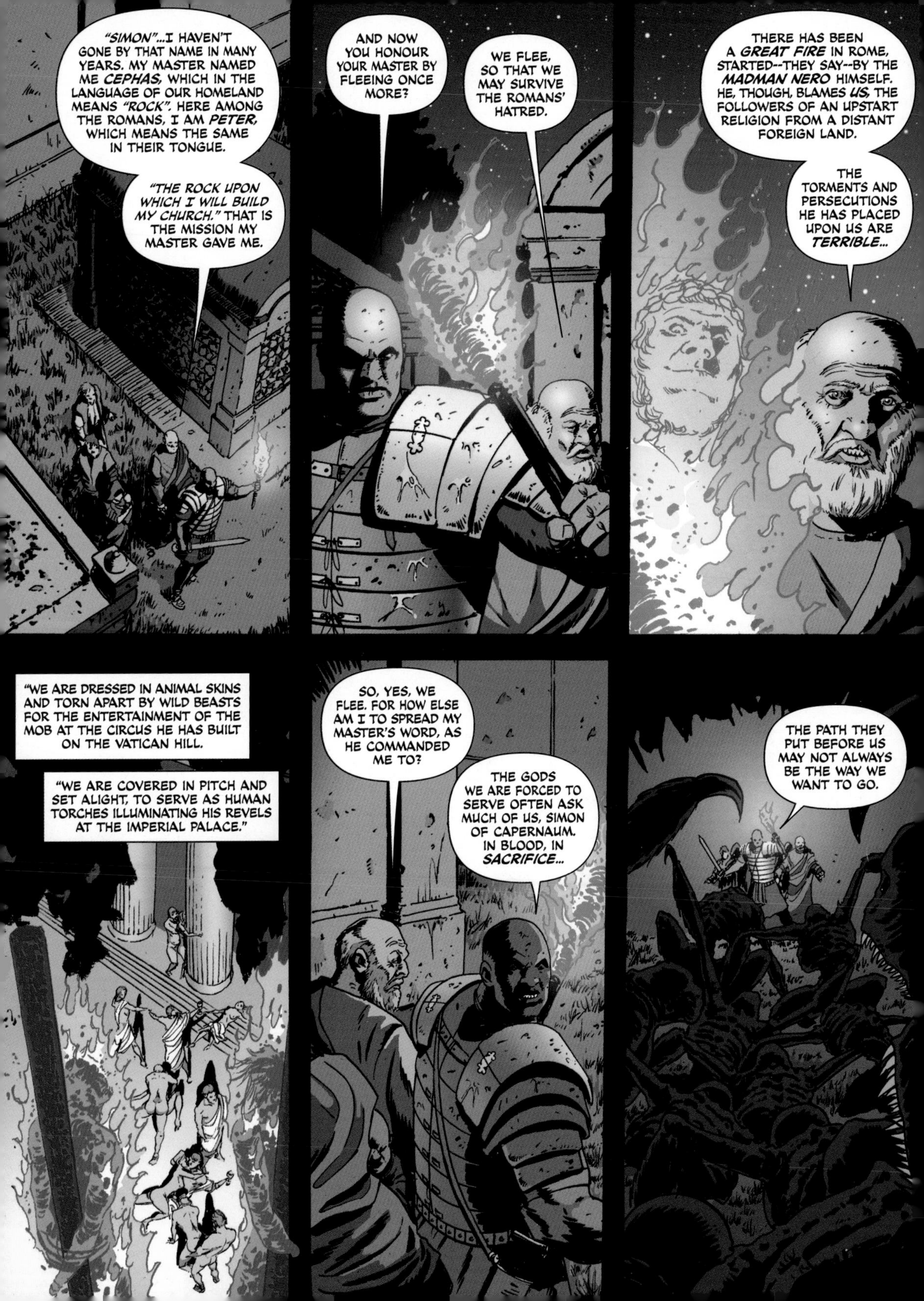
"SIMON"...I HAVEN'T GONE BY THAT NAME IN MANY YEARS. MY MASTER NAMED ME CEPHAS, WHICH IN THE LANGUAGE OF OUR HOMELAND MEANS "ROCK". HERE AMONG THE ROMANS, I AM PETER, WHICH MEANS THE SAME IN THEIR TONGUE.
"THE ROCK UPON WHICH I WILL BUILD MY CHURCH." THAT IS THE MISSION MY MASTER GAVE ME.
AND NOW YOU HONOUR YOUR MASTER BY FLEEING ONCE MORE?
WE FLEE, SO THAT WE MAY SURVIVE THE ROMANS' HATRED.
THERE HAS BEEN A GREAT FIRE IN ROME, STARTED--THEY SAY--BY THE MADMAN NERO HIMSELF. HE, THOUGH, BLAMES US, THE FOLLOWERS OF AN UPSTART RELIGION FROM A DISTANT FOREIGN LAND.
THE TORMENTS AND PERSECUTIONS HE HAS PLACED UPON US ARE TERRIBLE...
"WE ARE DRESSED IN ANIMAL SKINS AND TORN APART BY WILD BEASTS FOR THE ENTERTAINMENT OF THE MOB AT THE CIRCUS HE HAS BUILT ON THE VATICAN HILL.
"WE ARE COVERED IN PITCH AND SET ALIGHT, TO SERVE AS HUMAN TORCHES ILLUMINATING HIS REVELS AT THE IMPERIAL PALACE."
SO, YES, WE FLEE. FOR HOW ELSE AM I TO SPREAD MY MASTER'S WORD, AS HE COMMANDED ME TO?
THE GODS WE ARE FORCED TO SERVE OFTEN ASK MUCH OF US, SIMON OF CAPERNAUM. IN BLOOD, IN SACRIFICE...
THE PATH THEY PUT BEFORE US MAY NOT ALWAYS BE THE WAY WE WANT TO GO.

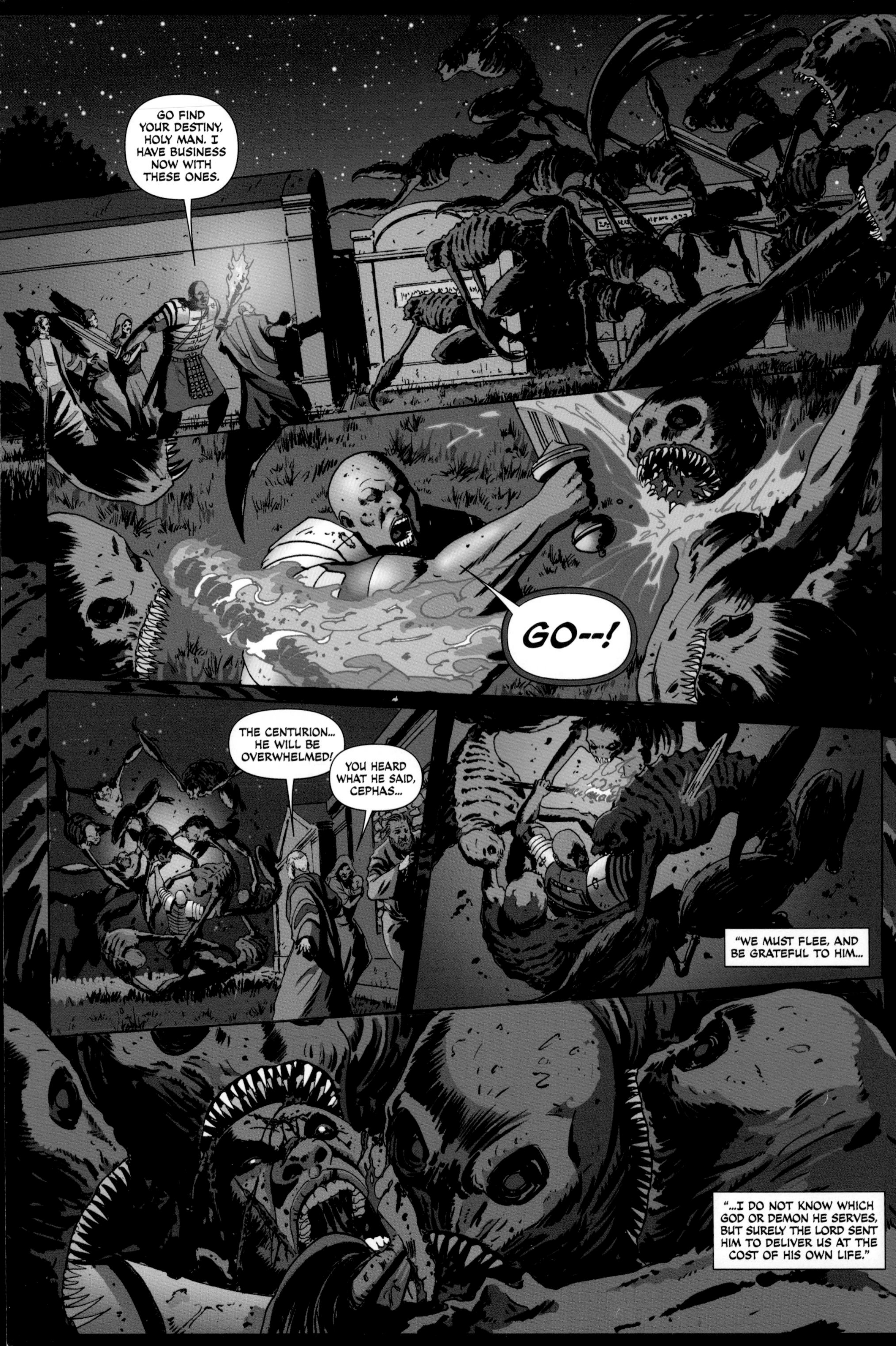
GO FIND YOUR DESTINY, HOLY MAN. I HAVE BUSINESS NOW WITH THESE ONES.
GO--!
THE CENTURION... HE WILL BE OVERWHELMED!
YOU HEARD WHAT HE SAID, CEPHAS...
"WE MUST FLEE, AND BE GRATEFUL TO HIM...
"...I DO NOT KNOW WHICH GOD OR DEMON HE SERVES, BUT SURELY THE LORD SENT HIM TO DELIVER US AT THE COST OF HIS OWN LIFE."

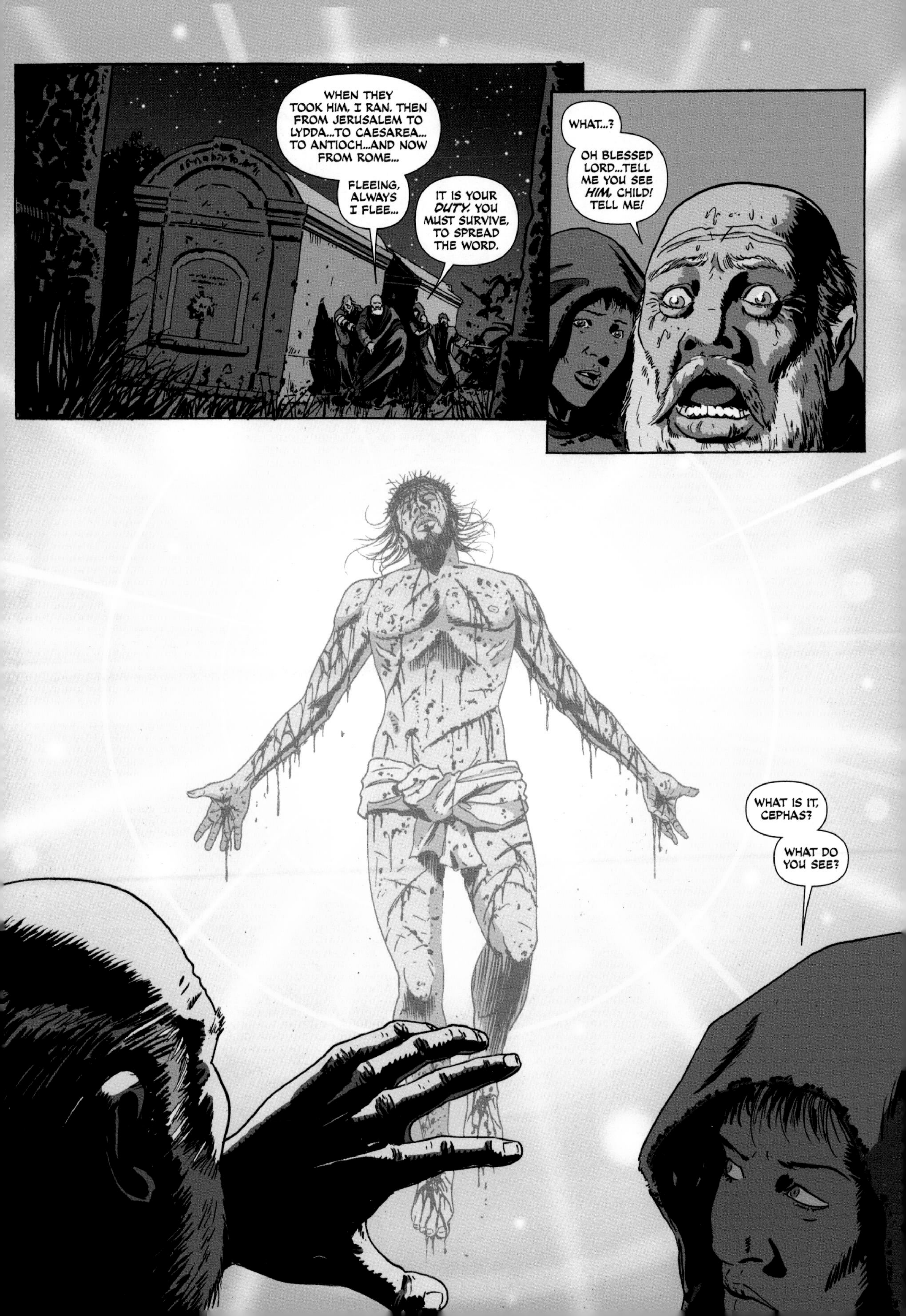
WHEN THEY TOOK HIM, I RAN. THEN FROM JERUSALEM TO LYDDA...TO CAESAREA... TO ANTIOCH...AND NOW FROM ROME...
FLEEING, ALWAYS I FLEE...
IT IS YOUR *DUTY.* YOU MUST SURVIVE, TO SPREAD THE WORD.
WHAT...?
OH BLESSED LORD...TELL ME YOU SEE *HIM,* CHILD! TELL ME!
WHAT IS IT, CEPHAS?
WHAT DO YOU SEE?

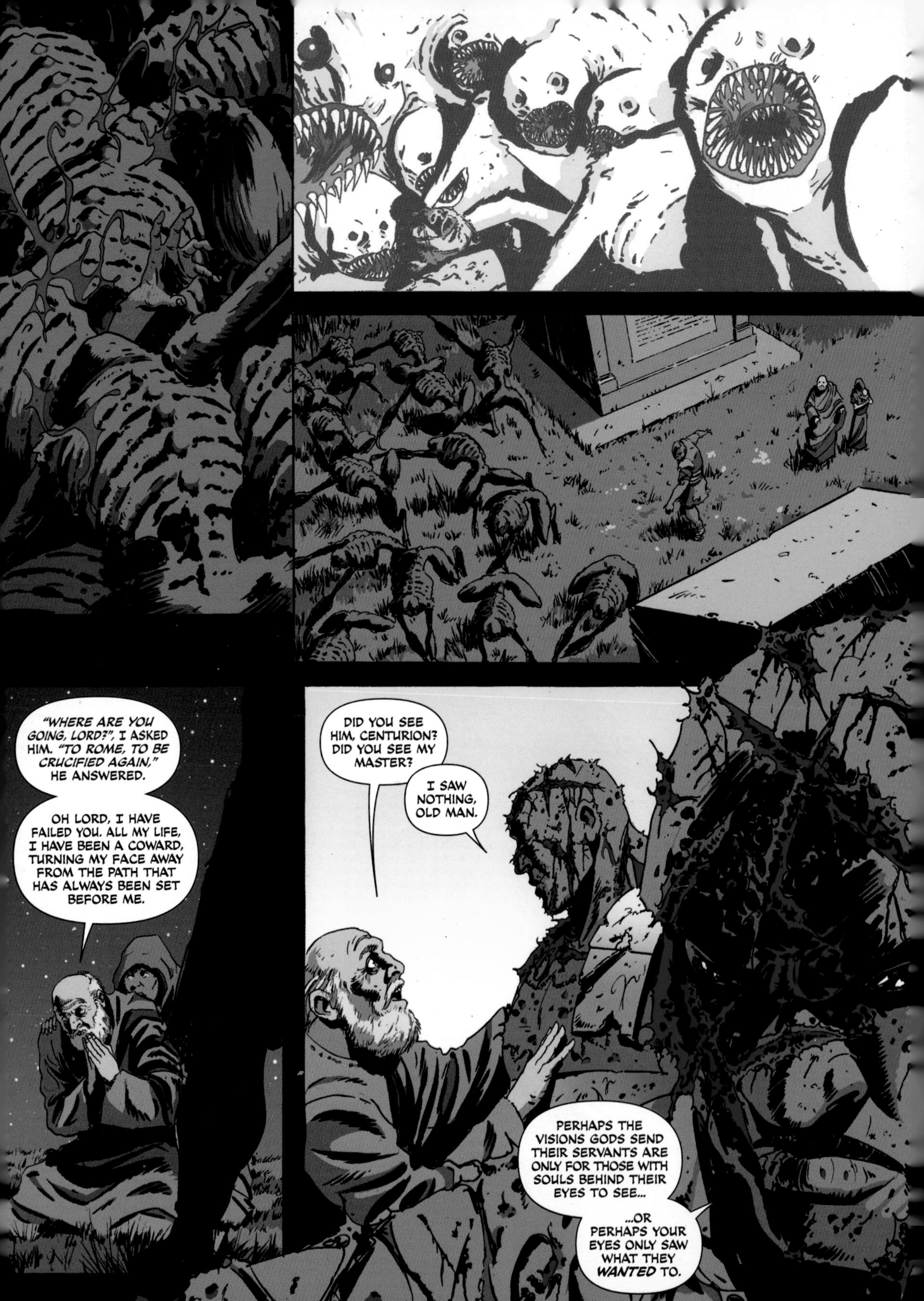
"WHERE ARE YOU GOING, LORD?", I ASKED HIM. "TO ROME, TO BE CRUCIFIED AGAIN," HE ANSWERED.
OH LORD, I HAVE FAILED YOU. ALL MY LIFE, I HAVE BEEN A COWARD, TURNING MY FACE AWAY FROM THE PATH THAT HAS ALWAYS BEEN SET BEFORE ME.
DID YOU SEE HIM, CENTURION? DID YOU SEE MY MASTER?
I SAW NOTHING, OLD MAN.
PERHAPS THE VISIONS GODS SEND THEIR SERVANTS ARE ONLY FOR THOSE WITH SOULS BEHIND THEIR EYES TO SEE...
...OR PERHAPS YOUR EYES ONLY SAW WHAT THEY *WANTED* TO.

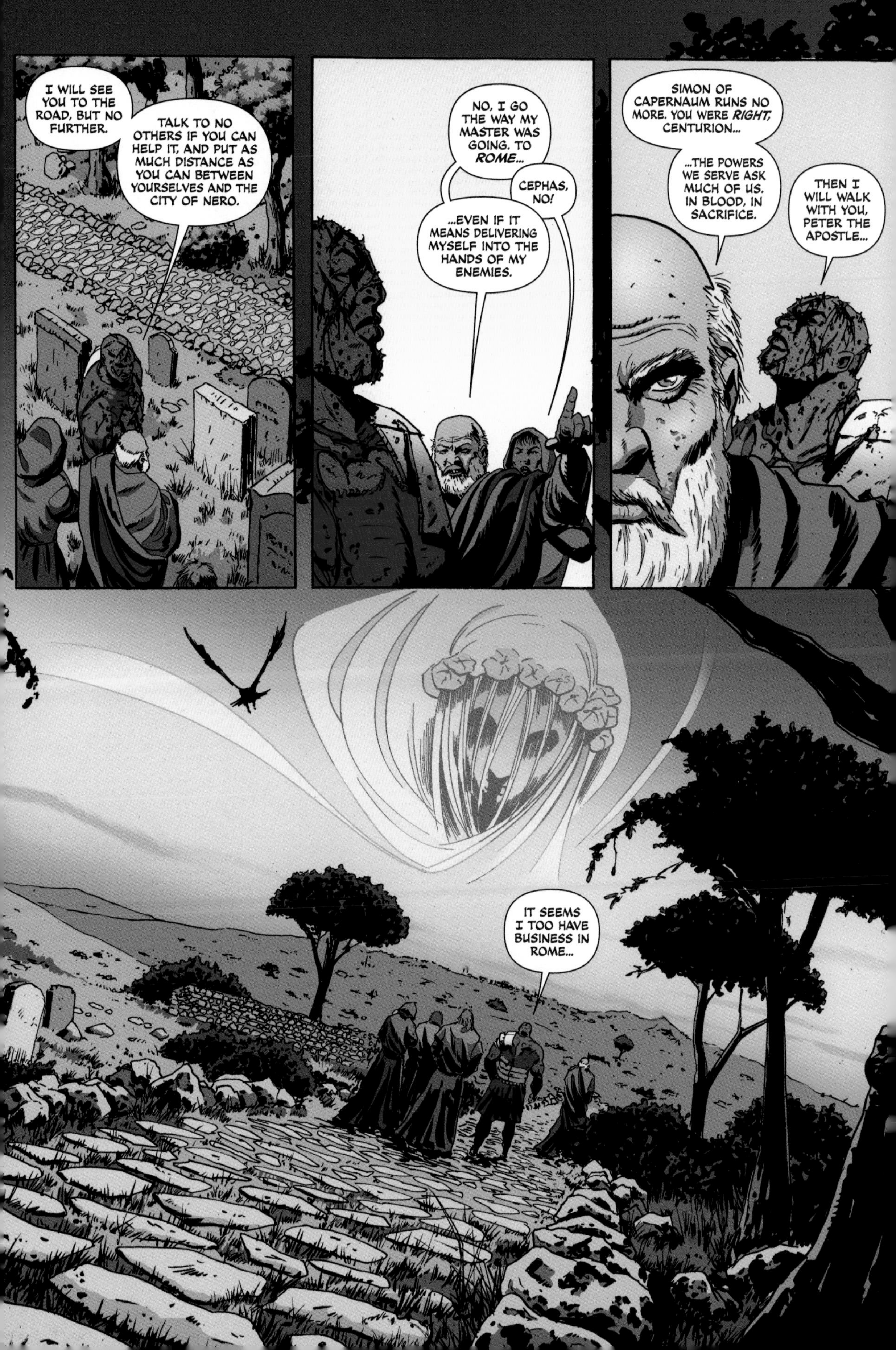
I WILL SEE YOU TO THE ROAD, BUT NO FURTHER.
TALK TO NO OTHERS IF YOU CAN HELP IT, AND PUT AS MUCH DISTANCE AS YOU CAN BETWEEN YOURSELVES AND THE CITY OF NERO.
NO, I GO THE WAY MY MASTER WAS GOING. TO *ROME*...
CEPHAS, NO!
...EVEN IF IT MEANS DELIVERING MYSELF INTO THE HANDS OF MY ENEMIES.
SIMON OF CAPERNAUM RUNS NO MORE. YOU WERE *RIGHT,* CENTURION...
...THE POWERS WE SERVE ASK MUCH OF US. IN BLOOD, IN SACRIFICE.
THEN I WILL WALK WITH YOU, PETER THE APOSTLE...
IT SEEMS I TOO HAVE BUSINESS IN ROME...

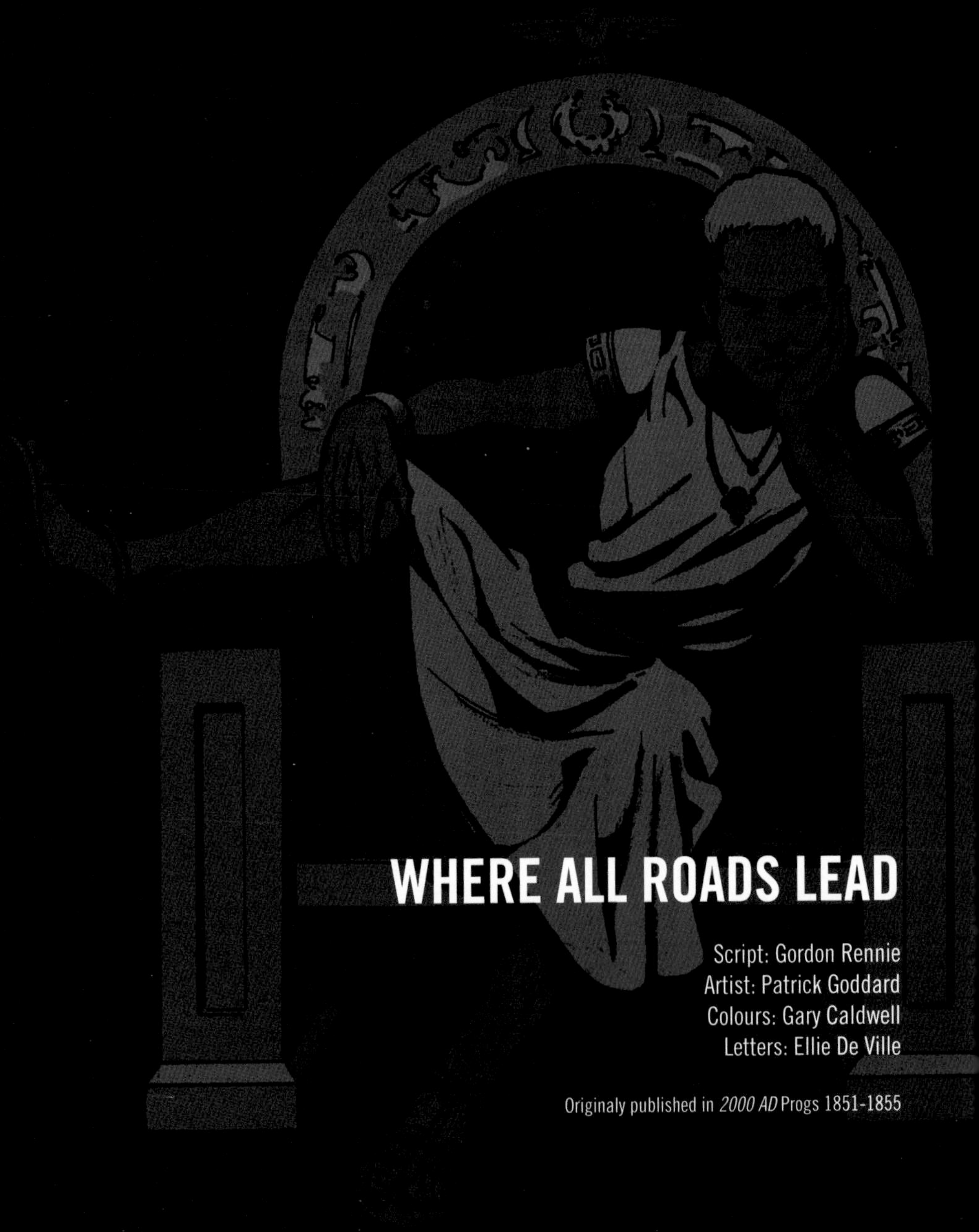

WHERE ALL ROADS LEAD

Script: Gordon Rennie
Artist: Patrick Goddard
Colours: Gary Caldwell
Letters: Ellie De Ville

Originaly published in *2000 AD* Progs 1851-1855

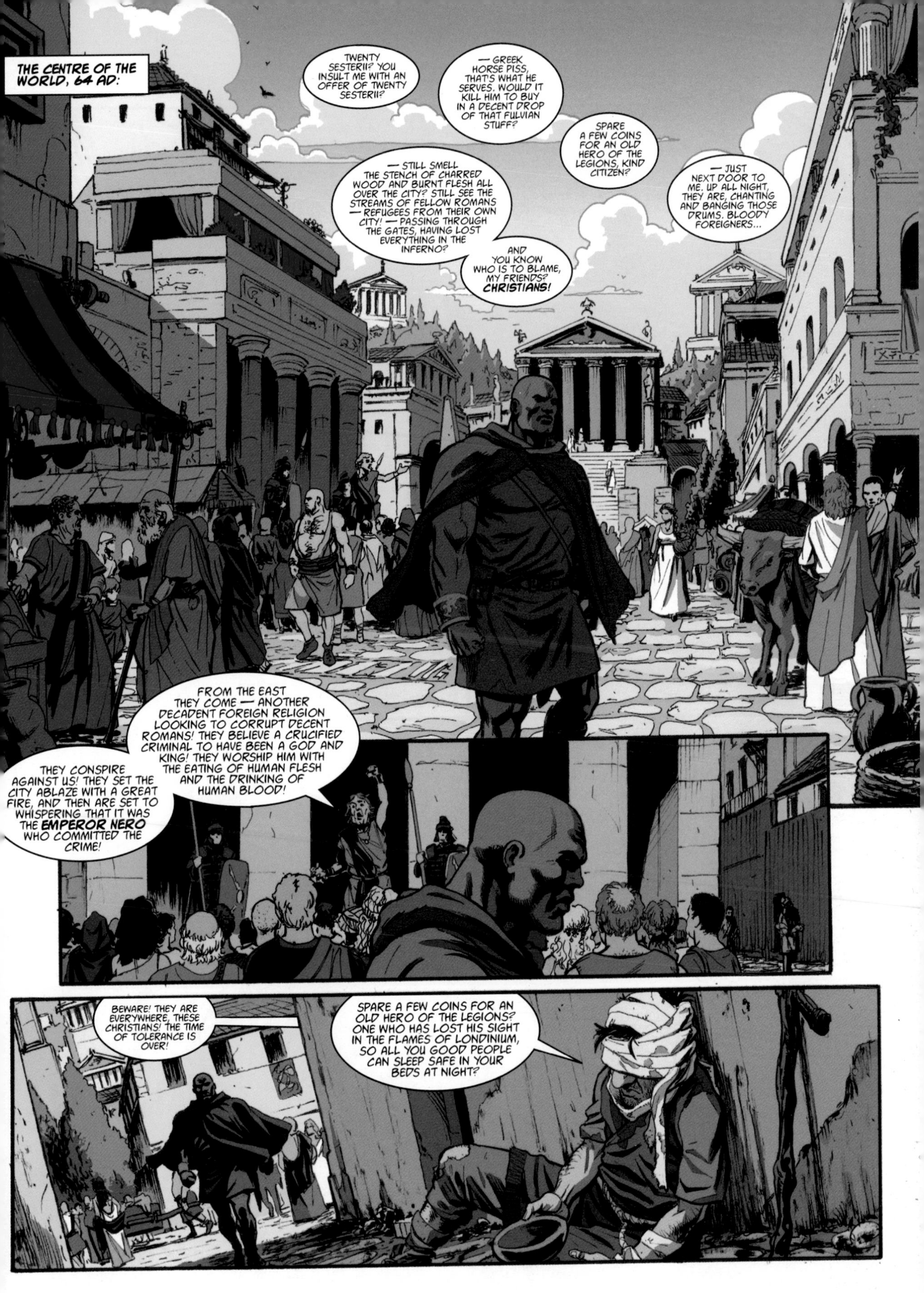
THE CENTRE OF THE WORLD, 64 AD:
TWENTY SESTERII? YOU INSULT ME WITH AN OFFER OF TWENTY SESTERII?
— GREEK HORSE PISS, THAT'S WHAT HE SERVES. WOULD IT KILL HIM TO BUY IN A DECENT DROP OF THAT FULVIAN STUFF?
SPARE A FEW COINS FOR AN OLD HERO OF THE LEGIONS, KIND CITIZEN?
— STILL SMELL THE STENCH OF CHARRED WOOD AND BURNT FLESH ALL OVER THE CITY? STILL SEE THE STREAMS OF FELLOW ROMANS — REFUGEES FROM THEIR OWN CITY! — PASSING THROUGH THE GATES, HAVING LOST EVERYTHING IN THE INFERNO?
AND YOU KNOW WHO IS TO BLAME, MY FRIENDS? **CHRISTIANS!**
— JUST NEXT DOOR TO ME. UP ALL NIGHT, THEY ARE, CHANTING AND BANGING THOSE DRUMS. BLOODY FOREIGNERS...
FROM THE EAST THEY COME — ANOTHER DECADENT FOREIGN RELIGION LOOKING TO CORRUPT DECENT ROMANS! THEY BELIEVE A CRUCIFIED CRIMINAL TO HAVE BEEN A GOD AND KING! THEY WORSHIP HIM WITH THE EATING OF HUMAN FLESH AND THE DRINKING OF HUMAN BLOOD!
THEY CONSPIRE AGAINST US! THEY SET THE CITY ABLAZE WITH A GREAT FIRE, AND THEN ARE SET TO WHISPERING THAT IT WAS THE **EMPEROR NERO** WHO COMMITTED THE CRIME!
BEWARE! THEY ARE EVERYWHERE, THESE CHRISTIANS! THE TIME OF TOLERANCE IS OVER!
SPARE A FEW COINS FOR AN OLD HERO OF THE LEGIONS? ONE WHO HAS LOST HIS SIGHT IN THE FLAMES OF LONDINIUM, SO ALL YOU GOOD PEOPLE CAN SLEEP SAFE IN YOUR BEDS AT NIGHT?

THANK YOU, GOOD MISTRESS. MAY ABUNDANTIA, LUCINA, VESTA AND THE BLESSINGS OF A DOZEN OTHER FINE GODDESSES SMILE UPON YOU AND YOUR —

EH — ?

BASTARD! POX-ROTTEN BALL OF GAULISH PIG CRAP!

DO YOU KNOW WHAT YOU DID TO ME? DO YOU KNOW WHAT I'VE WANTED TO DO TO YOU...?

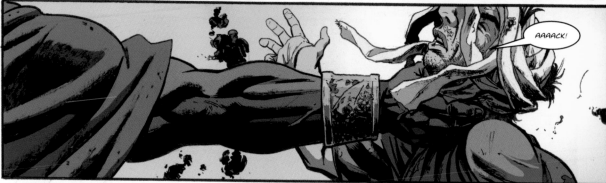

AAAACK!

FELIX FORTUNATUS, OPTIO OF THE FIFTH CENTURY OF THE EIGHTH COHORT OF THE EMPEROR'S FIGHTING NINTH.

IT'S BEEN A WHILE...

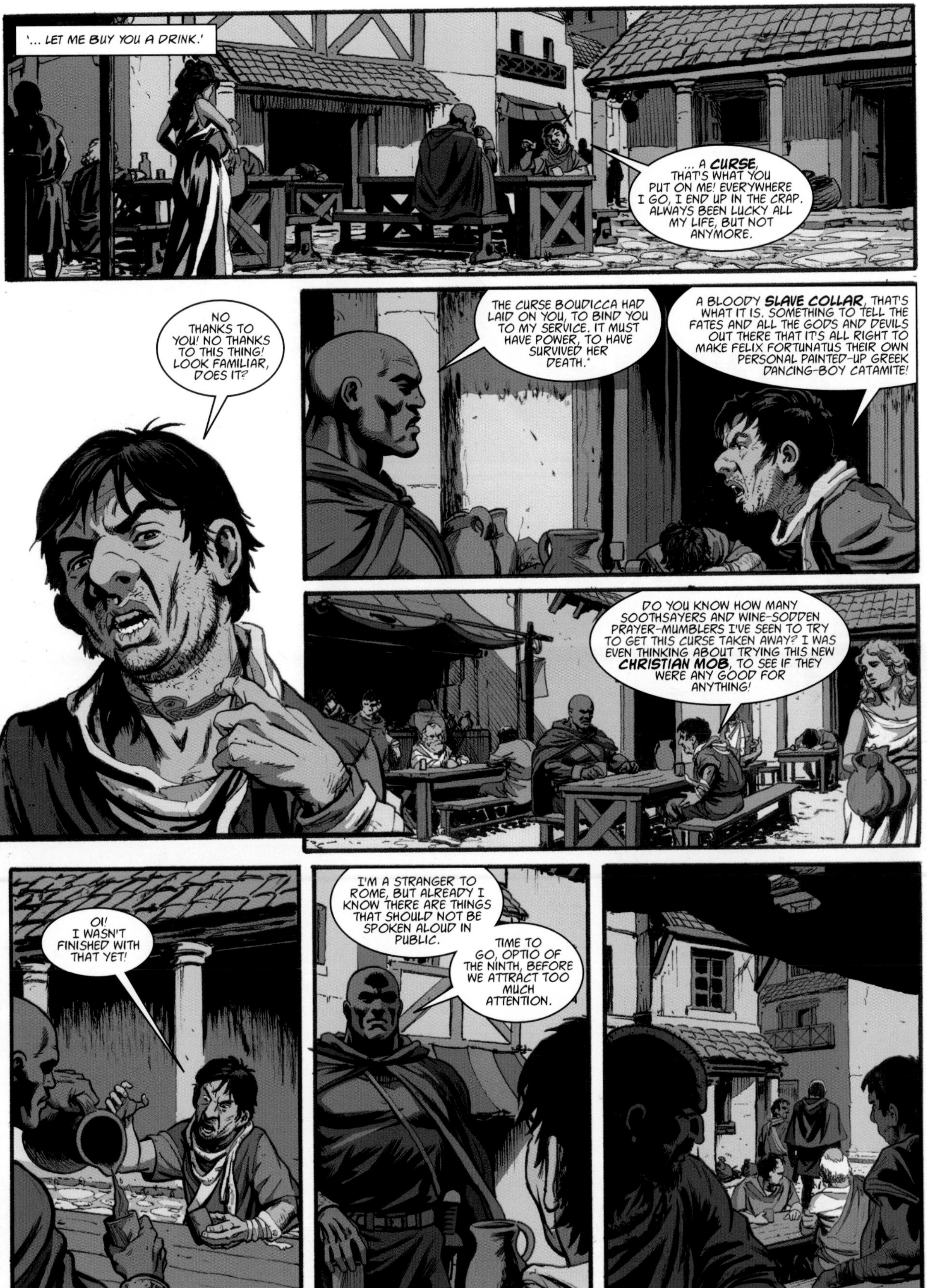
'... LET ME BUY YOU A DRINK.'
... A **CURSE**, THAT'S WHAT YOU PUT ON ME! EVERYWHERE I GO, I END UP IN THE CRAP. ALWAYS BEEN LUCKY ALL MY LIFE, BUT NOT ANYMORE.
NO THANKS TO YOU! NO THANKS TO THIS THING! LOOK FAMILIAR, DOES IT?
THE CURSE BOUDICCA HAD LAID ON YOU, TO BIND YOU TO MY SERVICE. IT MUST HAVE POWER, TO HAVE SURVIVED HER DEATH.*
A BLOODY **SLAVE COLLAR**, THAT'S WHAT IT IS. SOMETHING TO TELL THE FATES AND ALL THE GODS AND DEVILS OUT THERE THAT IT'S ALL RIGHT TO MAKE FELIX FORTUNATUS THEIR OWN PERSONAL PAINTED-UP GREEK DANCING-BOY CATAMITE!
DO YOU KNOW HOW MANY SOOTHSAYERS AND WINE-SODDEN PRAYER-MUMBLERS I'VE SEEN TO TRY TO GET THIS CURSE TAKEN AWAY? I WAS EVEN THINKING ABOUT TRYING THIS NEW **CHRISTIAN MOB**, TO SEE IF THEY WERE ANY GOOD FOR ANYTHING!
OI! I WASN'T FINISHED WITH THAT YET!
I'M A STRANGER TO ROME, BUT ALREADY I KNOW THERE ARE THINGS THAT SHOULD NOT BE SPOKEN ALOUD IN PUBLIC.
TIME TO GO, OPTIO OF THE NINTH, BEFORE WE ATTRACT TOO MUCH ATTENTION.

SO WHAT ARE YOU DOING HERE, IF IT'S YOUR FIRST TIME IN TOWN?

SOMETHING HAS ALWAYS WARNED ME AWAY FROM COMING HERE. ROME HAS TOO MANY ANGRY AND JEALOUS GODS OF ITS OWN TO TOLERATE THE SERVANT OF ANOTHER.

STILL, *SOMETHING* HAS LED ME HERE, ALTHOUGH I DO NOT YET KNOW WHY...

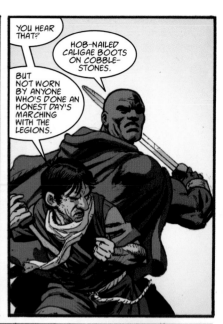

YOU HEAR THAT?

HOB-NAILED CALIGAE BOOTS ON COBBLE-STONES.

BUT NOT WORN BY ANYONE WHO'S DONE AN HONEST DAY'S MARCHING WITH THE LEGIONS.

SEE? WHAT DID I TELL YOU? BLOODY TOY-SOLDIER *PRAETORIANS.*

SEE HOW THE PROPHECY POISON BURNS THROUGH THE VEINS? SEE HOW THE BODY WRITHES AND CONTORTS? THESE ARE ALL GOOD SIGNS FOR THE POTENCY OF THE VISION.

THAT SOUND...

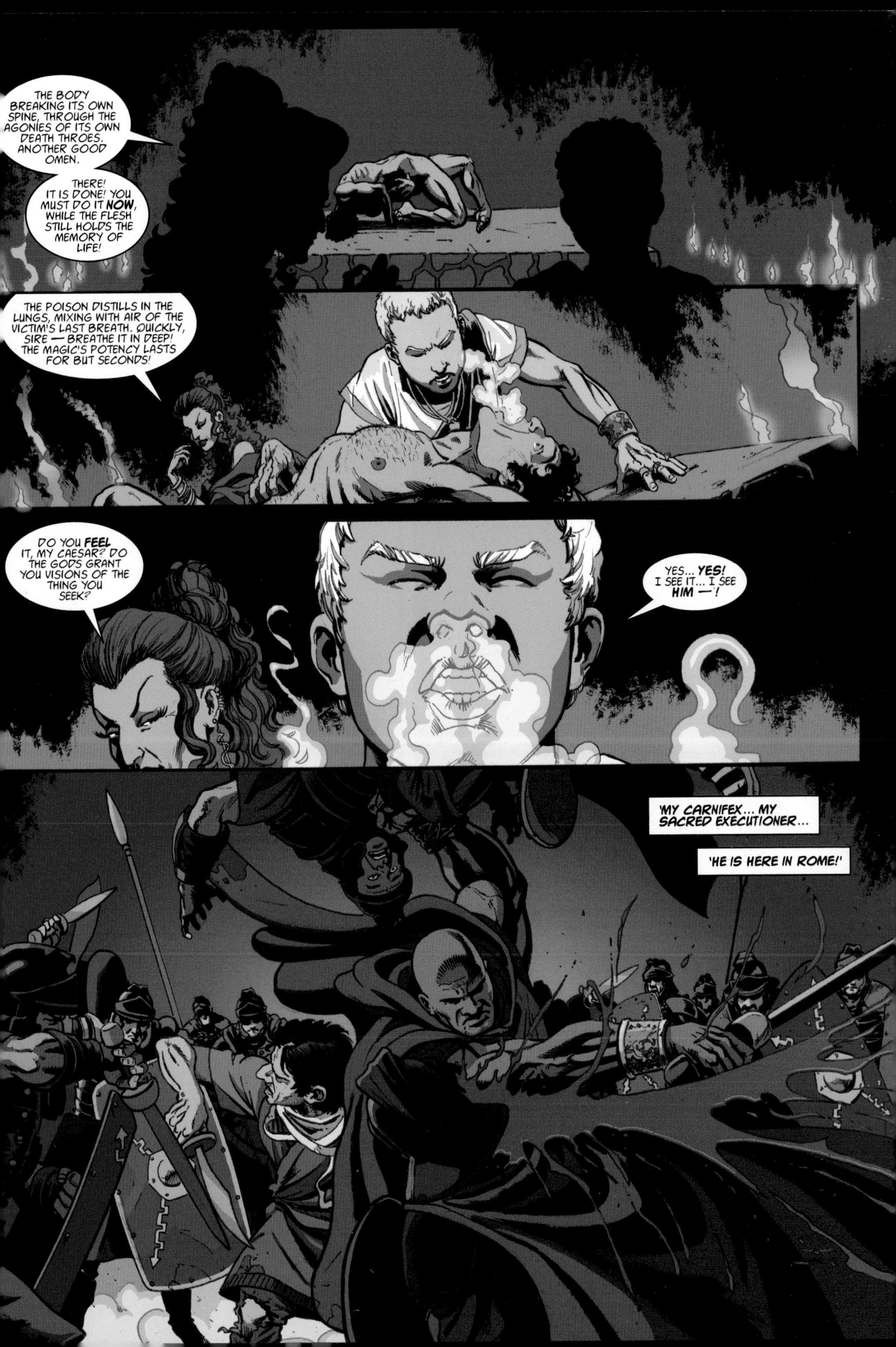
THE BODY BREAKING ITS OWN SPINE, THROUGH THE AGONIES OF ITS OWN DEATH THROES. ANOTHER GOOD OMEN.
THERE! IT IS DONE! YOU MUST DO IT NOW, WHILE THE FLESH STILL HOLDS THE MEMORY OF LIFE!
THE POISON DISTILLS IN THE LUNGS, MIXING WITH AIR OF THE VICTIM'S LAST BREATH. QUICKLY, SIRE — BREATHE IT IN DEEP! THE MAGIC'S POTENCY LASTS FOR BUT SECONDS!
DO YOU FEEL IT, MY CAESAR? DO THE GODS GRANT YOU VISIONS OF THE THING YOU SEEK?
YES... YES! I SEE IT... I SEE HIM —'!
'MY CARNIFEX... MY SACRED EXECUTIONER...
'HE IS HERE IN ROME!'

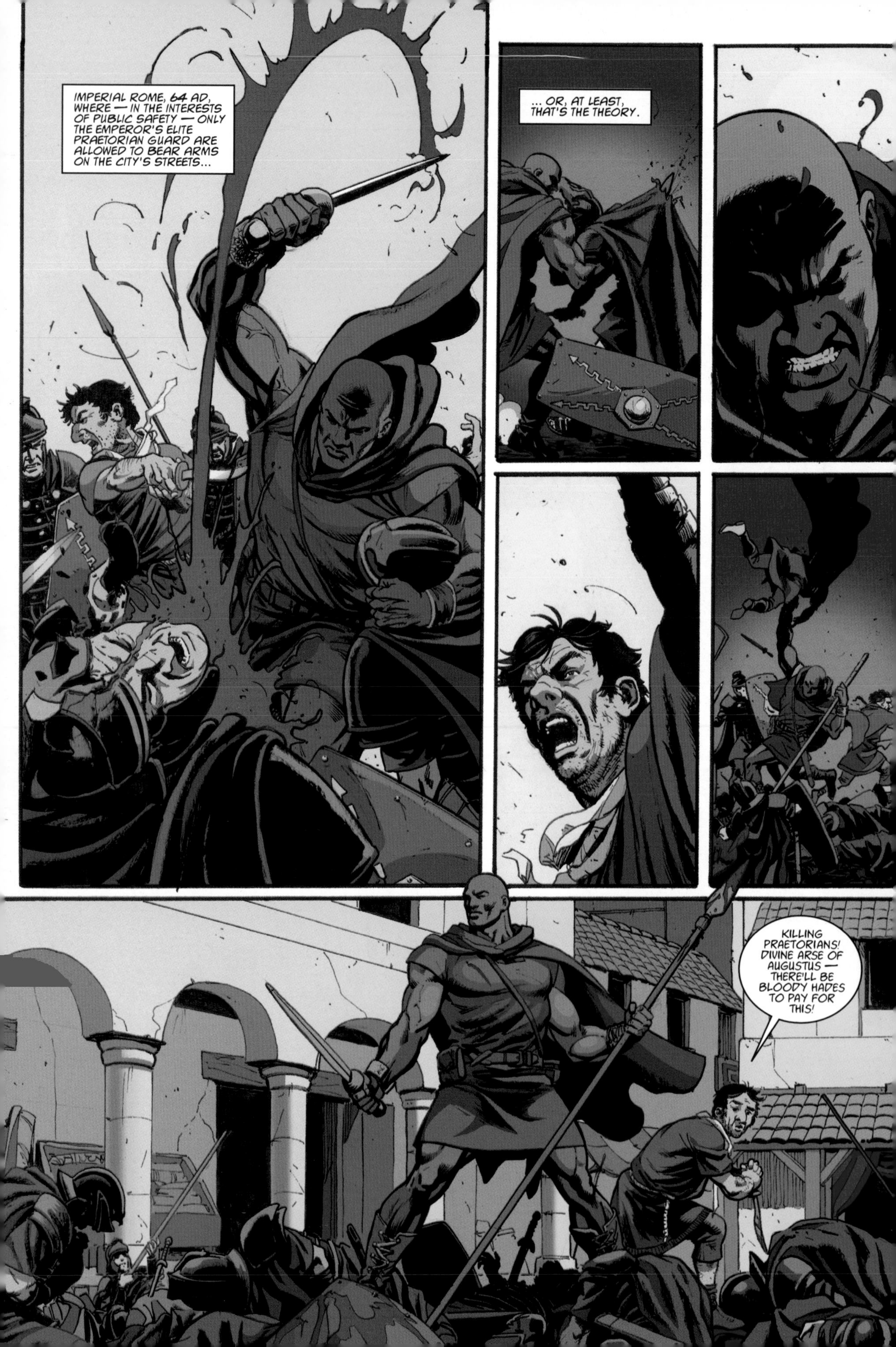
IMPERIAL ROME, 64 AD, WHERE — IN THE INTERESTS OF PUBLIC SAFETY — ONLY THE EMPEROR'S ELITE PRAETORIAN GUARD ARE ALLOWED TO BEAR ARMS ON THE CITY'S STREETS...
... OR, AT LEAST, THAT'S THE THEORY.
KILLING PRAETORIANS! DIVINE ARSE OF AUGUSTUS — THERE'LL BE BLOODY HADES TO PAY FOR THIS!

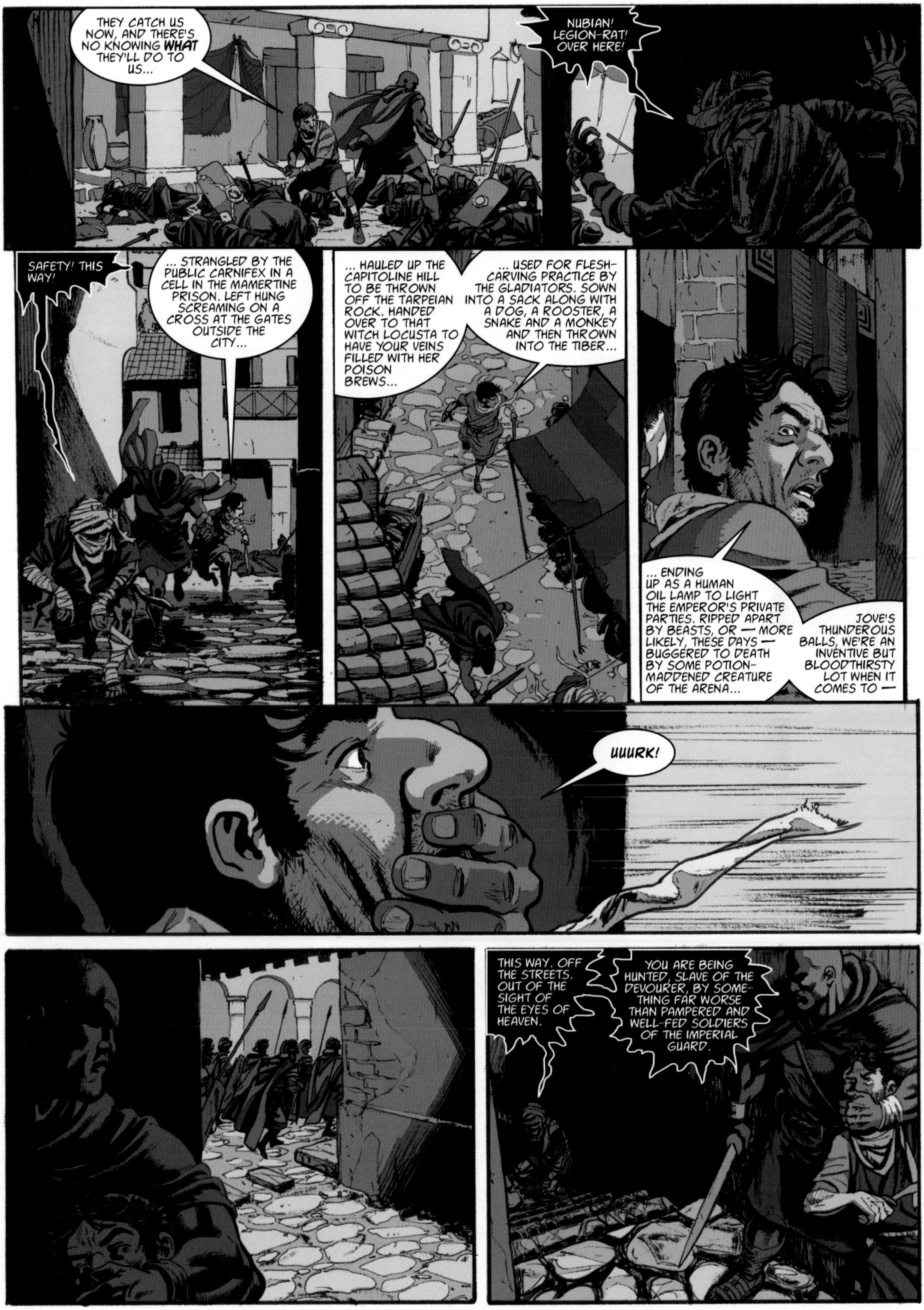
THEY CATCH US NOW, AND THERE'S NO KNOWING WHAT THEY'LL DO TO US...
NUBIAN! LEGION-RAT! OVER HERE!
SAFETY! THIS WAY!
... STRANGLED BY THE PUBLIC CARNIFEX IN A CELL IN THE MAMERTINE PRISON. LEFT HUNG SCREAMING ON A CROSS AT THE GATES OUTSIDE THE CITY...
... HAULED UP THE CAPITOLINE HILL TO BE THROWN OFF THE TARPEIAN ROCK. HANDED OVER TO THAT WITCH LOCUSTA TO HAVE YOUR VEINS FILLED WITH HER POISON BREWS...
... USED FOR FLESH-CARVING PRACTICE BY THE GLADIATORS. SOWN INTO A SACK ALONG WITH A DOG, A ROOSTER, A SNAKE AND A MONKEY AND THEN THROWN INTO THE TIBER...
... ENDING UP AS A HUMAN OIL LAMP TO LIGHT THE EMPEROR'S PRIVATE PARTIES. RIPPED APART BY BEASTS, OR — MORE LIKELY, THESE DAYS — BUGGERED TO DEATH BY SOME POTION-MADDENED CREATURE OF THE ARENA...
JOVE'S THUNDEROUS BALLS, WE'RE AN INVENTIVE BUT BLOODTHIRSTY LOT WHEN IT COMES TO —
UUURK!
THIS WAY. OFF THE STREETS. OUT OF THE SIGHT OF THE EYES OF HEAVEN.
YOU ARE BEING HUNTED, SLAVE OF THE DEVOURER, BY SOMETHING FAR WORSE THAN PAMPERED AND WELL-FED SOLDIERS OF THE IMPERIAL GUARD.

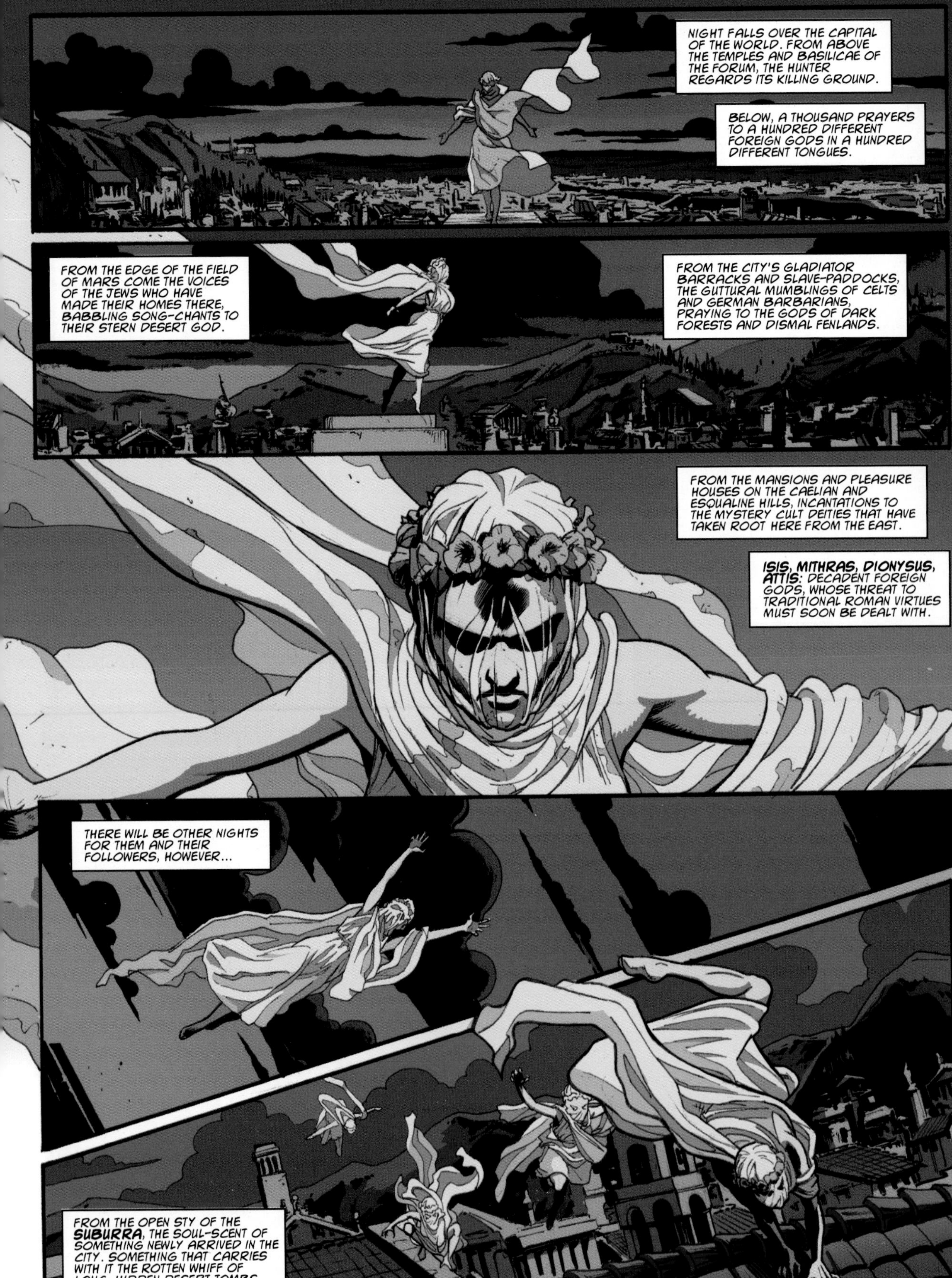
NIGHT FALLS OVER THE CAPITAL OF THE WORLD. FROM ABOVE THE TEMPLES AND BASILICAE OF THE FORUM, THE HUNTER REGARDS ITS KILLING GROUND.
BELOW, A THOUSAND PRAYERS TO A HUNDRED DIFFERENT FOREIGN GODS IN A HUNDRED DIFFERENT TONGUES.
FROM THE EDGE OF THE FIELD OF MARS COME THE VOICES OF THE JEWS WHO HAVE MADE THEIR HOMES THERE, BABBLING SONG-CHANTS TO THEIR STERN DESERT GOD.
FROM THE CITY'S GLADIATOR BARRACKS AND SLAVE-PADDOCKS, THE GUTTURAL MUMBLINGS OF CELTS AND GERMAN BARBARIANS, PRAYING TO THE GODS OF DARK FORESTS AND DISMAL FENLANDS.
FROM THE MANSIONS AND PLEASURE HOUSES ON THE CAELIAN AND ESQUALINE HILLS, INCANTATIONS TO THE MYSTERY CULT DEITIES THAT HAVE TAKEN ROOT HERE FROM THE EAST.
ISIS, MITHRAS, DIONYSUS, ATTIS: DECADENT FOREIGN GODS, WHOSE THREAT TO TRADITIONAL ROMAN VIRTUES MUST SOON BE DEALT WITH.
THERE WILL BE OTHER NIGHTS FOR THEM AND THEIR FOLLOWERS, HOWEVER...
FROM THE OPEN STY OF THE **SUBURRA**, THE SOUL-SCENT OF SOMETHING NEWLY ARRIVED IN THE CITY. SOMETHING THAT CARRIES WITH IT THE ROTTEN WHIFF OF LONG-HIDDEN DESERT TOMBS.

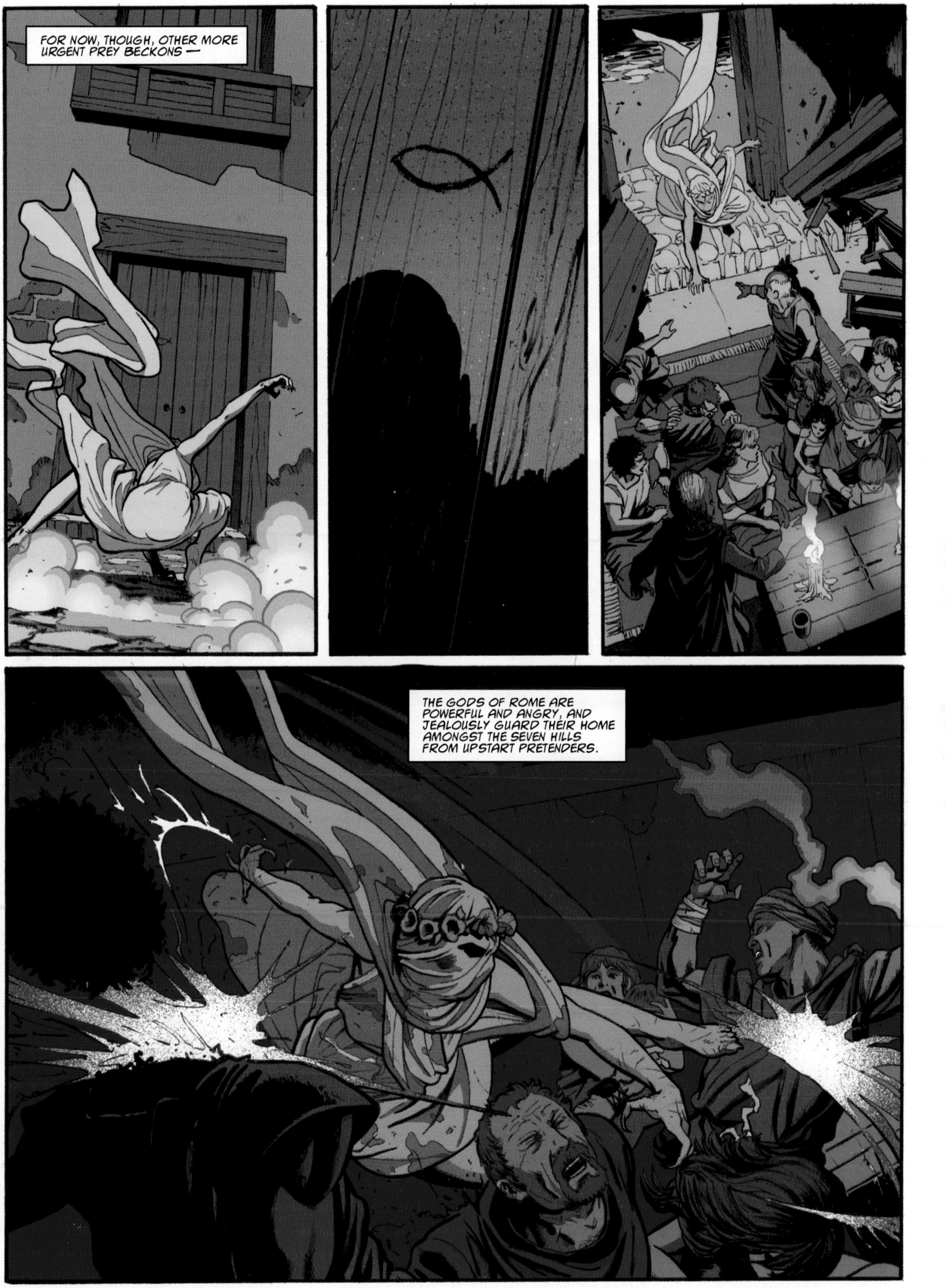
FOR NOW, THOUGH, OTHER MORE URGENT PREY BECKONS —
THE GODS OF ROME ARE POWERFUL AND ANGRY, AND JEALOUSLY GUARD THEIR HOME AMONGST THE SEVEN HILLS FROM UPSTART PRETENDERS.

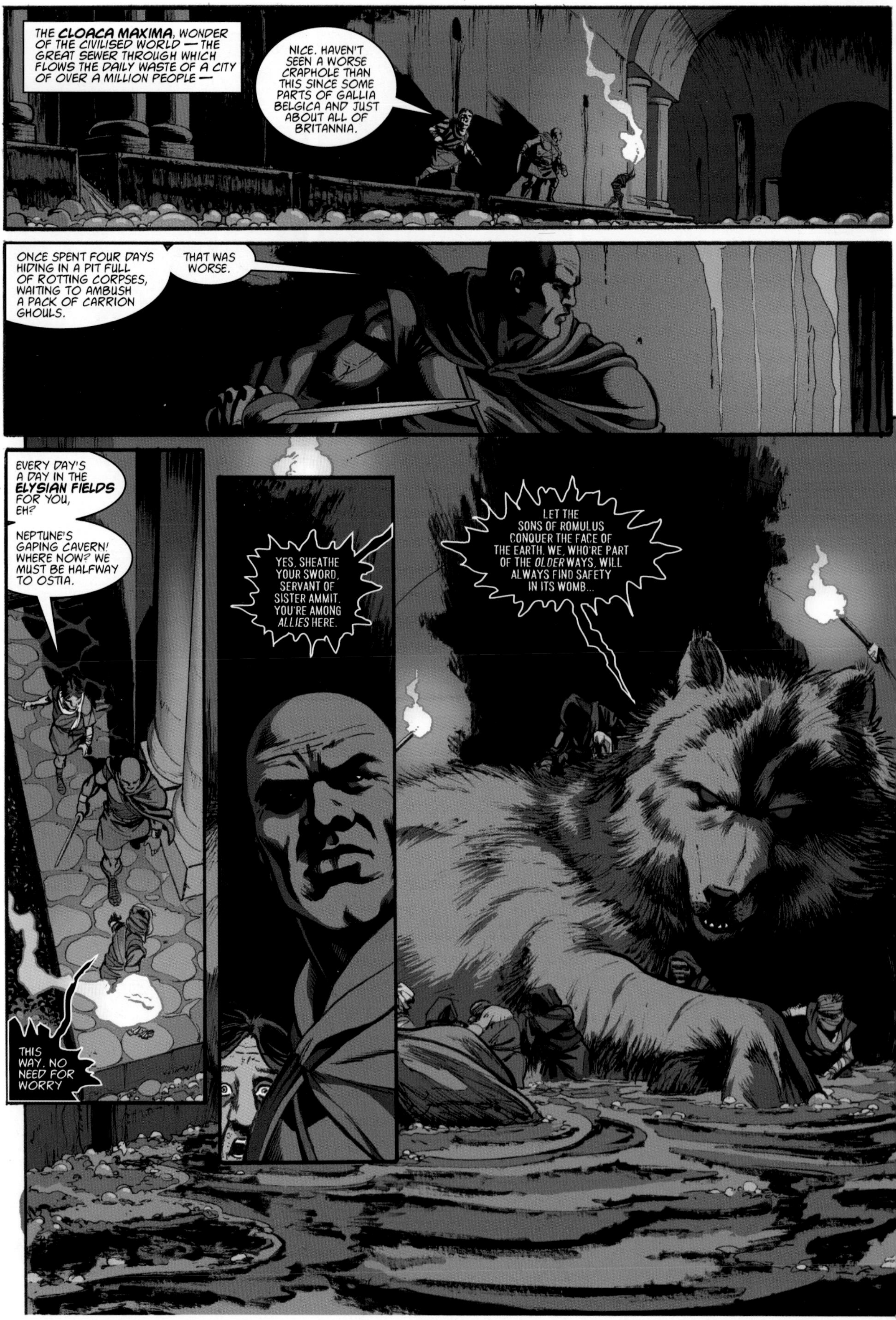
THE CLOACA MAXIMA, WONDER OF THE CIVILISED WORLD — THE GREAT SEWER THROUGH WHICH FLOWS THE DAILY WASTE OF A CITY OF OVER A MILLION PEOPLE —
NICE. HAVEN'T SEEN A WORSE CRAPHOLE THAN THIS SINCE SOME PARTS OF GALLIA BELGICA AND JUST ABOUT ALL OF BRITANNIA.
ONCE SPENT FOUR DAYS HIDING IN A PIT FULL OF ROTTING CORPSES, WAITING TO AMBUSH A PACK OF CARRION GHOULS.
THAT WAS WORSE.
EVERY DAY'S A DAY IN THE ELYSIAN FIELDS FOR YOU, EH?
NEPTUNE'S GAPING CAVERN! WHERE NOW? WE MUST BE HALFWAY TO OSTIA.
THIS WAY. NO NEED FOR WORRY
YES, SHEATHE YOUR SWORD, SERVANT OF SISTER AMMIT. YOU'RE AMONG ALLIES HERE.
LET THE SONS OF ROMULUS CONQUER THE FACE OF THE EARTH. WE, WHO'RE PART OF THE OLDER WAYS, WILL ALWAYS FIND SAFETY IN ITS WOMB...

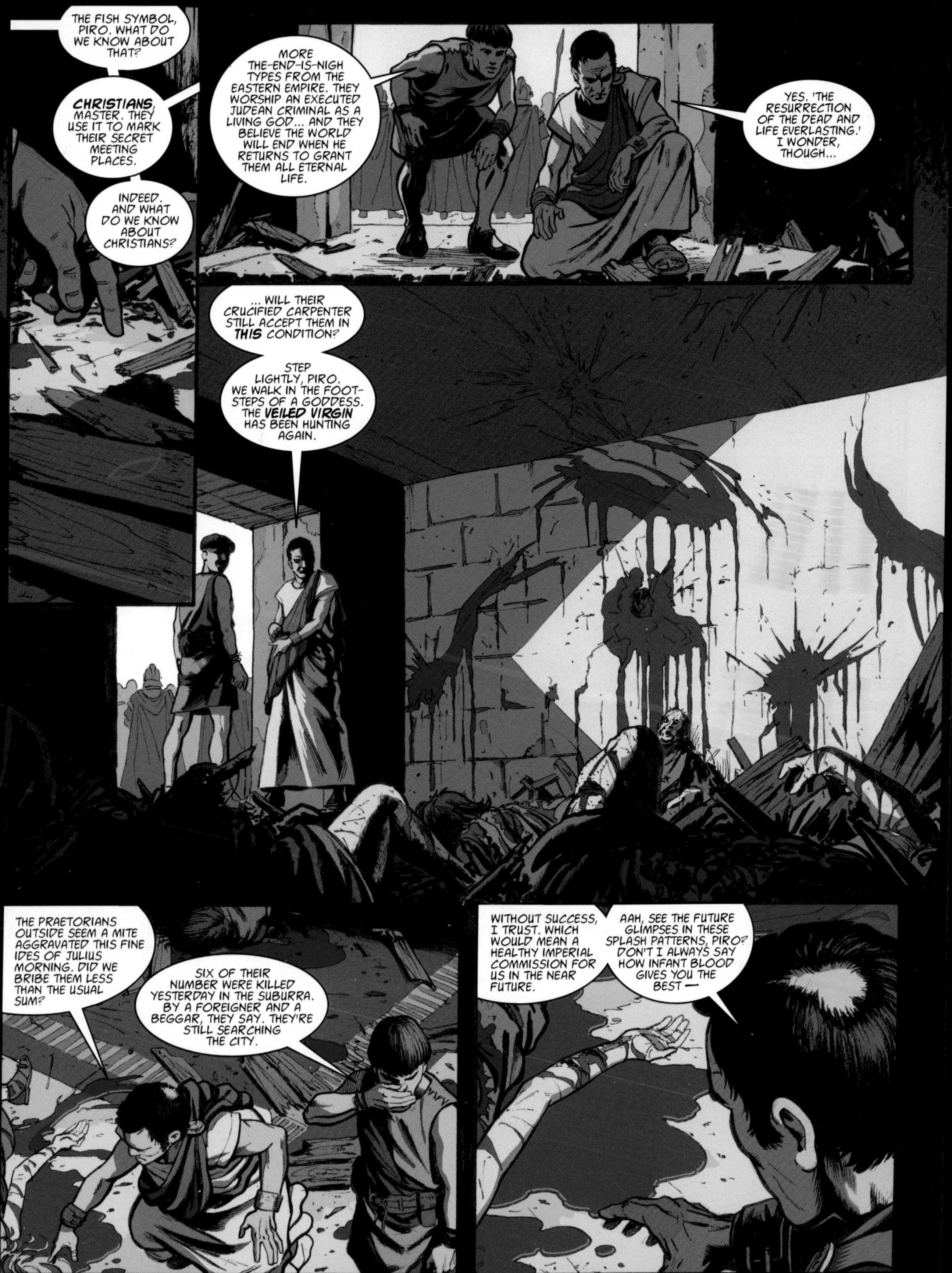
THE FISH SYMBOL, PIRO. WHAT DO WE KNOW ABOUT THAT?
CHRISTIANS, MASTER. THEY USE IT TO MARK THEIR SECRET MEETING PLACES.
INDEED. AND WHAT DO WE KNOW ABOUT CHRISTIANS?
MORE THE-END-IS-NIGH TYPES FROM THE EASTERN EMPIRE. THEY WORSHIP AN EXECUTED JUDEAN CRIMINAL AS A LIVING GOD... AND THEY BELIEVE THE WORLD WILL END WHEN HE RETURNS TO GRANT THEM ALL ETERNAL LIFE.
YES. 'THE RESURRECTION OF THE DEAD AND LIFE EVERLASTING.' I WONDER, THOUGH...
... WILL THEIR CRUCIFIED CARPENTER STILL ACCEPT THEM IN THIS CONDITION?
STEP LIGHTLY, PIRO. WE WALK IN THE FOOT-STEPS OF A GODDESS. THE VEILED VIRGIN HAS BEEN HUNTING AGAIN.
THE PRAETORIANS OUTSIDE SEEM A MITE AGGRAVATED THIS FINE IDES OF JULIUS MORNING. DID WE BRIBE THEM LESS THAN THE USUAL SUM?
SIX OF THEIR NUMBER WERE KILLED YESTERDAY IN THE SUBURRA. BY A FOREIGNER AND A BEGGAR, THEY SAY. THEY'RE STILL SEARCHING THE CITY.
WITHOUT SUCCESS, I TRUST. WHICH WOULD MEAN A HEALTHY IMPERIAL COMMISSION FOR US IN THE NEAR FUTURE.
AAH, SEE THE FUTURE GLIMPSES IN THESE SPLASH PATTERNS, PIRO? DON'T I ALWAYS SAY HOW INFANT BLOOD GIVES YOU THE BEST—

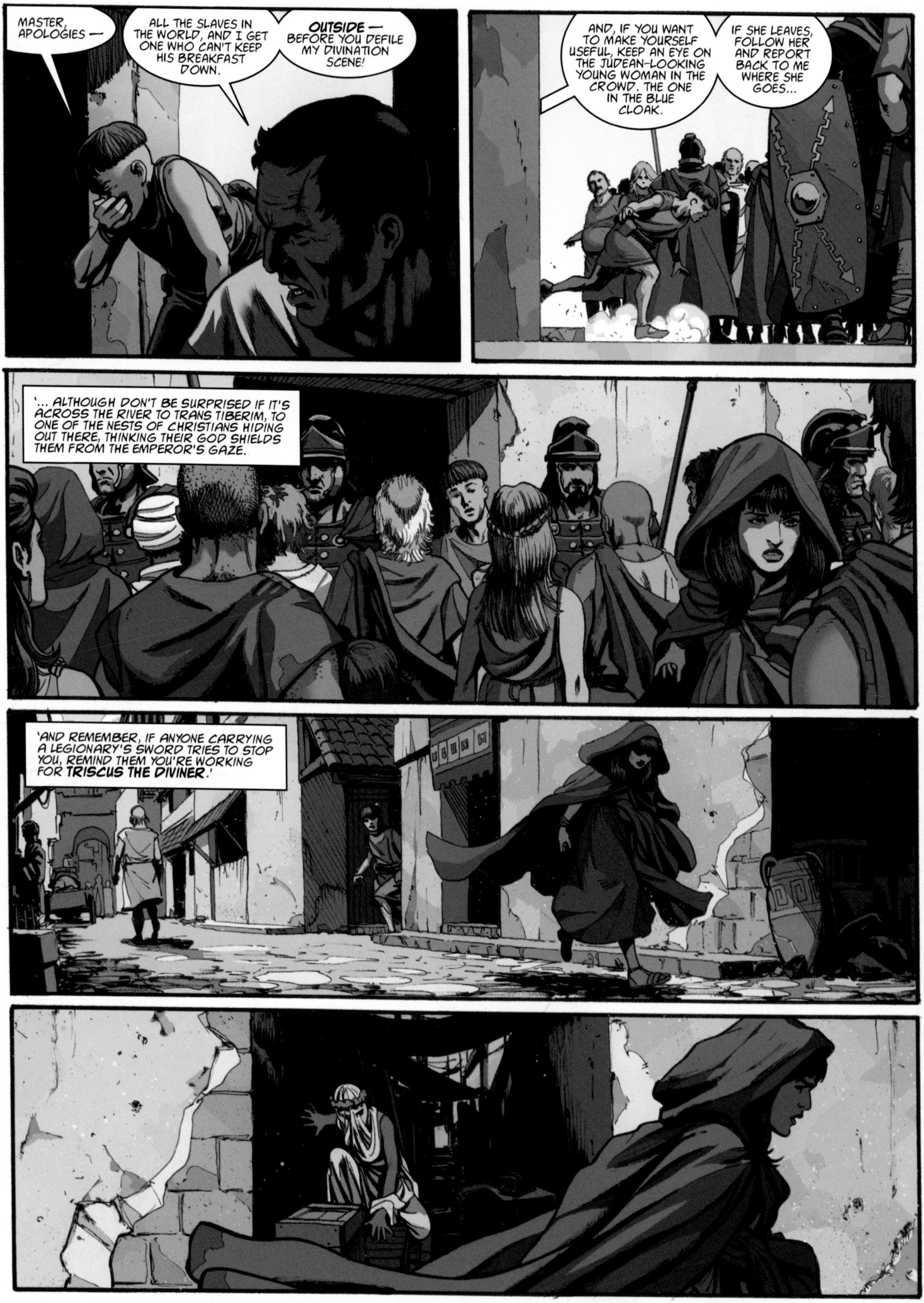
MASTER, APOLOGIES —
ALL THE SLAVES IN THE WORLD, AND I GET ONE WHO CAN'T KEEP HIS BREAKFAST DOWN.
OUTSIDE — BEFORE YOU DEFILE MY DIVINATION SCENE!
AND, IF YOU WANT TO MAKE YOURSELF USEFUL, KEEP AN EYE ON THE JUDEAN-LOOKING YOUNG WOMAN IN THE CROWD. THE ONE IN THE BLUE CLOAK.
IF SHE LEAVES, FOLLOW HER AND REPORT BACK TO ME WHERE SHE GOES...
'... ALTHOUGH DON'T BE SURPRISED IF IT'S ACROSS THE RIVER TO TRANS TIBERIM, TO ONE OF THE NESTS OF CHRISTIANS HIDING OUT THERE, THINKING THEIR GOD SHIELDS THEM FROM THE EMPEROR'S GAZE.
'AND REMEMBER, IF ANYONE CARRYING A LEGIONARY'S SWORD TRIES TO STOP YOU, REMIND THEM YOU'RE WORKING FOR TRISCUS THE DIVINER.'

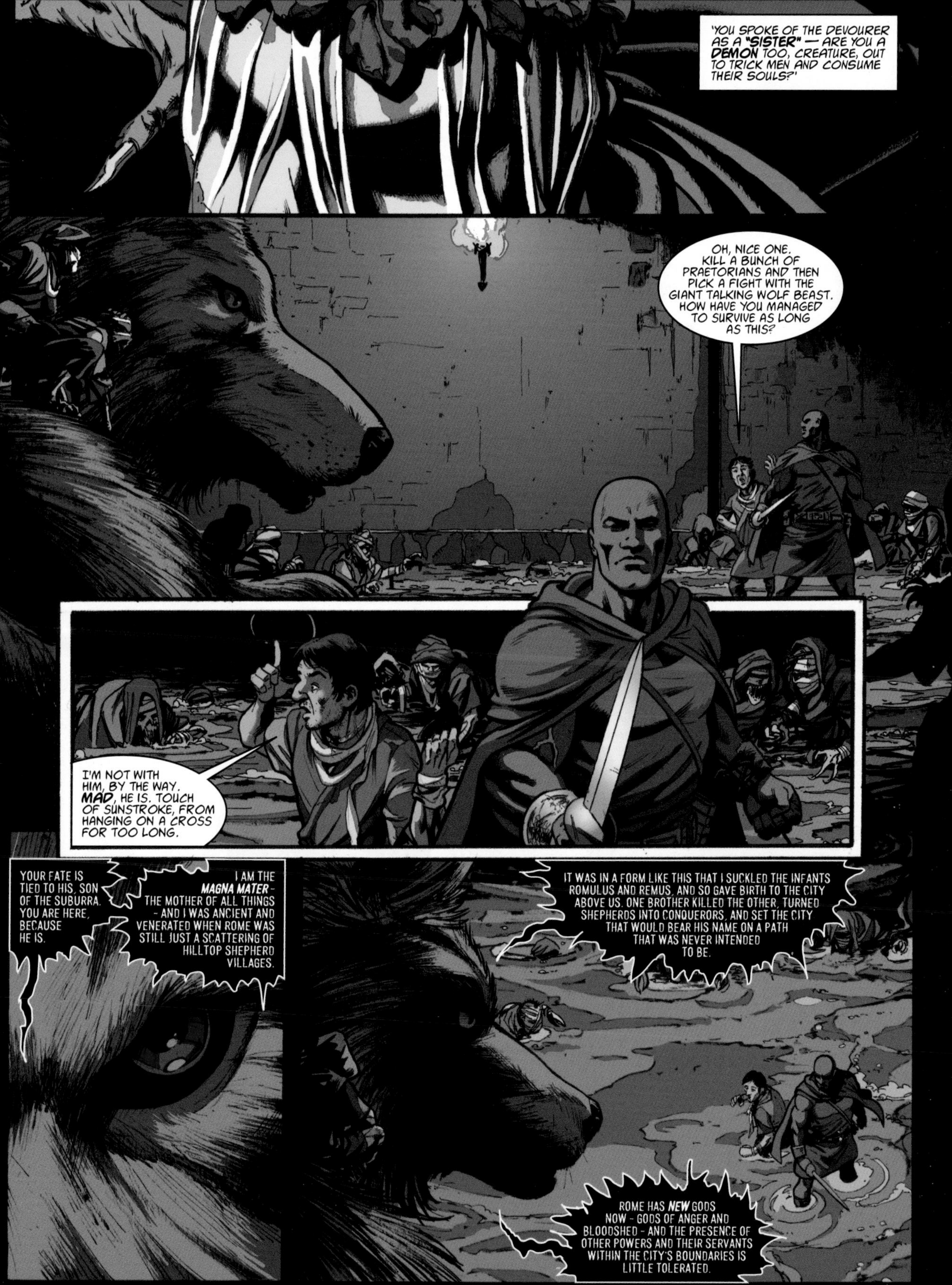

'YOU SPOKE OF THE DEVOURER AS A "SISTER" — ARE YOU A DEMON TOO, CREATURE, OUT TO TRICK MEN AND CONSUME THEIR SOULS?'
OH, NICE ONE. KILL A BUNCH OF PRAETORIANS AND THEN PICK A FIGHT WITH THE GIANT TALKING WOLF BEAST. HOW HAVE YOU MANAGED TO SURVIVE AS LONG AS THIS?
I'M NOT WITH HIM, BY THE WAY. MAD, HE IS. TOUCH OF SUNSTROKE, FROM HANGING ON A CROSS FOR TOO LONG.
YOUR FATE IS TIED TO HIS, SON OF THE SUBURRA. YOU ARE HERE, BECAUSE HE IS.
I AM THE MAGNA MATER - THE MOTHER OF ALL THINGS - AND I WAS ANCIENT AND VENERATED WHEN ROME WAS STILL JUST A SCATTERING OF HILLTOP SHEPHERD VILLAGES.
IT WAS IN A FORM LIKE THIS THAT I SUCKLED THE INFANTS ROMULUS AND REMUS, AND SO GAVE BIRTH TO THE CITY ABOVE US. ONE BROTHER KILLED THE OTHER, TURNED SHEPHERDS INTO CONQUERORS, AND SET THE CITY THAT WOULD BEAR HIS NAME ON A PATH THAT WAS NEVER INTENDED TO BE.
ROME HAS NEW GODS NOW - GODS OF ANGER AND BLOODSHED - AND THE PRESENCE OF OTHER POWERS AND THEIR SERVANTS WITHIN THE CITY'S BOUNDARIES IS LITTLE TOLERATED.

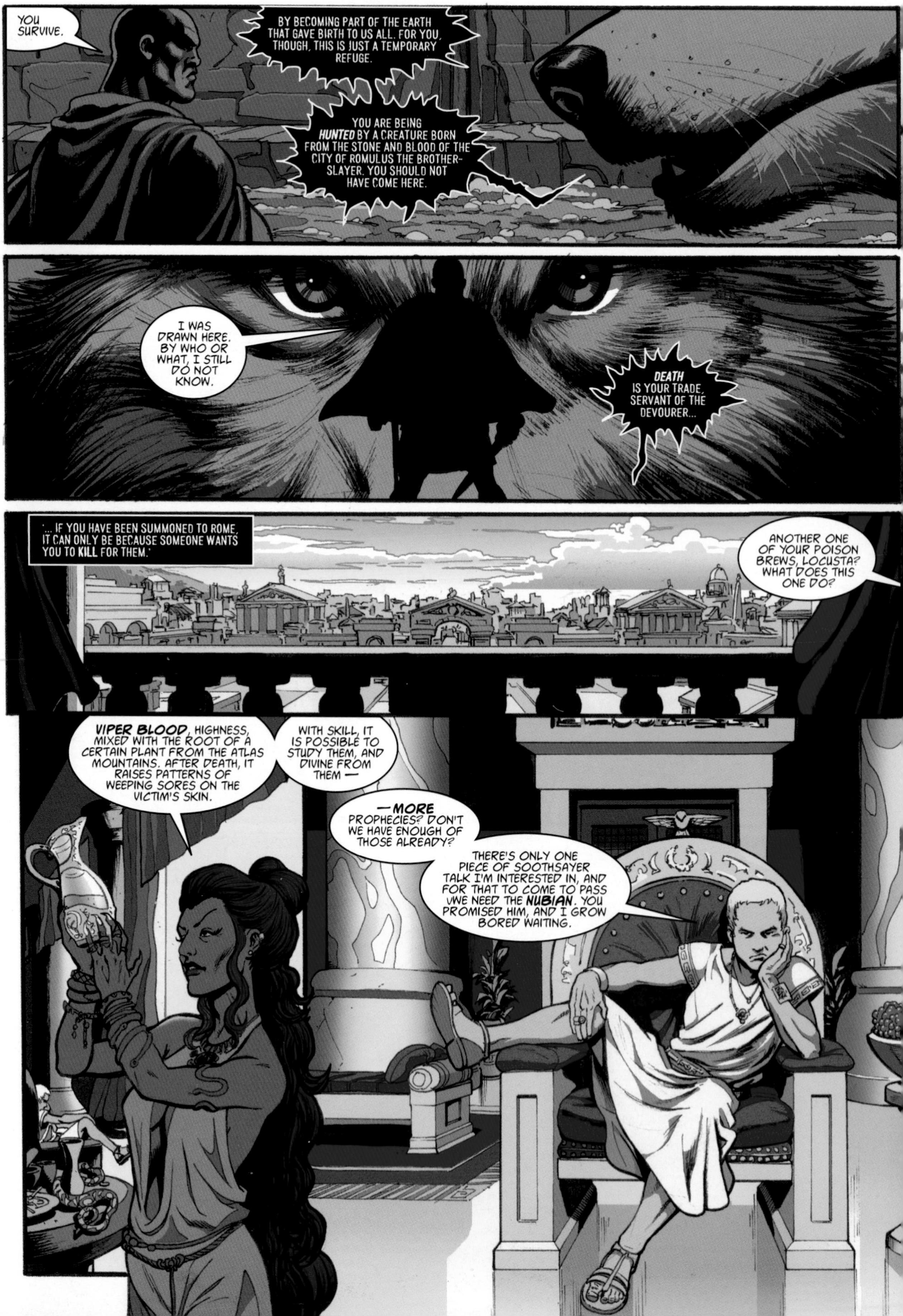
YOU SURVIVE.
BY BECOMING PART OF THE EARTH THAT GAVE BIRTH TO US ALL. FOR YOU, THOUGH, THIS IS JUST A TEMPORARY REFUGE.
YOU ARE BEING HUNTED BY A CREATURE BORN FROM THE STONE AND BLOOD OF THE CITY OF ROMULUS THE BROTHER-SLAYER. YOU SHOULD NOT HAVE COME HERE.
I WAS DRAWN HERE. BY WHO OR WHAT, I STILL DO NOT KNOW.
DEATH IS YOUR TRADE, SERVANT OF THE DEVOURER...
'... IF YOU HAVE BEEN SUMMONED TO ROME, IT CAN ONLY BE BECAUSE SOMEONE WANTS YOU TO KILL FOR THEM.'
ANOTHER ONE OF YOUR POISON BREWS, LOCUSTA? WHAT DOES THIS ONE DO?
VIPER BLOOD, HIGHNESS, MIXED WITH THE ROOT OF A CERTAIN PLANT FROM THE ATLAS MOUNTAINS. AFTER DEATH, IT RAISES PATTERNS OF WEEPING SORES ON THE VICTIM'S SKIN.
WITH SKILL, IT IS POSSIBLE TO STUDY THEM, AND DIVINE FROM THEM —
—MORE PROPHECIES? DON'T WE HAVE ENOUGH OF THOSE ALREADY?
THERE'S ONLY ONE PIECE OF SOOTHSAYER TALK I'M INTERESTED IN, AND FOR THAT TO COME TO PASS WE NEED THE NUBIAN. YOU PROMISED HIM, AND I GROW BORED WAITING.

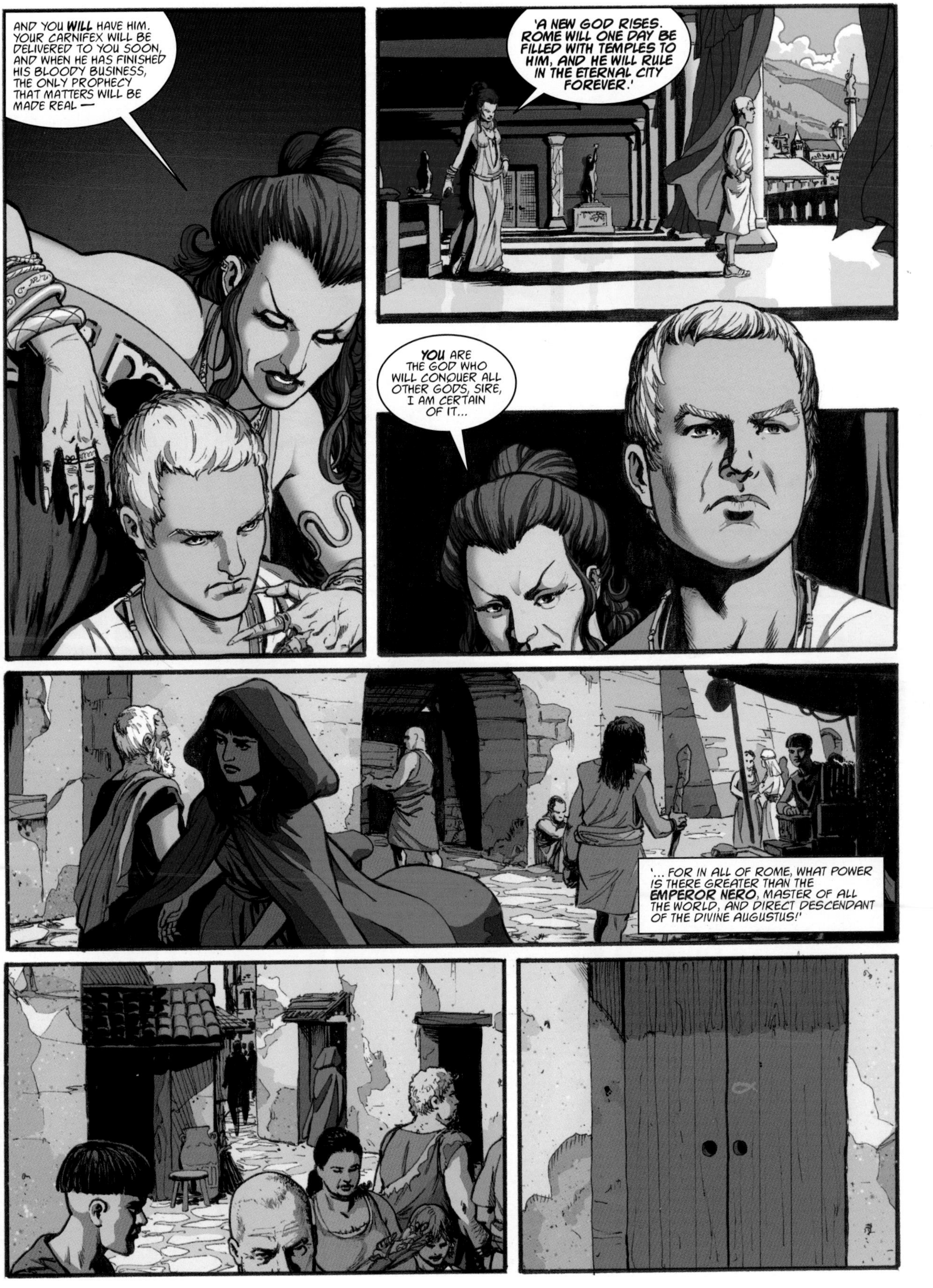

AND YOU WILL HAVE HIM. YOUR CARNIFEX WILL BE DELIVERED TO YOU SOON, AND WHEN HE HAS FINISHED HIS BLOODY BUSINESS, THE ONLY PROPHECY THAT MATTERS WILL BE MADE REAL —
'A NEW GOD RISES. ROME WILL ONE DAY BE FILLED WITH TEMPLES TO HIM, AND HE WILL RULE IN THE ETERNAL CITY FOREVER.'
YOU ARE THE GOD WHO WILL CONQUER ALL OTHER GODS, SIRE, I AM CERTAIN OF IT...
'... FOR IN ALL OF ROME, WHAT POWER IS THERE GREATER THAN THE EMPEROR NERO, MASTER OF ALL THE WORLD, AND DIRECT DESCENDANT OF THE DIVINE AUGUSTUS!'

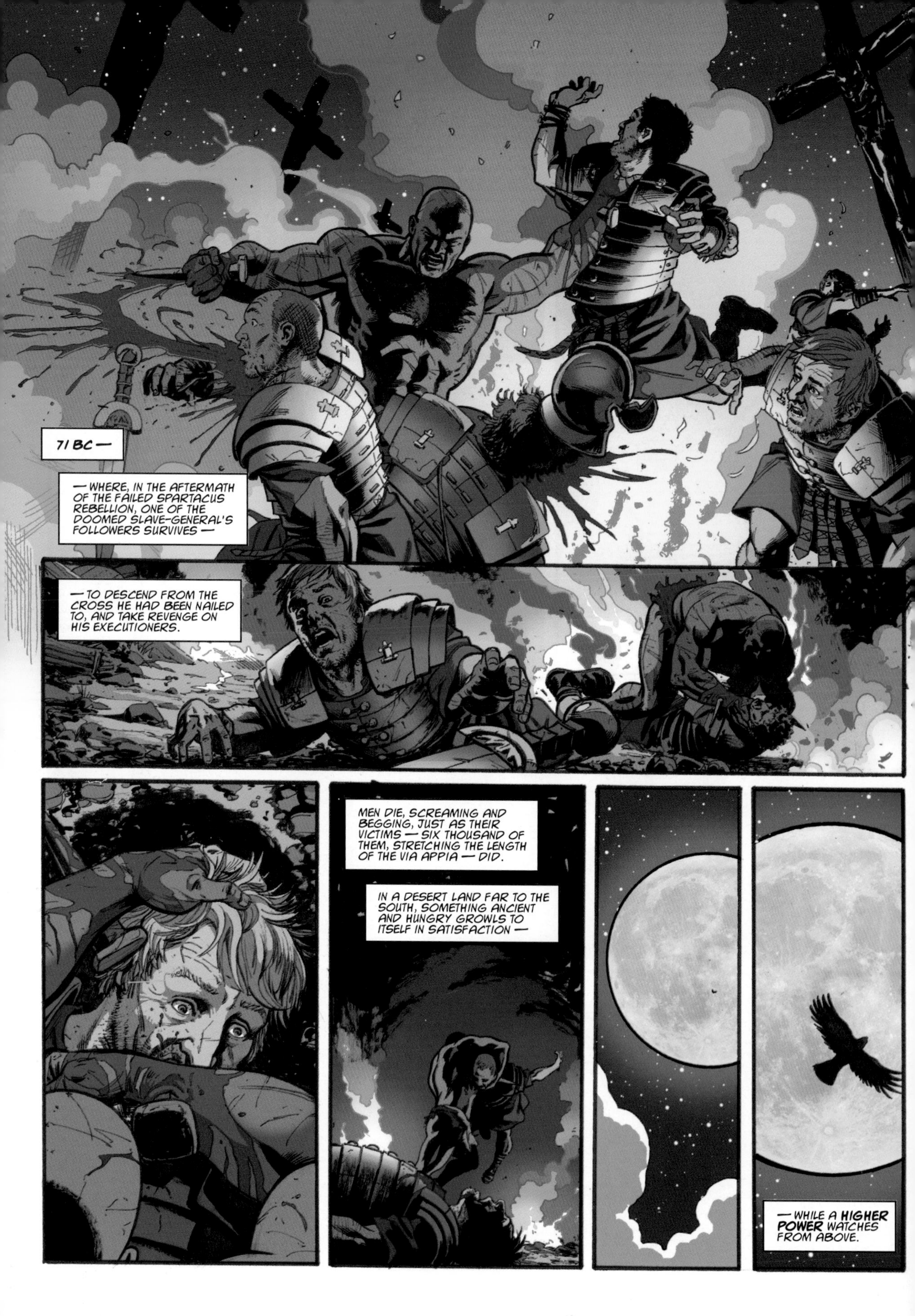
71 BC —
— WHERE, IN THE AFTERMATH OF THE FAILED SPARTACUS REBELLION, ONE OF THE DOOMED SLAVE-GENERAL'S FOLLOWERS SURVIVES —
— TO DESCEND FROM THE CROSS HE HAD BEEN NAILED TO, AND TAKE REVENGE ON HIS EXECUTIONERS.
MEN DIE, SCREAMING AND BEGGING, JUST AS THEIR VICTIMS — SIX THOUSAND OF THEM, STRETCHING THE LENGTH OF THE VIA APPIA — DID.
IN A DESERT LAND FAR TO THE SOUTH, SOMETHING ANCIENT AND HUNGRY GROWLS TO ITSELF IN SATISFACTION —
— WHILE A **HIGHER POWER** WATCHES FROM ABOVE.

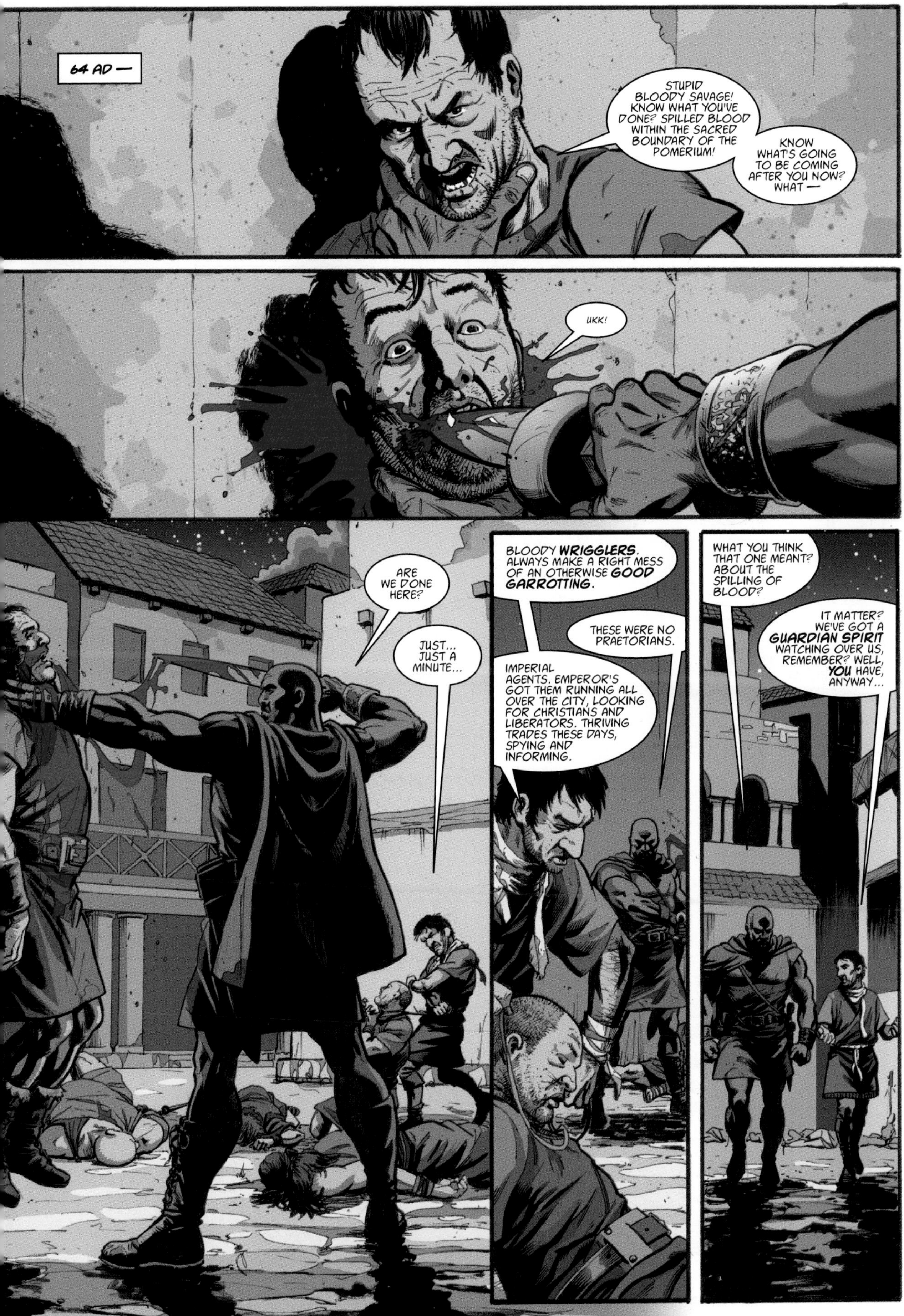
64 AD —
STUPID BLOODY SAVAGE! KNOW WHAT YOU'VE DONE? SPILLED BLOOD WITHIN THE SACRED BOUNDARY OF THE POMERIUM!
KNOW WHAT'S GOING TO BE COMING AFTER YOU NOW? WHAT —
UKK!
ARE WE DONE HERE?
JUST... JUST A MINUTE...
BLOODY WRIGGLERS. ALWAYS MAKE A RIGHT MESS OF AN OTHERWISE GOOD GARROTTING.
THESE WERE NO PRAETORIANS.
IMPERIAL AGENTS. EMPEROR'S GOT THEM RUNNING ALL OVER THE CITY, LOOKING FOR CHRISTIANS AND LIBERATORS. THRIVING TRADES THESE DAYS, SPYING AND INFORMING.
WHAT YOU THINK THAT ONE MEANT? ABOUT THE SPILLING OF BLOOD?
IT MATTER? WE'VE GOT A GUARDIAN SPIRIT WATCHING OVER US, REMEMBER? WELL, YOU HAVE, ANYWAY...

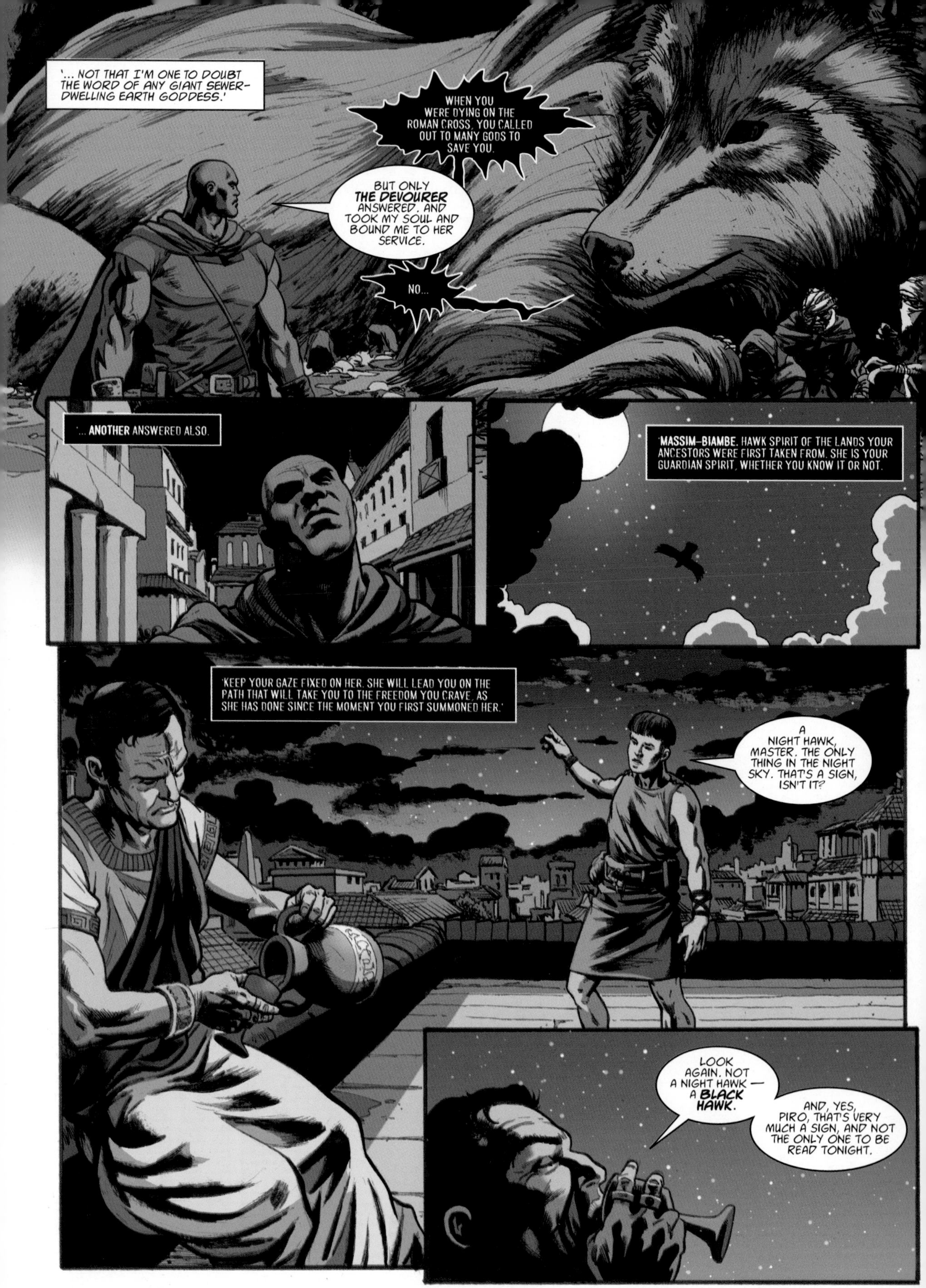
'... NOT THAT I'M ONE TO DOUBT THE WORD OF ANY GIANT SEWER-DWELLING EARTH GODDESS.'
WHEN YOU WERE DYING ON THE ROMAN CROSS, YOU CALLED OUT TO MANY GODS TO SAVE YOU.
BUT ONLY THE DEVOURER ANSWERED. AND TOOK MY SOUL AND BOUND ME TO HER SERVICE.
NO...
'... ANOTHER ANSWERED ALSO.
'MASSIM-BIAMBE. HAWK SPIRIT OF THE LANDS YOUR ANCESTORS WERE FIRST TAKEN FROM. SHE IS YOUR GUARDIAN SPIRIT, WHETHER YOU KNOW IT OR NOT.
'KEEP YOUR GAZE FIXED ON HER. SHE WILL LEAD YOU ON THE PATH THAT WILL TAKE YOU TO THE FREEDOM YOU CRAVE, AS SHE HAS DONE SINCE THE MOMENT YOU FIRST SUMMONED HER.'
A NIGHT HAWK, MASTER. THE ONLY THING IN THE NIGHT SKY. THAT'S A SIGN, ISN'T IT?
LOOK AGAIN. NOT A NIGHT HAWK — A BLACK HAWK.
AND, YES, PIRO, THAT'S VERY MUCH A SIGN, AND NOT THE ONLY ONE TO BE READ TONIGHT.

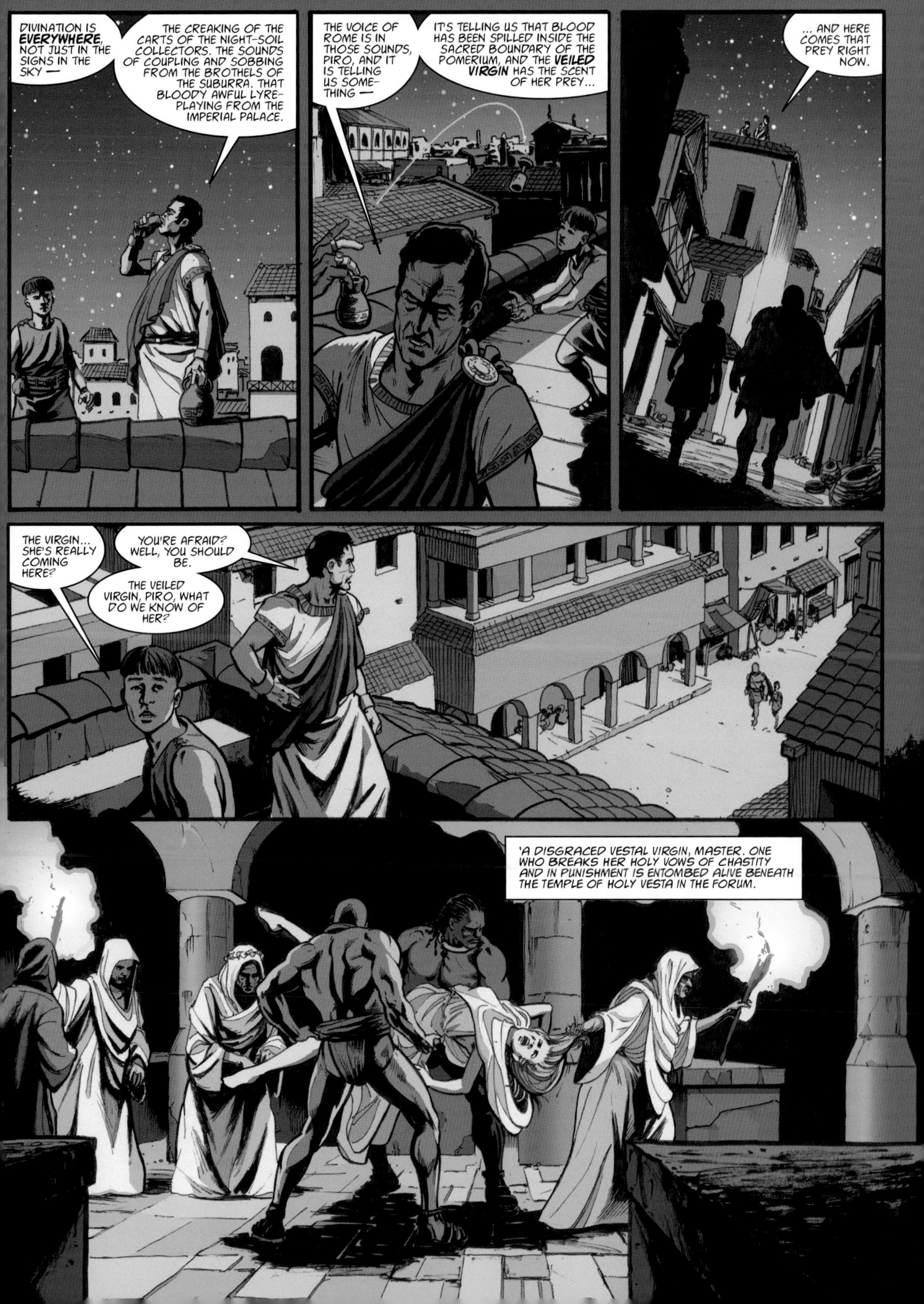
DIVINATION IS **EVERYWHERE**, NOT JUST IN THE SIGNS IN THE SKY —
THE CREAKING OF THE CARTS OF THE NIGHT-SOIL COLLECTORS. THE SOUNDS OF COUPLING AND SOBBING FROM THE BROTHELS OF THE SUBURRA. THAT BLOODY AWFUL LYRE-PLAYING FROM THE IMPERIAL PALACE.
THE VOICE OF ROME IS IN THOSE SOUNDS, PIRO, AND IT IS TELLING US SOME-THING —
IT'S TELLING US THAT BLOOD HAS BEEN SPILLED INSIDE THE SACRED BOUNDARY OF THE POMERIUM, AND THE **VEILED VIRGIN** HAS THE SCENT OF HER PREY...
... AND HERE COMES THAT PREY RIGHT NOW.
THE VIRGIN... SHE'S REALLY COMING HERE?
YOU'RE AFRAID? WELL, YOU SHOULD BE.
THE VEILED VIRGIN, PIRO, WHAT DO WE KNOW OF HER?
'A DISGRACED VESTAL VIRGIN, MASTER. ONE WHO BREAKS HER HOLY VOWS OF CHASTITY AND IN PUNISHMENT IS ENTOMBED ALIVE BENEATH THE TEMPLE OF HOLY VESTA IN THE FORUM.

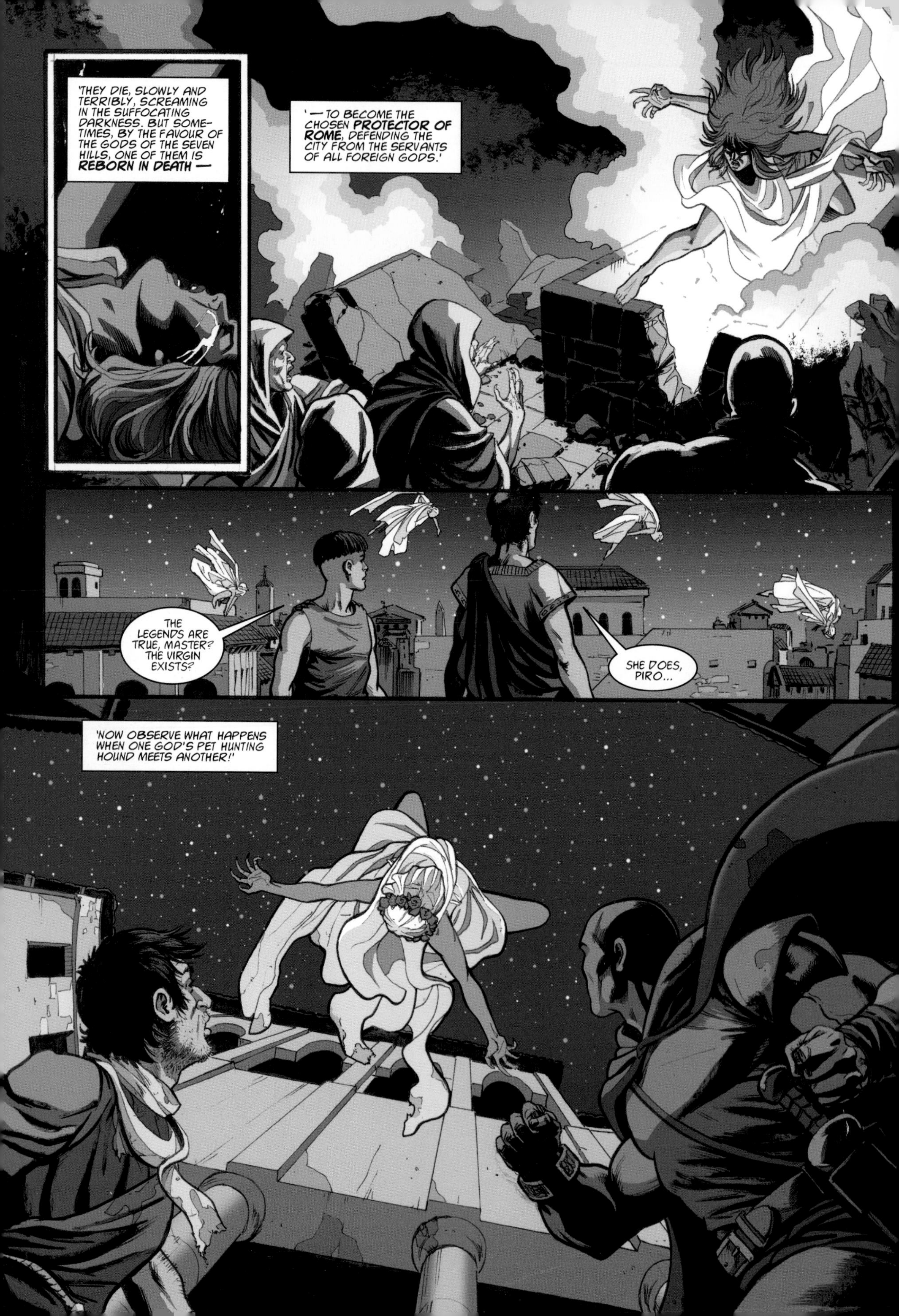
'THEY DIE, SLOWLY AND TERRIBLY, SCREAMING IN THE SUFFOCATING DARKNESS. BUT SOME-TIMES, BY THE FAVOUR OF THE GODS OF THE SEVEN HILLS, ONE OF THEM IS REBORN IN DEATH —
' — TO BECOME THE CHOSEN PROTECTOR OF ROME, DEFENDING THE CITY FROM THE SERVANTS OF ALL FOREIGN GODS.'
THE LEGENDS ARE TRUE, MASTER? THE VIRGIN EXISTS?
SHE DOES, PIRO...
'NOW OBSERVE WHAT HAPPENS WHEN ONE GOD'S PET HUNTING HOUND MEETS ANOTHER!'

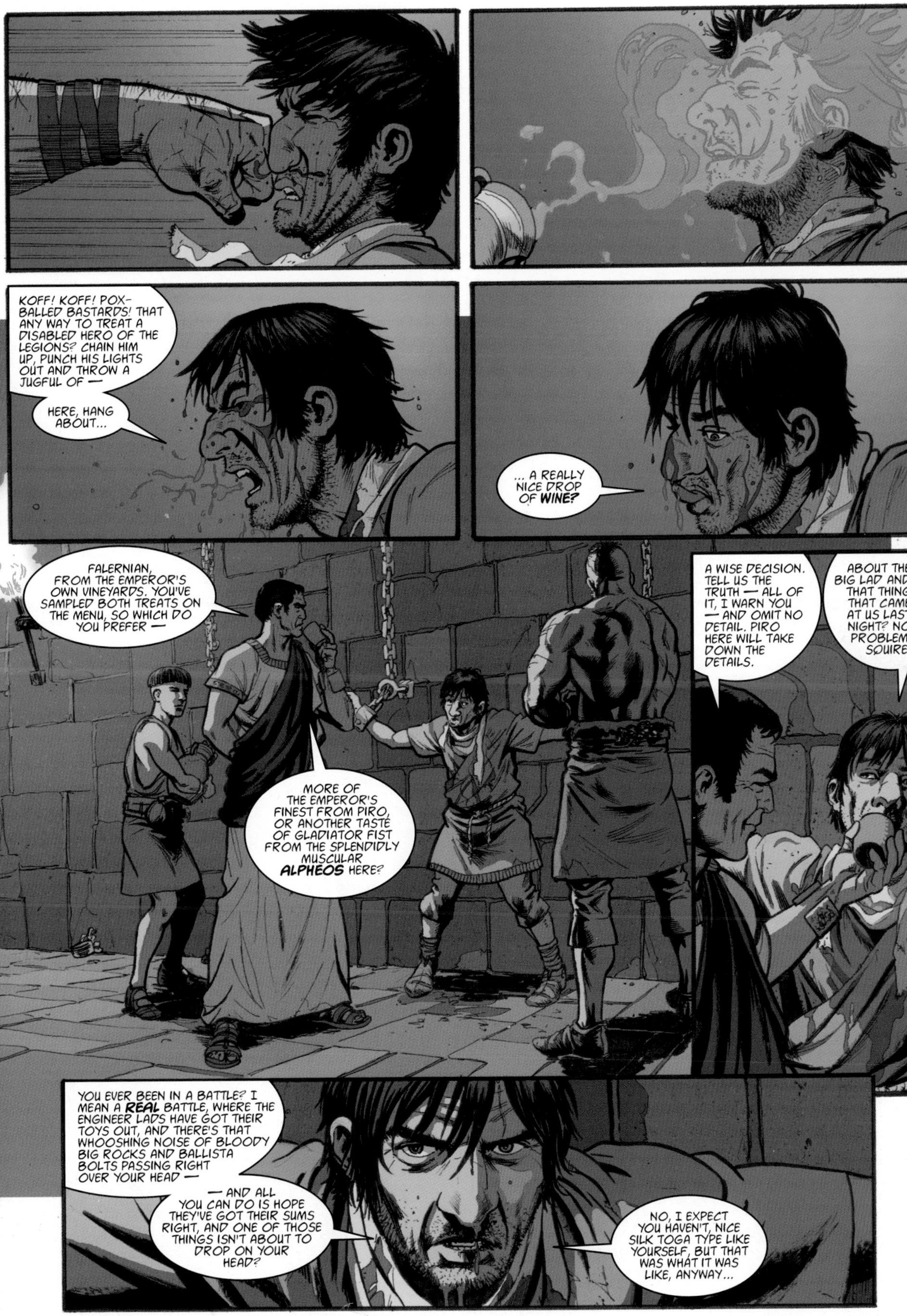
KOFF! KOFF! POX-BALLED BASTARDS! THAT ANY WAY TO TREAT A DISABLED HERO OF THE LEGIONS? CHAIN HIM UP, PUNCH HIS LIGHTS OUT AND THROW A JUGFUL OF —
HERE, HANG ABOUT...
... A REALLY NICE DROP OF WINE?
FALERNIAN, FROM THE EMPEROR'S OWN VINEYARDS. YOU'VE SAMPLED BOTH TREATS ON THE MENU, SO WHICH DO YOU PREFER —
MORE OF THE EMPEROR'S FINEST FROM PIRO, OR ANOTHER TASTE OF GLADIATOR FIST FROM THE SPLENDIDLY MUSCULAR ALPHEOS HERE?
A WISE DECISION. TELL US THE TRUTH — ALL OF IT, I WARN YOU — AND OMIT NO DETAIL. PIRO HERE WILL TAKE DOWN THE DETAILS.
ABOUT THE BIG LAD AND THAT THING THAT CAME AT US LAST NIGHT? NO PROBLEM, SQUIRE.
YOU EVER BEEN IN A BATTLE? I MEAN A REAL BATTLE, WHERE THE ENGINEER LADS HAVE GOT THEIR TOYS OUT, AND THERE'S THAT WHOOSHING NOISE OF BLOODY BIG ROCKS AND BALLISTA BOLTS PASSING RIGHT OVER YOUR HEAD —
— AND ALL YOU CAN DO IS HOPE THEY'VE GOT THEIR SUMS RIGHT, AND ONE OF THOSE THINGS ISN'T ABOUT TO DROP ON YOUR HEAD?
NO, I EXPECT YOU HAVEN'T, NICE SILK TOGA TYPE LIKE YOURSELF, BUT THAT WAS WHAT IT WAS LIKE, ANYWAY...

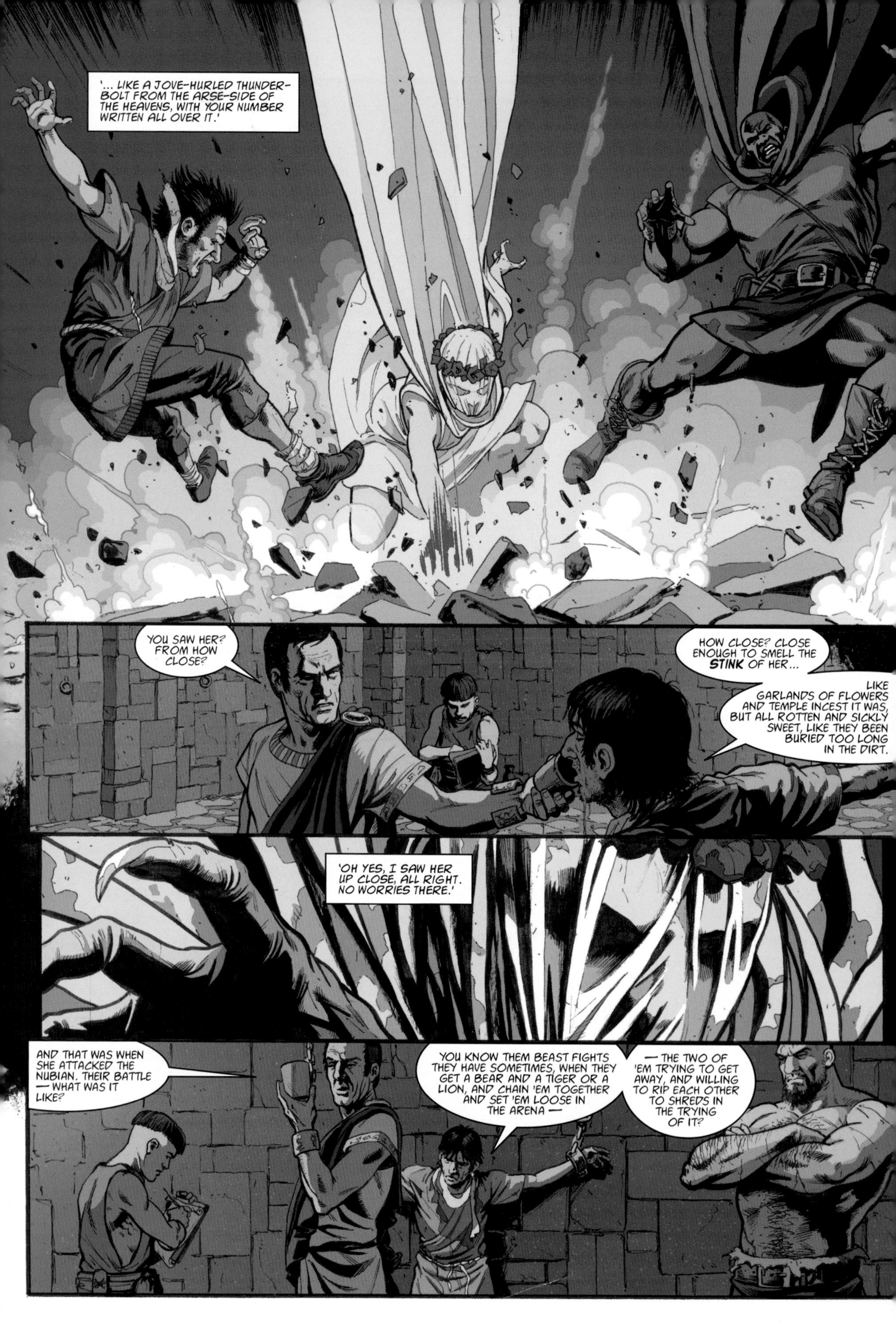
'... LIKE A JOVE-HURLED THUNDER-BOLT FROM THE ARSE-SIDE OF THE HEAVENS, WITH YOUR NUMBER WRITTEN ALL OVER IT.'
YOU SAW HER? FROM HOW CLOSE?
HOW CLOSE? CLOSE ENOUGH TO SMELL THE STINK OF HER...
LIKE GARLANDS OF FLOWERS AND TEMPLE INCEST IT WAS, BUT ALL ROTTEN AND SICKLY SWEET, LIKE THEY BEEN BURIED TOO LONG IN THE DIRT.
'OH YES, I SAW HER UP CLOSE, ALL RIGHT. NO WORRIES THERE.'
AND THAT WAS WHEN SHE ATTACKED THE NUBIAN. THEIR BATTLE — WHAT WAS IT LIKE?
YOU KNOW THEM BEAST FIGHTS THEY HAVE SOMETIMES, WHEN THEY GET A BEAR AND A TIGER OR A LION, AND CHAIN 'EM TOGETHER AND SET 'EM LOOSE IN THE ARENA —
— THE TWO OF 'EM TRYING TO GET AWAY, AND WILLING TO RIP EACH OTHER TO SHREDS IN THE TRYING OF IT?

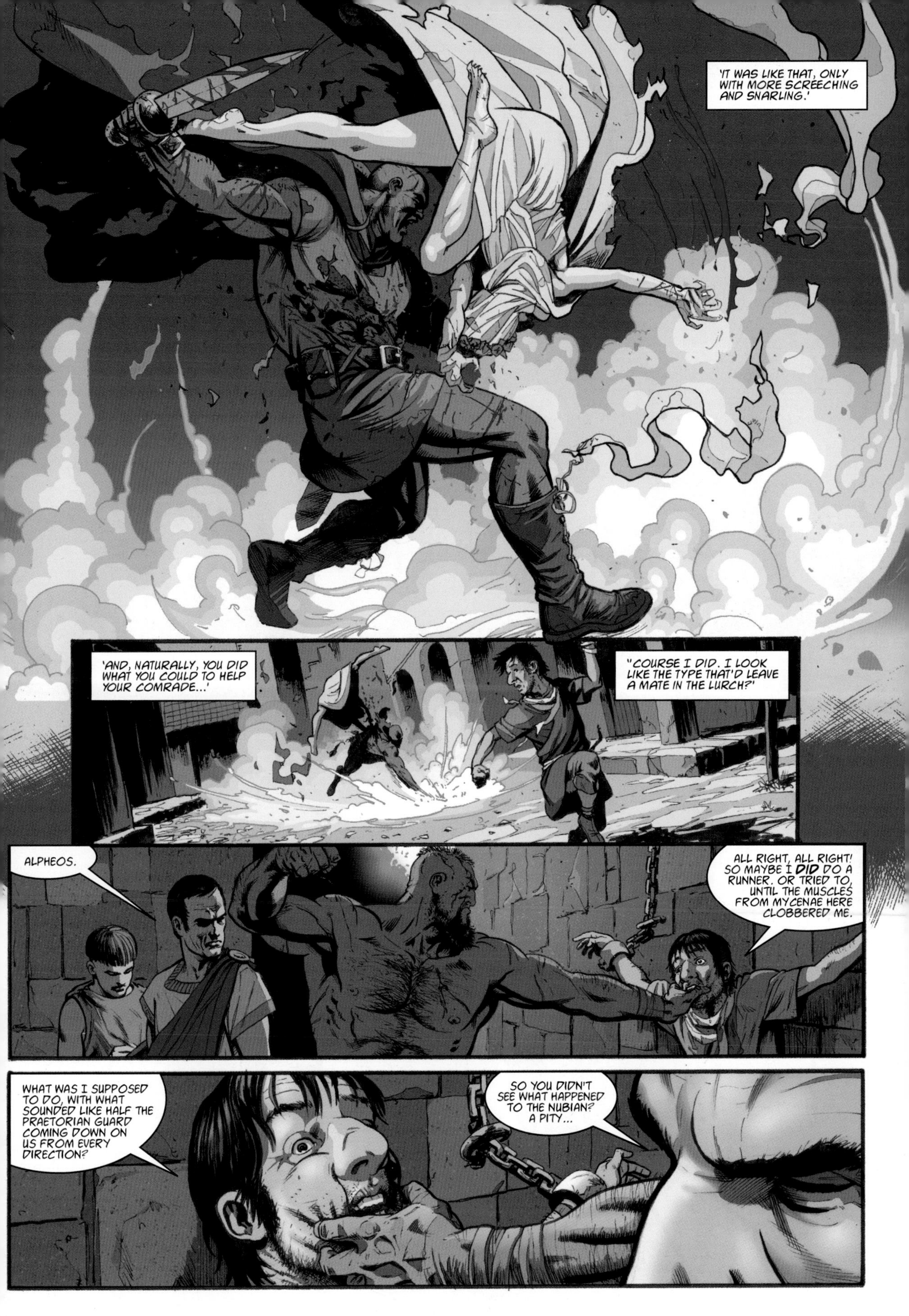
'IT WAS LIKE THAT, ONLY WITH MORE SCREECHING AND SNARLING.'
'AND, NATURALLY, YOU DID WHAT YOU COULD TO HELP YOUR COMRADE...'
"COURSE I DID. I LOOK LIKE THE TYPE THAT'D LEAVE A MATE IN THE LURCH?'
ALPHEOS.
ALL RIGHT, ALL RIGHT! SO MAYBE I **DID** DO A RUNNER. OR TRIED TO, UNTIL THE MUSCLES FROM MYCENAE HERE CLOBBERED ME.
WHAT WAS I SUPPOSED TO DO, WITH WHAT SOUNDED LIKE HALF THE PRAETORIAN GUARD COMING DOWN ON US FROM EVERY DIRECTION?
SO YOU DIDN'T SEE WHAT HAPPENED TO THE NUBIAN? A PITY...

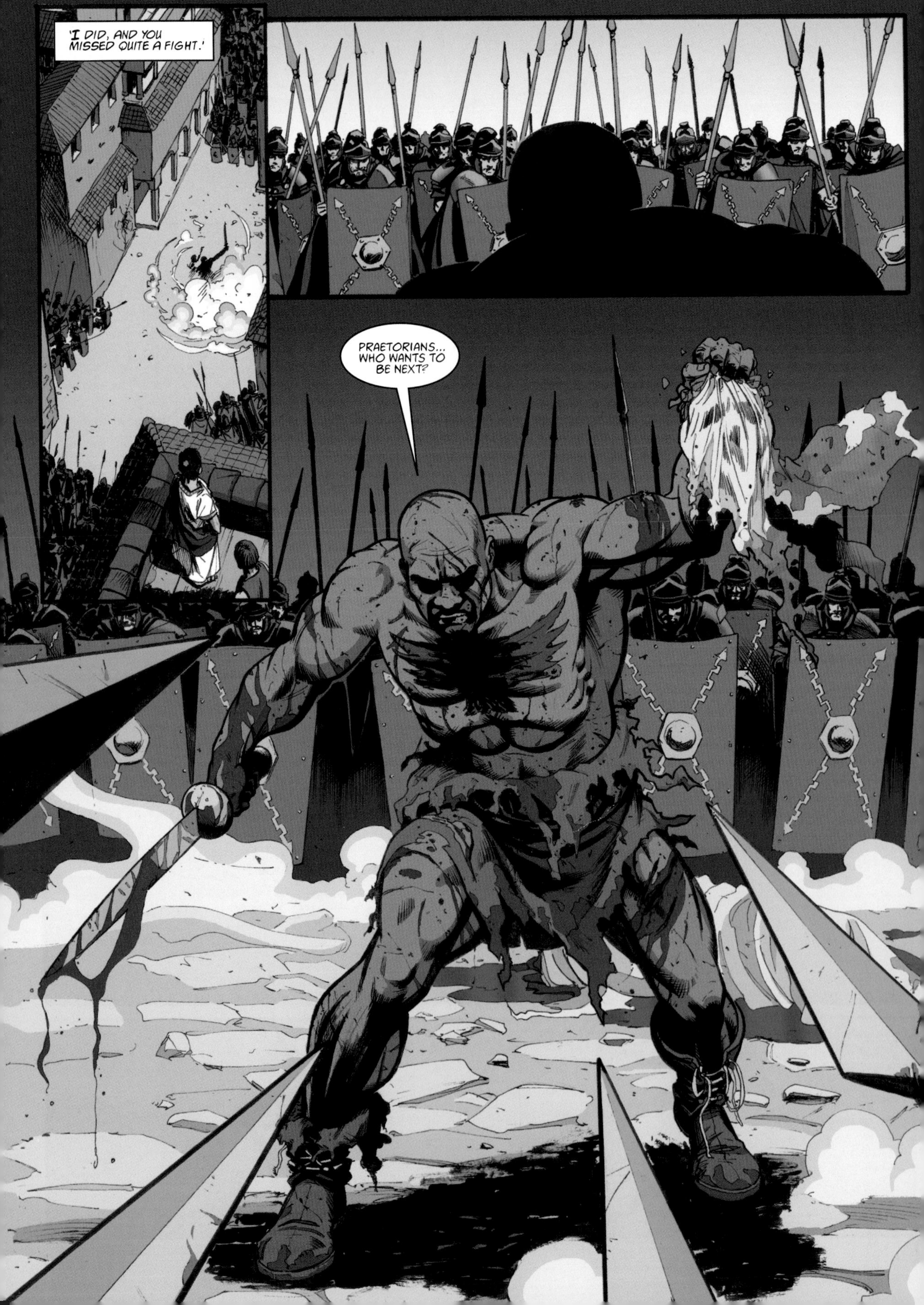
'I DID, AND YOU MISSED QUITE A FIGHT.'
PRAETORIANS... WHO WANTS TO BE NEXT?

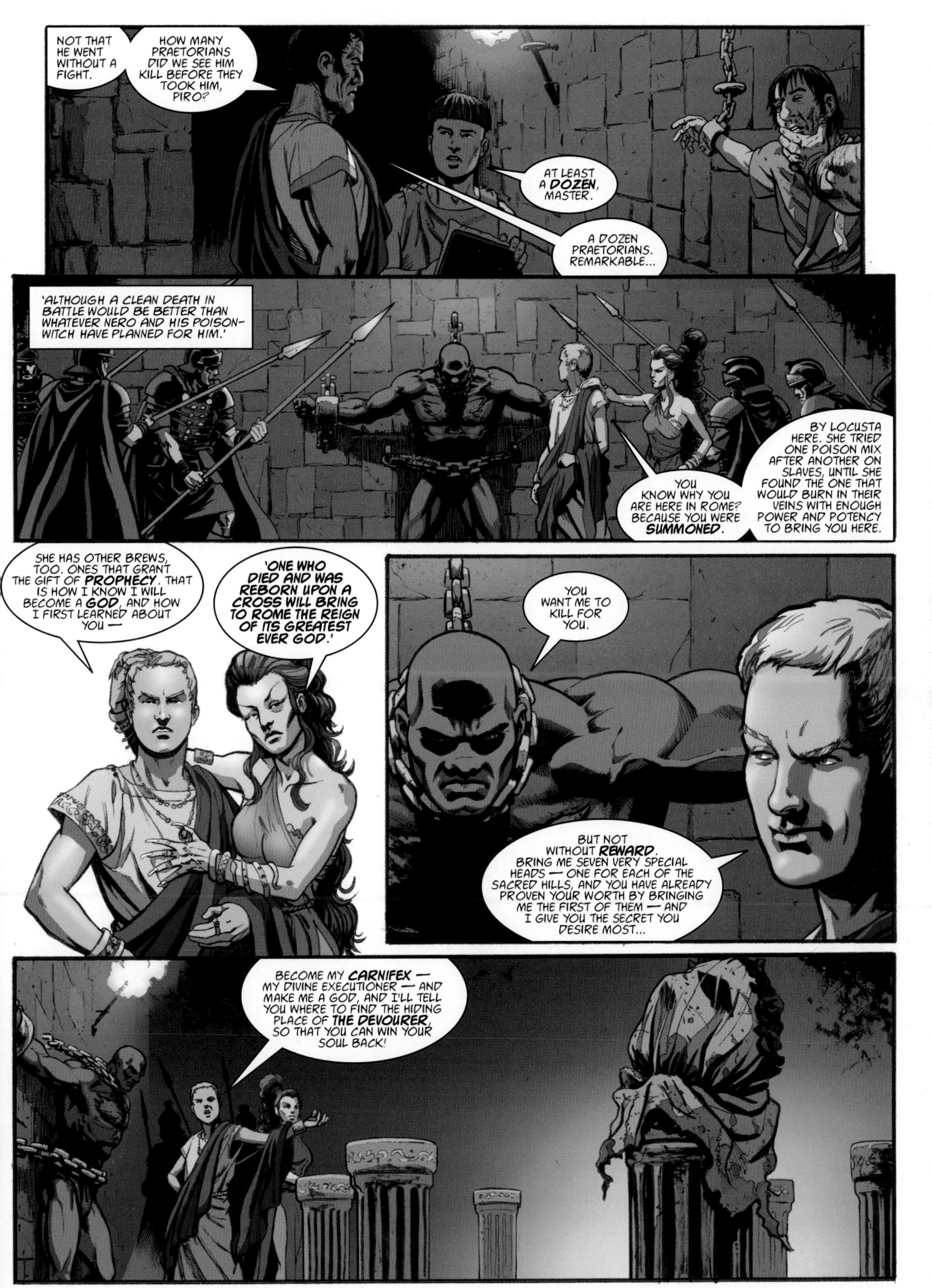
NOT THAT HE WENT WITHOUT A FIGHT.
HOW MANY PRAETORIANS DID WE SEE HIM KILL BEFORE THEY TOOK HIM, PIRO?
AT LEAST A DOZEN, MASTER.
A DOZEN PRAETORIANS. REMARKABLE...
'ALTHOUGH A CLEAN DEATH IN BATTLE WOULD BE BETTER THAN WHATEVER NERO AND HIS POISON-WITCH HAVE PLANNED FOR HIM.'
YOU KNOW WHY YOU ARE HERE IN ROME? BECAUSE YOU WERE SUMMONED.
BY LOCUSTA HERE. SHE TRIED ONE POISON MIX AFTER ANOTHER ON SLAVES, UNTIL SHE FOUND THE ONE THAT WOULD BURN IN THEIR VEINS WITH ENOUGH POWER AND POTENCY TO BRING YOU HERE.
SHE HAS OTHER BREWS, TOO. ONES THAT GRANT THE GIFT OF PROPHECY. THAT IS HOW I KNOW I WILL BECOME A GOD, AND HOW I FIRST LEARNED ABOUT YOU —
'ONE WHO DIED AND WAS REBORN UPON A CROSS WILL BRING TO ROME THE REIGN OF ITS GREATEST EVER GOD.'
YOU WANT ME TO KILL FOR YOU.
BUT NOT WITHOUT REWARD. BRING ME SEVEN VERY SPECIAL HEADS — ONE FOR EACH OF THE SACRED HILLS, AND YOU HAVE ALREADY PROVEN YOUR WORTH BY BRINGING ME THE FIRST OF THEM — AND I GIVE YOU THE SECRET YOU DESIRE MOST...
BECOME MY CARNIFEX — MY DIVINE EXECUTIONER — AND MAKE ME A GOD, AND I'LL TELL YOU WHERE TO FIND THE HIDING PLACE OF THE DEVOURER, SO THAT YOU CAN WIN YOUR SOUL BACK!

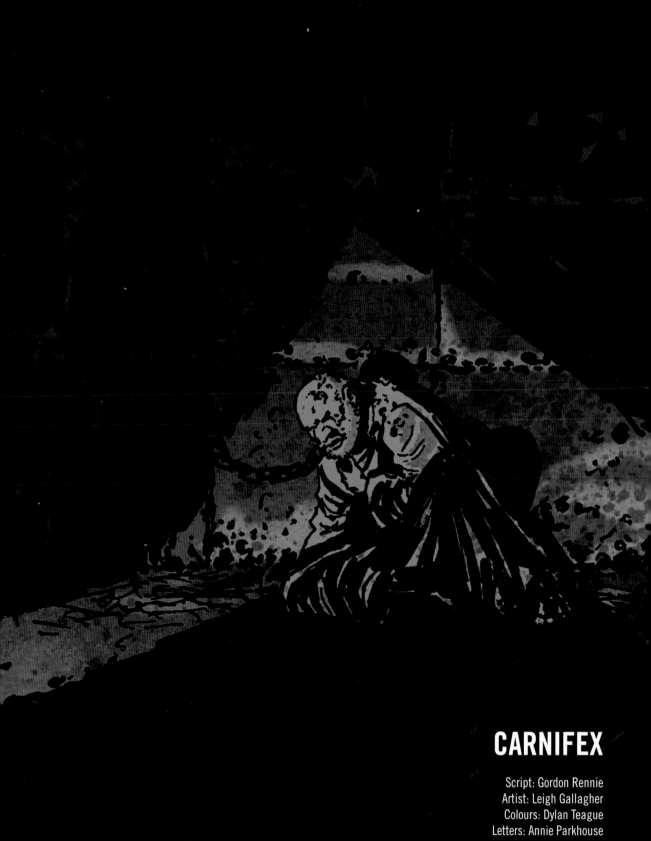

CARNIFEX

Script: Gordon Rennie
Artist: Leigh Gallagher
Colours: Dylan Teague
Letters: Annie Parkhouse

Originaly published in *2000 AD* Progs 1890-1899

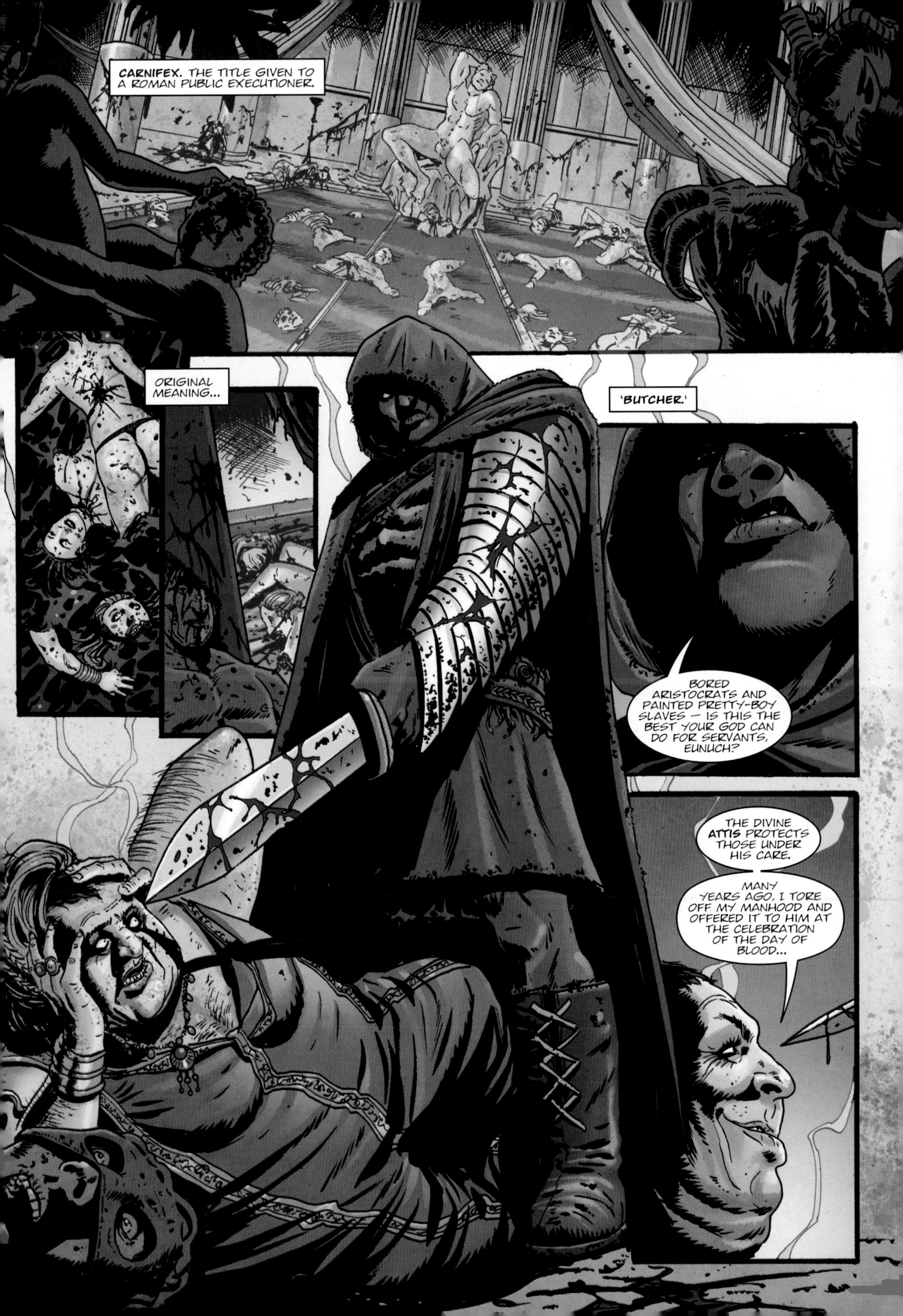
CARNIFEX. THE TITLE GIVEN TO A ROMAN PUBLIC EXECUTIONER.
ORIGINAL MEANING...
'BUTCHER.'
BORED ARISTOCRATS AND PAINTED PRETTY-BOY SLAVES — IS THIS THE BEST YOUR GOD CAN DO FOR SERVANTS, EUNUCH?
THE DIVINE ATTIS PROTECTS THOSE UNDER HIS CARE.
MANY YEARS AGO, I TORE OFF MY MANHOOD AND OFFERED IT TO HIM AT THE CELEBRATION OF THE DAY OF BLOOD...

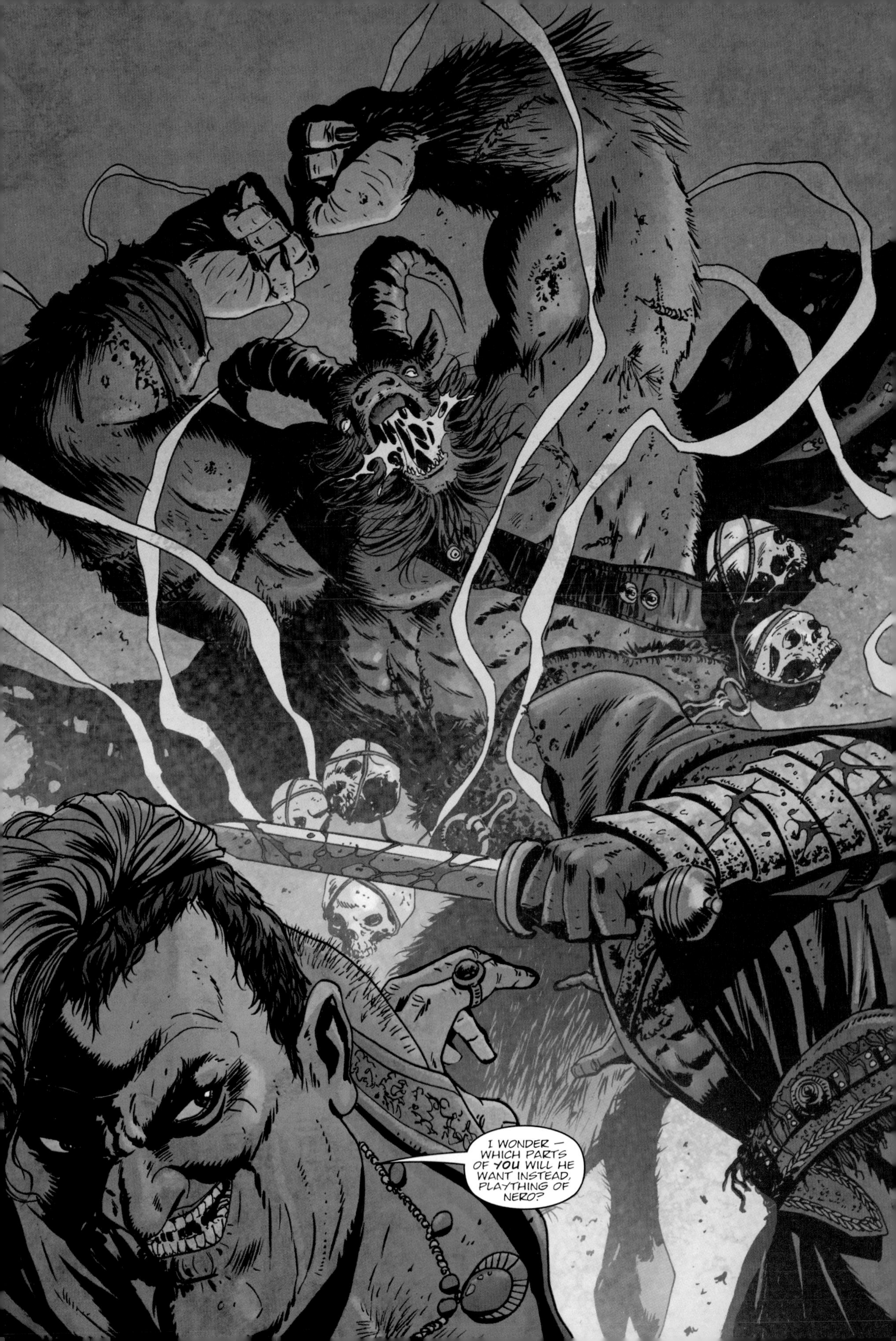
I WONDER — WHICH PARTS OF YOU WILL HE WANT INSTEAD, PLAYTHING OF NERO?

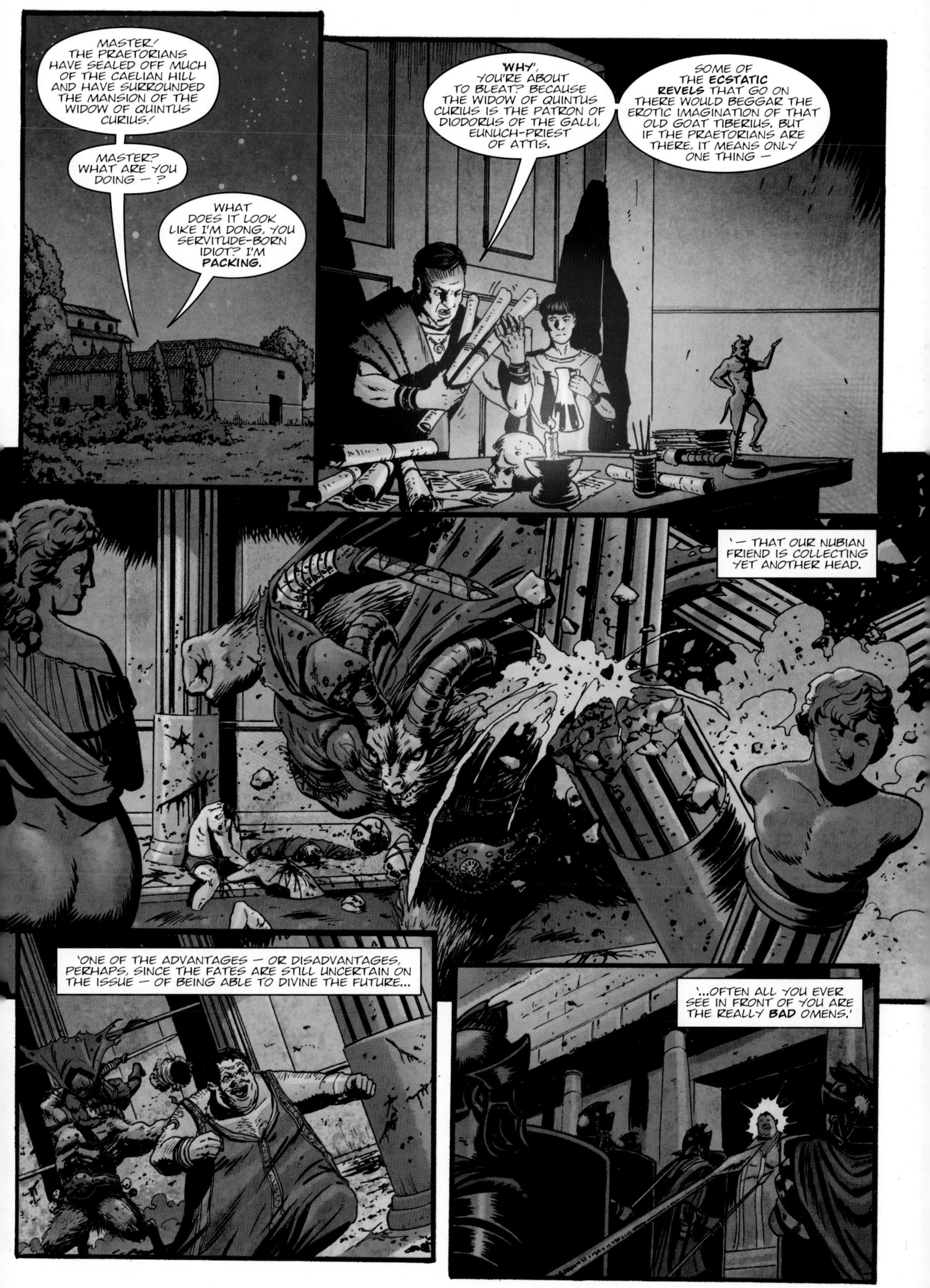
MASTER! THE PRAETORIANS HAVE SEALED OFF MUCH OF THE CAELIAN HILL AND HAVE SURROUNDED THE MANSION OF THE WIDOW OF QUINTUS CURIUS!
MASTER? WHAT ARE YOU DOING — ?
WHAT DOES IT LOOK LIKE I'M DONG, YOU SERVITUDE-BORN IDIOT? I'M **PACKING.**
'WHY', YOU'RE ABOUT TO BLEAT? BECAUSE THE WIDOW OF QUINTUS CURIUS IS THE PATRON OF DIODORUS OF THE GALLI, EUNUCH-PRIEST OF ATTIS.
SOME OF THE **ECSTATIC REVELS** THAT GO ON THERE WOULD BEGGAR THE EROTIC IMAGINATION OF THAT OLD GOAT TIBERIUS. BUT IF THE PRAETORIANS ARE THERE, IT MEANS ONLY ONE THING —
'— THAT OUR NUBIAN FRIEND IS COLLECTING YET ANOTHER HEAD.
'ONE OF THE ADVANTAGES — OR DISADVANTAGES, PERHAPS, SINCE THE FATES ARE STILL UNCERTAIN ON THE ISSUE — OF BEING ABLE TO DIVINE THE FUTURE...
'...OFTEN ALL YOU EVER SEE IN FRONT OF YOU ARE THE REALLY **BAD** OMENS.'

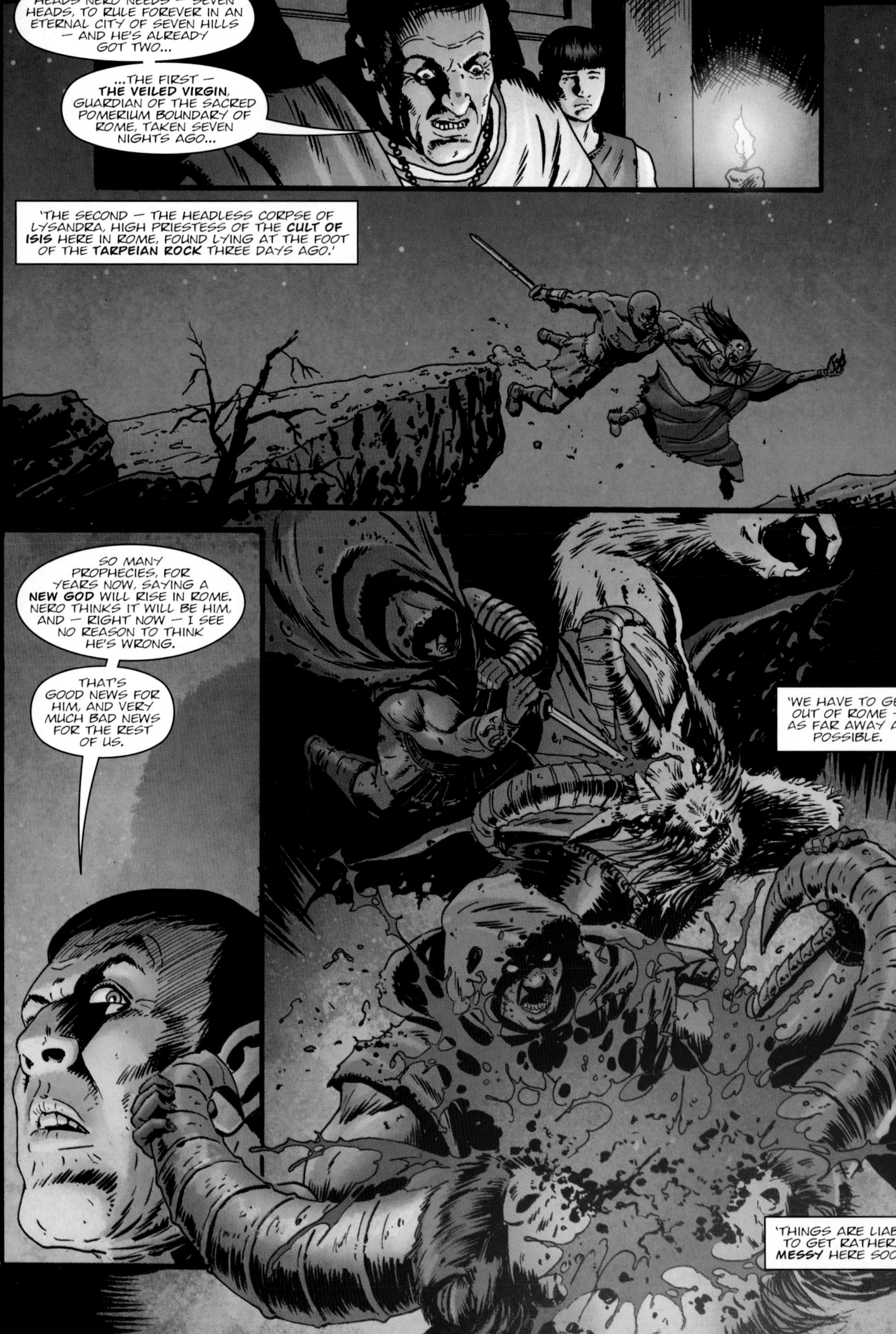
SEVEN GODLY HEADS NERO NEEDS — SEVEN HEADS, TO RULE FOREVER IN AN ETERNAL CITY OF SEVEN HILLS — AND HE'S ALREADY GOT TWO...
...THE FIRST — THE VEILED VIRGIN, GUARDIAN OF THE SACRED POMERIUM BOUNDARY OF ROME, TAKEN SEVEN NIGHTS AGO...
'THE SECOND — THE HEADLESS CORPSE OF LYSANDRA, HIGH PRIESTESS OF THE CULT OF ISIS HERE IN ROME, FOUND LYING AT THE FOOT OF THE TARPEIAN ROCK THREE DAYS AGO.'
SO MANY PROPHECIES, FOR YEARS NOW, SAYING A NEW GOD WILL RISE IN ROME. NERO THINKS IT WILL BE HIM, AND — RIGHT NOW — I SEE NO REASON TO THINK HE'S WRONG.
THAT'S GOOD NEWS FOR HIM, AND VERY MUCH BAD NEWS FOR THE REST OF US.
'WE HAVE TO GET OUT OF ROME — AS FAR AWAY AS POSSIBLE.
'THINGS ARE LIABLE TO GET RATHER... MESSY HERE SOON.'

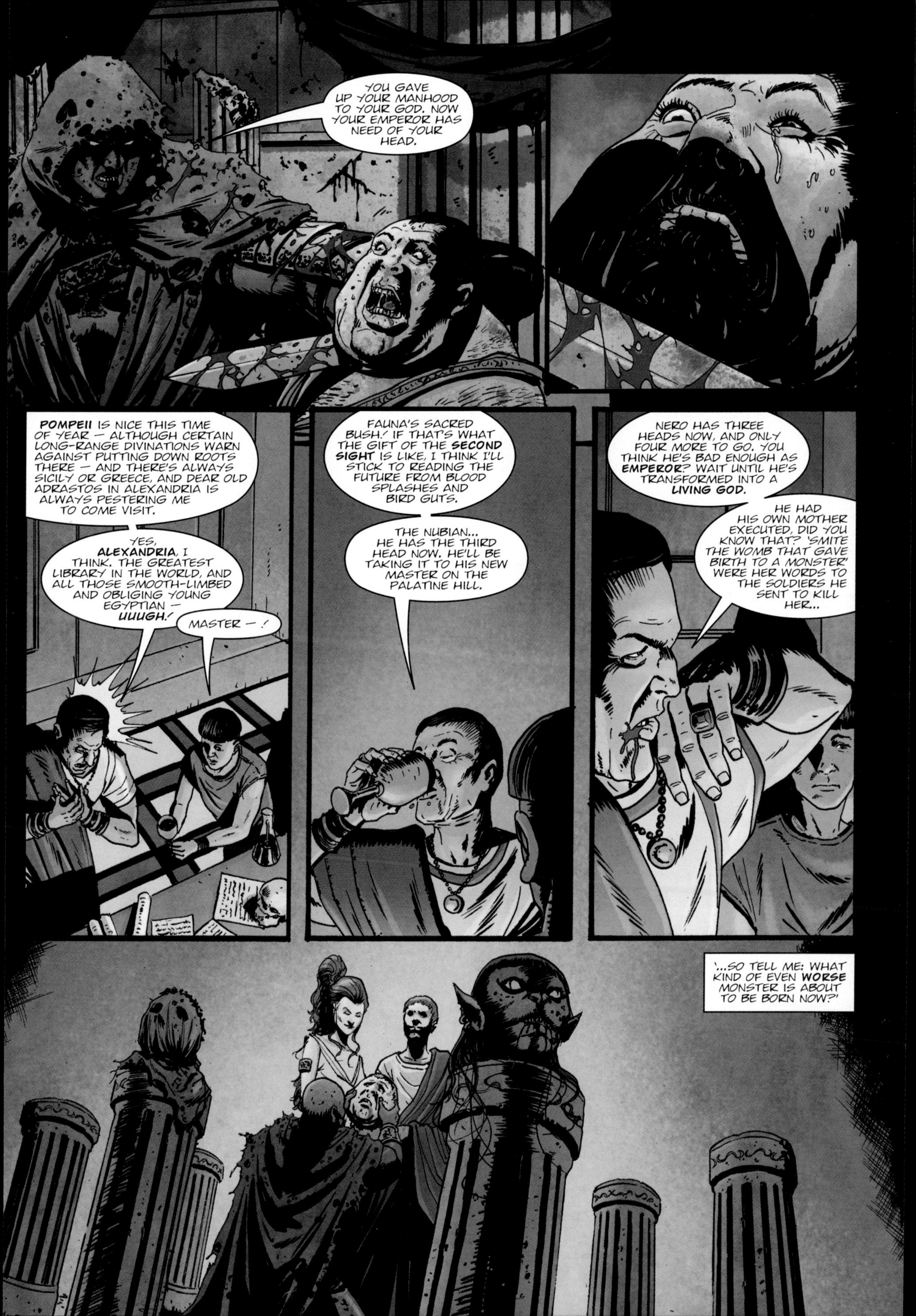
YOU GAVE UP YOUR MANHOOD TO YOUR GOD. NOW YOUR EMPEROR HAS NEED OF YOUR HEAD.
POMPEII IS NICE THIS TIME OF YEAR — ALTHOUGH CERTAIN LONG-RANGE DIVINATIONS WARN AGAINST PUTTING DOWN ROOTS THERE — AND THERE'S ALWAYS SICILY OR GREECE, AND DEAR OLD ADRASTOS IN ALEXANDRIA IS ALWAYS PESTERING ME TO COME VISIT.
YES, ALEXANDRIA, I THINK. THE GREATEST LIBRARY IN THE WORLD, AND ALL THOSE SMOOTH-LIMBED AND OBLIGING YOUNG EGYPTIAN — UUUGH!
MASTER — !
FAUNA'S SACRED BUSH! IF THAT'S WHAT THE GIFT OF THE SECOND SIGHT IS LIKE, I THINK I'LL STICK TO READING THE FUTURE FROM BLOOD SPLASHES AND BIRD GUTS.
THE NUBIAN... HE HAS THE THIRD HEAD NOW. HE'LL BE TAKING IT TO HIS NEW MASTER ON THE PALATINE HILL.
NERO HAS THREE HEADS NOW, AND ONLY FOUR MORE TO GO. YOU THINK HE'S BAD ENOUGH AS EMPEROR? WAIT UNTIL HE'S TRANSFORMED INTO A LIVING GOD.
HE HAD HIS OWN MOTHER EXECUTED, DID YOU KNOW THAT? 'SMITE THE WOMB THAT GAVE BIRTH TO A MONSTER' WERE HER WORDS TO THE SOLDIERS HE SENT TO KILL HER...
'...SO TELL ME: WHAT KIND OF EVEN WORSE MONSTER IS ABOUT TO BE BORN NOW?'

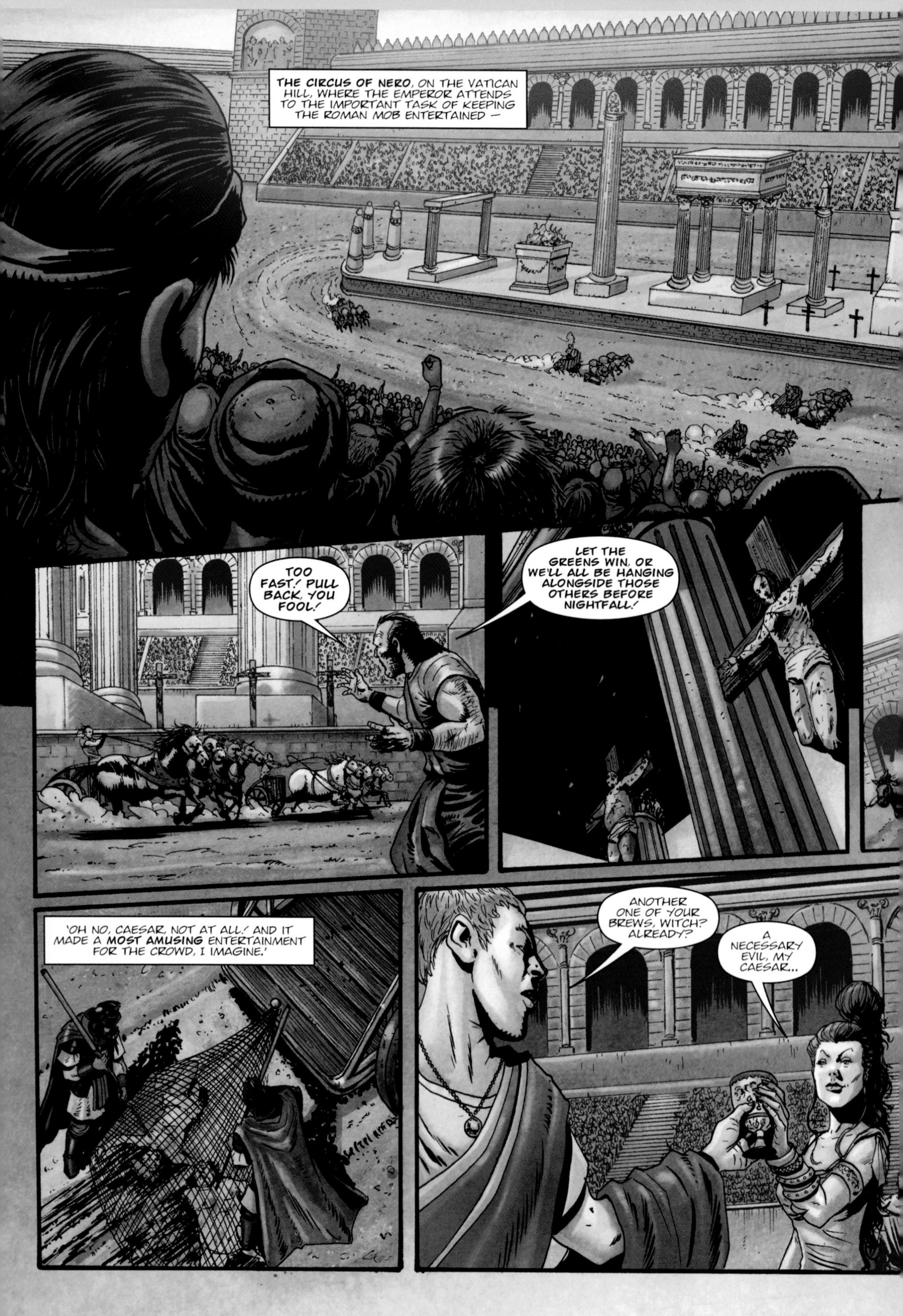
THE CIRCUS OF NERO, ON THE VATICAN HILL, WHERE THE EMPEROR ATTENDS TO THE IMPORTANT TASK OF KEEPING THE ROMAN MOB ENTERTAINED —
TOO FAST! PULL BACK, YOU FOOL!
LET THE GREENS WIN, OR WE'LL ALL BE HANGING ALONGSIDE THOSE OTHERS BEFORE NIGHTFALL!
'OH NO, CAESAR, NOT AT ALL.' AND IT MADE A MOST AMUSING ENTERTAINMENT FOR THE CROWD, I IMAGINE.'
ANOTHER ONE OF YOUR BREWS, WITCH? ALREADY?
A NECESSARY EVIL, MY CAESAR...

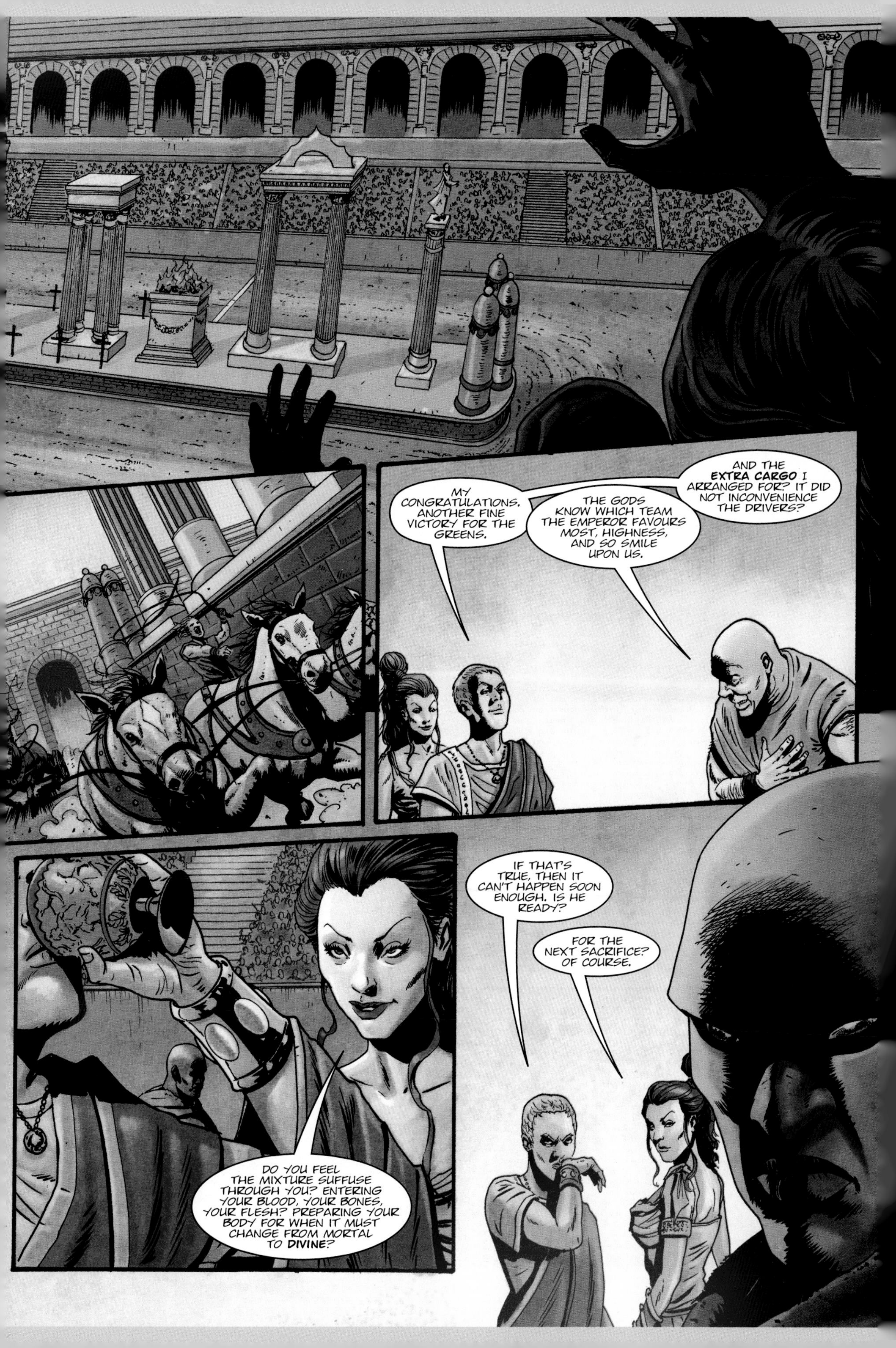
MY CONGRATULATIONS. ANOTHER FINE VICTORY FOR THE GREENS.
AND THE **EXTRA CARGO** I ARRANGED FOR? IT DID NOT INCONVENIENCE THE DRIVERS?
THE GODS KNOW WHICH TEAM THE EMPEROR FAVOURS MOST, HIGHNESS, AND SO SMILE UPON US.
DO YOU FEEL THE MIXTURE SUFFUSE THROUGH YOU? ENTERING YOUR BLOOD, YOUR BONES, YOUR FLESH? PREPARING YOUR BODY FOR WHEN IT MUST CHANGE FROM MORTAL TO **DIVINE**?
IF THAT'S TRUE, THEN IT CAN'T HAPPEN SOON ENOUGH. IS HE READY?
FOR THE NEXT SACRIFICE? OF COURSE.

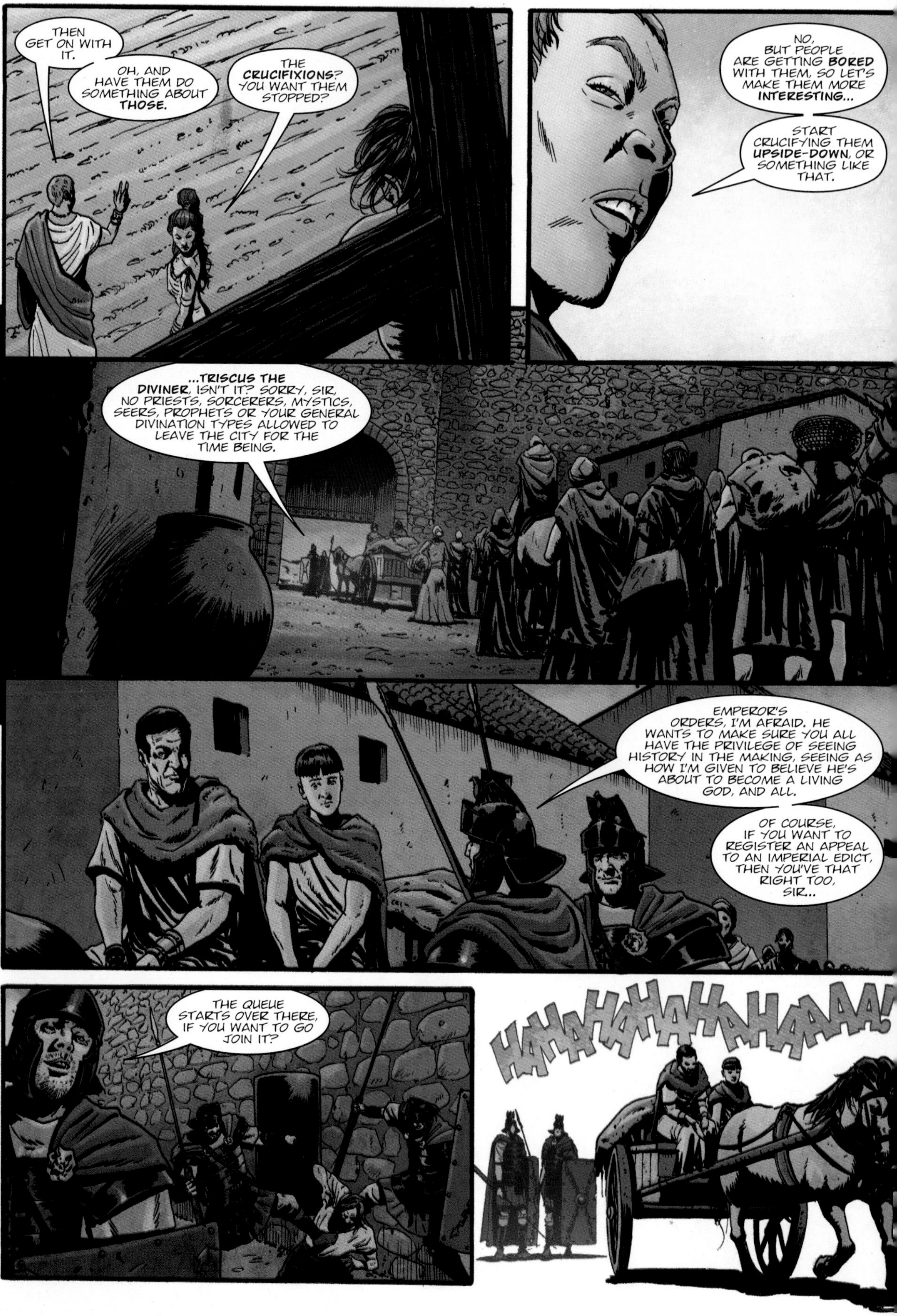
THEN GET ON WITH IT.
OH, AND HAVE THEM DO SOMETHING ABOUT THOSE.
THE CRUCIFIXIONS? YOU WANT THEM STOPPED?
NO, BUT PEOPLE ARE GETTING BORED WITH THEM, SO LET'S MAKE THEM MORE INTERESTING...
START CRUCIFYING THEM UPSIDE-DOWN, OR SOMETHING LIKE THAT.
...TRISCUS THE DIVINER, ISN'T IT? SORRY, SIR, NO PRIESTS, SORCERERS, MYSTICS, SEERS, PROPHETS OR YOUR GENERAL DIVINATION TYPES ALLOWED TO LEAVE THE CITY FOR THE TIME BEING.
EMPEROR'S ORDERS, I'M AFRAID. HE WANTS TO MAKE SURE YOU ALL HAVE THE PRIVILEGE OF SEEING HISTORY IN THE MAKING, SEEING AS HOW I'M GIVEN TO BELIEVE HE'S ABOUT TO BECOME A LIVING GOD, AND ALL.
OF COURSE, IF YOU WANT TO REGISTER AN APPEAL TO AN IMPERIAL EDICT, THEN YOU'VE THAT RIGHT TOO, SIR...
THE QUEUE STARTS OVER THERE, IF YOU WANT TO GO JOIN IT?
HAHAHAHAHAHAHAAAA!

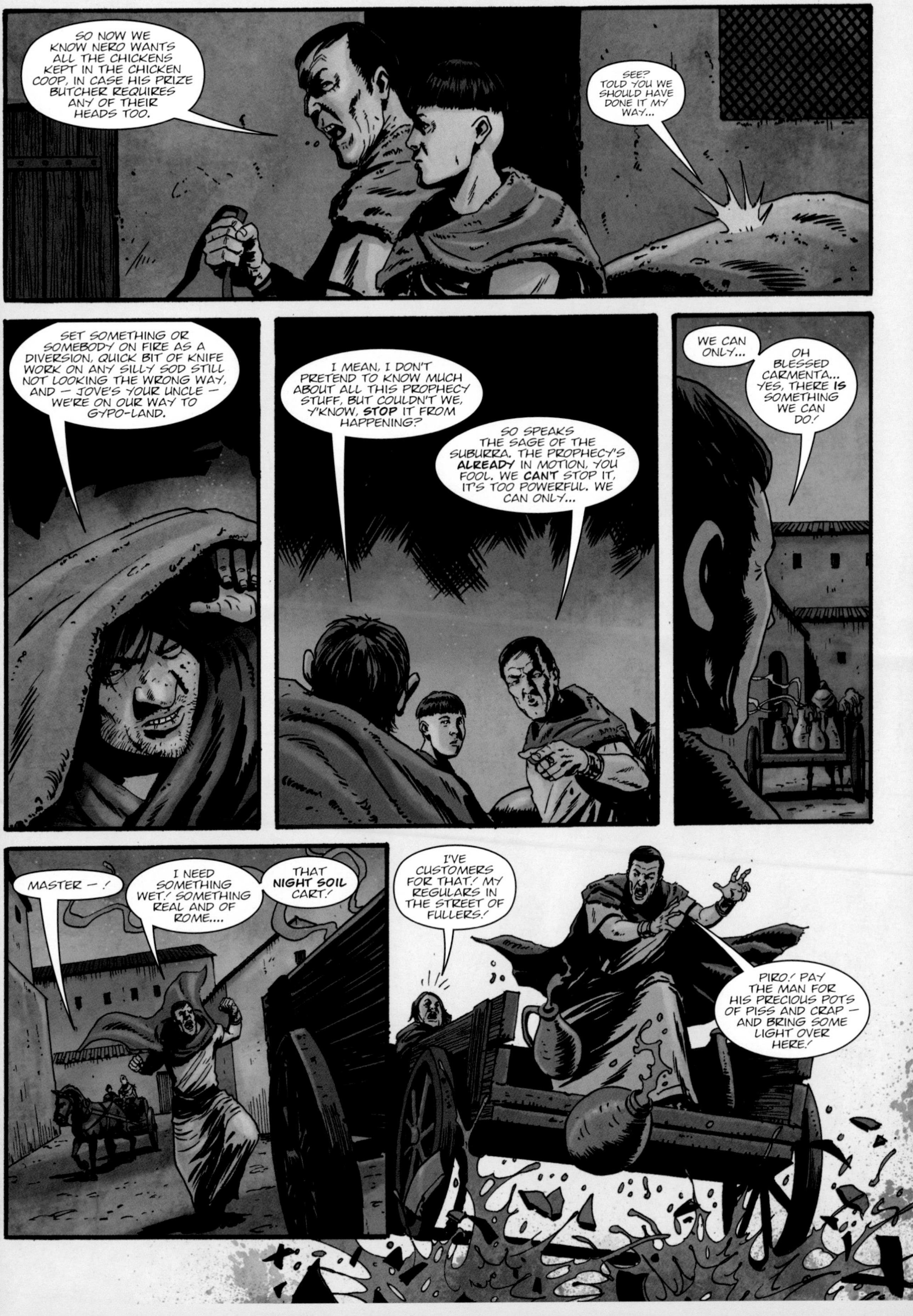
SO NOW WE KNOW NERO WANTS ALL THE CHICKENS KEPT IN THE CHICKEN COOP, IN CASE HIS PRIZE BUTCHER REQUIRES ANY OF THEIR HEADS TOO.
SEE? TOLD YOU WE SHOULD HAVE DONE IT MY WAY...
SET SOMETHING OR SOMEBODY ON FIRE AS A DIVERSION, QUICK BIT OF KNIFE WORK ON ANY SILLY SOD STILL NOT LOOKING THE WRONG WAY, AND — JOVE'S YOUR UNCLE — WE'RE ON OUR WAY TO GYPO-LAND.
I MEAN, I DON'T PRETEND TO KNOW MUCH ABOUT ALL THIS PROPHECY STUFF, BUT COULDN'T WE, Y'KNOW, STOP IT FROM HAPPENING?
SO SPEAKS THE SAGE OF THE SUBURRA. THE PROPHECY'S ALREADY IN MOTION, YOU FOOL. WE CAN'T STOP IT, IT'S TOO POWERFUL. WE CAN ONLY...
WE CAN ONLY...
OH BLESSED CARMENTA... YES, THERE IS SOMETHING WE CAN DO!
MASTER — !
I NEED SOMETHING WET! SOMETHING REAL AND OF ROME....
THAT NIGHT SOIL CART!
I'VE CUSTOMERS FOR THAT! MY REGULARS IN THE STREET OF FULLERS!
PIRO! PAY THE MAN FOR HIS PRECIOUS POTS OF PISS AND CRAP — AND BRING SOME LIGHT OVER HERE!

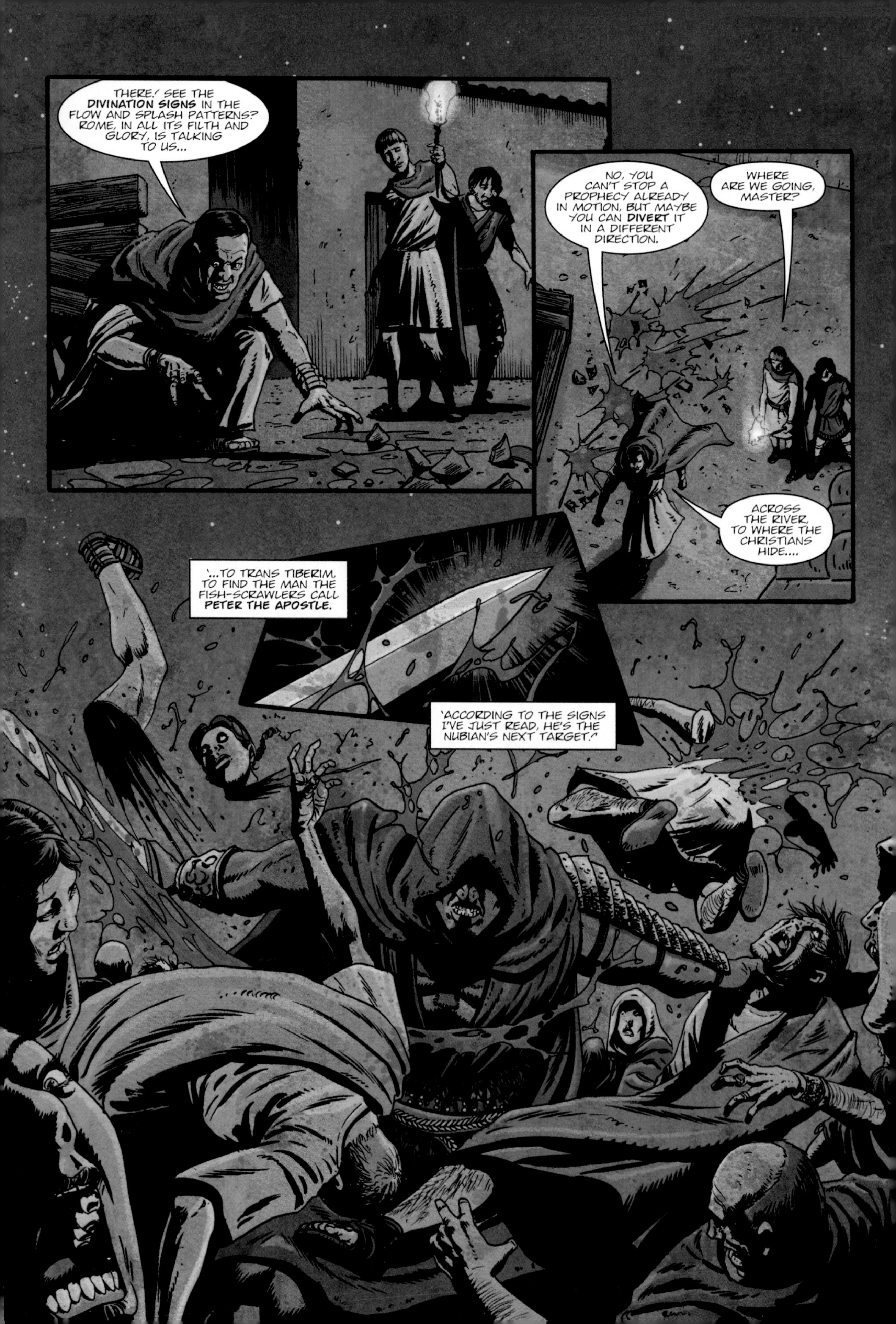
THERE! SEE THE DIVINATION SIGNS IN THE FLOW AND SPLASH PATTERNS? ROME, IN ALL ITS FILTH AND GLORY, IS TALKING TO US...
NO, YOU CAN'T STOP A PROPHECY ALREADY IN MOTION, BUT MAYBE YOU CAN DIVERT IT IN A DIFFERENT DIRECTION.
WHERE ARE WE GOING, MASTER?
ACROSS THE RIVER, TO WHERE THE CHRISTIANS HIDE....
'...TO TRANS TIBERIM, TO FIND THE MAN THE FISH-SCRAWLERS CALL PETER THE APOSTLE.
'ACCORDING TO THE SIGNS I'VE JUST READ, HE'S THE NUBIAN'S NEXT TARGET.'

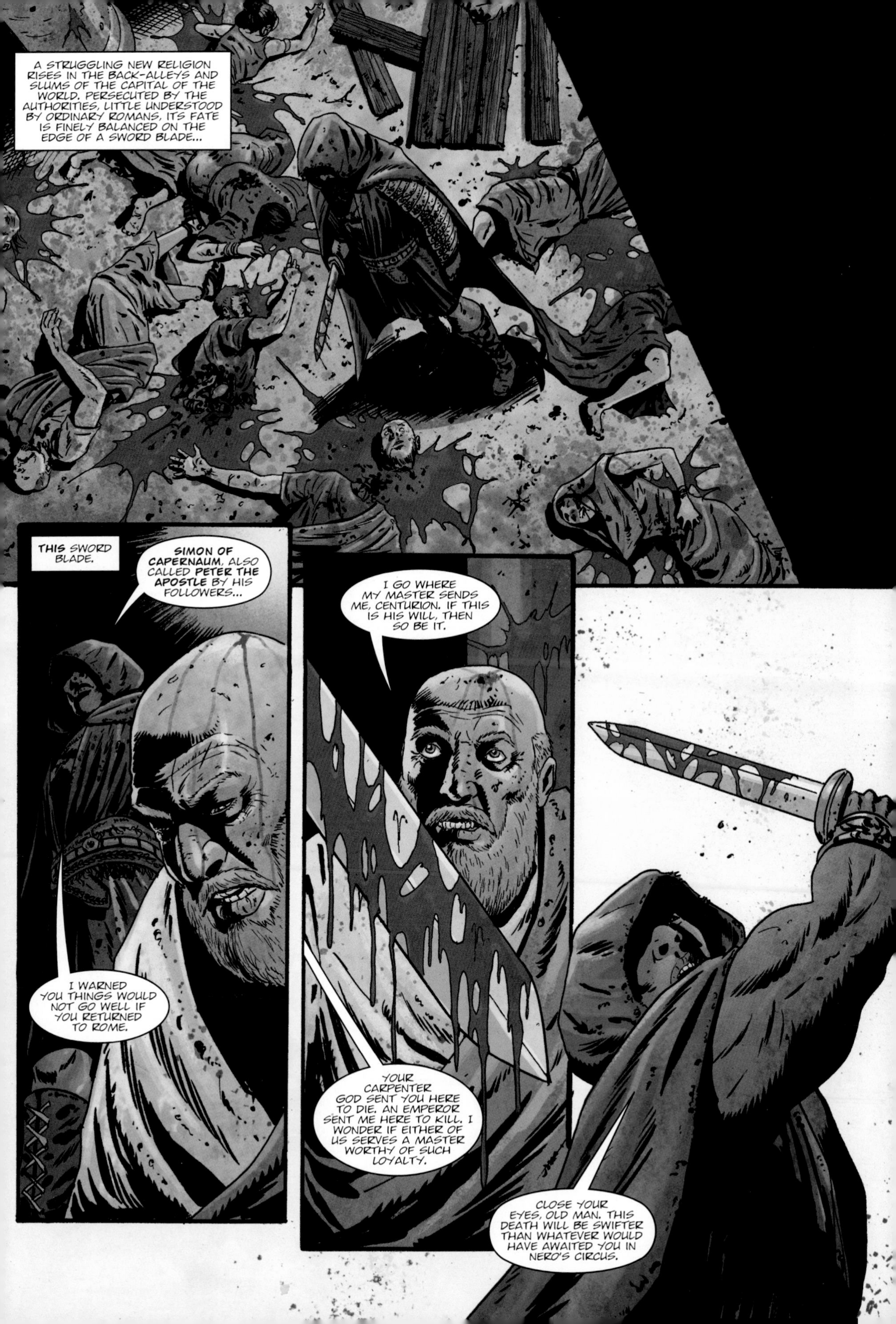
A STRUGGLING NEW RELIGION RISES IN THE BACK-ALLEYS AND SLUMS OF THE CAPITAL OF THE WORLD. PERSECUTED BY THE AUTHORITIES, LITTLE UNDERSTOOD BY ORDINARY ROMANS, ITS FATE IS FINELY BALANCED ON THE EDGE OF A SWORD BLADE...
THIS SWORD BLADE.
SIMON OF CAPERNAUM, ALSO CALLED PETER THE APOSTLE BY HIS FOLLOWERS...
I WARNED YOU THINGS WOULD NOT GO WELL IF YOU RETURNED TO ROME.
I GO WHERE MY MASTER SENDS ME, CENTURION. IF THIS IS HIS WILL, THEN SO BE IT.
YOUR CARPENTER GOD SENT YOU HERE TO DIE. AN EMPEROR SENT ME HERE TO KILL. I WONDER IF EITHER OF US SERVES A MASTER WORTHY OF SUCH LOYALTY.
CLOSE YOUR EYES, OLD MAN. THIS DEATH WILL BE SWIFTER THAN WHATEVER WOULD HAVE AWAITED YOU IN NERO'S CIRCUS.

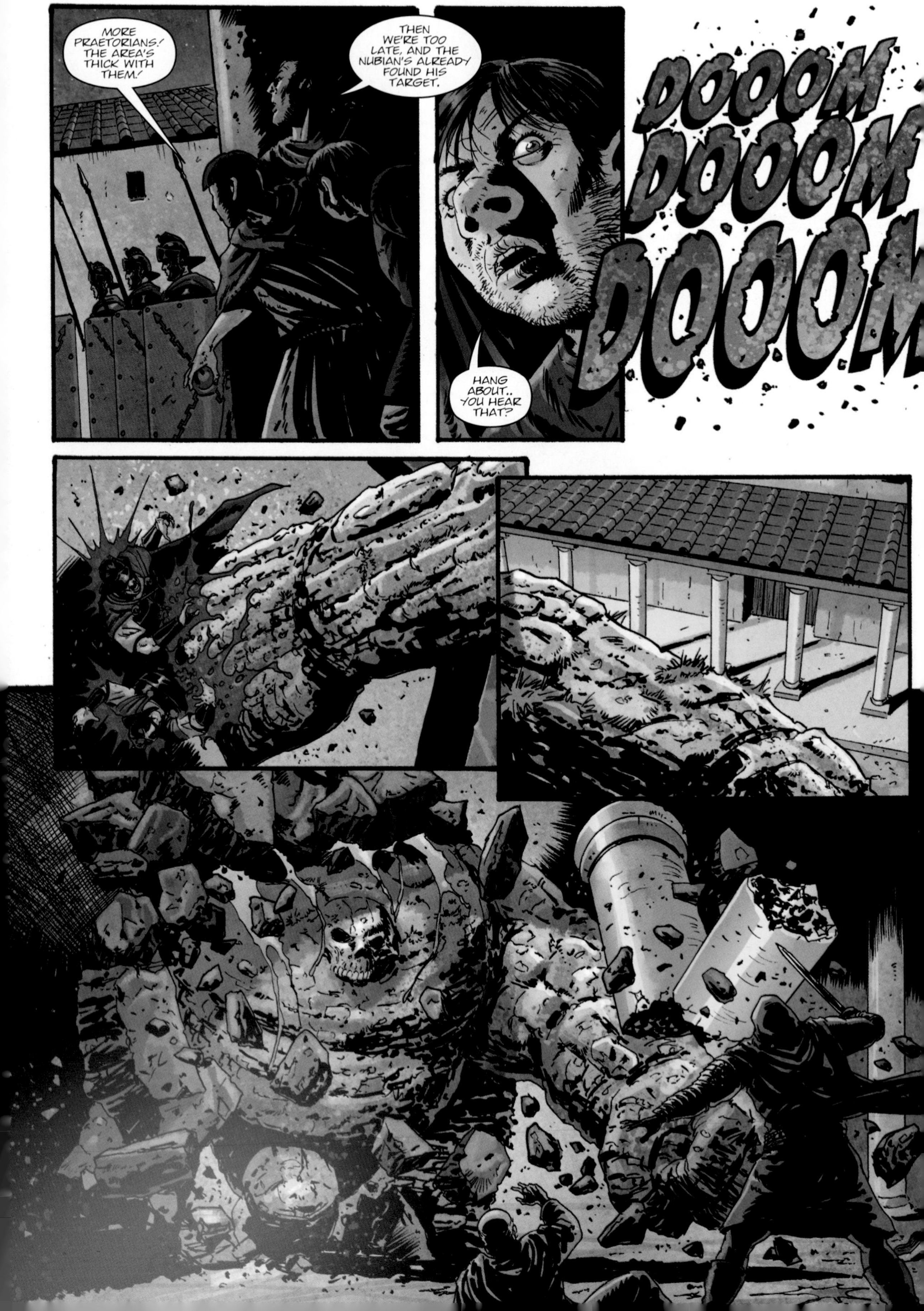

MORE PRAETORIANS! THE AREA'S THICK WITH THEM!
THEN WE'RE TOO LATE, AND THE NUBIAN'S ALREADY FOUND HIS TARGET.
HANG ABOUT.. YOU HEAR THAT?
DOOOM
DOOOM
DOOOM

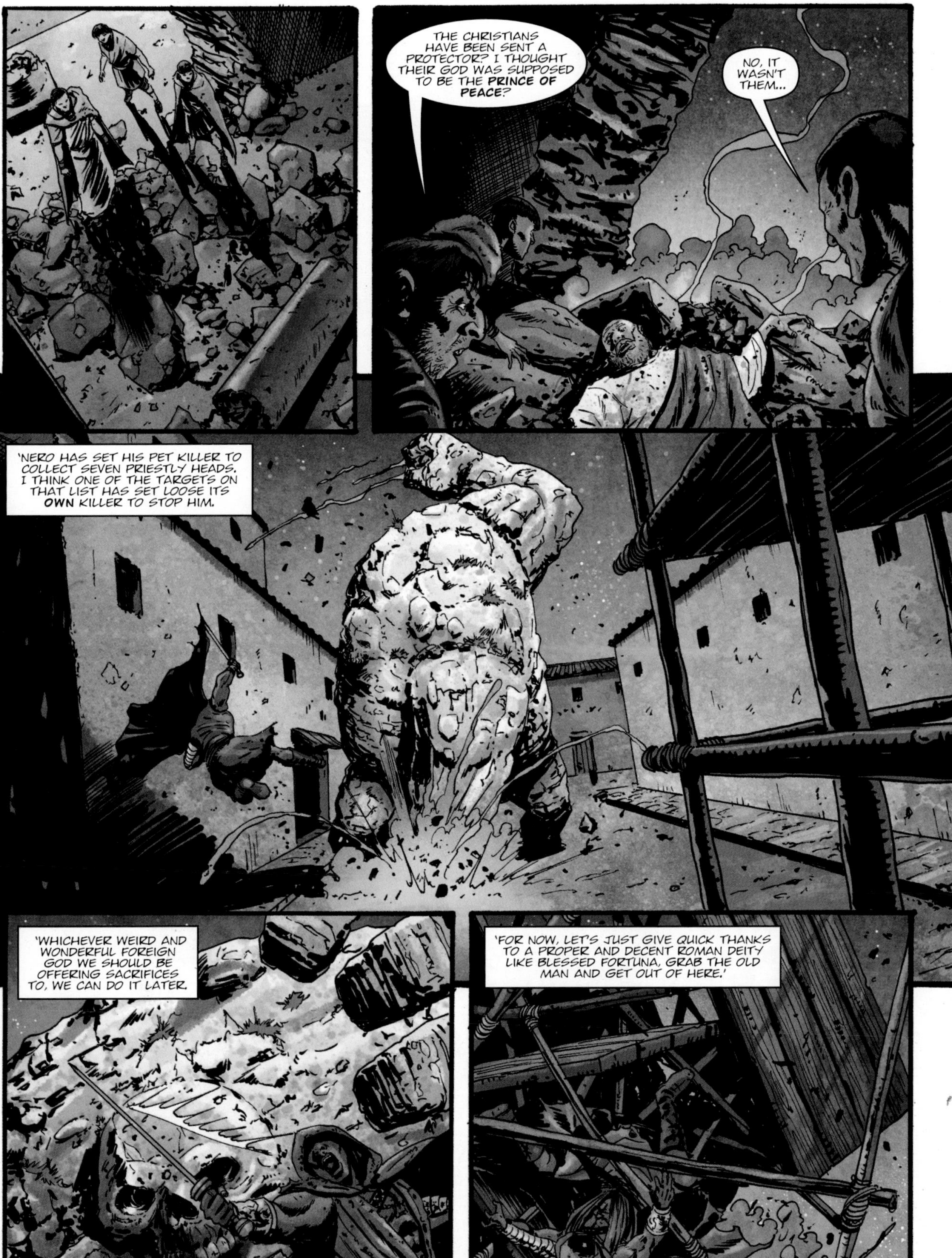
THE CHRISTIANS HAVE BEEN SENT A PROTECTOR? I THOUGHT THEIR GOD WAS SUPPOSED TO BE THE **PRINCE OF PEACE**?
NO, IT WASN'T THEM...
'NERO HAS SET HIS PET KILLER TO COLLECT SEVEN PRIESTLY HEADS. I THINK ONE OF THE TARGETS ON THAT LIST HAS SET LOOSE ITS **OWN** KILLER TO STOP HIM.
'WHICHEVER WEIRD AND WONDERFUL FOREIGN GOD WE SHOULD BE OFFERING SACRIFICES TO, WE CAN DO IT LATER.
'FOR NOW, LET'S JUST GIVE QUICK THANKS TO A PROPER AND DECENT ROMAN DEITY LIKE BLESSED FORTUNA, GRAB THE OLD MAN AND GET OUT OF HERE.'

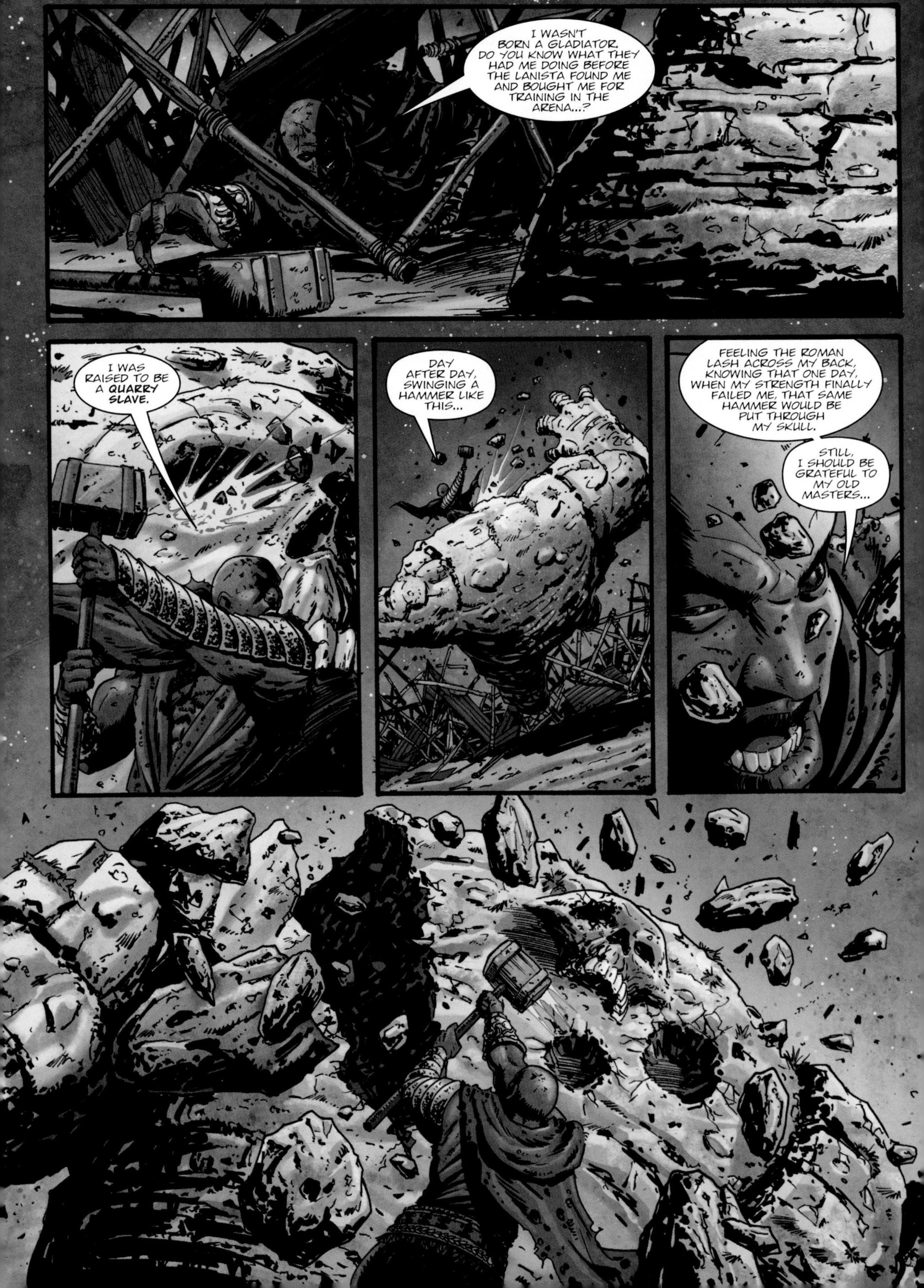
I WASN'T BORN A GLADIATOR. DO YOU KNOW WHAT THEY HAD ME DOING BEFORE THE LANISTA FOUND ME AND BOUGHT ME FOR TRAINING IN THE ARENA...?
I WAS RAISED TO BE A **QUARRY SLAVE.**
DAY AFTER DAY, SWINGING A HAMMER LIKE THIS...
FEELING THE ROMAN LASH ACROSS MY BACK, KNOWING THAT ONE DAY, WHEN MY STRENGTH FINALLY FAILED ME, THAT SAME HAMMER WOULD BE PUT THROUGH MY SKULL.
STILL, I SHOULD BE GRATEFUL TO MY OLD MASTERS...

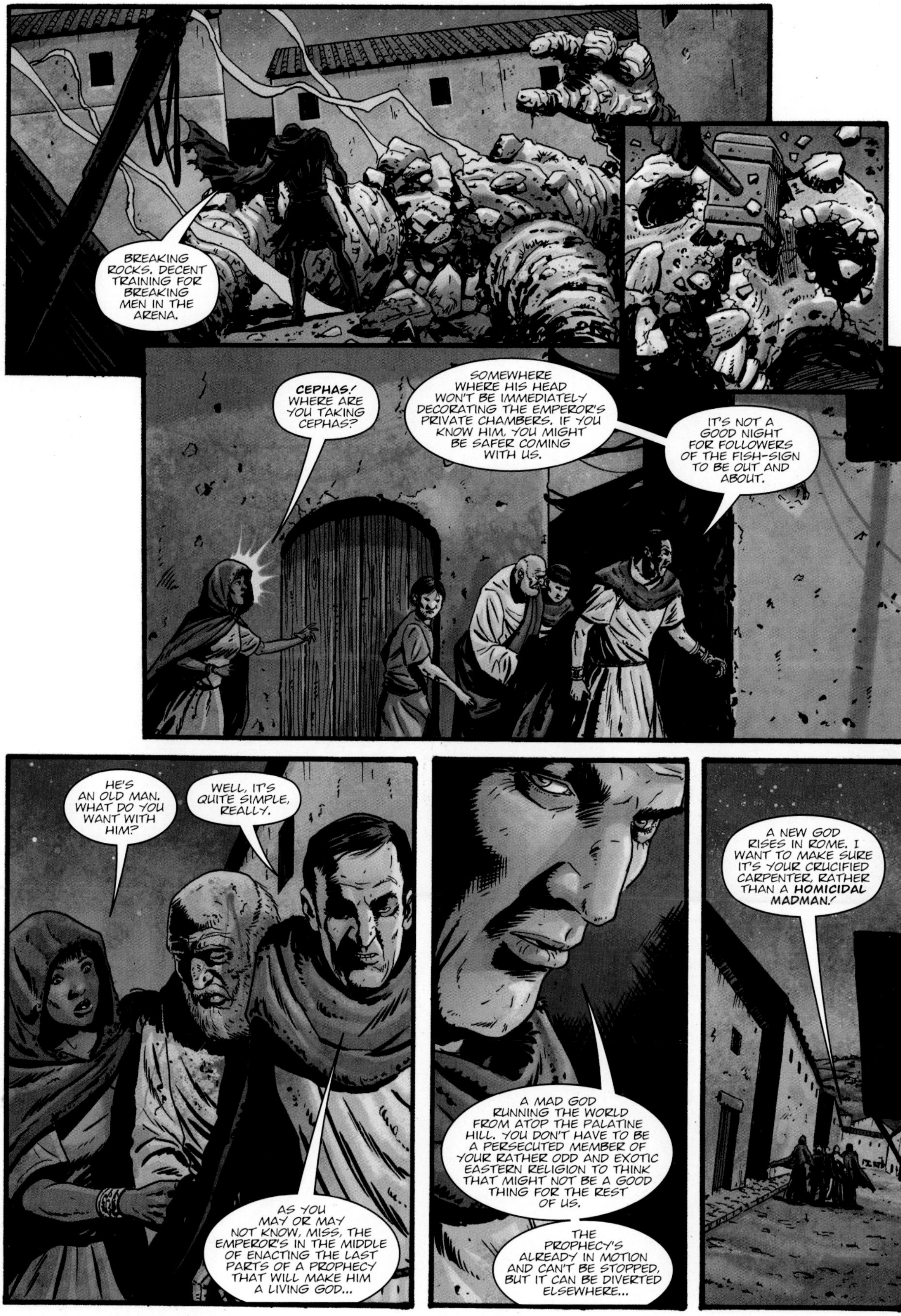
BREAKING ROCKS. DECENT TRAINING FOR BREAKING MEN IN THE ARENA.
CEPHAS! WHERE ARE YOU TAKING CEPHAS?
SOMEWHERE WHERE HIS HEAD WON'T BE IMMEDIATELY DECORATING THE EMPEROR'S PRIVATE CHAMBERS. IF YOU KNOW HIM, YOU MIGHT BE SAFER COMING WITH US.
IT'S NOT A GOOD NIGHT FOR FOLLOWERS OF THE FISH-SIGN TO BE OUT AND ABOUT.
HE'S AN OLD MAN. WHAT DO YOU WANT WITH HIM?
WELL, IT'S QUITE SIMPLE, REALLY.
AS YOU MAY OR MAY NOT KNOW, MISS, THE EMPEROR'S IN THE MIDDLE OF ENACTING THE LAST PARTS OF A PROPHECY THAT WILL MAKE HIM A LIVING GOD...
A MAD GOD RUNNING THE WORLD FROM ATOP THE PALATINE HILL. YOU DON'T HAVE TO BE A PERSECUTED MEMBER OF YOUR RATHER ODD AND EXOTIC EASTERN RELIGION TO THINK THAT MIGHT NOT BE A GOOD THING FOR THE REST OF US.
THE PROPHECY'S ALREADY IN MOTION AND CAN'T BE STOPPED, BUT IT CAN BE DIVERTED ELSEWHERE...
A NEW GOD RISES IN ROME. I WANT TO MAKE SURE IT'S YOUR CRUCIFIED CARPENTER, RATHER THAN A HOMICIDAL MADMAN!

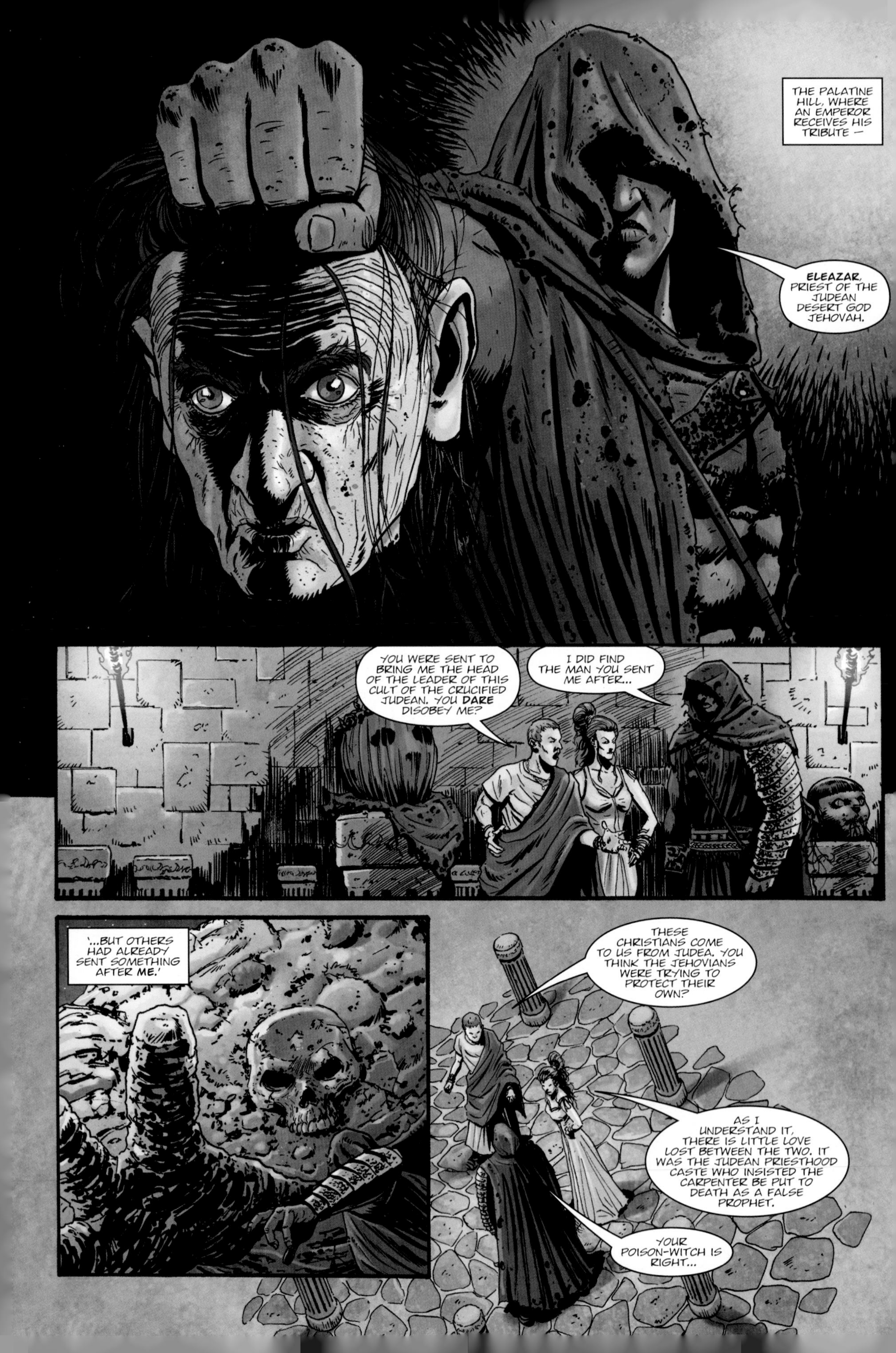
THE PALATINE HILL, WHERE AN EMPEROR RECEIVES HIS TRIBUTE —
ELEAZAR, PRIEST OF THE JUDEAN DESERT GOD JEHOVAH.
YOU WERE SENT TO BRING ME THE HEAD OF THE LEADER OF THIS CULT OF THE CRUCIFIED JUDEAN. YOU DARE DISOBEY ME?
I DID FIND THE MAN YOU SENT ME AFTER...
'...BUT OTHERS HAD ALREADY SENT SOMETHING AFTER ME.'
THESE CHRISTIANS COME TO US FROM JUDEA. YOU THINK THE JEHOVIANS WERE TRYING TO PROTECT THEIR OWN?
AS I UNDERSTAND IT, THERE IS LITTLE LOVE LOST BETWEEN THE TWO. IT WAS THE JUDEAN PRIESTHOOD CASTE WHO INSISTED THE CARPENTER BE PUT TO DEATH AS A FALSE PROPHET.
YOUR POISON-WITCH IS RIGHT...

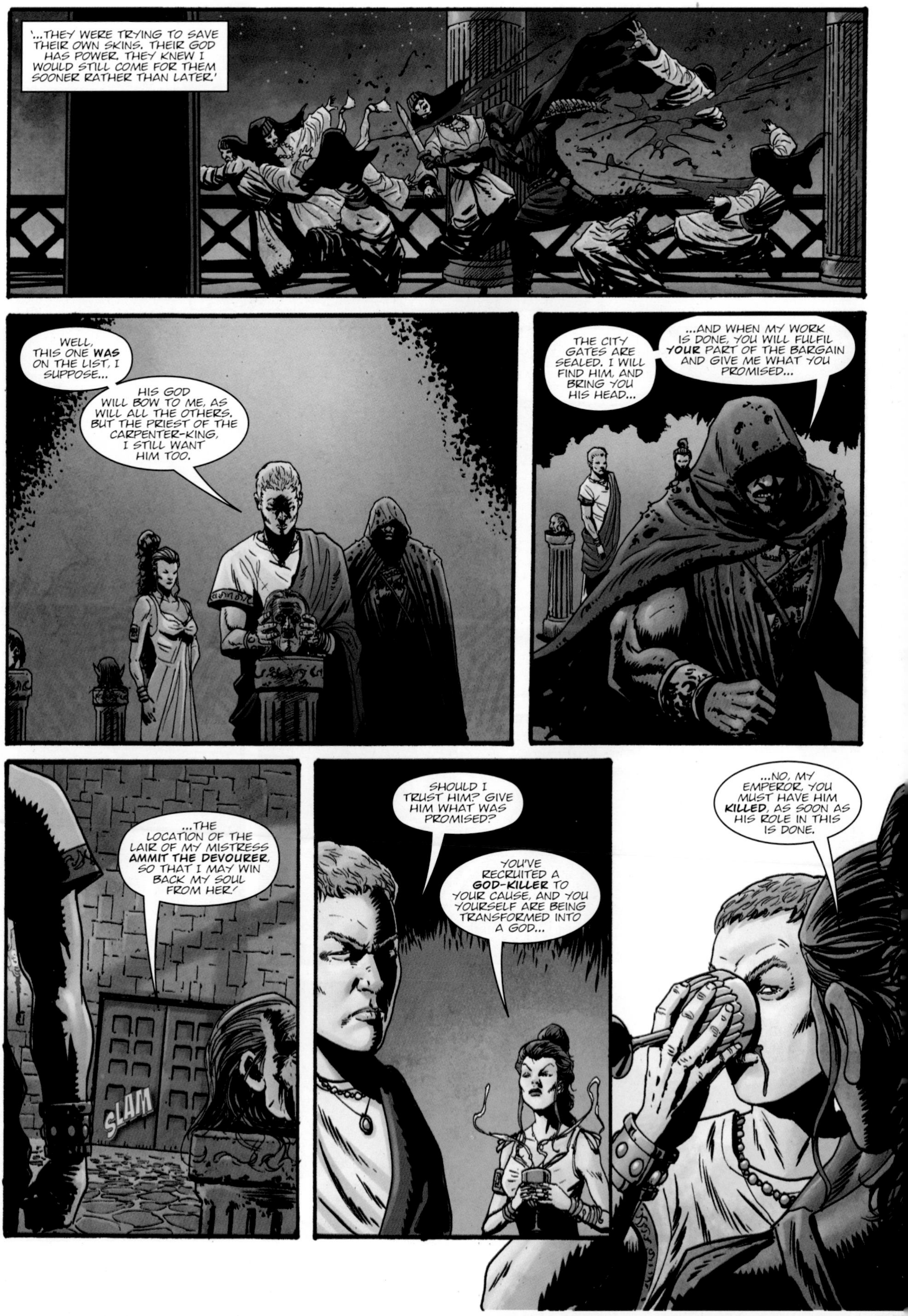
'...THEY WERE TRYING TO SAVE THEIR OWN SKINS. THEIR GOD HAS POWER. THEY KNEW I WOULD STILL COME FOR THEM SOONER RATHER THAN LATER.'
WELL, THIS ONE WAS ON THE LIST, I SUPPOSE...
HIS GOD WILL BOW TO ME, AS WILL ALL THE OTHERS. BUT THE PRIEST OF THE CARPENTER-KING, I STILL WANT HIM TOO.
THE CITY GATES ARE SEALED. I WILL FIND HIM, AND BRING YOU HIS HEAD...
...AND WHEN MY WORK IS DONE, YOU WILL FULFIL YOUR PART OF THE BARGAIN AND GIVE ME WHAT YOU PROMISED...
...THE LOCATION OF THE LAIR OF MY MISTRESS AMMIT THE DEVOURER, SO THAT I MAY WIN BACK MY SOUL FROM HER.'
SLAM
SHOULD I TRUST HIM? GIVE HIM WHAT WAS PROMISED?
YOU'VE RECRUITED A GOD-KILLER TO YOUR CAUSE, AND YOU YOURSELF ARE BEING TRANSFORMED INTO A GOD...
...NO, MY EMPEROR, YOU MUST HAVE HIM KILLED, AS SOON AS HIS ROLE IN THIS IS DONE.

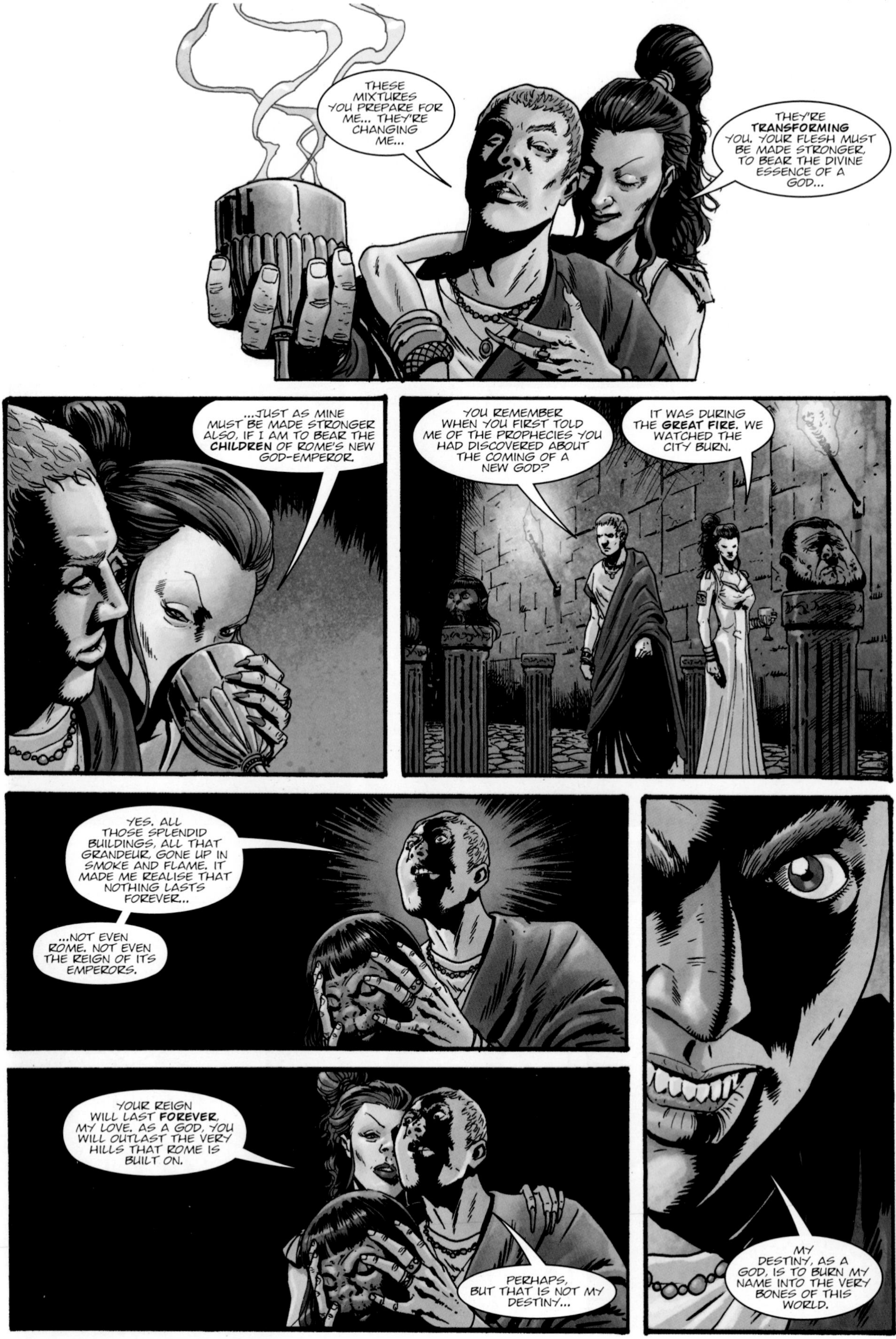
THESE MIXTURES YOU PREPARE FOR ME... THEY'RE CHANGING ME...
THEY'RE **TRANSFORMING** YOU. YOUR FLESH MUST BE MADE STRONGER, TO BEAR THE DIVINE ESSENCE OF A GOD...
...JUST AS MINE MUST BE MADE STRONGER ALSO, IF I AM TO BEAR THE **CHILDREN** OF ROME'S NEW GOD-EMPEROR.
YOU REMEMBER WHEN YOU FIRST TOLD ME OF THE PROPHECIES YOU HAD DISCOVERED ABOUT THE COMING OF A NEW GOD?
IT WAS DURING THE **GREAT FIRE**. WE WATCHED THE CITY BURN.
YES. ALL THOSE SPLENDID BUILDINGS, ALL THAT GRANDEUR, GONE UP IN SMOKE AND FLAME. IT MADE ME REALISE THAT NOTHING LASTS FOREVER...
...NOT EVEN ROME. NOT EVEN THE REIGN OF ITS EMPERORS.
YOUR REIGN WILL LAST **FOREVER**, MY LOVE. AS A GOD, YOU WILL OUTLAST THE VERY HILLS THAT ROME IS BUILT ON.
PERHAPS, BUT THAT IS NOT MY DESTINY...
MY DESTINY, AS A GOD, IS TO BURN MY NAME INTO THE VERY BONES OF THIS WORLD.

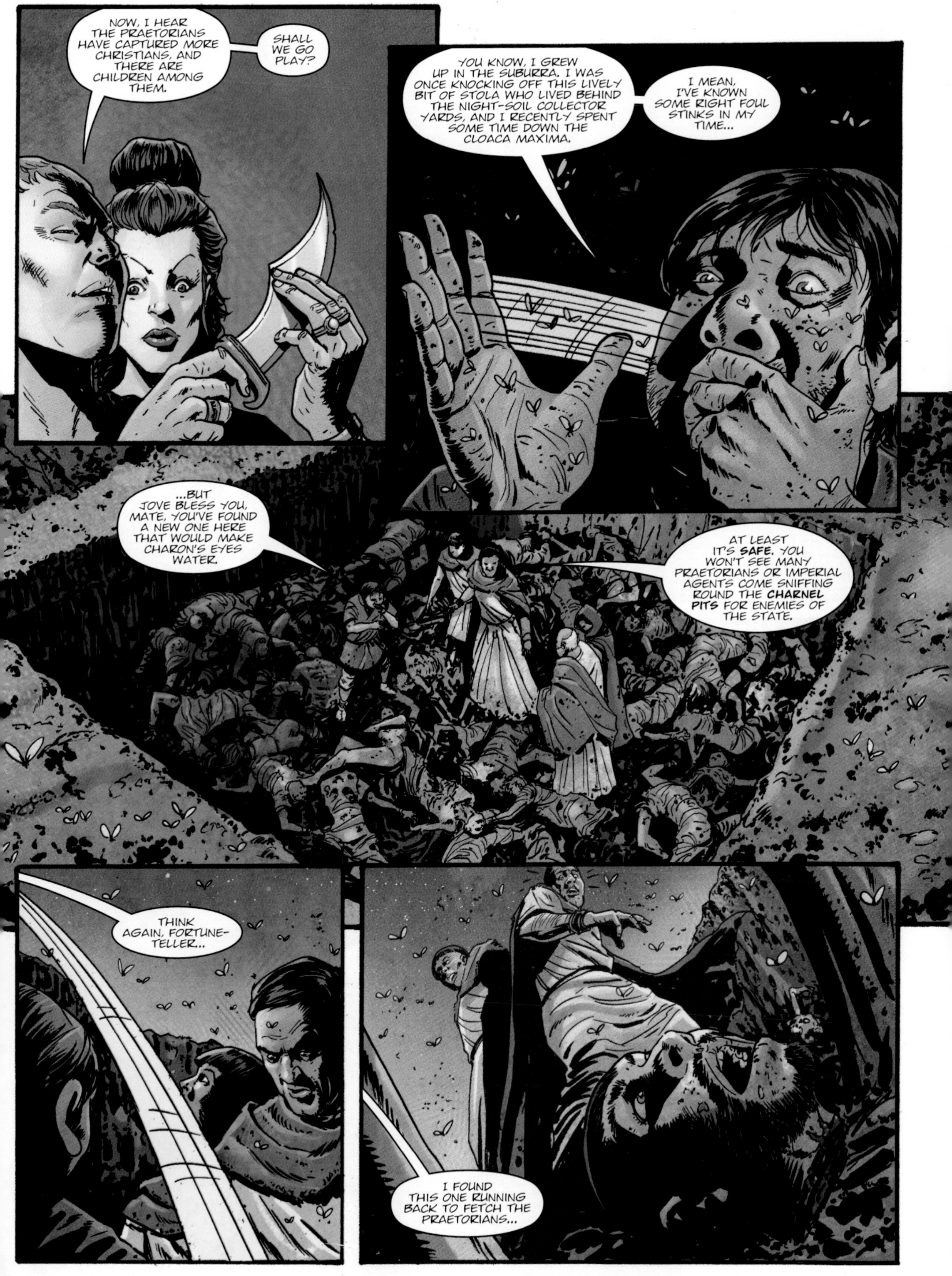
NOW, I HEAR THE PRAETORIANS HAVE CAPTURED MORE CHRISTIANS, AND THERE ARE CHILDREN AMONG THEM.
SHALL WE GO PLAY?
YOU KNOW, I GREW UP IN THE SUBURRA. I WAS ONCE KNOCKING OFF THIS LIVELY BIT OF STOLA WHO LIVED BEHIND THE NIGHT-SOIL COLLECTOR YARDS, AND I RECENTLY SPENT SOME TIME DOWN THE CLOACA MAXIMA.
I MEAN, I'VE KNOWN SOME RIGHT FOUL STINKS IN MY TIME...
...BUT JOVE BLESS YOU, MATE, YOU'VE FOUND A NEW ONE HERE THAT WOULD MAKE CHARON'S EYES WATER.
AT LEAST IT'S **SAFE.** YOU WON'T SEE MANY PRAETORIANS OR IMPERIAL AGENTS COME SNIFFING ROUND THE **CHARNEL PITS** FOR ENEMIES OF THE STATE.
THINK AGAIN, FORTUNE-TELLER...
I FOUND THIS ONE RUNNING BACK TO FETCH THE PRAETORIANS...

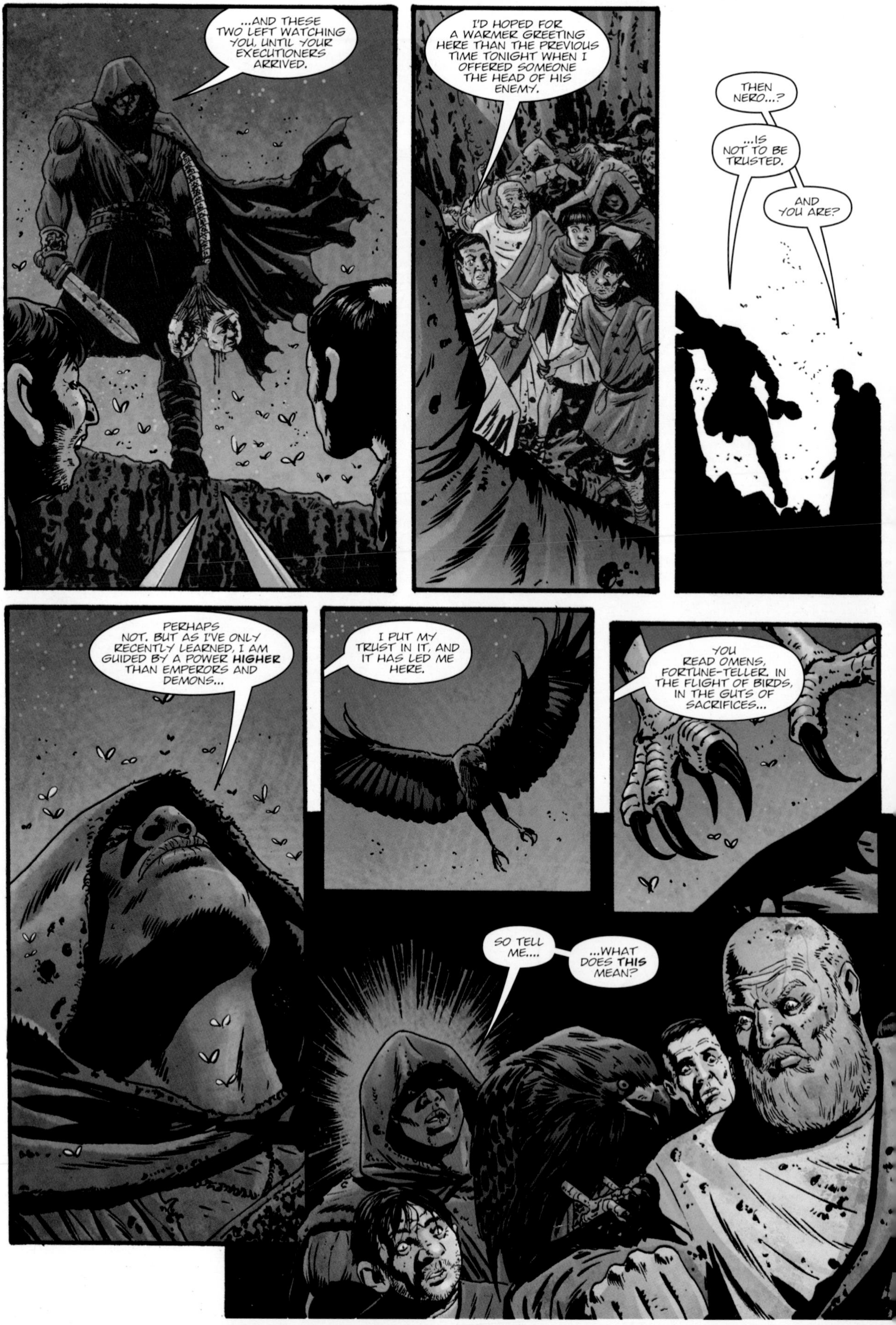
...AND THESE TWO LEFT WATCHING YOU, UNTIL YOUR EXECUTIONERS ARRIVED.
I'D HOPED FOR A WARMER GREETING HERE THAN THE PREVIOUS TIME TONIGHT WHEN I OFFERED SOMEONE THE HEAD OF HIS ENEMY.
THEN NERO...?
...IS NOT TO BE TRUSTED.
AND YOU ARE?
PERHAPS NOT. BUT AS I'VE ONLY RECENTLY LEARNED, I AM GUIDED BY A POWER HIGHER THAN EMPERORS AND DEMONS...
I PUT MY TRUST IN IT, AND IT HAS LED ME HERE.
YOU READ OMENS, FORTUNE-TELLER, IN THE FLIGHT OF BIRDS, IN THE GUTS OF SACRIFICES...
SO TELL ME....
...WHAT DOES THIS MEAN?

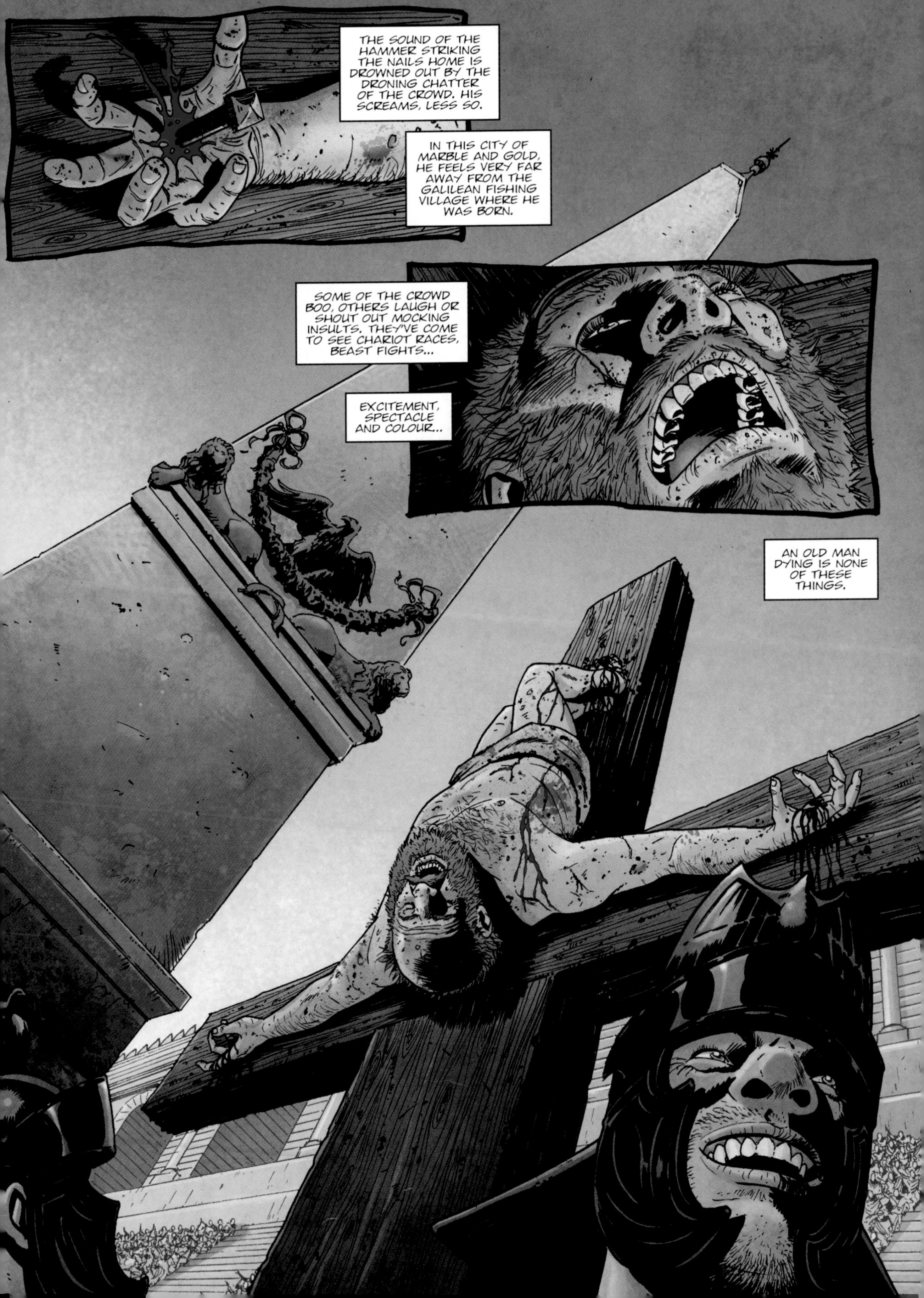
THE SOUND OF THE HAMMER STRIKING THE NAILS HOME IS DROWNED OUT BY THE DRONING CHATTER OF THE CROWD. HIS SCREAMS, LESS SO.
IN THIS CITY OF MARBLE AND GOLD, HE FEELS VERY FAR AWAY FROM THE GALILEAN FISHING VILLAGE WHERE HE WAS BORN.
SOME OF THE CROWD BOO, OTHERS LAUGH OR SHOUT OUT MOCKING INSULTS. THEY'VE COME TO SEE CHARIOT RACES, BEAST FIGHTS...
EXCITEMENT, SPECTACLE AND COLOUR...
AN OLD MAN DYING IS NONE OF THESE THINGS.

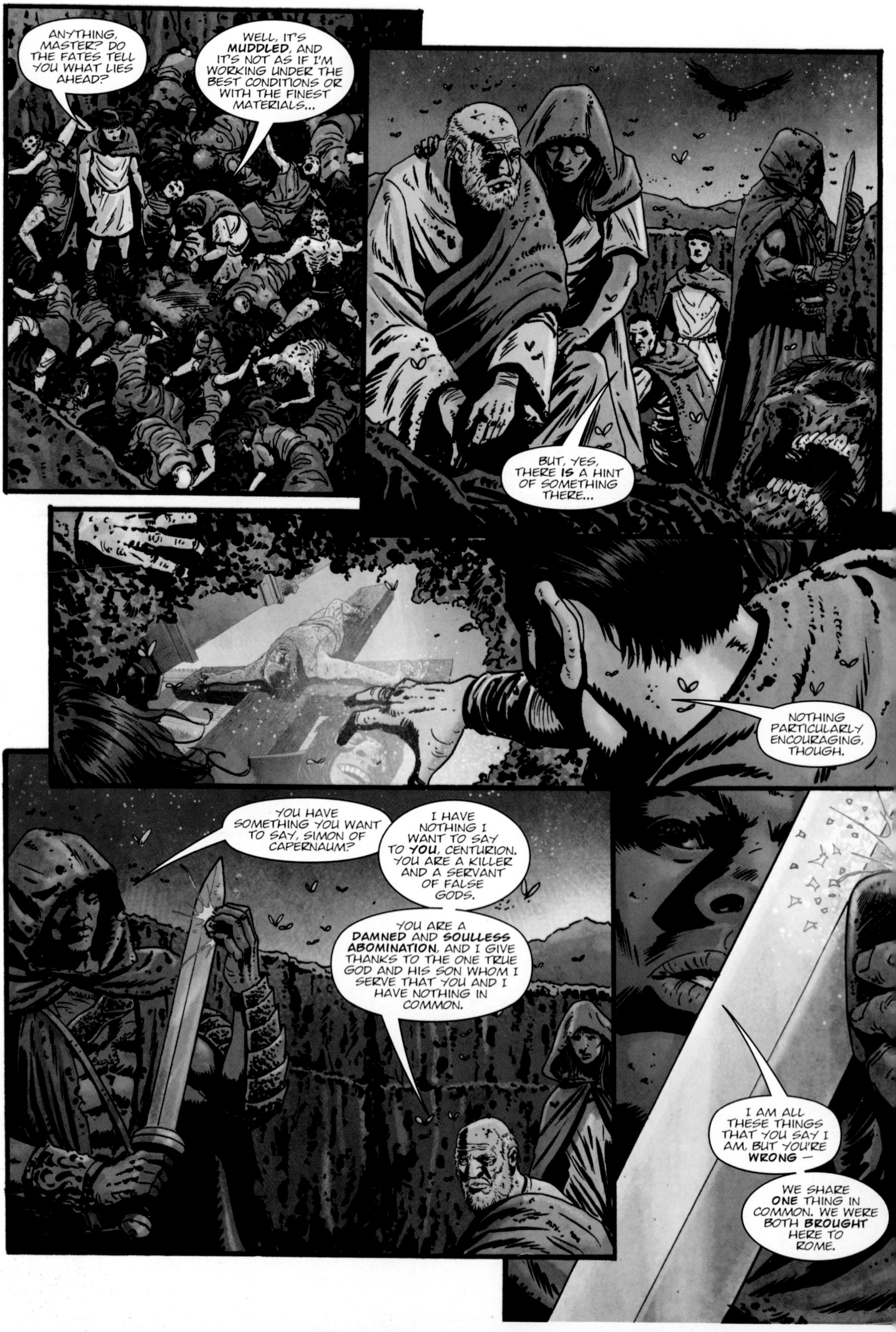
ANYTHING, MASTER? DO THE FATES TELL YOU WHAT LIES AHEAD?
WELL, IT'S MUDDLED, AND IT'S NOT AS IF I'M WORKING UNDER THE BEST CONDITIONS OR WITH THE FINEST MATERIALS...
BUT, YES, THERE IS A HINT OF SOMETHING THERE...
NOTHING PARTICULARLY ENCOURAGING, THOUGH.
YOU HAVE SOMETHING YOU WANT TO SAY, SIMON OF CAPERNAUM?
I HAVE NOTHING I WANT TO SAY TO YOU, CENTURION. YOU ARE A KILLER AND A SERVANT OF FALSE GODS.
YOU ARE A DAMNED AND SOULLESS ABOMINATION, AND I GIVE THANKS TO THE ONE TRUE GOD AND HIS SON WHOM I SERVE THAT YOU AND I HAVE NOTHING IN COMMON.
I AM ALL THESE THINGS THAT YOU SAY I AM, BUT YOU'RE WRONG —
WE SHARE ONE THING IN COMMON. WE WERE BOTH BROUGHT HERE TO ROME.

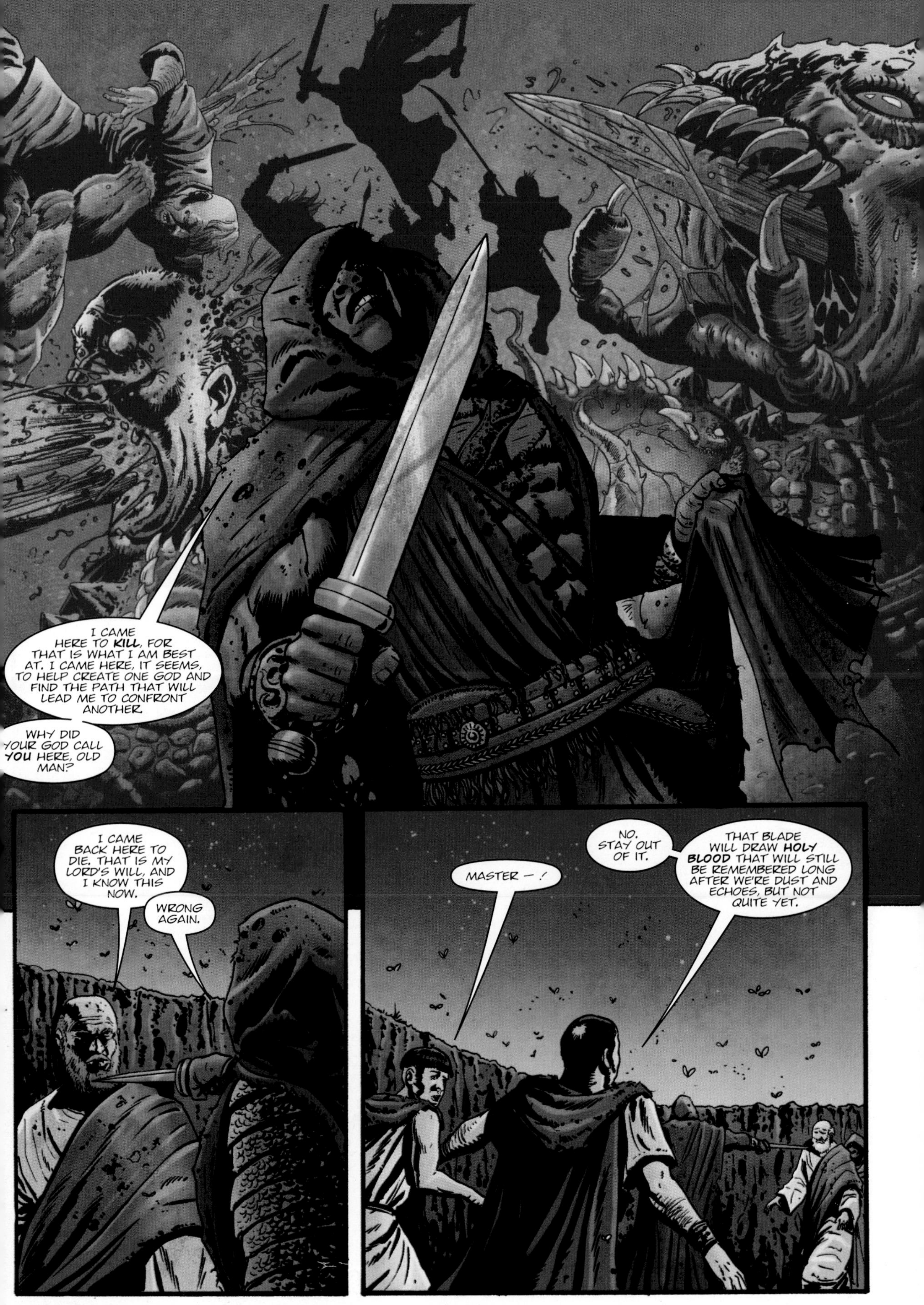

I CAME HERE TO KILL, FOR THAT IS WHAT I AM BEST AT. I CAME HERE, IT SEEMS, TO HELP CREATE ONE GOD AND FIND THE PATH THAT WILL LEAD ME TO CONFRONT ANOTHER.
WHY DID YOUR GOD CALL YOU HERE, OLD MAN?
I CAME BACK HERE TO DIE. THAT IS MY LORD'S WILL, AND I KNOW THIS NOW.
WRONG AGAIN.
MASTER — !
NO. STAY OUT OF IT.
THAT BLADE WILL DRAW HOLY BLOOD THAT WILL STILL BE REMEMBERED LONG AFTER WE'RE DUST AND ECHOES, BUT NOT QUITE YET.

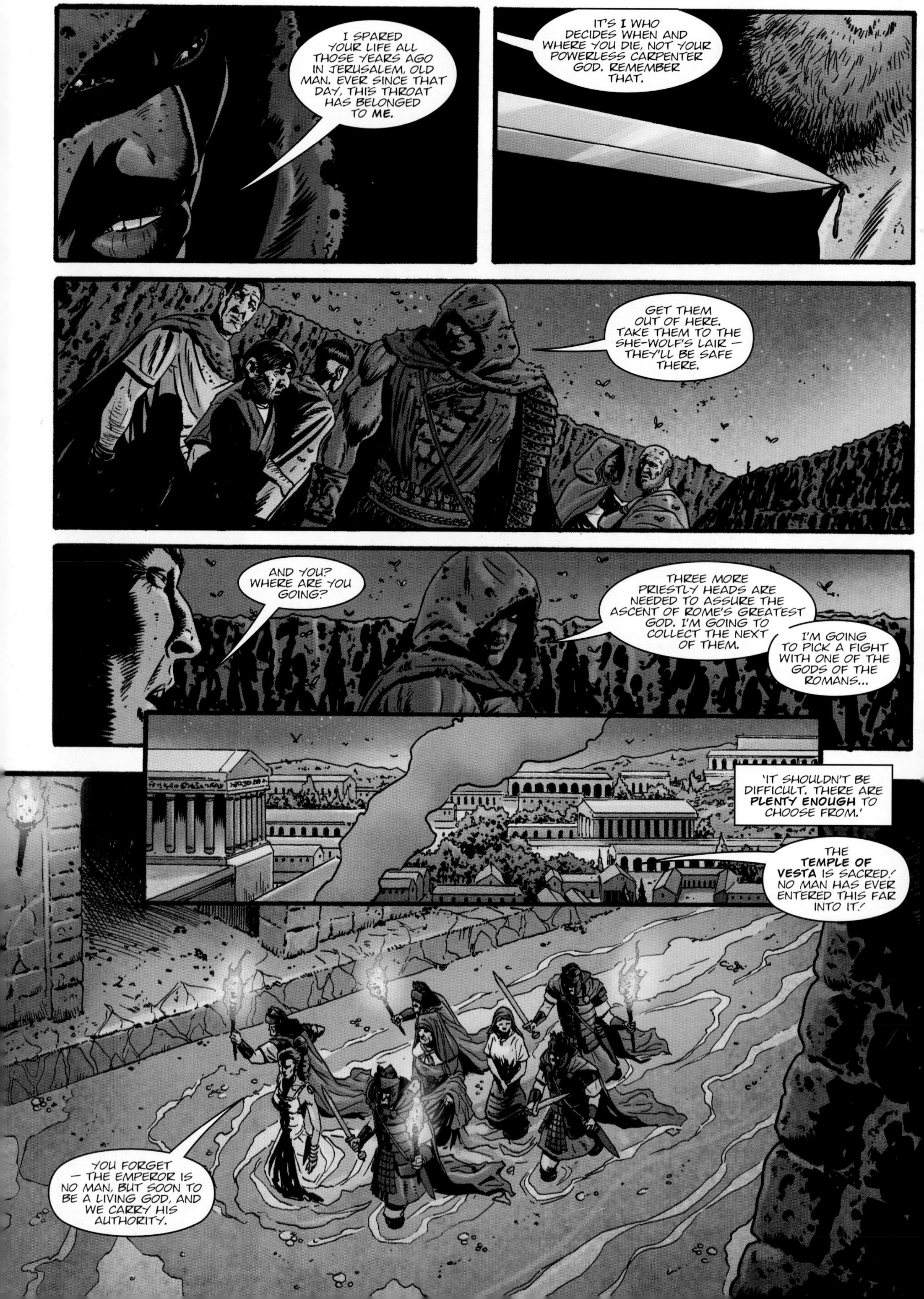
I SPARED YOUR LIFE ALL THOSE YEARS AGO IN JERUSALEM, OLD MAN. EVER SINCE THAT DAY, THIS THROAT HAS BELONGED TO **ME.**
IT'S **I** WHO DECIDES WHEN AND WHERE YOU DIE, NOT YOUR POWERLESS CARPENTER GOD. REMEMBER THAT.
GET THEM OUT OF HERE. TAKE THEM TO THE SHE-WOLF'S LAIR — THEY'LL BE SAFE THERE.
AND YOU? WHERE ARE YOU GOING?
THREE MORE PRIESTLY HEADS ARE NEEDED TO ASSURE THE ASCENT OF ROME'S GREATEST GOD. I'M GOING TO COLLECT THE NEXT OF THEM.
I'M GOING TO PICK A FIGHT WITH ONE OF THE GODS OF THE ROMANS...
'IT SHOULDN'T BE DIFFICULT. THERE ARE **PLENTY ENOUGH** TO CHOOSE FROM.'
THE **TEMPLE OF VESTA** IS SACRED! NO MAN HAS EVER ENTERED THIS FAR INTO IT!
YOU FORGET — THE EMPEROR IS NO MAN, BUT SOON TO BE A LIVING GOD, AND WE CARRY HIS AUTHORITY.

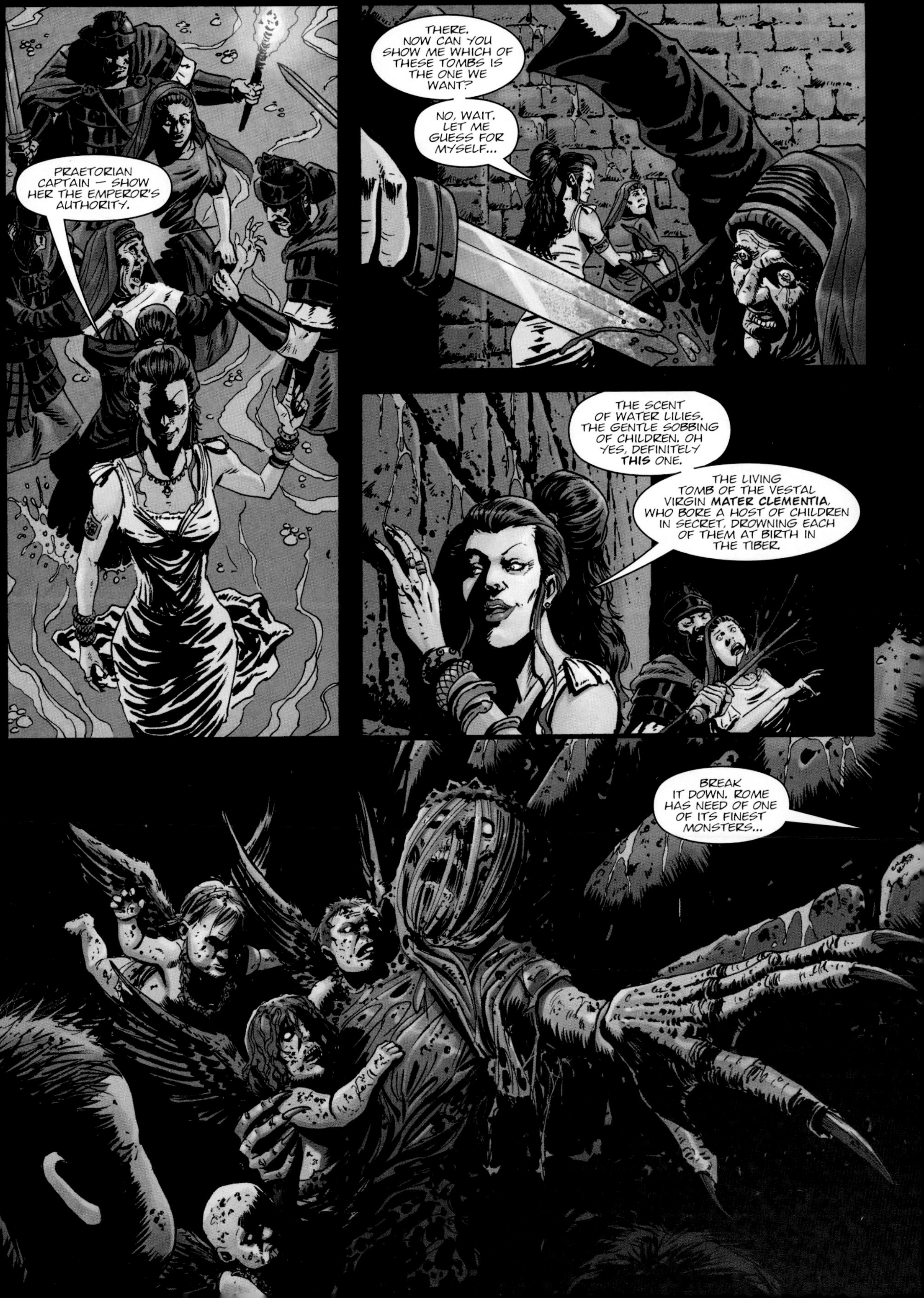
PRAETORIAN CAPTAIN — SHOW HER THE EMPEROR'S AUTHORITY.
THERE. NOW CAN YOU SHOW ME WHICH OF THESE TOMBS IS THE ONE WE WANT?
NO, WAIT. LET ME GUESS FOR MYSELF...
THE SCENT OF WATER LILIES. THE GENTLE SOBBING OF CHILDREN. OH YES, DEFINITELY **THIS** ONE.
THE LIVING TOMB OF THE VESTAL VIRGIN **MATER CLEMENTIA**, WHO BORE A HOST OF CHILDREN IN SECRET, DROWNING EACH OF THEM AT BIRTH IN THE TIBER.
BREAK IT DOWN. ROME HAS NEED OF ONE OF ITS FINEST MONSTERS...

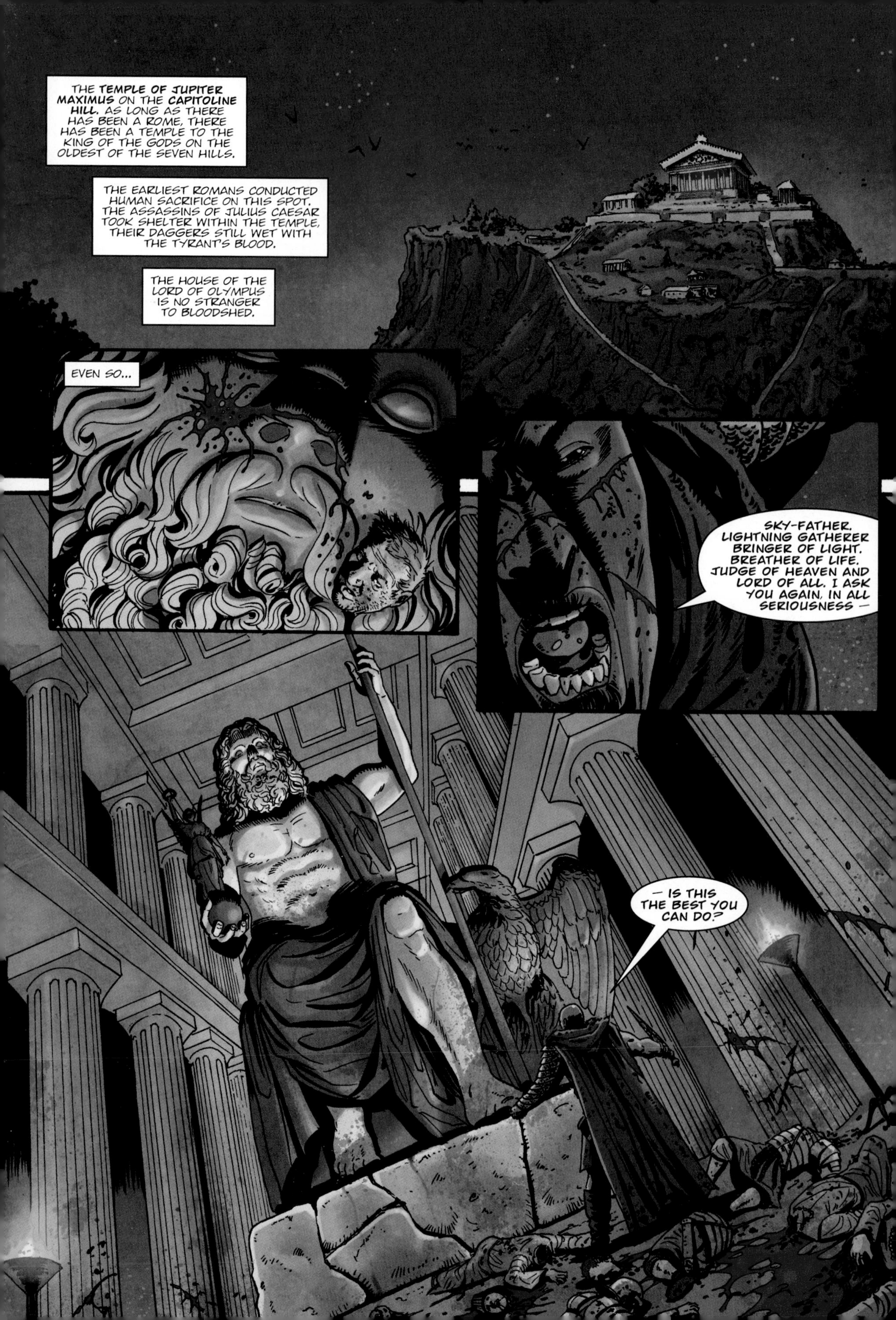
THE TEMPLE OF JUPITER MAXIMUS ON THE CAPITOLINE HILL. AS LONG AS THERE HAS BEEN A ROME, THERE HAS BEEN A TEMPLE TO THE KING OF THE GODS ON THE OLDEST OF THE SEVEN HILLS.
THE EARLIEST ROMANS CONDUCTED HUMAN SACRIFICE ON THIS SPOT. THE ASSASSINS OF JULIUS CAESAR TOOK SHELTER WITHIN THE TEMPLE, THEIR DAGGERS STILL WET WITH THE TYRANT'S BLOOD.
THE HOUSE OF THE LORD OF OLYMPUS IS NO STRANGER TO BLOODSHED.
EVEN SO...
SKY-FATHER. LIGHTNING GATHERER BRINGER OF LIGHT. BREATHER OF LIFE. JUDGE OF HEAVEN AND LORD OF ALL. I ASK YOU AGAIN, IN ALL SERIOUSNESS —
— IS THIS THE BEST YOU CAN DO?

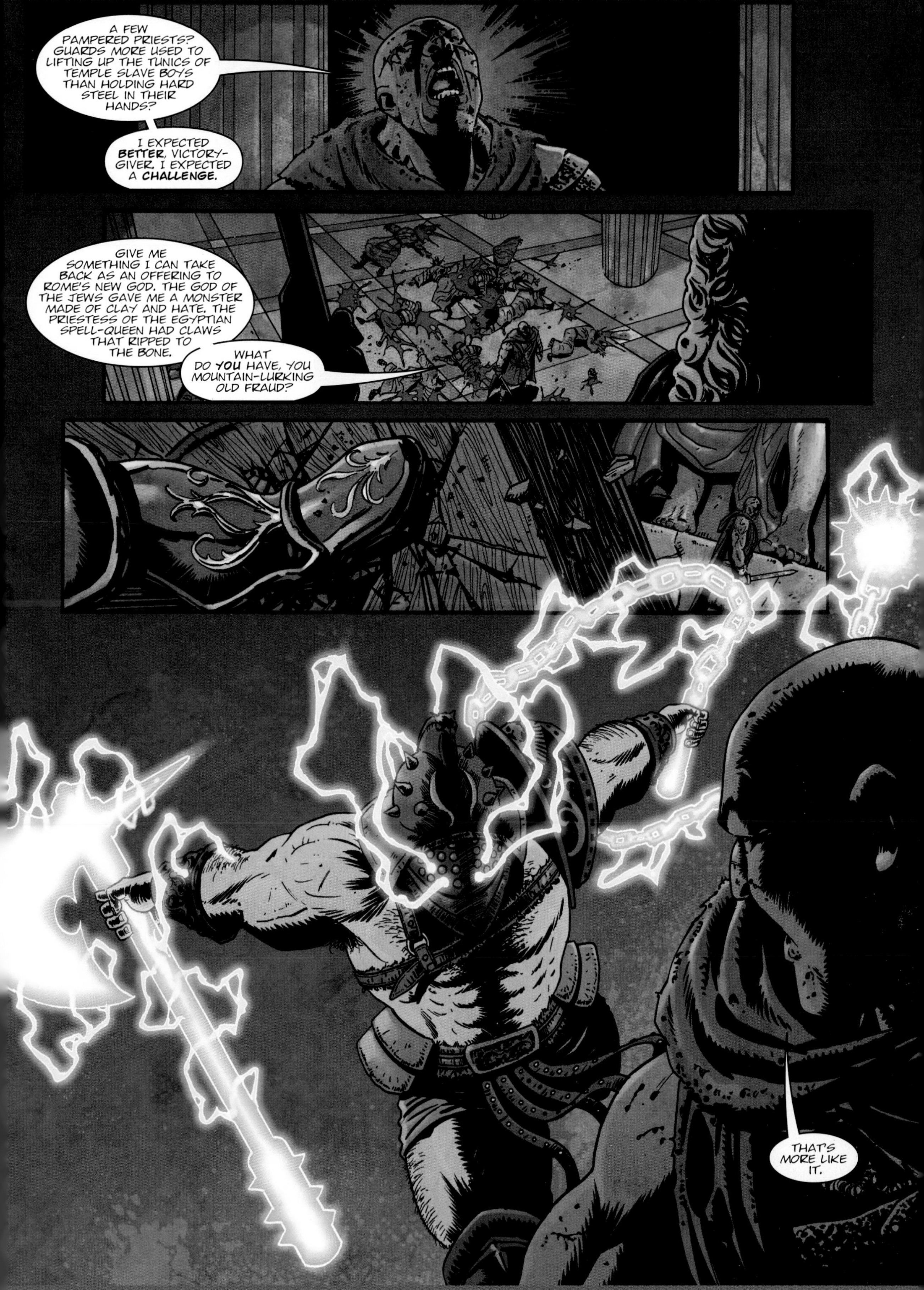
A FEW PAMPERED PRIESTS? GUARDS MORE USED TO LIFTING UP THE TUNICS OF TEMPLE SLAVE BOYS THAN HOLDING HARD STEEL IN THEIR HANDS?
I EXPECTED BETTER, VICTORY-GIVER. I EXPECTED A CHALLENGE.
GIVE ME SOMETHING I CAN TAKE BACK AS AN OFFERING TO ROME'S NEW GOD. THE GOD OF THE JEWS GAVE ME A MONSTER MADE OF CLAY AND HATE. THE PRIESTESS OF THE EGYPTIAN SPELL-QUEEN HAD CLAWS THAT RIPPED TO THE BONE.
WHAT DO YOU HAVE, YOU MOUNTAIN-LURKING OLD FRAUD?
THAT'S MORE LIKE IT.

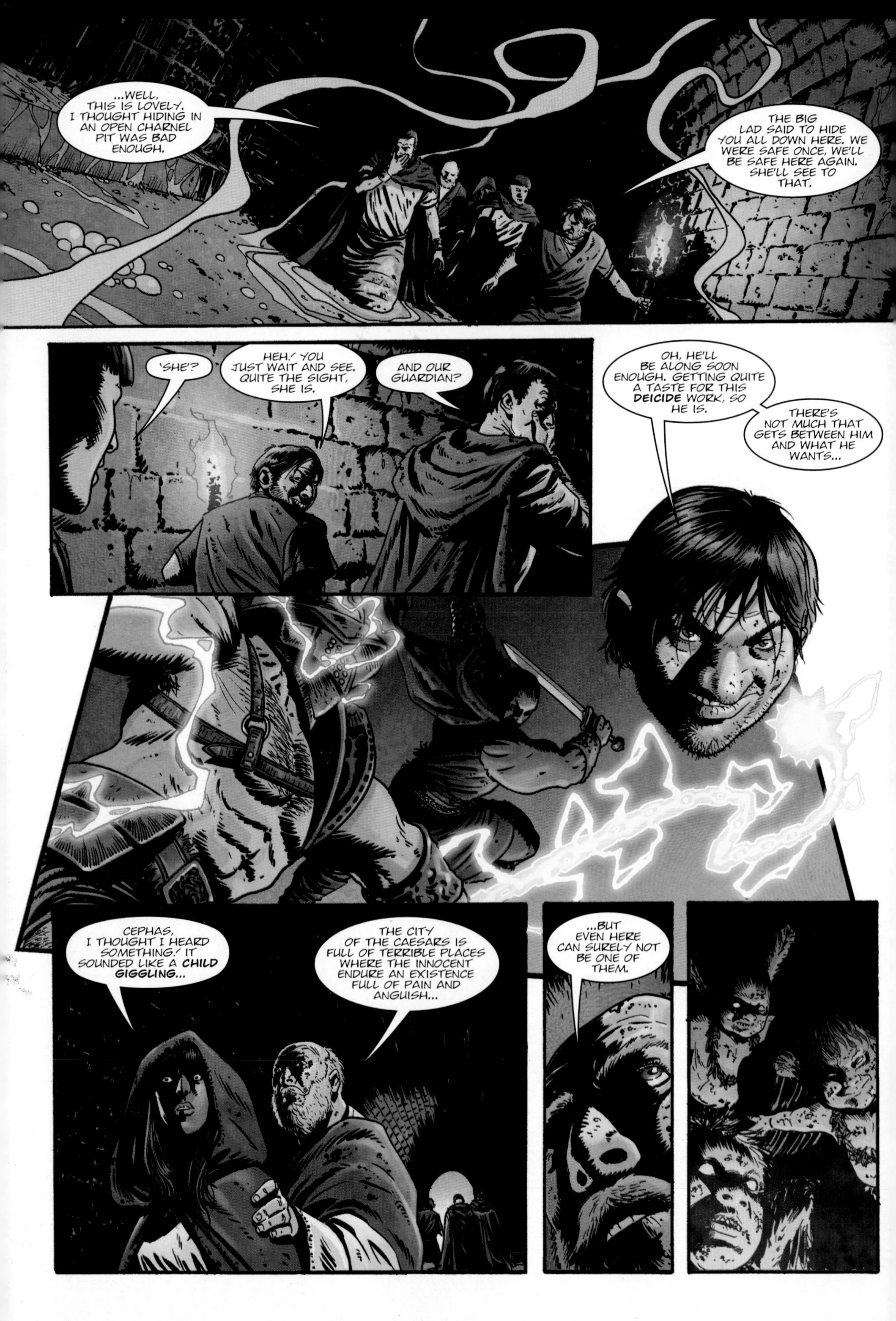
...WELL, THIS IS LOVELY. I THOUGHT HIDING IN AN OPEN CHARNEL PIT WAS BAD ENOUGH.
THE BIG LAD SAID TO HIDE YOU ALL DOWN HERE. WE WERE SAFE ONCE, WE'LL BE SAFE HERE AGAIN. SHE'LL SEE TO THAT.
'SHE'?
HEH! YOU JUST WAIT AND SEE. QUITE THE SIGHT, SHE IS.
AND OUR GUARDIAN?
OH, HE'LL BE ALONG SOON ENOUGH. GETTING QUITE A TASTE FOR THIS DEICIDE WORK, SO HE IS.
THERE'S NOT MUCH THAT GETS BETWEEN HIM AND WHAT HE WANTS...
CEPHAS, I THOUGHT I HEARD SOMETHING! IT SOUNDED LIKE A CHILD GIGGLING...
THE CITY OF THE CAESARS IS FULL OF TERRIBLE PLACES WHERE THE INNOCENT ENDURE AN EXISTENCE FULL OF PAIN AND ANGUISH...
...BUT EVEN HERE CAN SURELY NOT BE ONE OF THEM.

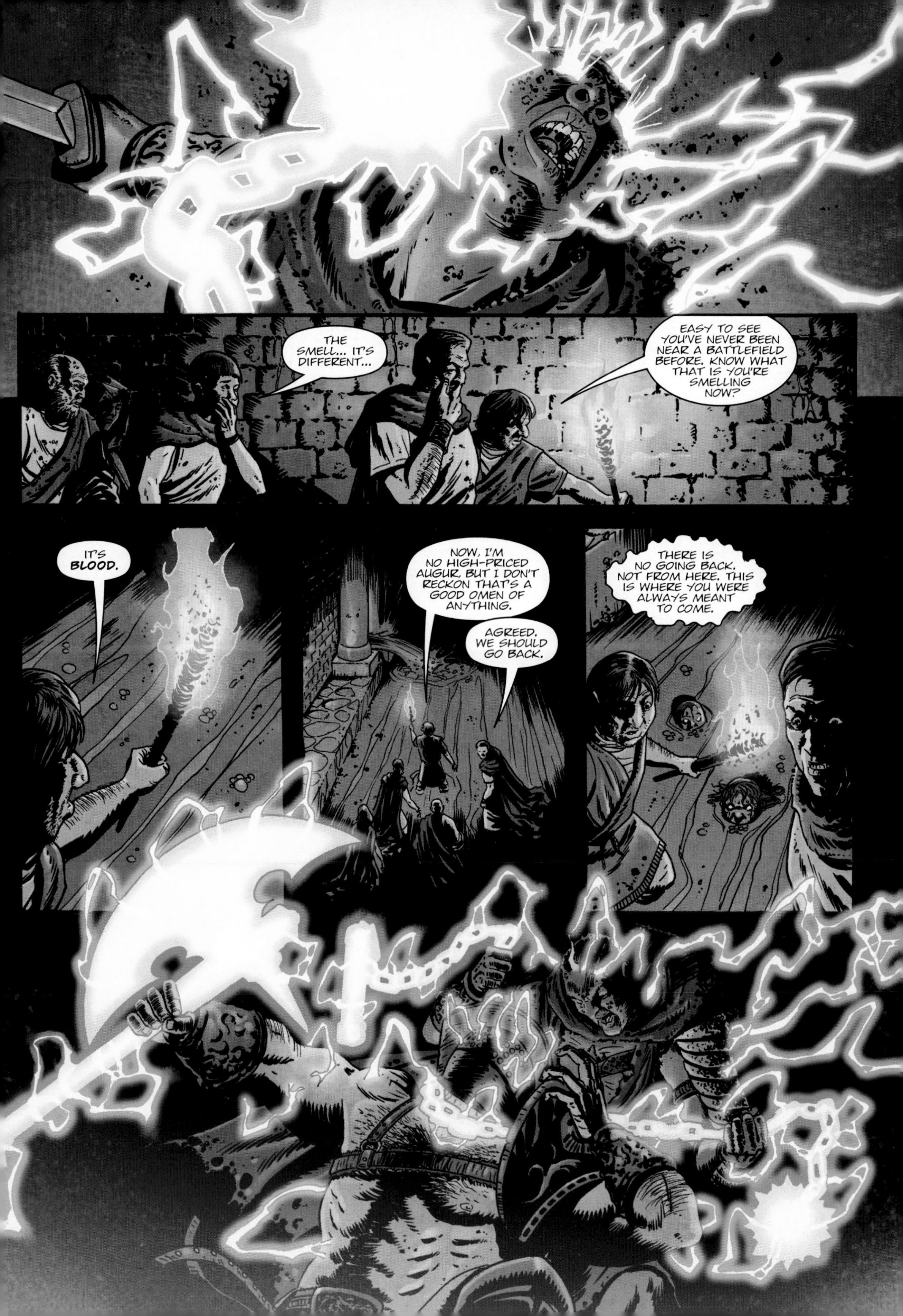
THE SMELL... IT'S DIFFERENT...
EASY TO SEE YOU'VE NEVER BEEN NEAR A BATTLEFIELD BEFORE. KNOW WHAT THAT IS YOU'RE SMELLING NOW?
IT'S **BLOOD.**
NOW, I'M NO HIGH-PRICED AUGUR, BUT I DON'T RECKON THAT'S A GOOD OMEN OF ANYTHING.
AGREED. WE SHOULD GO BACK.
THERE IS NO GOING BACK. NOT FROM HERE. THIS IS WHERE YOU WERE ALWAYS MEANT TO COME.

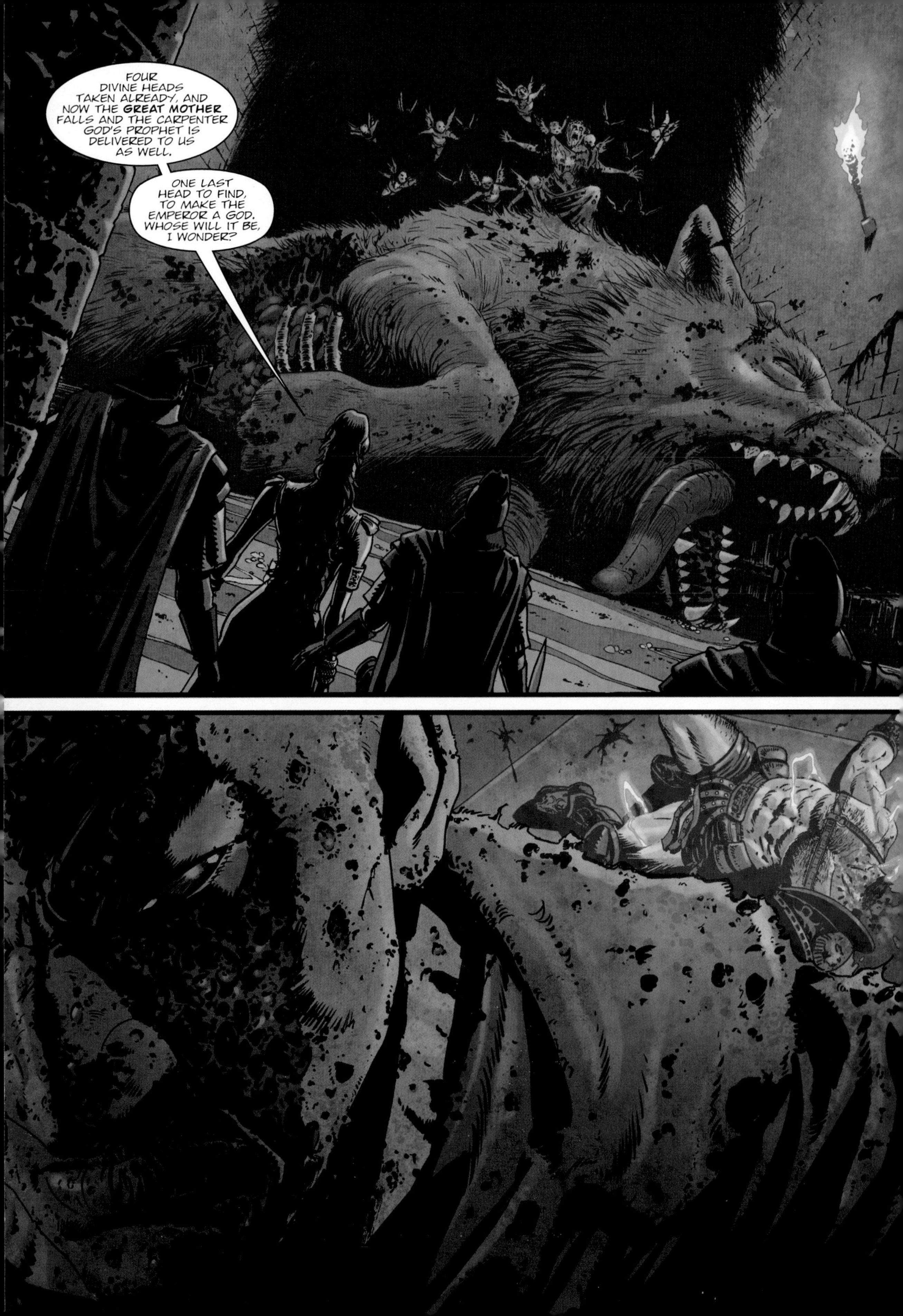
FOUR DIVINE HEADS TAKEN ALREADY, AND NOW THE **GREAT MOTHER** FALLS AND THE CARPENTER GOD'S PROPHET IS DELIVERED TO US AS WELL.
ONE LAST HEAD TO FIND, TO MAKE THE EMPEROR A GOD. WHOSE WILL IT BE, I WONDER?

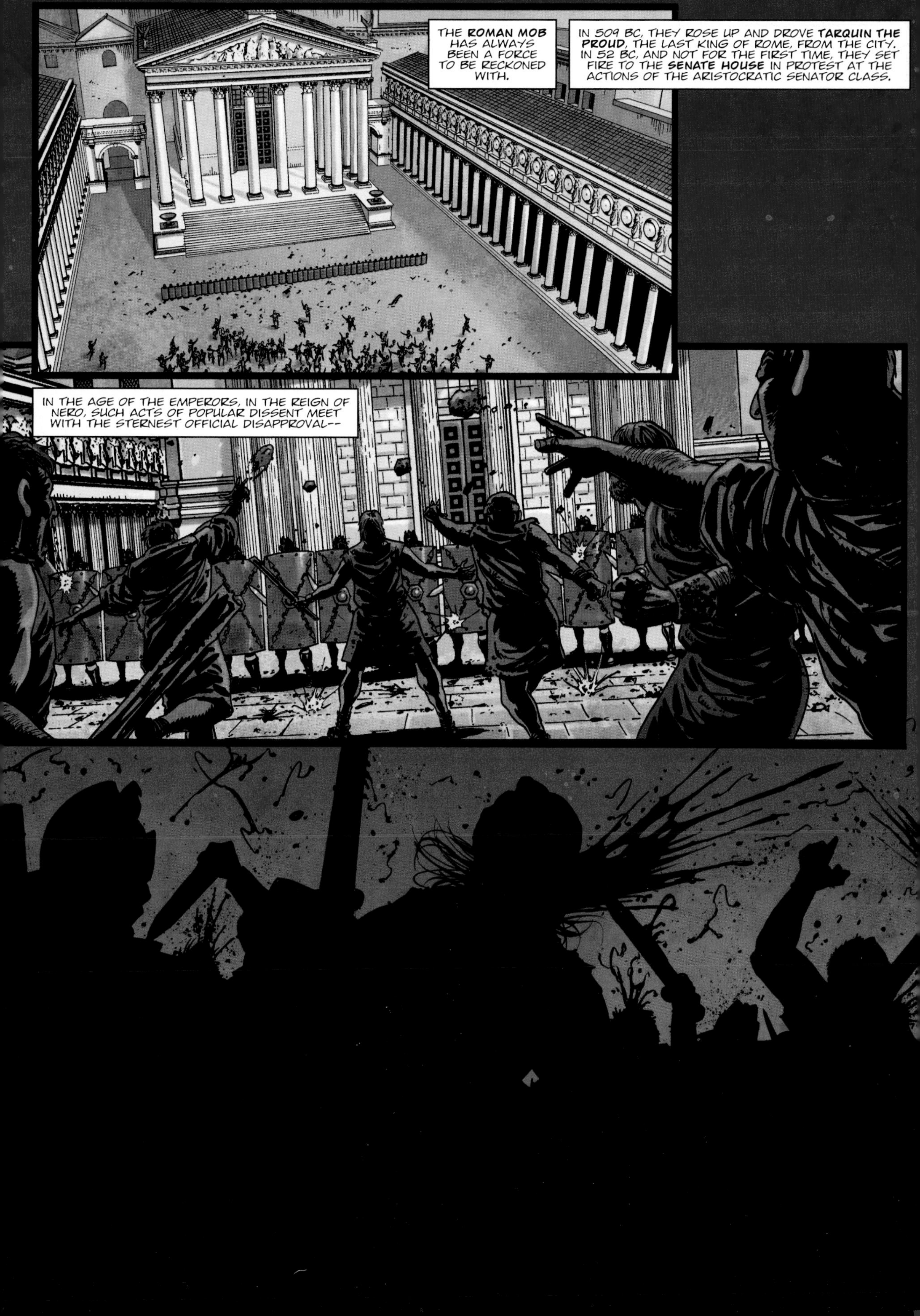
THE **ROMAN MOB** HAS ALWAYS BEEN A FORCE TO BE RECKONED WITH.
IN 509 BC, THEY ROSE UP AND DROVE **TARQUIN THE PROUD**, THE LAST KING OF ROME, FROM THE CITY. IN 52 BC, AND NOT FOR THE FIRST TIME, THEY SET FIRE TO THE **SENATE HOUSE** IN PROTEST AT THE ACTIONS OF THE ARISTOCRATIC SENATOR CLASS.
IN THE AGE OF THE EMPERORS, IN THE REIGN OF NERO, SUCH ACTS OF POPULAR DISSENT MEET WITH THE STERNEST OFFICIAL DISAPPROVAL--

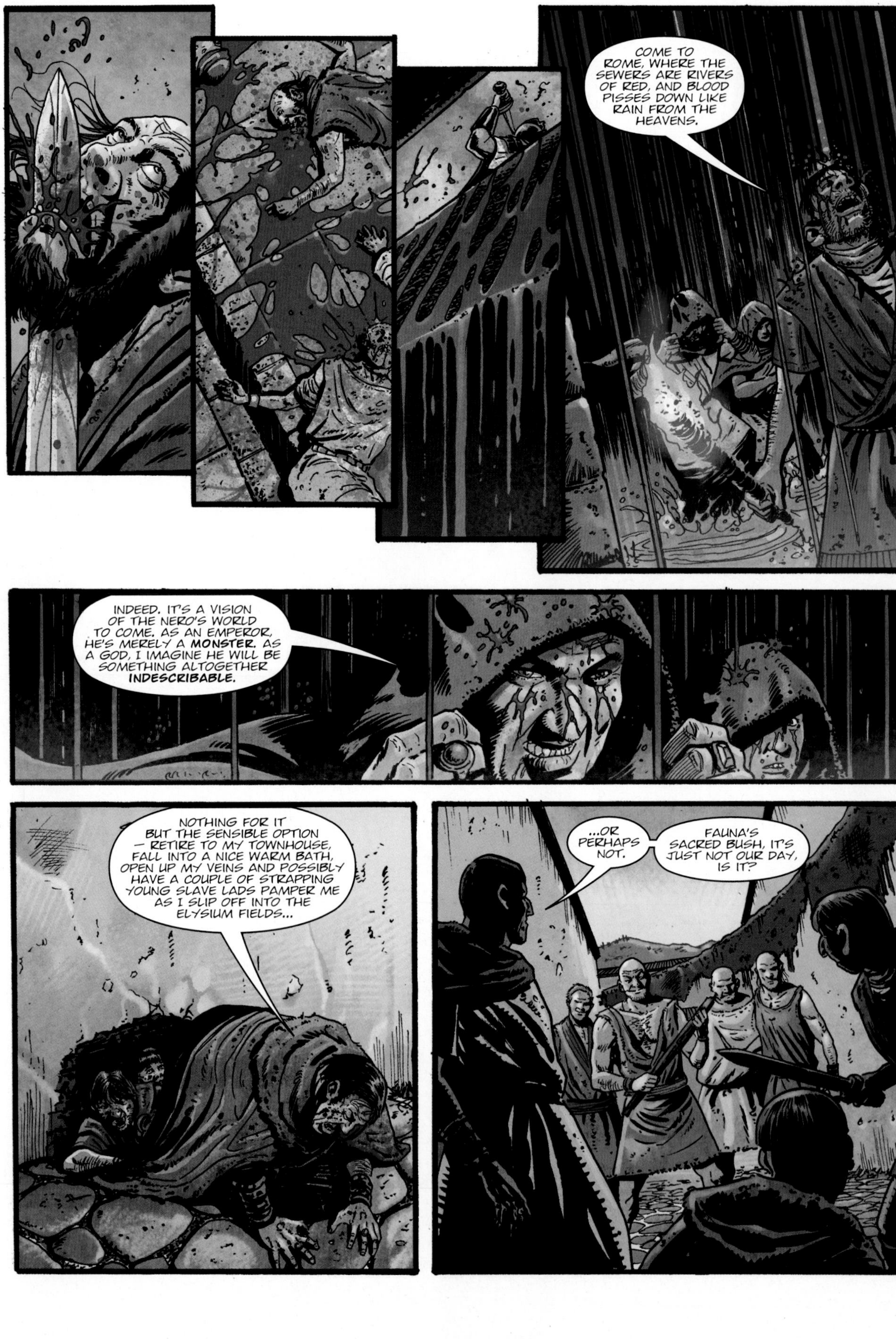
COME TO ROME, WHERE THE SEWERS ARE RIVERS OF RED, AND BLOOD PISSES DOWN LIKE RAIN FROM THE HEAVENS.
INDEED. IT'S A VISION OF THE NERO'S WORLD TO COME. AS AN EMPEROR, HE'S MERELY A **MONSTER**. AS A GOD, I IMAGINE HE WILL BE SOMETHING ALTOGETHER **INDESCRIBABLE**.
NOTHING FOR IT BUT THE SENSIBLE OPTION — RETIRE TO MY TOWNHOUSE, FALL INTO A NICE WARM BATH, OPEN UP MY VEINS AND POSSIBLY HAVE A COUPLE OF STRAPPING YOUNG SLAVE LADS PAMPER ME AS I SLIP OFF INTO THE ELYSIUM FIELDS...
...OR PERHAPS NOT.
FAUNA'S SACRED BUSH, IT'S JUST NOT OUR DAY, IS IT?

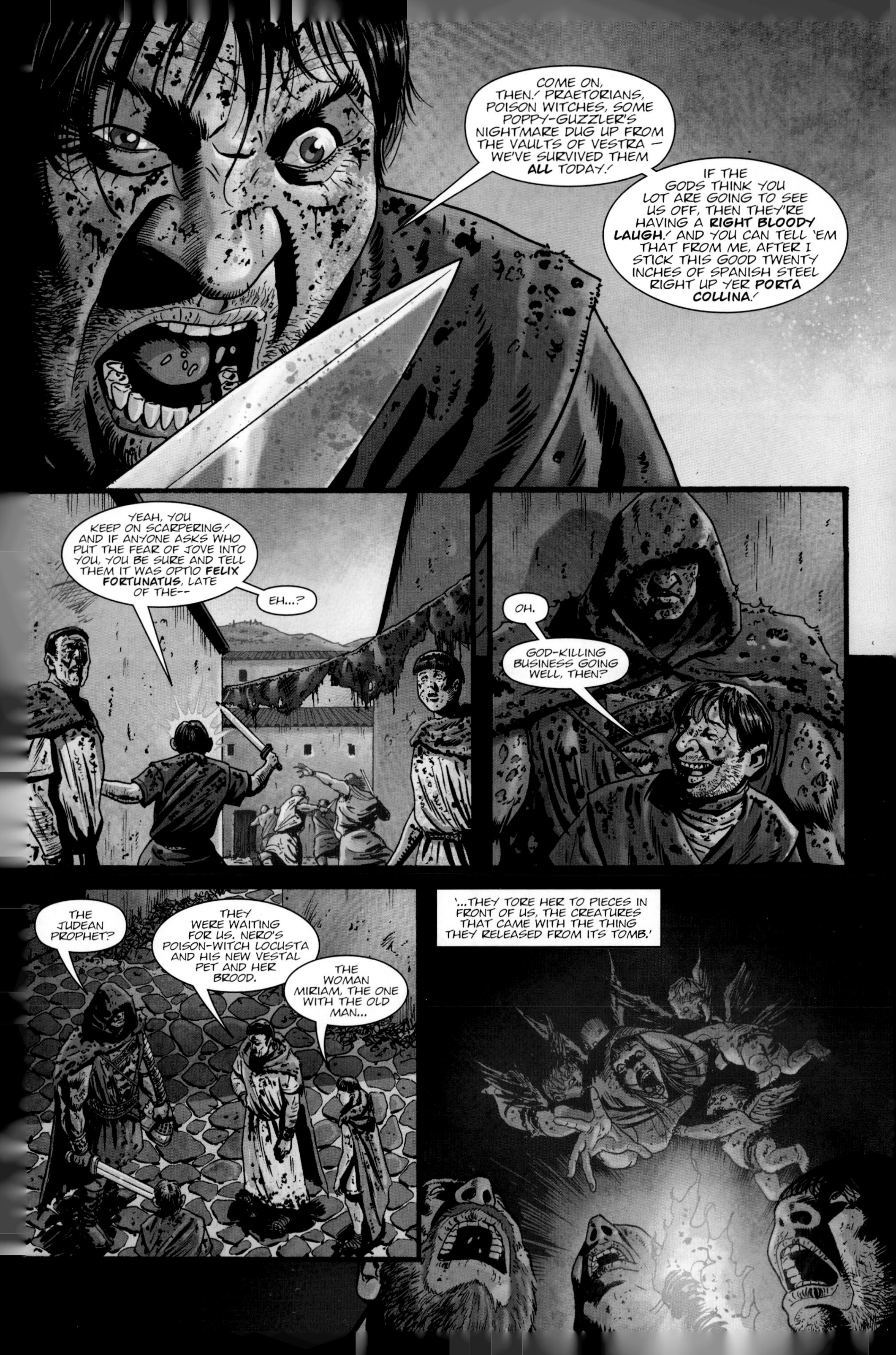
COME ON, THEN! PRAETORIANS, POISON WITCHES, SOME POPPY-GUZZLER'S NIGHTMARE DUG UP FROM THE VAULTS OF VESTRA — WE'VE SURVIVED THEM ALL TODAY!
IF THE GODS THINK YOU LOT ARE GOING TO SEE US OFF, THEN THEY'RE HAVING A RIGHT BLOODY LAUGH! AND YOU CAN TELL 'EM THAT FROM ME, AFTER I STICK THIS GOOD TWENTY INCHES OF SPANISH STEEL RIGHT UP YER PORTA COLLINA!
YEAH, YOU KEEP ON SCARPERING! AND IF ANYONE ASKS WHO PUT THE FEAR OF JOVE INTO YOU, YOU BE SURE AND TELL THEM IT WAS OPTIO FELIX FORTUNATUS, LATE OF THE--
EH...?
OH.
GOD-KILLING BUSINESS GOING WELL, THEN?
THE JUDEAN PROPHET?
THEY WERE WAITING FOR US. NERO'S POISON-WITCH LOCUSTA AND HIS NEW VESTAL PET AND HER BROOD.
THE WOMAN MIRIAM, THE ONE WITH THE OLD MAN...
'...THEY TORE HER TO PIECES IN FRONT OF US, THE CREATURES THAT CAME WITH THE THING THEY RELEASED FROM ITS TOMB.'

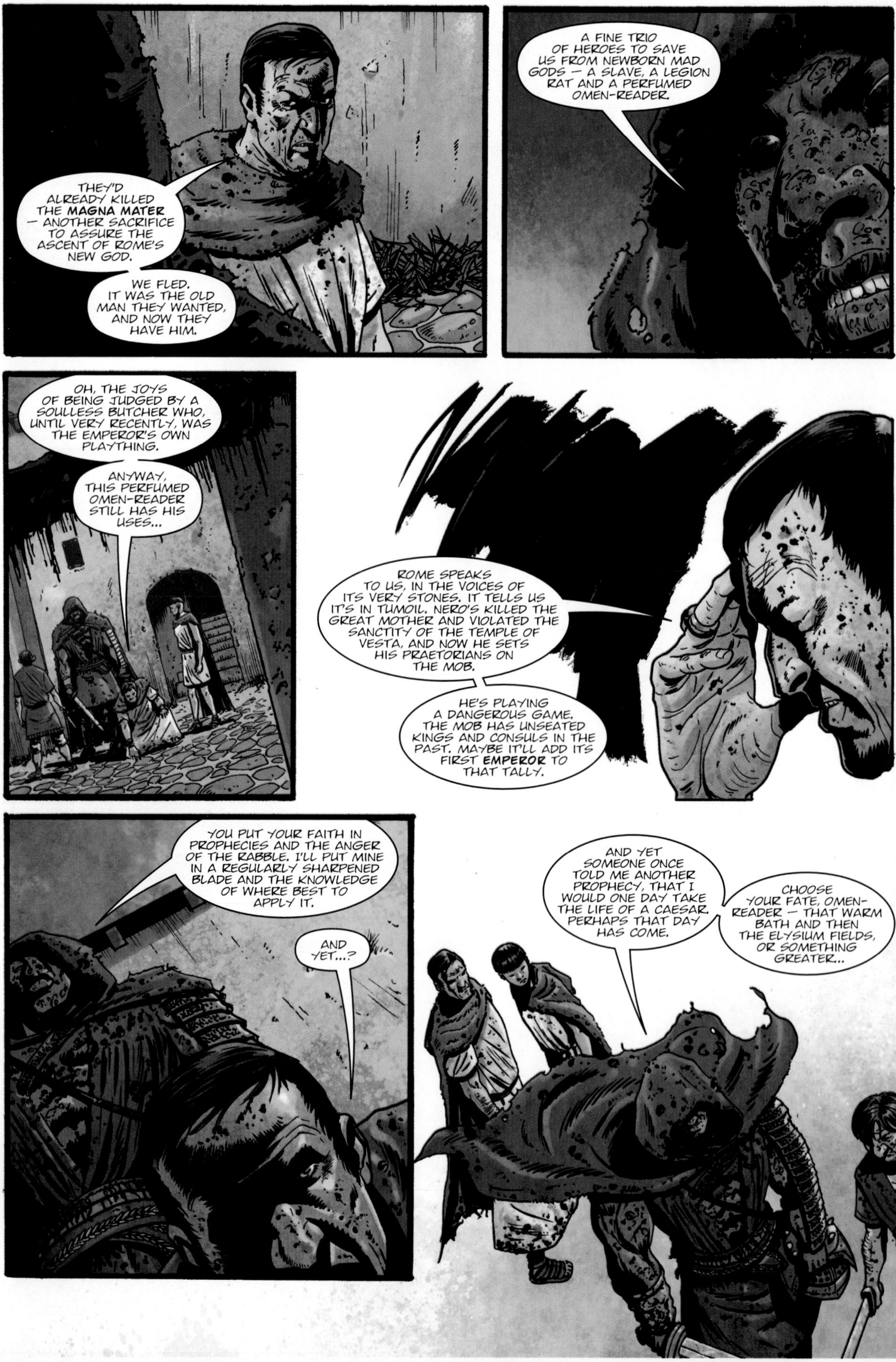
THEY'D ALREADY KILLED THE MAGNA MATER — ANOTHER SACRIFICE TO ASSURE THE ASCENT OF ROME'S NEW GOD.
WE FLED. IT WAS THE OLD MAN THEY WANTED, AND NOW THEY HAVE HIM.
A FINE TRIO OF HEROES TO SAVE US FROM NEWBORN MAD GODS — A SLAVE, A LEGION RAT AND A PERFUMED OMEN-READER.
OH, THE JOYS OF BEING JUDGED BY A SOULLESS BUTCHER WHO, UNTIL VERY RECENTLY, WAS THE EMPEROR'S OWN PLAYTHING.
ANYWAY, THIS PERFUMED OMEN-READER STILL HAS HIS USES...
ROME SPEAKS TO US, IN THE VOICES OF ITS VERY STONES. IT TELLS US IT'S IN TUMOIL. NERO'S KILLED THE GREAT MOTHER AND VIOLATED THE SANCTITY OF THE TEMPLE OF VESTA, AND NOW HE SETS HIS PRAETORIANS ON THE MOB.
HE'S PLAYING A DANGEROUS GAME. THE MOB HAS UNSEATED KINGS AND CONSULS IN THE PAST. MAYBE IT'LL ADD ITS FIRST EMPEROR TO THAT TALLY.
YOU PUT YOUR FAITH IN PROPHECIES AND THE ANGER OF THE RABBLE. I'LL PUT MINE IN A REGULARLY SHARPENED BLADE AND THE KNOWLEDGE OF WHERE BEST TO APPLY IT.
AND YET...?
AND YET SOMEONE ONCE TOLD ME ANOTHER PROPHECY, THAT I WOULD ONE DAY TAKE THE LIFE OF A CAESAR. PERHAPS THAT DAY HAS COME.
CHOOSE YOUR FATE, OMEN-READER — THAT WARM BATH AND THEN THE ELYSIUM FIELDS, OR SOMETHING GREATER...

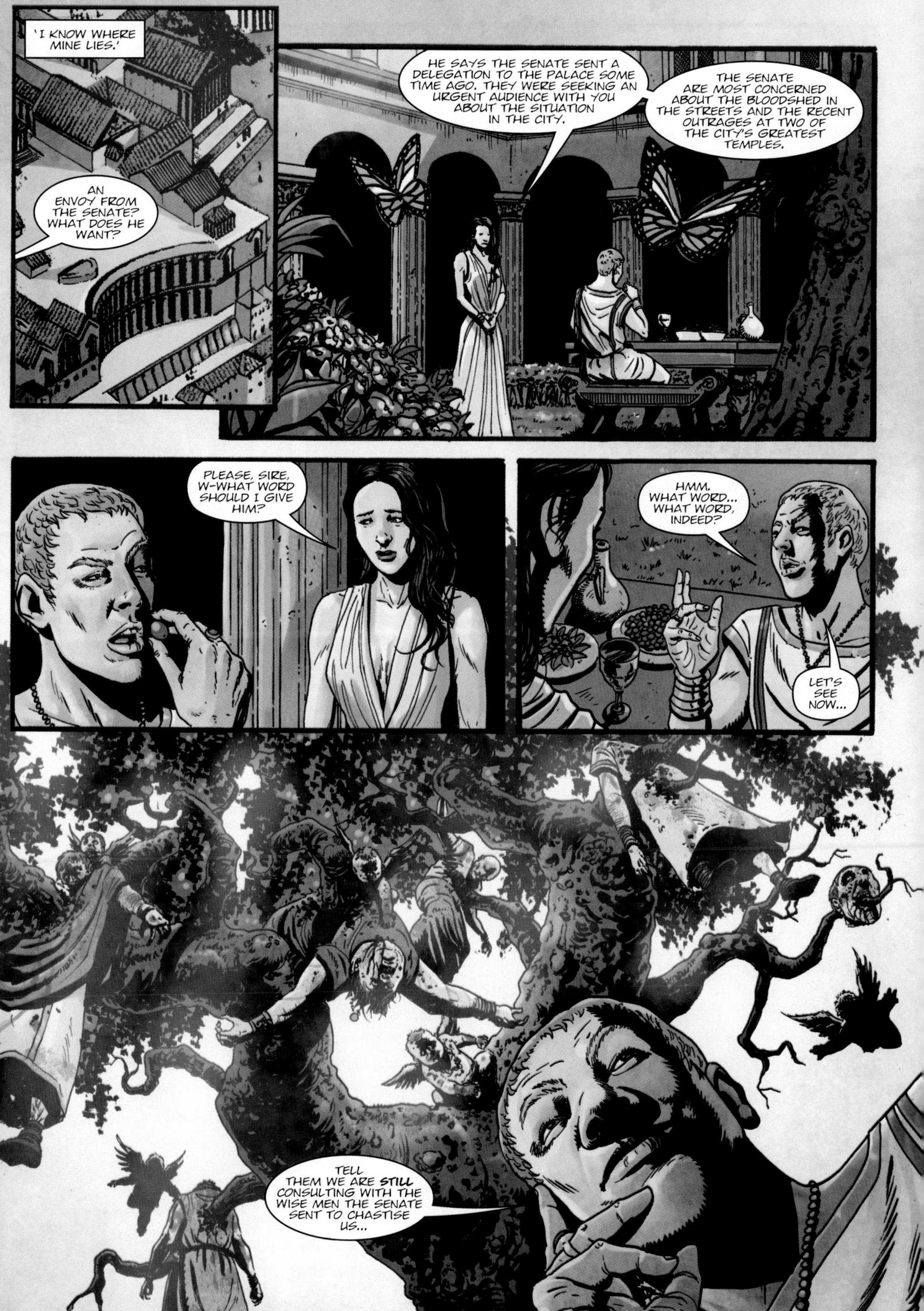
'I KNOW WHERE MINE LIES.'
AN ENVOY FROM THE SENATE? WHAT DOES HE WANT?
HE SAYS THE SENATE SENT A DELEGATION TO THE PALACE SOME TIME AGO. THEY WERE SEEKING AN URGENT AUDIENCE WITH YOU ABOUT THE SITUATION IN THE CITY.
THE SENATE ARE MOST CONCERNED ABOUT THE BLOODSHED IN THE STREETS AND THE RECENT OUTRAGES AT TWO OF THE CITY'S GREATEST TEMPLES.
PLEASE, SIRE, W-WHAT WORD SHOULD I GIVE HIM?
HMM. WHAT WORD... WHAT WORD, INDEED?
LET'S SEE NOW...
TELL THEM WE ARE **STILL** CONSULTING WITH THE WISE MEN THE SENATE SENT TO CHASTISE US...

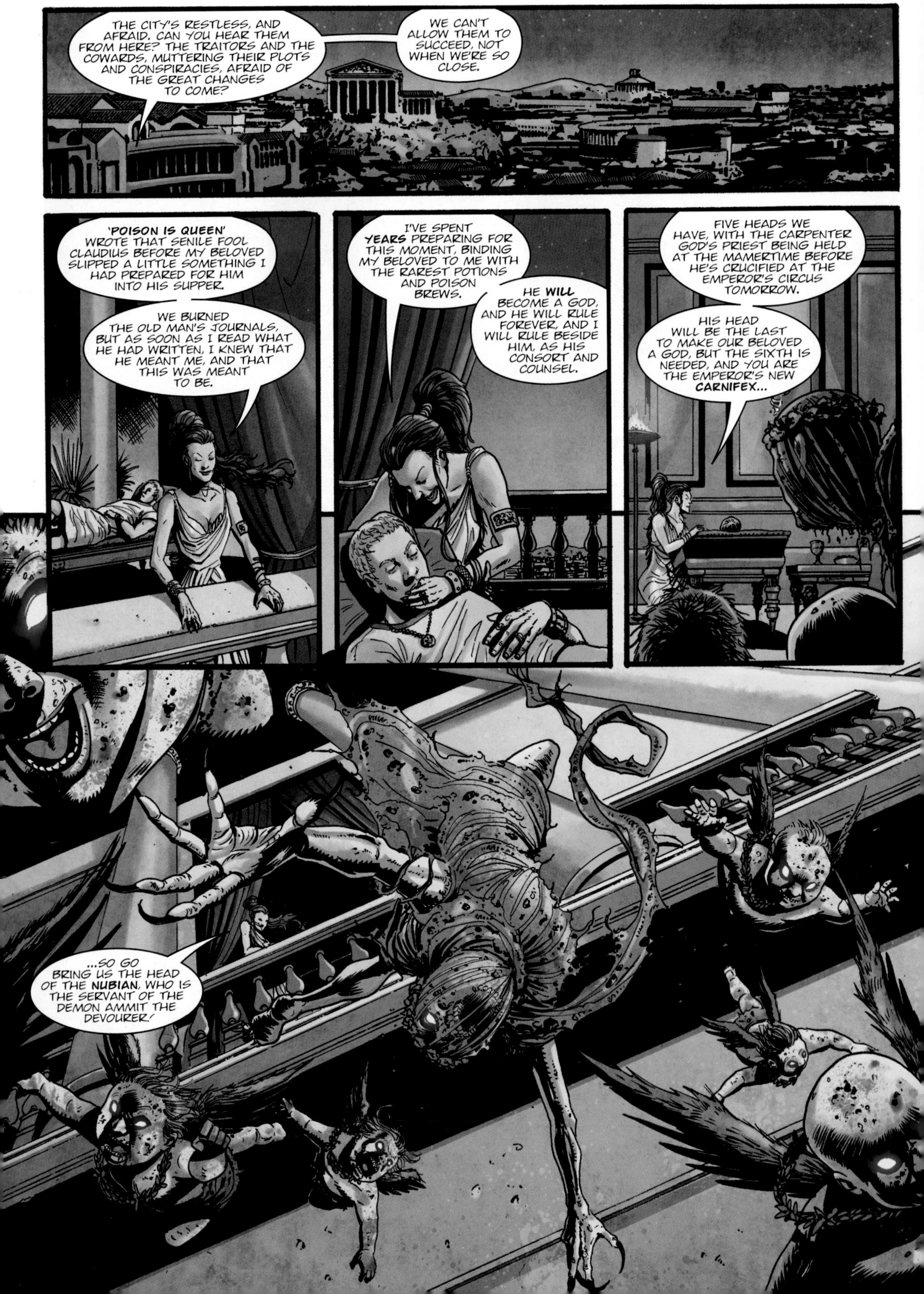
THE CITY'S RESTLESS, AND AFRAID. CAN YOU HEAR THEM FROM HERE? THE TRAITORS AND THE COWARDS, MUTTERING THEIR PLOTS AND CONSPIRACIES, AFRAID OF THE GREAT CHANGES TO COME?
WE CAN'T ALLOW THEM TO SUCCEED, NOT WHEN WE'RE SO CLOSE.
'POISON IS QUEEN' WROTE THAT SENILE FOOL CLAUDIUS BEFORE MY BELOVED SLIPPED A LITTLE SOMETHING I HAD PREPARED FOR HIM INTO HIS SUPPER.
WE BURNED THE OLD MAN'S JOURNALS, BUT AS SOON AS I READ WHAT HE HAD WRITTEN, I KNEW THAT HE MEANT ME, AND THAT THIS WAS MEANT TO BE.
I'VE SPENT YEARS PREPARING FOR THIS MOMENT, BINDING MY BELOVED TO ME WITH THE RAREST POTIONS AND POISON BREWS.
HE WILL BECOME A GOD, AND HE WILL RULE FOREVER, AND I WILL RULE BESIDE HIM, AS HIS CONSORT AND COUNSEL.
FIVE HEADS WE HAVE, WITH THE CARPENTER GOD'S PRIEST BEING HELD AT THE MAMERTIME BEFORE HE'S CRUCIFIED AT THE EMPEROR'S CIRCUS TOMORROW.
HIS HEAD WILL BE THE LAST TO MAKE OUR BELOVED A GOD, BUT THE SIXTH IS NEEDED, AND YOU ARE THE EMPEROR'S NEW CARNIFEX...
...SO GO BRING US THE HEAD OF THE NUBIAN, WHO IS THE SERVANT OF THE DEMON AMMIT THE DEVOURER.'

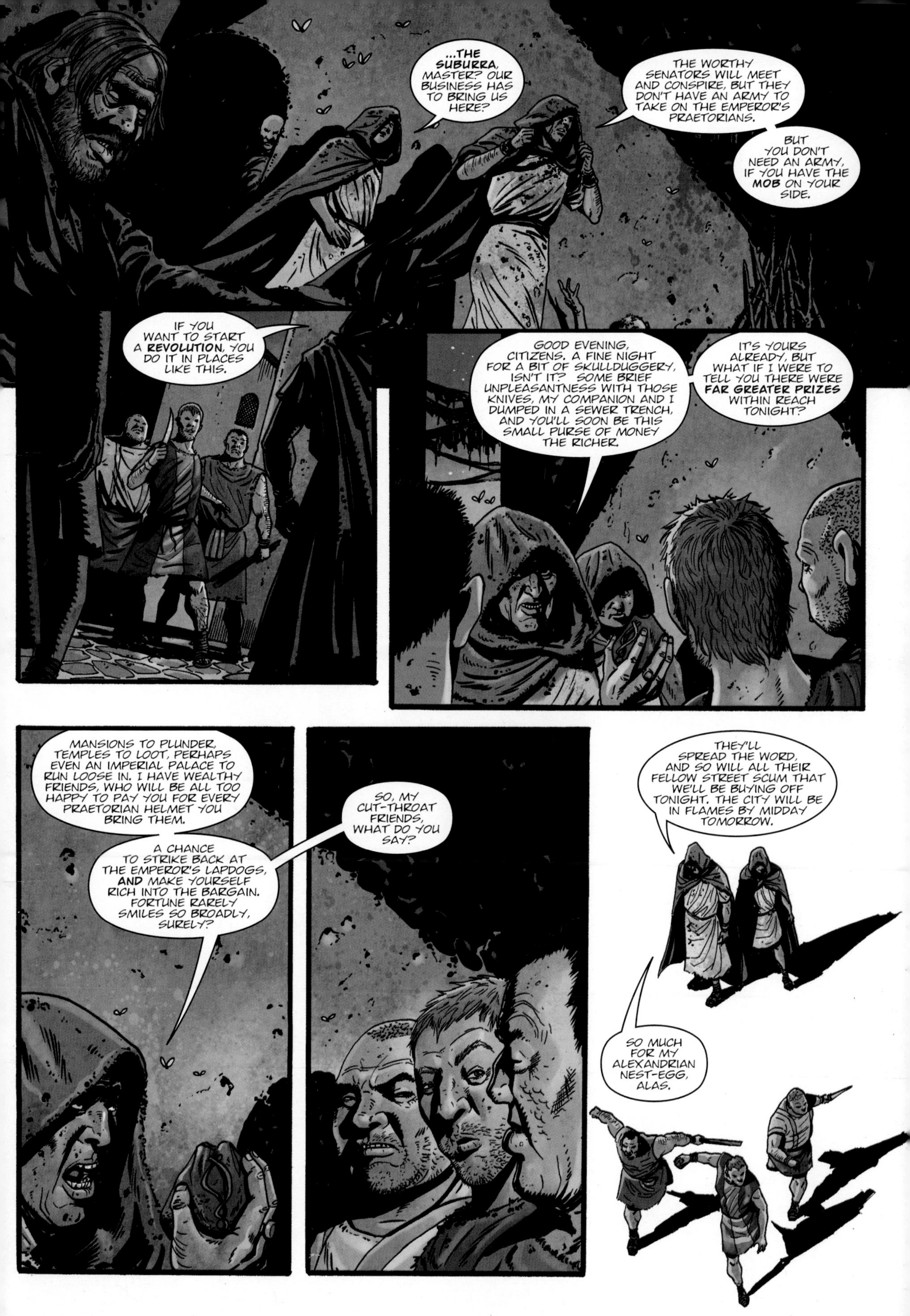
...THE SUBURRA, MASTER? OUR BUSINESS HAS TO BRING US HERE?
THE WORTHY SENATORS WILL MEET AND CONSPIRE, BUT THEY DON'T HAVE AN ARMY TO TAKE ON THE EMPEROR'S PRAETORIANS.
BUT YOU DON'T NEED AN ARMY, IF YOU HAVE THE MOB ON YOUR SIDE.
IF YOU WANT TO START A REVOLUTION, YOU DO IT IN PLACES LIKE THIS.
GOOD EVENING, CITIZENS. A FINE NIGHT FOR A BIT OF SKULLDUGGERY, ISN'T IT? SOME BRIEF UNPLEASANTNESS WITH THOSE KNIVES, MY COMPANION AND I DUMPED IN A SEWER TRENCH, AND YOU'LL SOON BE THIS SMALL PURSE OF MONEY THE RICHER.
IT'S YOURS ALREADY, BUT WHAT IF I WERE TO TELL YOU THERE WERE FAR GREATER PRIZES WITHIN REACH TONIGHT?
MANSIONS TO PLUNDER, TEMPLES TO LOOT, PERHAPS EVEN AN IMPERIAL PALACE TO RUN LOOSE IN. I HAVE WEALTHY FRIENDS, WHO WILL BE ALL TOO HAPPY TO PAY YOU FOR EVERY PRAETORIAN HELMET YOU BRING THEM.
A CHANCE TO STRIKE BACK AT THE EMPEROR'S LAPDOGS, AND MAKE YOURSELF RICH INTO THE BARGAIN. FORTUNE RARELY SMILES SO BROADLY, SURELY?
SO, MY CUT-THROAT FRIENDS, WHAT DO YOU SAY?
THEY'LL SPREAD THE WORD, AND SO WILL ALL THEIR FELLOW STREET SCUM THAT WE'LL BE BUYING OFF TONIGHT. THE CITY WILL BE IN FLAMES BY MIDDAY TOMORROW.
SO MUCH FOR MY ALEXANDRIAN NEST-EGG, ALAS.

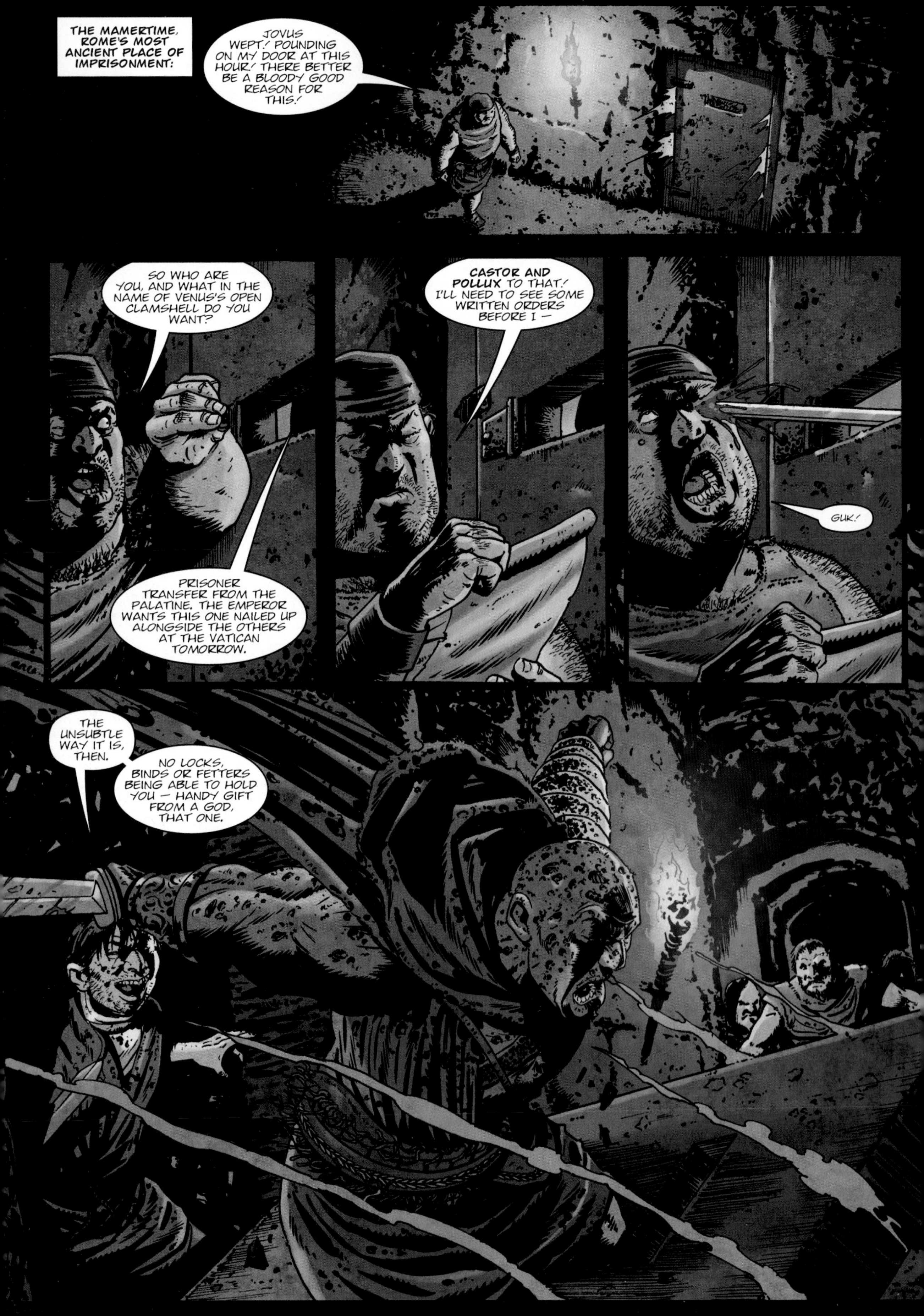
THE MAMERTIME, ROME'S MOST ANCIENT PLACE OF IMPRISONMENT:
JOVUS WEPT! POUNDING ON MY DOOR AT THIS HOUR! THERE BETTER BE A BLOODY GOOD REASON FOR THIS!
SO WHO ARE YOU, AND WHAT IN THE NAME OF VENUS'S OPEN CLAMSHELL DO YOU WANT?
PRISONER TRANSFER FROM THE PALATINE. THE EMPEROR WANTS THIS ONE NAILED UP ALONGSIDE THE OTHERS AT THE VATICAN TOMORROW.
CASTOR AND POLLUX TO THAT! I'LL NEED TO SEE SOME WRITTEN ORDERS BEFORE I —
GUK!
THE UNSUBTLE WAY IT IS, THEN.
NO LOCKS, BINDS OR FETTERS BEING ABLE TO HOLD YOU — HANDY GIFT FROM A GOD, THAT ONE.

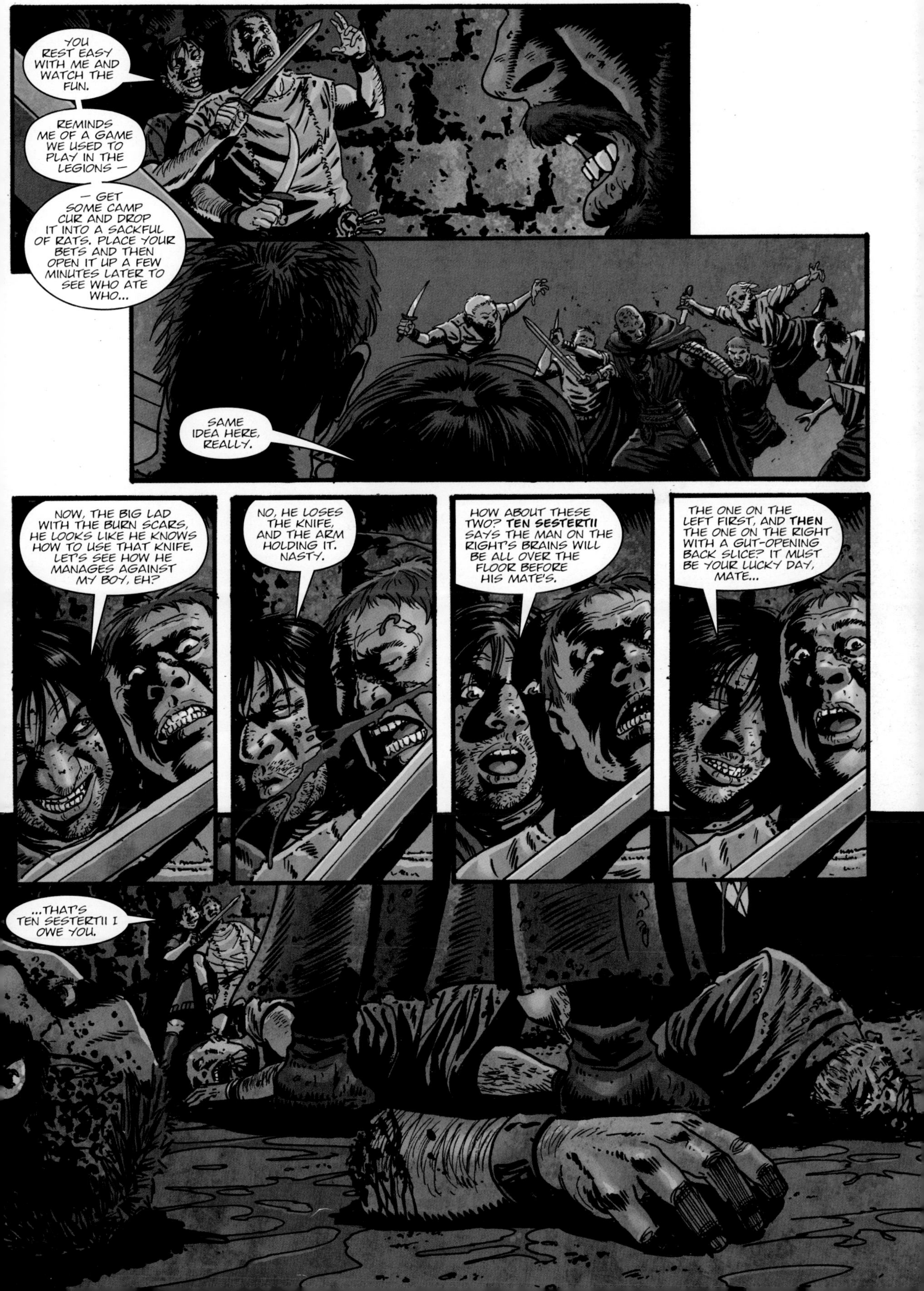
YOU REST EASY WITH ME AND WATCH THE FUN.
REMINDS ME OF A GAME WE USED TO PLAY IN THE LEGIONS —
— GET SOME CAMP CUR AND DROP IT INTO A SACKFUL OF RATS. PLACE YOUR BETS AND THEN OPEN IT UP A FEW MINUTES LATER TO SEE WHO ATE WHO...
SAME IDEA HERE, REALLY.
NOW, THE BIG LAD WITH THE BURN SCARS, HE LOOKS LIKE HE KNOWS HOW TO USE THAT KNIFE. LET'S SEE HOW HE MANAGES AGAINST MY BOY, EH?
NO, HE LOSES THE KNIFE, AND THE ARM HOLDING IT. NASTY.
HOW ABOUT THESE TWO? **TEN SESTERTII** SAYS THE MAN ON THE RIGHT'S BRAINS WILL BE ALL OVER THE FLOOR BEFORE HIS MATE'S.
THE ONE ON THE LEFT FIRST, AND **THEN** THE ONE ON THE RIGHT WITH A GUT-OPENING BACK SLICE? IT MUST BE YOUR LUCKY DAY, MATE...
...THAT'S TEN SESTERTII I OWE YOU.

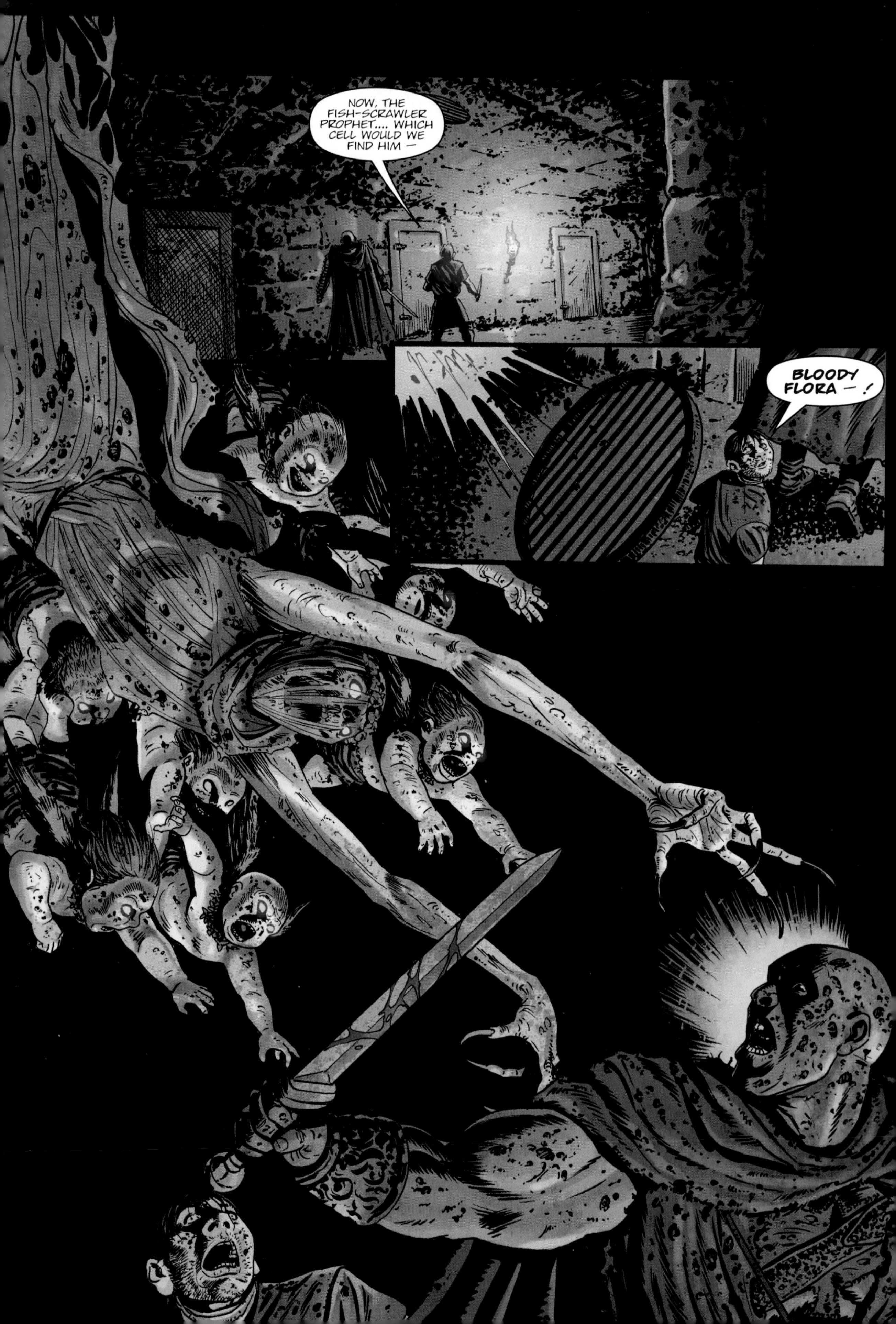
NOW, THE FISH-SCRAWLER PROPHET.... WHICH CELL WOULD WE FIND HIM —
BLOODY FLORA — !

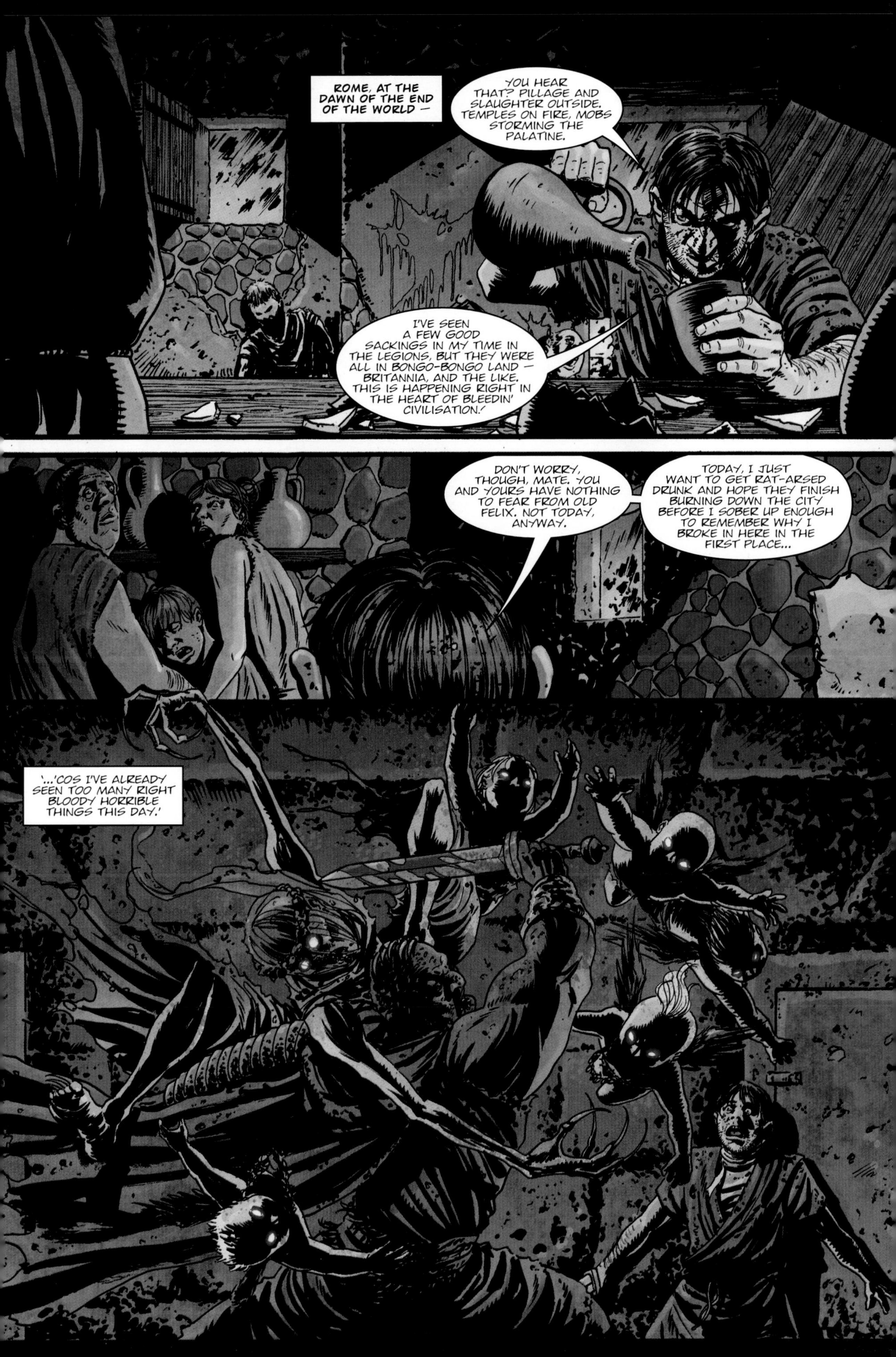
ROME, AT THE DAWN OF THE END OF THE WORLD —
YOU HEAR THAT? PILLAGE AND SLAUGHTER OUTSIDE. TEMPLES ON FIRE, MOBS STORMING THE PALATINE.
I'VE SEEN A FEW GOOD SACKINGS IN MY TIME IN THE LEGIONS, BUT THEY WERE ALL IN BONGO-BONGO LAND — BRITANNIA, AND THE LIKE. THIS IS HAPPENING RIGHT IN THE HEART OF BLEEDIN' CIVILISATION.'
DON'T WORRY, THOUGH, MATE. YOU AND YOURS HAVE NOTHING TO FEAR FROM OLD FELIX. NOT TODAY, ANYWAY.
TODAY, I JUST WANT TO GET RAT-ARSED DRUNK AND HOPE THEY FINISH BURNING DOWN THE CITY BEFORE I SOBER UP ENOUGH TO REMEMBER WHY I BROKE IN HERE IN THE FIRST PLACE...
'...'COS I'VE ALREADY SEEN TOO MANY RIGHT BLOODY HORRIBLE THINGS THIS DAY.'

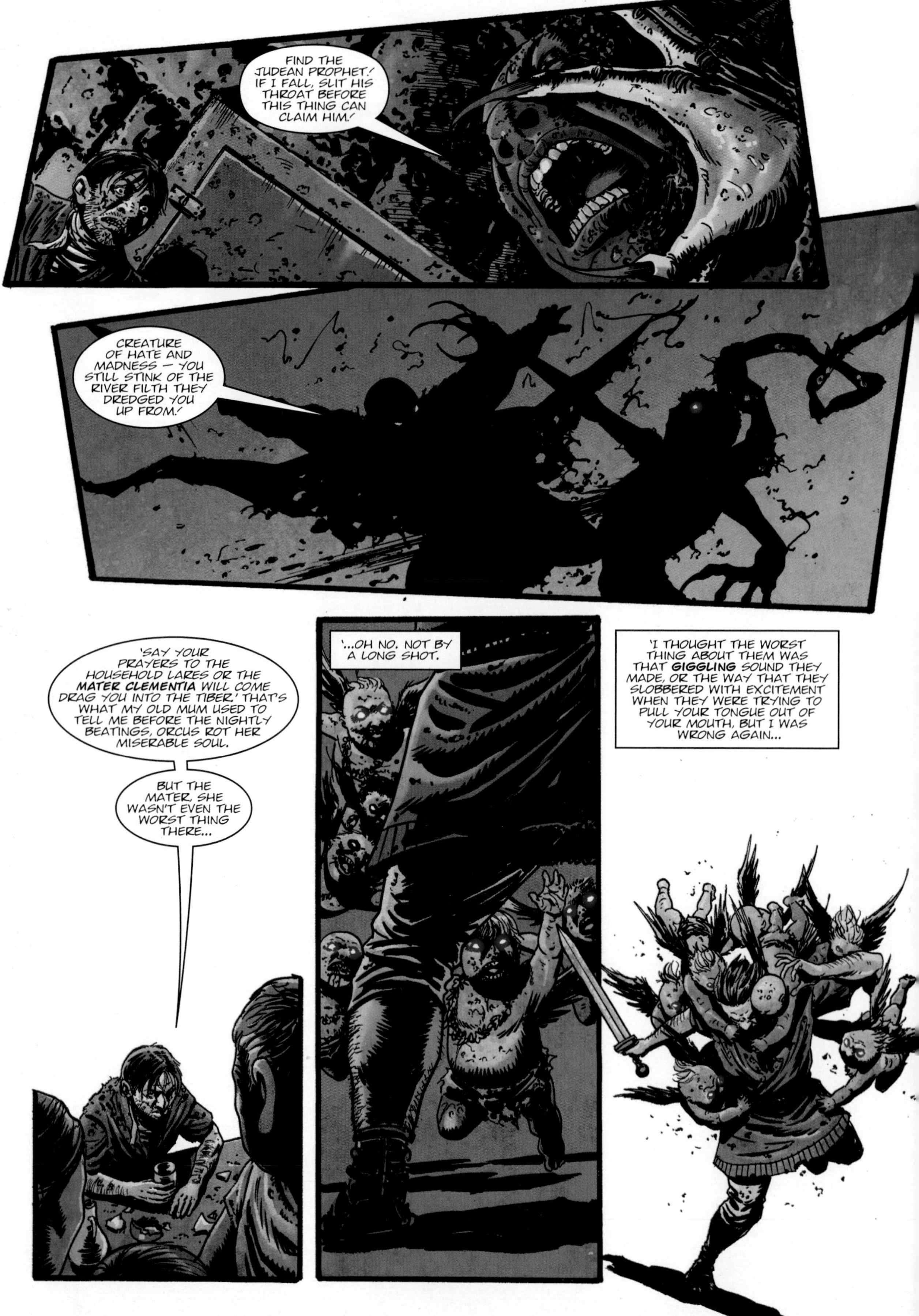

FIND THE JUDEAN PROPHET! IF I FALL, SLIT HIS THROAT BEFORE THIS THING CAN CLAIM HIM!
CREATURE OF HATE AND MADNESS — YOU STILL STINK OF THE RIVER FILTH THEY DREDGED YOU UP FROM!
'SAY YOUR PRAYERS TO THE HOUSEHOLD LARES OR THE **MATER CLEMENTIA** WILL COME DRAG YOU INTO THE TIBER.' THAT'S WHAT MY OLD MUM USED TO TELL ME BEFORE THE NIGHTLY BEATINGS, ORCUS ROT HER MISERABLE SOUL.
BUT THE MATER, SHE WASN'T EVEN THE WORST THING THERE...
'...OH NO. NOT BY A LONG SHOT.
'I THOUGHT THE WORST THING ABOUT THEM WAS THAT **GIGGLING** SOUND THEY MADE, OR THE WAY THAT THEY SLOBBERED WITH EXCITEMENT WHEN THEY WERE TRYING TO PULL YOUR TONGUE OUT OF YOUR MOUTH, BUT I WAS WRONG AGAIN...

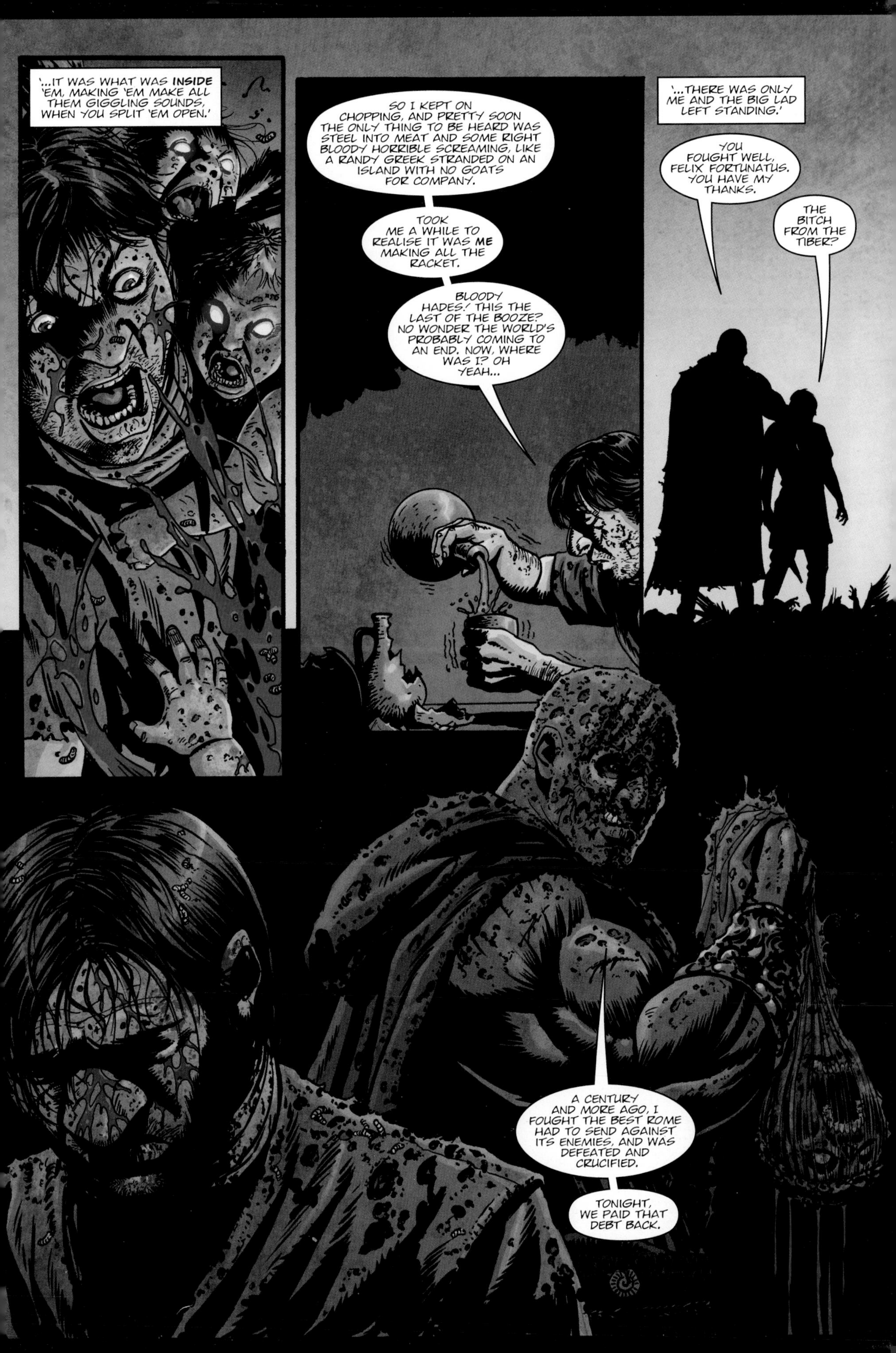
'...IT WAS WHAT WAS INSIDE 'EM, MAKING 'EM MAKE ALL THEM GIGGLING SOUNDS, WHEN YOU SPLIT 'EM OPEN.'
SO I KEPT ON CHOPPING, AND PRETTY SOON THE ONLY THING TO BE HEARD WAS STEEL INTO MEAT AND SOME RIGHT BLOODY HORRIBLE SCREAMING, LIKE A RANDY GREEK STRANDED ON AN ISLAND WITH NO GOATS FOR COMPANY.
TOOK ME A WHILE TO REALISE IT WAS ME MAKING ALL THE RACKET.
BLOODY HADES! THIS THE LAST OF THE BOOZE? NO WONDER THE WORLD'S PROBABLY COMING TO AN END. NOW, WHERE WAS I? OH YEAH...
'...THERE WAS ONLY ME AND THE BIG LAD LEFT STANDING.'
YOU FOUGHT WELL, FELIX FORTUNATUS. YOU HAVE MY THANKS.
THE BITCH FROM THE TIBER?
A CENTURY AND MORE AGO, I FOUGHT THE BEST ROME HAD TO SEND AGAINST ITS ENEMIES, AND WAS DEFEATED AND CRUCIFIED.
TONIGHT, WE PAID THAT DEBT BACK.

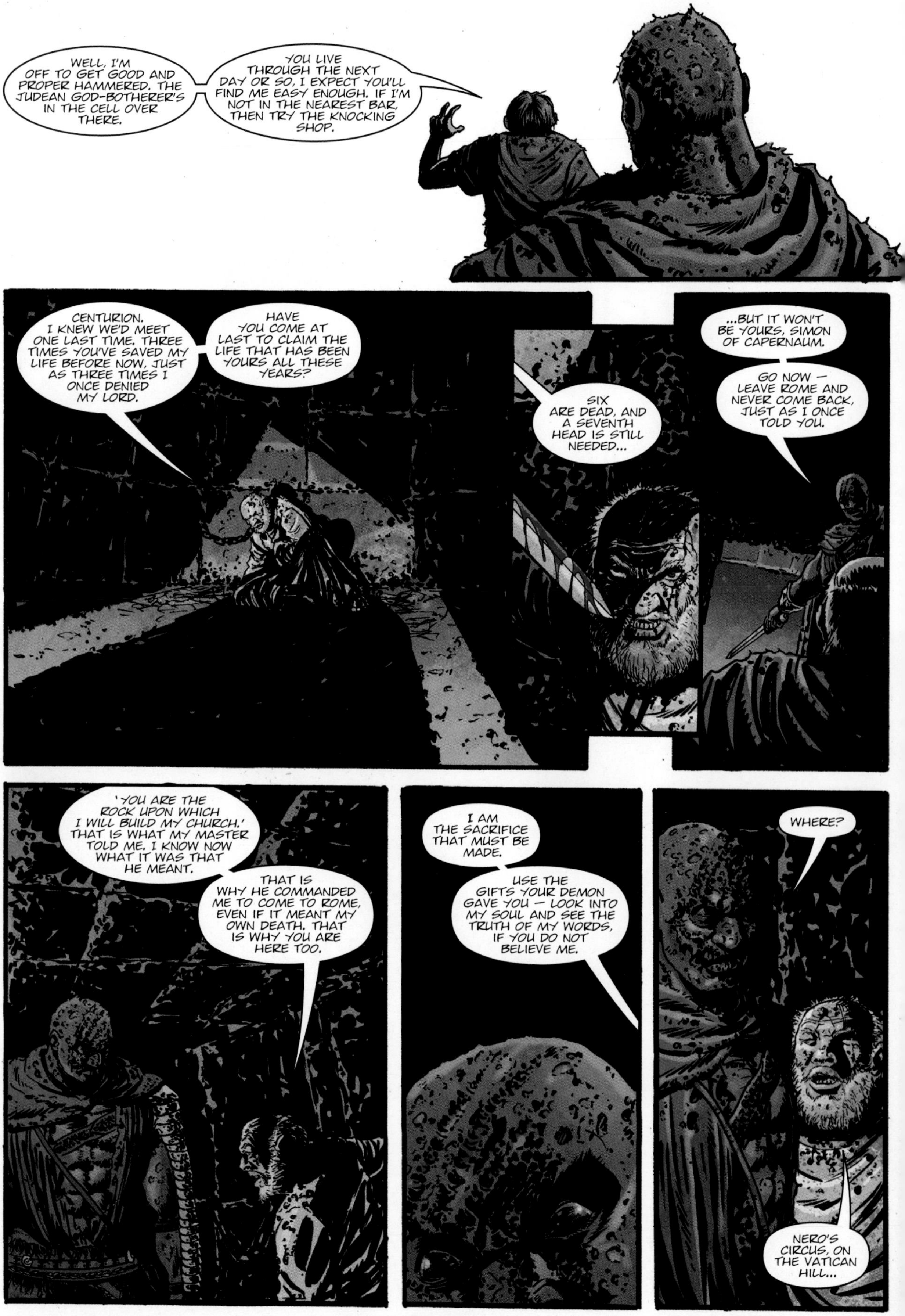
WELL, I'M OFF TO GET GOOD AND PROPER HAMMERED. THE JUDEAN GOD-BOTHERER'S IN THE CELL OVER THERE.
YOU LIVE THROUGH THE NEXT DAY OR SO, I EXPECT YOU'LL FIND ME EASY ENOUGH. IF I'M NOT IN THE NEAREST BAR, THEN TRY THE KNOCKING SHOP.
CENTURION. I KNEW WE'D MEET ONE LAST TIME. THREE TIMES YOU'VE SAVED MY LIFE BEFORE NOW, JUST AS THREE TIMES I ONCE DENIED MY LORD.
HAVE YOU COME AT LAST TO CLAIM THE LIFE THAT HAS BEEN YOURS ALL THESE YEARS?
SIX ARE DEAD, AND A SEVENTH HEAD IS STILL NEEDED...
...BUT IT WON'T BE YOURS, SIMON OF CAPERNAUM.
GO NOW — LEAVE ROME AND NEVER COME BACK, JUST AS I ONCE TOLD YOU.
'YOU ARE THE ROCK UPON WHICH I WILL BUILD MY CHURCH.' THAT IS WHAT MY MASTER TOLD ME. I KNOW NOW WHAT IT WAS THAT HE MEANT.
THAT IS WHY HE COMMANDED ME TO COME TO ROME, EVEN IF IT MEANT MY OWN DEATH. THAT IS WHY YOU ARE HERE TOO.
I AM THE SACRIFICE THAT MUST BE MADE.
USE THE GIFTS YOUR DEMON GAVE YOU — LOOK INTO MY SOUL AND SEE THE TRUTH OF MY WORDS, IF YOU DO NOT BELIEVE ME.
WHERE?
NERO'S CIRCUS, ON THE VATICAN HILL...

'...THAT IS WHERE WE WILL BEGIN TO BUILD MY MASTER'S CHURCH.'

THE CIRCUS OF NERO —

AN OLD MAN DIES IN AGONY. A NEW GOD'S POWER RISES IN ROME.

FOR BETTER OR FOR WORSE, THE WORLD WILL NEVER BE THE SAME AGAIN.

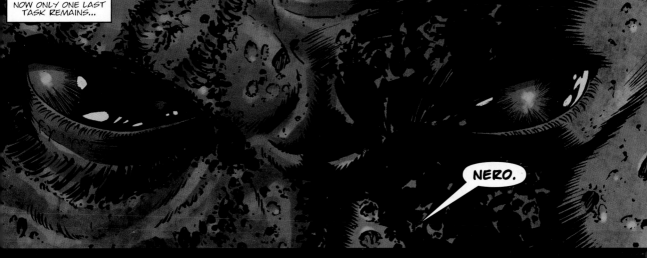

NOW ONLY ONE LAST TASK REMAINS...

NERO.

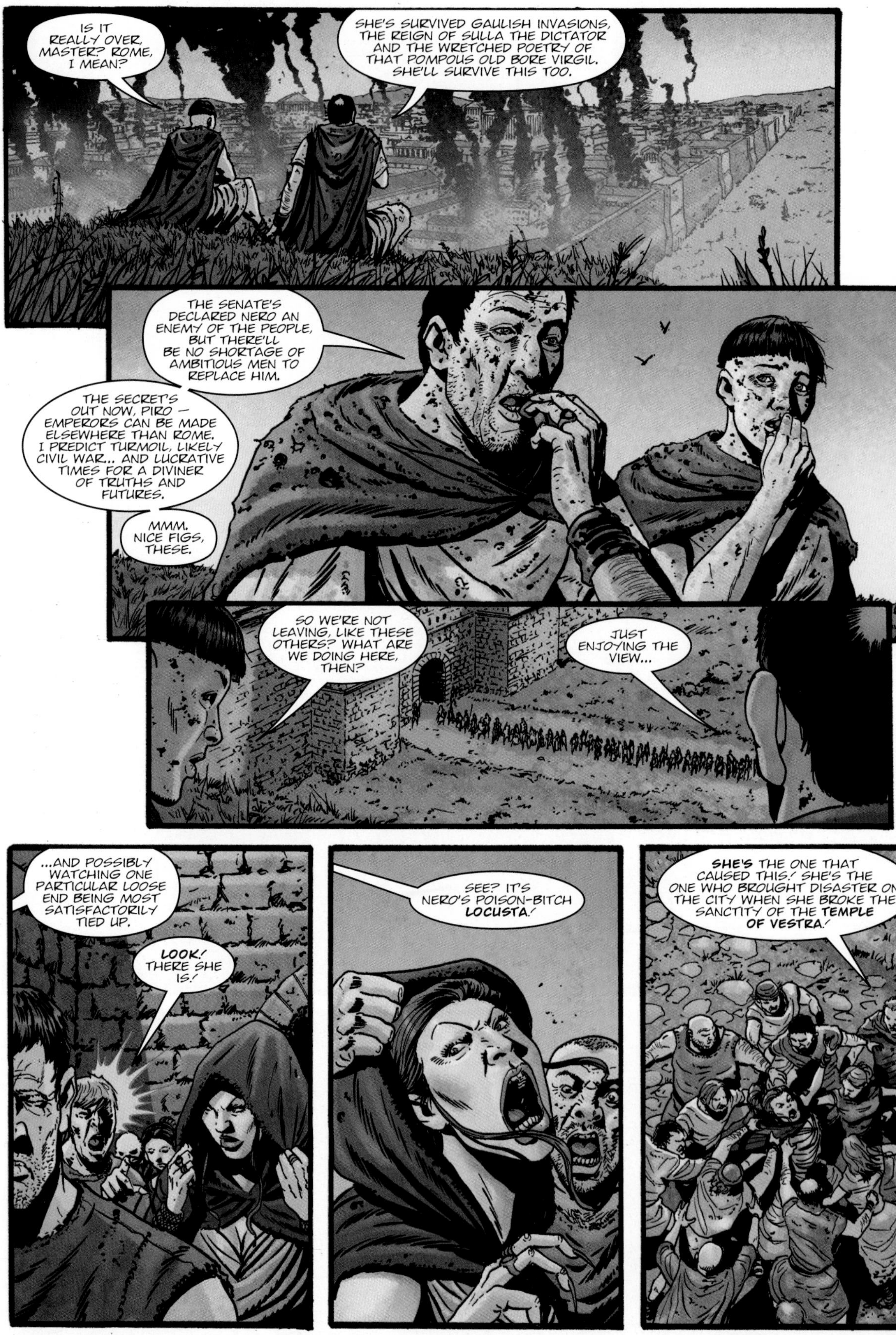
IS IT REALLY OVER, MASTER? ROME, I MEAN?
SHE'S SURVIVED GAULISH INVASIONS, THE REIGN OF SULLA THE DICTATOR AND THE WRETCHED POETRY OF THAT POMPOUS OLD BORE VIRGIL. SHE'LL SURVIVE THIS TOO.
THE SENATE'S DECLARED NERO AN ENEMY OF THE PEOPLE, BUT THERE'LL BE NO SHORTAGE OF AMBITIOUS MEN TO REPLACE HIM.
THE SECRET'S OUT NOW, PIRO — EMPERORS CAN BE MADE ELSEWHERE THAN ROME. I PREDICT TURMOIL, LIKELY CIVIL WAR... AND LUCRATIVE TIMES FOR A DIVINER OF TRUTHS AND FUTURES.
MMM. NICE FIGS, THESE.
SO WE'RE NOT LEAVING, LIKE THESE OTHERS? WHAT ARE WE DOING HERE, THEN?
JUST ENJOYING THE VIEW...
...AND POSSIBLY WATCHING ONE PARTICULAR LOOSE END BEING MOST SATISFACTORILY TIED UP.
LOOK! THERE SHE IS!
SEE? IT'S NERO'S POISON-BITCH LOCUSTA!
SHE'S THE ONE THAT CAUSED THIS! SHE'S THE ONE WHO BROUGHT DISASTER ON THE CITY WHEN SHE BROKE THE SANCTITY OF THE TEMPLE OF VESTRA!

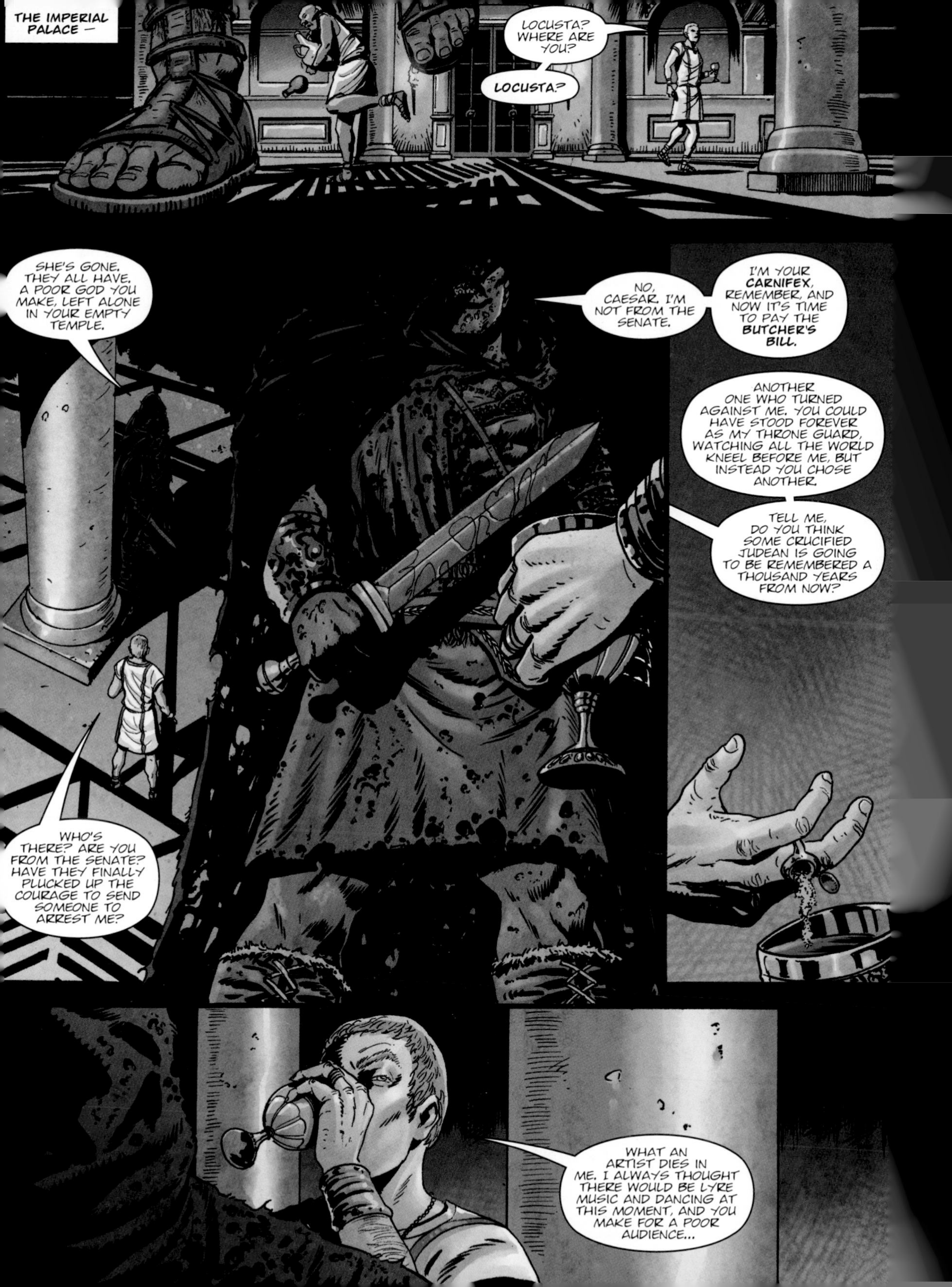
THE IMPERIAL PALACE —
LOCUSTA? WHERE ARE YOU?
LOCUSTA?
SHE'S GONE. THEY ALL HAVE. A POOR GOD YOU MAKE, LEFT ALONE IN YOUR EMPTY TEMPLE.
WHO'S THERE? ARE YOU FROM THE SENATE? HAVE THEY FINALLY PLUCKED UP THE COURAGE TO SEND SOMEONE TO ARREST ME?
NO, CAESAR. I'M NOT FROM THE SENATE.
I'M YOUR CARNIFEX, REMEMBER, AND NOW IT'S TIME TO PAY THE BUTCHER'S BILL.
ANOTHER ONE WHO TURNED AGAINST ME. YOU COULD HAVE STOOD FOREVER AS MY THRONE GUARD, WATCHING ALL THE WORLD KNEEL BEFORE ME, BUT INSTEAD YOU CHOSE ANOTHER.
TELL ME, DO YOU THINK SOME CRUCIFIED JUDEAN IS GOING TO BE REMEMBERED A THOUSAND YEARS FROM NOW?
WHAT AN ARTIST DIES IN ME. I ALWAYS THOUGHT THERE WOULD BE LYRE MUSIC AND DANCING AT THIS MOMENT, AND YOU MAKE FOR A POOR AUDIENCE...

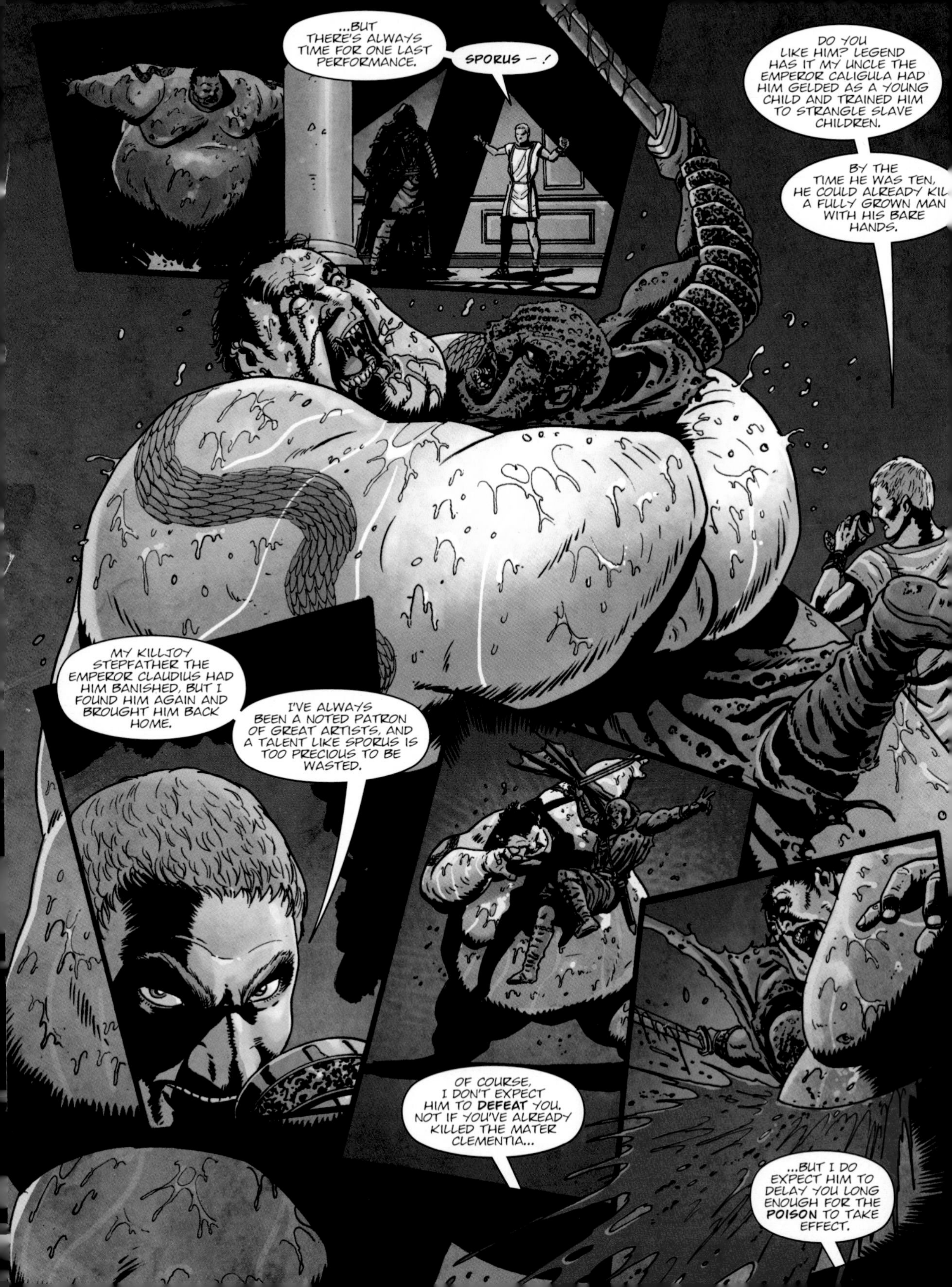
...BUT THERE'S ALWAYS TIME FOR ONE LAST PERFORMANCE.
SPORUS — !
DO YOU LIKE HIM? LEGEND HAS IT MY UNCLE THE EMPEROR CALIGULA HAD HIM GELDED AS A YOUNG CHILD AND TRAINED HIM TO STRANGLE SLAVE CHILDREN.
BY THE TIME HE WAS TEN, HE COULD ALREADY KIL A FULLY GROWN MAN WITH HIS BARE HANDS.
MY KILLJOY STEPFATHER THE EMPEROR CLAUDIUS HAD HIM BANISHED, BUT I FOUND HIM AGAIN AND BROUGHT HIM BACK HOME.
I'VE ALWAYS BEEN A NOTED PATRON OF GREAT ARTISTS, AND A TALENT LIKE SPORUS IS TOO PRECIOUS TO BE WASTED.
OF COURSE, I DON'T EXPECT HIM TO **DEFEAT** YOU. NOT IF YOU'VE ALREADY KILLED THE MATER CLEMENTIA...
...BUT I DO EXPECT HIM TO DELAY YOU LONG ENOUGH FOR THE **POISON** TO TAKE EFFECT.

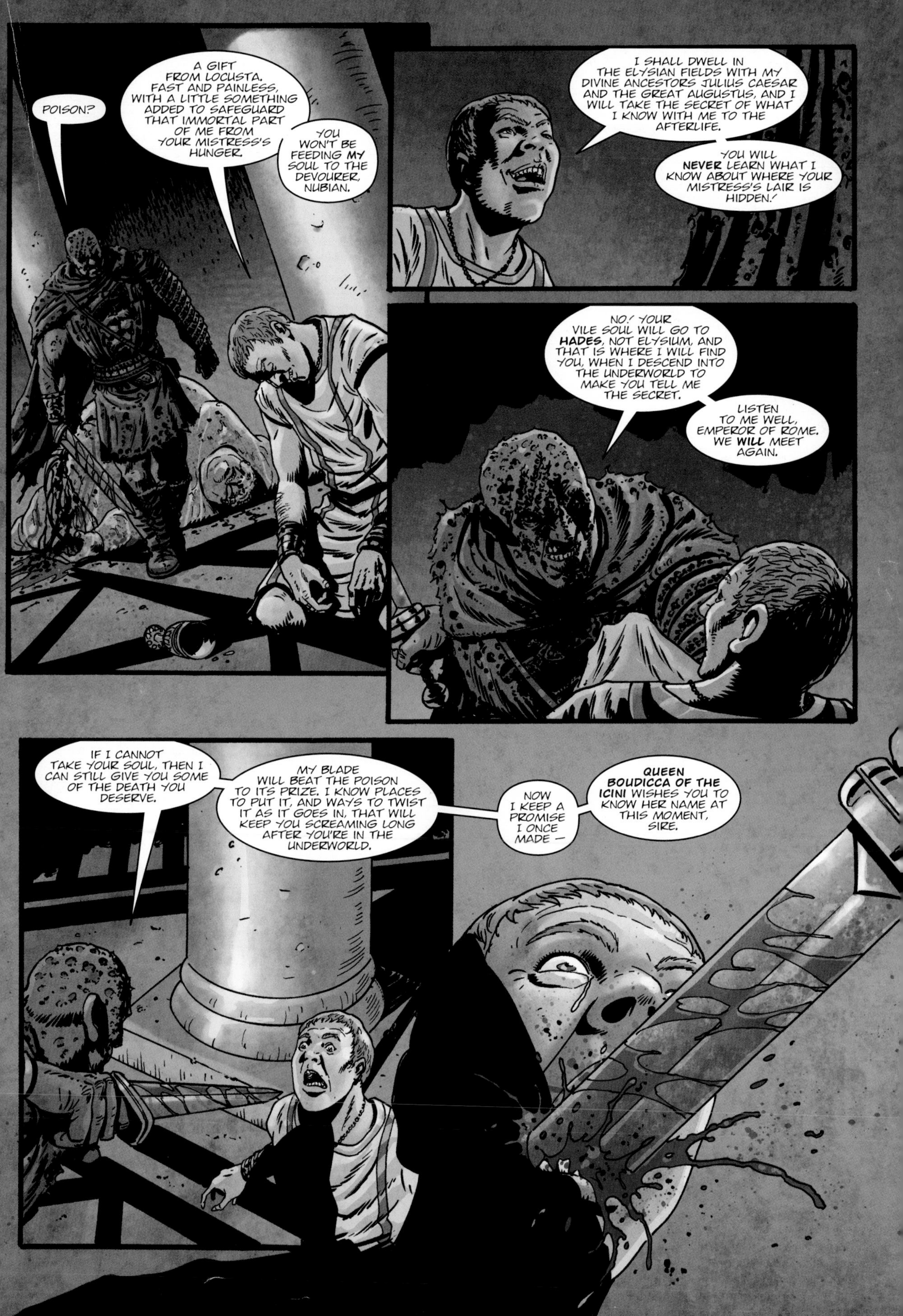
POISON?
A GIFT FROM LOCUSTA. FAST AND PAINLESS, WITH A LITTLE SOMETHING ADDED TO SAFEGUARD THAT IMMORTAL PART OF ME FROM YOUR MISTRESS'S HUNGER.
YOU WON'T BE FEEDING MY SOUL TO THE DEVOURER, NUBIAN.
I SHALL DWELL IN THE ELYSIAN FIELDS WITH MY DIVINE ANCESTORS JULIUS CAESAR AND THE GREAT AUGUSTUS, AND I WILL TAKE THE SECRET OF WHAT I KNOW WITH ME TO THE AFTERLIFE.
YOU WILL NEVER LEARN WHAT I KNOW ABOUT WHERE YOUR MISTRESS'S LAIR IS HIDDEN!
NO! YOUR VILE SOUL WILL GO TO HADES, NOT ELYSIUM, AND THAT IS WHERE I WILL FIND YOU, WHEN I DESCEND INTO THE UNDERWORLD TO MAKE YOU TELL ME THE SECRET.
LISTEN TO ME WELL, EMPEROR OF ROME. WE WILL MEET AGAIN.
IF I CANNOT TAKE YOUR SOUL, THEN I CAN STILL GIVE YOU SOME OF THE DEATH YOU DESERVE.
MY BLADE WILL BEAT THE POISON TO ITS PRIZE. I KNOW PLACES TO PUT IT, AND WAYS TO TWIST IT AS IT GOES IN, THAT WILL KEEP YOU SCREAMING LONG AFTER YOU'RE IN THE UNDERWORLD.
NOW I KEEP A PROMISE I ONCE MADE —
QUEEN BOUDICCA OF THE ICINI WISHES YOU TO KNOW HER NAME AT THIS MOMENT, SIRE.

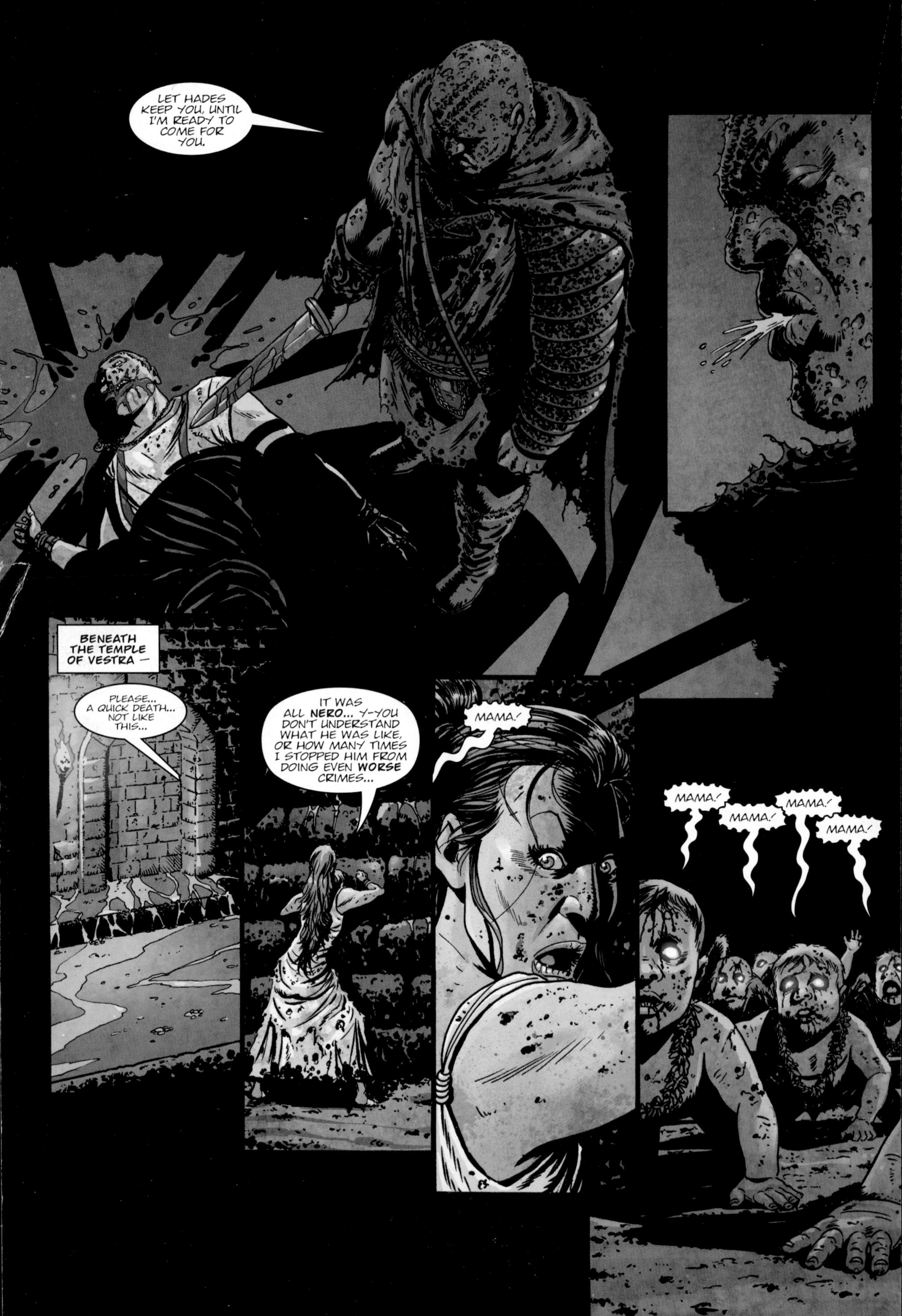
LET HADES KEEP YOU, UNTIL I'M READY TO COME FOR YOU.
BENEATH THE TEMPLE OF VESTRA —
PLEASE... A QUICK DEATH... NOT LIKE THIS...
IT WAS ALL NERO... Y-YOU DON'T UNDERSTAND WHAT HE WAS LIKE, OR HOW MANY TIMES I STOPPED HIM FROM DOING EVEN WORSE CRIMES...
MAMA!
MAMA!
MAMA!
MAMA!
MAMA!

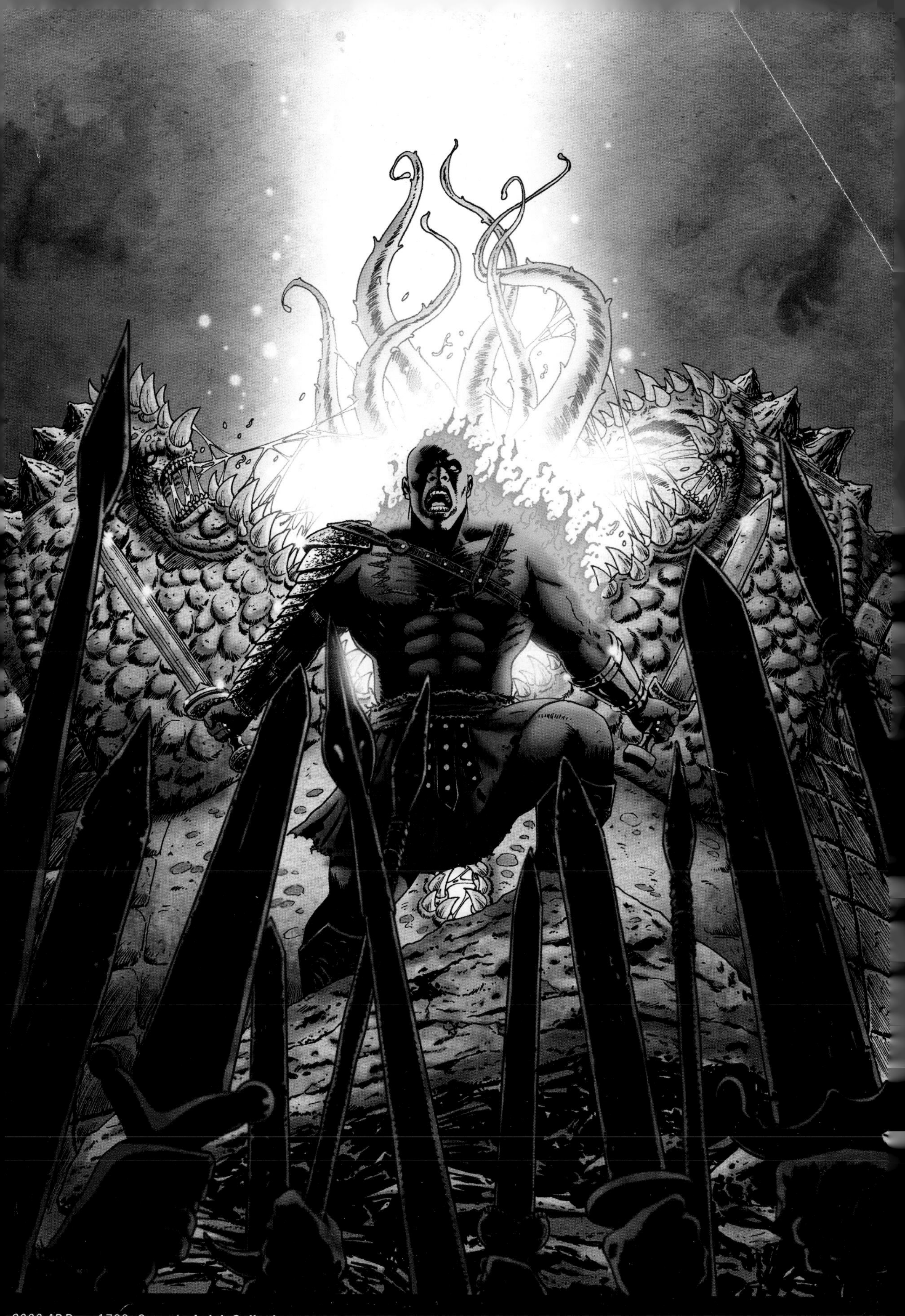

2000 AD Prog 1793: Cover by **Leigh Gallagher**

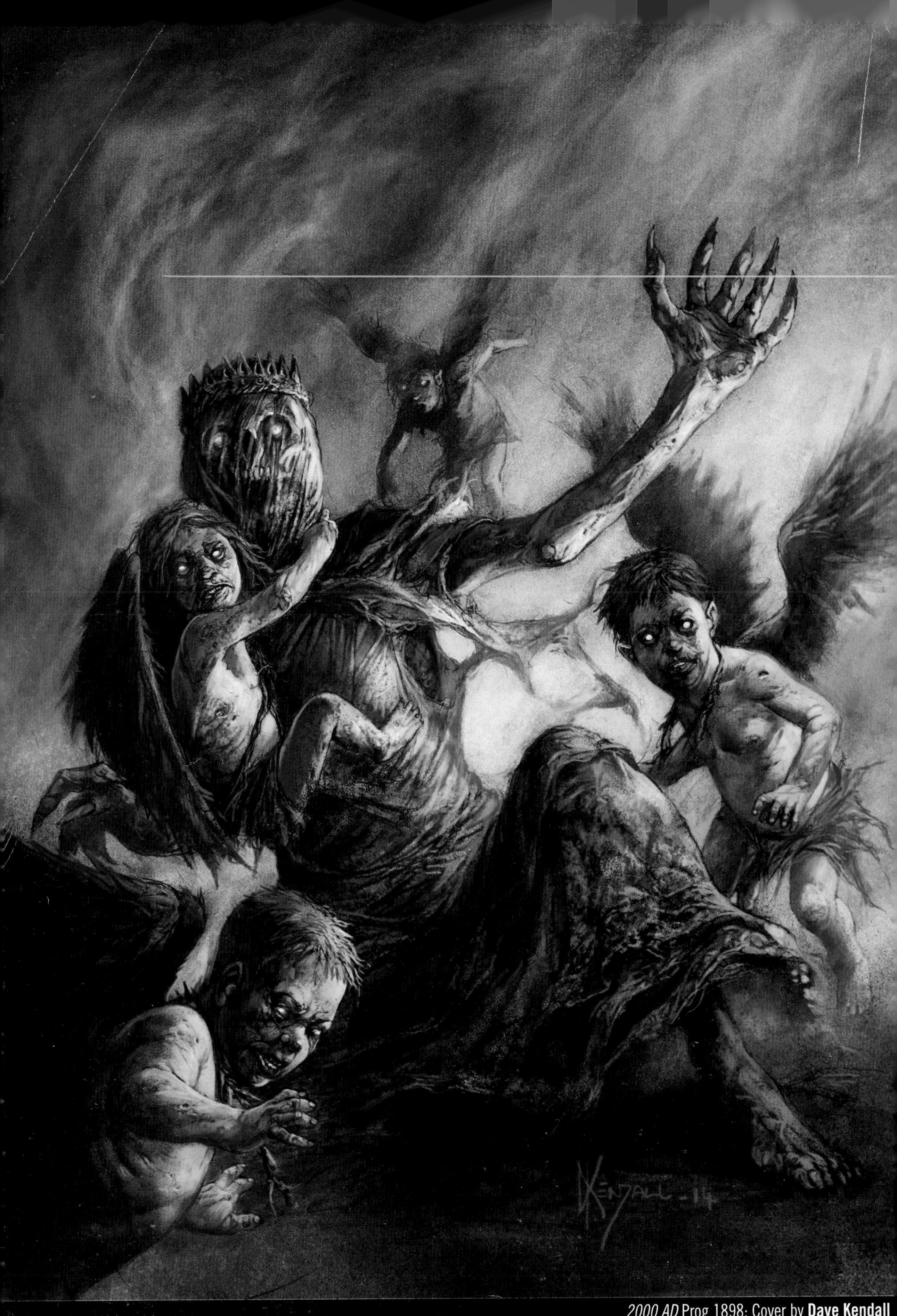

2000 AD Prog 1898: Cover by **Dave Kendall**